Hypnosis and Conscious States

Hypnosis and Conscious States: The Cognitive Neuroscience Perspective

Edited by

Graham A Jamieson

Lecturer in Human Neuropsychology,
School of Psychology,
University of New England,
Armidale, Australia

OXFORD
UNIVERSITY PRESS

OXFORD

UNIVERSITY PRESS

Great Clarendon Street, Oxford OX2 6DP

Oxford University Press is a department of the University of Oxford.
It furthers the University's objective of excellence in research, scholarship,
and education by publishing worldwide in

Oxford New York

Athens Auckland Bangkok Bogotá Buenos Aires Cape Town
Chennai Dar es Salaam Delhi Florence Hong Kong Istanbul Karachi
Kolkata Kuala Lumpur Madrid Melbourne Mexico City Mumbai Nairobi
Paris São Paulo Shanghai Singapore Taipei Tokyo Toronto Warsaw
with associated companies in Berlin Ibadan

Oxford is a registered trade mark of Oxford University Press
in the UK and in certain other countries

Published in the United States
by Oxford University Press Inc., New York

British Library Cataloguing in Publication Data

Data available

Library of Congress Cataloguing in Publication Data

ISBN 13: 978-0-19-856979-4 (Hbk)
ISBN 13: 978-0-19-856980-0 (Pbk)

10 9 8 7 6 5 4 3 2 1

Typeset in Minion
by Cepha Imaging Pvt Ltd, Bangalore, India
Printed in Great Britain
on acid-free paper by
Biddles Ltd., King's Lynn, Norfolk

Preface

For over 200 years, the phenomenon of hypnosis has provided a rich paradigm for those seeking to understand the processes that underlie the construction of the conscious self and its associated experiences. Within a few minutes of hypnotic induction, some 10–15 per cent of healthy alert individuals are able to demonstrate profound alterations in many aspects of their conscious experience. In response to suggestion, they may experience a lack of control over their own actions, the inability to recall recent events, the absence of pain and other specific sensations or, conversely, the apparent reality of illusory events. These rapid, non-pathological and reversible changes in conscious awareness and cognitive processes encountered in hypnosis provide an intriguing domain as well as a (largely unexploited) tool of research in the cognitive neurosciences. Clinically these phenomena may provide new models for understanding many disorders of psychological self-regulation. Hypnosis is already widely used in conjunction with other therapies in the treatment of a range of psychological and physical disorders.

The previous generation of hypnosis researchers focused strongly on the social psychology of the hypnotic situation and the cognitive processes of the hypnotized person. Their achievements remain crucial to any complete understanding of hypnotic phenomena. However, the sad loss of so many major figures in recent years has resulted in a generational change in ideas and perspectives amongst those engaging with the field. In recent years, I have had the opportunity to meet with many exciting (mostly younger) researchers from the UK, Europe, North America, Japan and Australia, with emerging ideas and challenging findings. A clear theme of these contributions is their close reciprocal links with wider scientific developments in the scientific study of consciousness, for example the use of imaging technologies to study state-like networks of functional activation in the brain, the analysis of complexity and non-linear synchronization in the large-scale organization of cortical oscillations (EEG and MEG), evolutionary psychology and genetics. The goal of this book then is to provide a framework to assist those researchers now entering the field to delineate candidate models and to articulate cohesive research agendas for a cognitive neuroscience of hypnosis and of conscious states. Each chapter has been commissioned to make a distinctive contribution to the task of constructing a cognitive neuroscience of hypnosis and has been independently reviewed and revised before final acceptance.

Cognitive neuroscience is a distinctly different intellectual project from either cognitive psychology or neuroscience. It offers a different approach from that of relying solely upon the primacy of functional cognitive models based largely on behavioural data. It sees the traffic between cognitive and neurophysiological data and models going both ways (and at the same time), providing the possibility for a synthesis, which is definitely not just the sum of its parts. Rather than one layer swallowing another (the reductionist model) or one autonomous layer being added alongside another (the functionalist model), the cognitive neuroscience approach is leading to a synthesis in which previously separated domains of enquiry are now able usefully to inform, influence and constrain one another. The chapters in this volume are by no means exclusively focused upon the neurophysiological domain. They frequently draw upon (but move beyond) existing behavioural, experiential, interpersonal, affective and cognitive paradigms. This reflects the diversity of approaches required to build a cognitive neuroscience of hypnosis and conscious states. The cognitive neuroscience framework advocated here both draws upon and contributes to the development of each of these ongoing forms of investigation. The phenomena of hypnosis are fundamentally phenomena of the construction and dissolution of conscious states. Collectively and individually, these chapters must also be seen as contributions to the wider project of constructing a cognitive neuroscience of conscious states.

This work is dedicated to the late George Farquhar Jamieson and to Agnes Fraser Jamieson (nee Craig), my father and mother.

Graham Jamieson

Acknowledgements

I would like to thank Peter Sheehan my teacher and mentor in the field of hypnosis research for his support and encouragement. He has been a wonderful example of committed intellectual and professional life. I also thank John Gruzelier and the Institute for Frontier Areas of Psychology and Mental Health (Freiburg), for a life-changing post-doctoral experience and all the old crew at Imperial College London with whom I sailed on the good ship Cognitive Neuroscience. Thanks to Colin MacLeod who enthusiastically supported the book and who came up with its title. My gratitude also goes to those who acted as anonymous reviewers of the manuscripts which appear in this book. Finally, I wish to thank my wife and children for their very real practical support throughout the course of this project.

Contents

List of Contributors

Tim Bayne,
Department of Philosophy,
Macquarie University,
Sydney, Australia

Melanie Boly,
Centre de Recherches du Cyclotron,
Department of Neurology,
University of Liege, Belgium

Adrian Burgess,
Department of Psychology,
University of Wales,
Swansea, UK

Vilfredo de Pascalis,
Department of Psychology,
University of Rome, La Sapienza,
Rome, Italy

Zoltan Dienes,
Department of Psychology,
University of Sussex,
Brighton, UK

Tobias Egner,
fMRI Research Center,
Columbia University,
New York, USA

Oliver W Fassler
Department of Psychology
Binghamton University
Binghamton NY, USA

Marie-Elisabeth Faymonville,
Pain Clinic, Liege University Hospital,
Sart-Tilman, Belgium

Harutomo Hasegawa,
Imperial College,
London, UK

Graham A Jamieson,
School of Psychology,
University of New England,
Armidale, NSW, Australia

Irving Kirsch,
School of Psychology,
University of Plymouth, UK

Josh Knox,
Psychology Department,
Binghamton University,
Binghamton NY, USA

V Krishna Kumar,
School of Psychology,
West Chester University of Pennsylvania,
West Chester, USA

Steven Laureys,
Centre de Recherches du Cyclotron,
Department of Neurology,
University of Liege, Belgium

Scott O Lilienfeld,
Department of Psychology,
Emory University,
Atlanta GA, USA

Steven Jay Lynn,
Psychology Department,
Binghamton University,
Binghamton NY, USA

Pierre Maquet,
Centre de Recherches du Cyclotron,
Department of Neurology,
University of Liege, Belgium

Wolfgang H R Miltner,
Department of Biological and Clinical
Psychology,
Friedrich Schiller University,
Jena, Germany

Peter L N Naish,
Department of Psychology,
Open University,
Milton Keynes, UK

Ulrich Ott,
Bender Institute of Neuroimaging,
Justus Liebig University,
Giessen, Germany

Ronald J Pekala,
Biofeedback Clinic,
Coatesville V A Medical Center,
Coatesville PA, USA

Josef Perner,
Department of Psychology,
University of Salzburg, Austria

William J Ray,
Department of Psychology,
Penn State University,
University Park PA, USA

Amir Raz,
New York State Psychiatric Institute,
New York, USA

Henry Szechtman,
Department of Psychiatry and
Behavioural Sciences,
McMaster University,
Hamilton ON, Canada

Brent Vogt,
Cingulum Neurosciences Institute,
Manlius NY, USA

Thomas Weiss,
Department of Biological and Clinical
Psychology,
Friedrich Schiller University,
Jena, Germany

Erik Woody,
Department of Psychology,
University of Waterloo,
Waterloo ON, Canada

Chapter 1

Previews and prospects for the cognitive neuroscience of hypnosis and conscious states

Graham A Jamieson

1.1 Introduction

This chapter aims to provide an overview of core issues in the development of the cognitive neuroscience of hypnosis and conscious states as they emerge in the following chapters. The integration of neurophysiological, behavioural and phenomenological data into broad theoretical frameworks spanning across traditionally discreet levels of analysis is highlighted. Functional connectivity is identified as a unifying theme for future electrophysiological and imaging studies of hypnosis and conscious states. Careful attention to the ecological context of functionally significant neurophysiological systems is argued to be an essential component to building such integrated models. It both previews individual contributions and locates them within this wider framework of issues and themes in the cognitive neuroscience of conscious states. The case is made for the ongoing development of a mutually informative dialogue between the emerging cognitive neuroscience of consciousness and hypnosis research.

1.2 Functional connection in brain networks of consciousness

Historically and down to the present day the relief of pain has been one of the major clinical applications of hypnotic suggestion. Functional neuroimaging studies of hypnotic analgesia (HA) have revealed important new information about the neural representation of pain experience and the nature of hypnosis itself (Maquet *et al.* 1999; Rainville *et al.* 1999). The generation of pain experience is now known to rely not on a single area but instead on a functionally heterogeneous network spanning multiple cortical and subcortical regions (Jones *et al.* 1991). Pain is a psychologically complex phenomenon, and the nature of the pain experience corresponds to synchronized activity within this network.

Boly *et al.* (Chapter 2) describe their systematic, long-term and ongoing programme of functional imaging studies to uncover the neurophysiological networks underling HA. Their studies utilize hypnotic procedures drawn directly from the highly successful programme of clinical HA under the direction of Marie Faymonville at the University Hospital of Liège. Hypnotic suggestions for the revivification of pleasant autobiographical memories are contrasted with the effects of mental imagery for similar material under non-hypnotic conditions. Boly *et al.* describe both similarities and differences between the wide networks of activation observed in hypnosis and mental imagery. A major difference between these networks is the relative deactivation of medial parietal cortex (the precuneus) in the hypnosis condition (a finding also observed by Rainville *et al.* 1999). Subsequent studies by this group have identified activation in midcingulate cortex area 24a′ as directly mediating the changes in pain perception specific to their HA suggestion. Whilst the nodes of a network are critical to understanding its functional properties so to are the specific functional connections between nodes. Faymonville *et al.* (2003) next studied changes in cerebral regional connectivity directly associated with the effects of HA. HA was found to significantly enhance functional modulation between midcingulate area 24a′ and a wide network of sensory, affective, cognitive and motor-related brain regions. Boly *et al.* have recently extended the work of this group from positron emission tomography (PET) to functional magnetic resonance imaging (fMRI), enabling hypnosis-related changes in pain processing brain networks to be studied at an individual level.

Egner and Raz (Chapter 3) provide an encouraging example of researchers working together to find common ground across a divide of conflicting empirical findings and theoretical perspectives. Together they seek to locate hypnotic phenomena in the context of cognitive control. Egner *et al.* (2005) utilized fMRI to demonstrate that the Stroop-induced conflict response in (dorsal) anterior cingulate cortex (ACC) is enhanced following hypnosis for individuals of high but not of low susceptibility. However, Raz *et al.* (2002, 2003) found Stroop interference effects to be abolished in hypnotized highly susceptible individuals with the post-hypnotic suggestion to perceive words as meaningless symbols. Raz *et al.* (2005) combined electroencephalography (EEG) and fMRI to demonstrate the effect of their post-hypnotic suggestion in downregulating neural activation both earlier in the visual pathway and later in the (rostral) ACC. Together, Egner and Raz carefully set out what we can and cannot learn about cognitive control from Stroop interference measures, such as those used in their own and other studies. They argue that, in their traditional form, these measures cannot differentiate between conflict detection and cognitive control in contemporary imaging and EEG [or magnetoencephalography (MEG)] experiments. In future, they propose a number of paradigms capable of dissociating conflict detection (monitoring the need for control) and subsequent adaptive adjustments in control as a response to the detection of changing levels of conflict.

Egner and Raz find parallels between their own findings and an influential earlier study (Sheehan *et al.* 1988) of Stroop and hypnosis which reported *both* an increase in Stroop interference in highly susceptible hypnotized individuals *and* a decrease in Stroop interference in these same individuals when given the hypnotic suggestion to focus their attention on a portion of the colour so the word became obscured (individuals of low susceptibilty did not show this pattern of change from the non-hypnotized condition). Egner and Raz conclude that the critical difference between high and low susceptible individuals occurs in hypnosis either without or with specific suggestions for the reduction of Stroop interference. They propose that flexible adaptation in cognitive control is impaired in hypnosis but that this very condition may be the key to enabling the hypnotized person to implement the specific suggestions, when made by the hypnotist, without interference from higher order monitoring systems. Within this framework, Egner and Raz provide specific predictions and specific research methodologies with which to test them.

Jamieson and Sheehan (2004) found no impact for suggestions to rehearse task instructions or for increased effort on responses to Stroop conflict trials, i.e. the specific content of the conflict-reducing suggestions may also be critical to their impact on those who are highly susceptible. The suggestions used successfully by Sheehan *et al.* (1988) and Raz *et al.* (2002) have in common the demand for a shift in attention to the spatial pattern of the visual (word) stimuli. In the case of Raz *et al.* (2005), this attentional instruction was demonstrated to reduce perceptual processing in the early visual pathway. This suggests a complex interplay (at least in highly hypnotically susceptible individuals) between attentional networks for conflict monitoring and flexible cognitive control on the one hand, and attentional networks for visuospatial processing on the other. If this is so, the research programme proposed by Egner and Raz will also require a detailed exploration of both these major attentional networks and the nature of the possible interactions between them. Such a focus on functional interaction between anterior and posterior cortical networks makes this a rich paradigm for basic cognitive neuroscience research.

Miltner, Weiss and colleagues (Chapter 4; Trippe *et al.* 2004) used laser-evoked potentials (LEPs) of noxious heat stimuli to compare the mechanisms responsible for pain control in attentional distraction and HA. While both psychological methods were effective in reducing perceived pain, only distraction significantly reduced sensory processing components of the corresponding somatosensory evoked potentials (an EEG measure), i.e. attentional distraction (but not HA) resulted in a reduction of the flow of pain-related information to the primary somatosensory cortex, strongly suggesting the involvement of a thalamo-cortical filter in implementing the pain control effects of attentional distraction. In contrast, primary somatosensory cortex appears to receive an unimpeded (possibly even enhanced) flow of information from pain stimuli during HA. In Chapter 4, Miltner and Weiss report a breakdown in EEG functional connectivity (coherence) in the gamma band (associated with the binding of cell assemblies) between somatosensory and frontal cortical regions. Presenting further evidence drawn from a combination of fMRI and EEG source analyses, they build the case that HA specifically results from inhibitory influences on the S2/insula regions from a source in the right lateral prefrontal cortex. More broadly, Miltner and Weiss argue that hypnosis is characterized by a breakdown of coherent large-scale cortical oscillations organized and controlled by regions within the frontal cortex.

De Pascalis (Chapter 5) focuses more specifically on the role of synchronized fast frequency cortical oscillations (gamma) in the creation, maintenance and dissolution of the succession of neural ensembles that correspond to the contents of human mental life. In particular, De Pascalis emphasizes the critical role of timing or phase relationships of gamma oscillations in synchronizing or coordinating distributed neural activity. He surveys a range of tools and analytical techniques available in the current signal processing toolbox for the analysis of phase and timing of gamma oscillations. De Pascalis presents a wide range of studies in support of his contention that the modulation of gamma oscillations plays a key role in the (re)construction of hypnotic consciousness. He points out the importance of largely neglected but highly reliable correlates of hypnotizability such as proneness to perceptual illusions and the frequent occurrence of quasi-hallucinatory distortions in everyday experience as potential paradigms for the investigation of the role of gamma oscillations in the generation of hypnotic experience. A much broader question hinted at by the contributions of both De Pascalis and Miltner and Weiss is the role played by slower frequency oscillations in the coordination of gamma activity and neural cell assembly formation. In order to specify such a role, it will be essential for contemporary researchers to design studies around methods designed to represent the dynamics of timing relationships in cortical oscillations rather than the simple presence or magnitude of gamma in the EEG (which can be observed even in coma).

1.3 Connection and disconnection

Many of the phenomena which arise in the study of conscious states raise fundamental questions in the philosophy of mind; what is the self, the nature of volition, the relationship between phenomenal consciousness and access to output systems. Consequently the scientific study of conscious states has developed a mutual, critical and open dialogue with contemporary philosophers of mind. Perhaps no phenomenon in the field of hypnosis is more difficult to interpret conceptually than that of the hidden observer. It has long been observed that even in the most profoundly hallucinatory or deluded experiences which arise during hypnosis, a portion of the mind appears to remain in contact with and capable of responding to the actual reality of the person (Gill and Brenman 1959; Schilder 1921). Made famous by Ernest Hilgard and co-workers, the hidden observer is the most dramatic example of this wider phenomenon. At the heart of the hidden observer lies a profound dissociation between the separate and apparent self experiencing a hypnotic suggestion (such as HA) and another apparent self able to report their experience of the real situation (such as pain). Taken at face value, it seems to challenge the most basic assumption of the unity of conscious experience in the human subject. Philosopher of mind Tim Bayne (Chapter 6) gives careful conceptual scrutiny to the literature on the hidden observer from Hilgard's initial reports down to the most recent studies and discussions. Traditionally this literature has been viewed as closely tied to the dispute between state and non-state accounts of hypnosis. Bayne takes a fresh perspective and analyses the evidence and arguments from the perspective of what they imply for the unity of consciousness. He identifies three possible models of the hidden observer which he dubs the two streams model, the zombie model and the switching model. Bayne draws an important parallel with the interpretation of split brain studies. Ultimately he argues that the switching model (also capable of accounting for split brain data) gives the most parsimonious account of the hidden observer.

Jamieson and Woody (Chapter 7) agree that divided consciousness fails to provide an adequate model for hypnotic dissociation and, following the lead of Ken Bowers (1990, 1992), seek to develop an alternative model with deep roots in Hilgard's wider framework of a hierarchy of cognitive subsystems coordinated at the highest level by an executive system with both monitoring and control functions. This model understands hypnotic dissociation as resulting from a disruption in the normal processes of integration and higher order control. Woody and Bowers (1994) proposed that rather than a dissociation between two streams of consciousness, hypnotic dissociation consists of a dissociation in control between the flexible and conscious executive supervisory attentional system (SAS; Norman and Shallice 1986) and an automatic contention scheduling system. The former was held to be mediated by anterior networks and the latter by more posterior networks, thus dissociated control theory posits a breakdown in functional connectivity between anterior and posterior cortical regions. Subsequent neuropsychological evidence suggests that while important aspects of SAS functioning are compromised (Jamieson and Sheehan 2004), hypnosis cannot be explained on the basis of rigid contention scheduling alone or of a simple global shutdown in frontal activation or connectivity with posterior regions. Current evidence points toward a relative disconnection between monitoring and control functions within the SAS. Such a disconnection is instantiated as a breakdown in feedback between dorsal ACC conflict monitoring and adaptive adjustment of task set representations in dorsolateral prefrontal cortex (see also Egner and Raz, Chapter 3). This conclusion supports an extension of dissociated control theory more in line with Hilgard's original framework and suggests that aspects of experience and control (rather than autonomous streams of awareness) may be dissociated in hypnosis.

1.4 Methodological issues in the study of states of consciousness

The capacity of the hypnotized person to experience suggested alterations in their subjective experience of self and world, profoundly at odds with objective reality, is part of the very essence of hypnosis (Orne 1979). Whether or not these changes in experience should be explained as due to the existence of a fundamental alteration in conscious state is one of the oldest questions in the field and can be traced back to at least the nineteenth century (Spanos and Chaves 1991). However, before we can judge whether or not hypnosis can be explained as a state of consciousness, we must first have clear methods and concepts for defining, describing and investigating what constitutes a state of consciousness. Only then will we be in a position to consider whether hypnosis is such an altered state of consciousness and if so to determine its specific nature. Many have declared the state–non-state controversy decisively won (by one side or the other), a clear indication that the debate is far from settled. Others argue that it is at best a non-issue and at worst a useless waste of scarce research resources. Contrary to these claims, Chapters 8–11 in particular attest to the continued vitality and relevance of states of consciousness as a central topic within the cognitive neuroscience of hypnosis and one of wide importance to the scientific study of consciousness.

Jamieson and Hasegawa (Chapter 8) provide an important background to the modern debate within the hypnosis literature for those approaching it from other fields. A thorough familiarity with the arguments, methods and findings of this literature is essential if contemporary researchers are to avoid labouring simply to 'reinvent the wheel'. Jamieson and Hasegawa draw links between Sheehan and Perry's (1976) model of cross-paradigm hypnosis research and the implications of recent statements of biological naturalism (Searle 1998, 2004) for cognitive neuroscience research. In this context, they develop Tart's (1983, 2000) phenomenological model of states of states of consciousness as a conceptual framework for assessing neurophysiological methods and descriptions capable of providing informative data on brain states related to different modes of conscious functioning.

Prominent non-state theorists Steven Jay Lynn and Irving Kirsch in conjunction with their collaborators Josh Knox and Scott Lilienfeld provide an important statement of the modern non-state position and a valuable critique of those arguments that leap too readily from evidence of neurophysiological differences to conclusions of an altered state of consciousness (Chapter 9). As they point out, non-state theories also predict brain changes in responding to hypnotic suggestions. For example, one of the leading non-state accounts, response expectancy theory, can be directly related to an important general issue within cognitive neuroscience, that of the interplay between top-down and bottom-up processes in the emergence of coherent high level neural states linked with the contents of conscious experience (Kirsch 2000). This can be viewed as a parallel with Friston's account (e.g. Friston 2002) of the role of predictive coding in the functional integration of brain states. Indeed Friston's development of logical models for testing predictive coding hypotheses in functional imaging data sets provides a natural framework for the elaboration and development of response expectancy-based research paradigms in cognitive neuroscience. Lynn *et al.* carefully criticize the logic of inference from existing studies and highlight the unsettled issue of what is to count as an appropriate control condition if inferences are to be drawn (one way or another) about the presence of a hypnotic state.

The study of functional brain networks underlying different conscious states requires at some stage the employment of phenomenological self-report measures which can identify individual differences in the organization of conscious experience across various experimental (e.g. hypnotic and non-hypnotic) conditions. Pekala and Kumar (Chapter 10) detail the development of an instrument, the Phenomenology of Consciousness Inventory (PCI), capable of assessing core elements in Tart's model of states of consciousness, which they have applied extensively in hypnosis research. This instrument is a 53-item questionnaire which asks untrained observers to make retrospective quantitative ratings of 12 major and 14 minor dimensions of their experience in a short prior experimental interval. A similar approach in PET applied to studies has identified distinct cortical and subcortical networks modulating the experience of relaxation and absorption in hypnotized subjects (Rainville and Price 2003). Pekala and Kumar provide specific and easy to apply methods for the quantitative assessment of differences in intensity and different patterns of relationship between subsystems of consciousness across different experimental conditions. One finding from this method of immediate importance for cognitive researchers of hypnosis and conscious states is that discrete clusters of association between conscious subsystems can be identified amongst (and within) high, medium and low hypnotically susceptible individuals in hypnosis, i.e. hypnosis may correspond not to one but to several distinct patterns of conscious organization, even amongst those of the same susceptibility level. Investigation of the networks of functional connectivity associated with these distinct 'trance typology profiles' should now be an immediate priority for cognitive neuroscience researchers.

Just as PET and fMRI investigators have focused on identifying networks of functional connectivity associated with hypnosis, so do Adrian Burgess (Chapter 11) and other EEG researchers (e.g. Miltner and Weiss, Chapter 4; De Pascalis, Chapter 5) focus on describing and assessing the characteristic dynamics of these systems as revealed in cortical oscillations beyond the temporal resolution of current imaging technology. Burgess does not take sides in the state–non-state debate, but instead asks how we could identify such a state if it were present. He carefully surveys previous approaches and identifies important weaknesses in their logic. A range of alternative methods derived from recent applications of advances in signal processing to EEG analysis are introduced and their potential application to questions regarding conscious states is explored. Burgess makes important practical suggestions as to how these techniques can be applied to hypnosis data and what general form these results may be expected to take under state and non-state models, respectively. One potential weakness in Burgess's approach, associated with the poor spatial resolution of EEG, is its relative neglect of the specific neuroanatomical foci comprising functional networks. As Jamieson and Hasegawa argue in Chapter 8, a convergent inquiry between EEG and neuroimaging researchers is most probably called for in this case.

1.5 Psychobiology of trance experience

As many contributors to the present volume have observed, hypnotizabilty is a stable trait of adults, and phenomena similar to hypnosis may be observed in all cultures. Bill Ray (Chapter 12) reviews evidence that demonstrates a genetic basis for hypnotic susceptibility. Ray argues that as a genetically rooted and species-wide attribute, hypnosis must have its origins in the evolutionary, neurobiological and developmental history of human behaviour. He views successive waves of brain–behaviour evolution as a process of growing internalization and flexibility of control each requiring additional layers of neural regulation and circuitry. Ray asks us to consider which level in this multilayered system regulates the expression of hypnotic phenomena. He argues that it is the level of affective, and in particular attachment-related, limbic structures and their consequent pattern of interaction with higher cortical structures. The ACC is argued by Ray to be the primary anatomical focus of networks regulating attachment-related patterns of affect, behaviour and cognition. Ray proposes that the EEG theta rhythm, which is often observed to be stronger in some hypnotic conditions, may be the common mechanism whereby the ACC regulates its interaction with other cortical structures (Ray and Tucker 2003). If he is correct, then the new tools for assessing the dynamics of phase and timing relationships (described by Burgess, Chapter 11) in the theta rhythm between various ACC and other cortical sources will play an essential role in future research to test or develop his general framework.

Whilst Woody and Bowers (1994) focused previously on the experience of non-volition as a core feature of the phenomenology of hypnosis, another core feature of hypnotic phenomenology is the distortion in 'feelings of knowing' what is real and what is not. Orne's (1959) real-simulating paradigm identifies 'trance logic' (tolerance of logical incongruity) and delusion as part of the essence of hypnosis, and Sheehan and McConkey's (1982) work with the experiential analysis technique confirms the complex ways in which the awareness of reality is interwoven with hypnotic responses which at the same time deny aspects of that reality. Woody and Szechtman (Chapter 13) examine the role of the affective and motivational component of these epistemic states, not simply their propositional (cognitive) content, in producing hypnotic responses. This unique motivational quality of hypnotic responsiveness, termed *rapport*, was widely recognized in the earlier hypnosis literature (Shor 1979) but has dropped from view in recent times in exclusively cognitive research paradigms. Woody and Szechtman correct this omission by placing these feeling states in a *cognitive and affective* neuroscience context. Their approach further highlights the intrinsic interpersonal context of such feeling states. This perspective is closely related to but extends many of the elements in the framework proposed by Ray (Chapter 12).

Hypnosis itself is an example of a wider human capacity to experience temporary, but profound, alterations in conscious experience which are personally and socially valued. This capacity is directly reflected in the psychological trait labelled 'absorption' (Tellegen and Atkinson 1974). This trait was originally discovered in the search for personality correlates of hypnotizability and has been conceptualized by its discoverer Tellegen (1981) as a predisposition, in appropriate circumstances, to surrender what he terms an 'instrumental' mental set for a radical restructuring of the experience of self and world that he terms an 'experiential' mental set. Growing evidence suggests that absorption is an important trait in mediating the success of differing psychological interventions in the self-regulation of internal psychophysiological states (Jamieson 2005). In Chapter 14, Ulrich Ott outlines the contemporary research for the psychobiological roots of the trait absorption and the accompanying capacity for a socially important group of altered states of experience. Ott's chapter starts with a detailed description of the Tellegen Absorption Scale and other questionnaires that include similar factors such as the scale 'Self-transcendence' from Cloninger's Temperament and Character Inventory, which is frequently used in biologically oriented personality research. Studies of heritability show approximately 40 per cent of this personality trait to be genetically determined. Ott's own psychophysiological research identifies absorption-related individual differences in autonomic sensitivity and the ability selectively to inhibit some aspects of cortical processing. He presents a theory of the brain mechanisms underpinning states of absorption which links the dynamic nature of the psychological procedures used to induce many absorption-related states with the role of central brain structures and neurotransmitters so far found to be involved. In conclusion, he sets out a detailed programme for future research including genetic analyses of neurotransmitter-related polymorphisms (already underway), a training-based approach studying the plasticity of absorption capacity (e.g. long-term studies of training in concentrative meditation) and a self-regulation approach based on specific EEG and fMRI biofeedback protocols.

A robust and reliable but relatively neglected finding from the study of hypnotic consciousness is the retrospective shortening of the estimated duration of events which occurred in the hypnotic session. Peter Naish (Chapter 15) considers several explanations for this important empirical finding. According to the logic of Orne's (1979) real-simulating paradigm, the 'essence' of hypnosis is to be found in those aspects of hypnotic phenomena which remain when other elements which can potentially be explained by 'ordinary' social psychological processes are stripped away. Attempts to identify this essence have found that most overt behavioural responses to hypnotic suggestions can also be produced by simulators. Instead the key differences that have been observed between real and simulating subjects are found to occur largely at the level of subjective experience. It is therefore a very important result that retrospective time shortening is not reported by simulators. This leads Naish to propose that subjective 'time shortening' may be a feature of the 'essence' long sought by Orne. Naish's presents recent findings from his own work on retro- and pro-spective time estimation which support the conclusion that an internal clock mechanism runs slow during hypnosis. His results demonstrate that, when calculated appropriately, there is a correlation between hypnotic susceptibility and the rate of time slowing during hypnosis. Naish identifies that the ticking of the internal clock corresponds to successive states of Jeffrey Gray's (1995) comparator system for monitoring the match or mismatch between predicted and actual states in the interplay between neural systems and the world. In Gray's model, these states also correspond to successive moments of conscious experience. Naish hypothesizes that in highly susceptible individuals hypnosis disrupts the operation of this monitoring and prediction circuitry (in which the ACC plays a critical role), leading to a breakdown in reality checking which leads to a lower 'tick rate' in the cycle of conscious moments. Naish concludes that hypnosis is indeed an altered state of consciousness in which 'time is of the essence'.

Zoltan Dienes and Josef Perner (Chapter 16) approach hypnosis as a case study in the application of the Higher Order Thought (HOT) theory of consciousness recently developed by Rosenthal (2002). They argue that hypnosis is an example of a highly novel prediction from their hierarchy of explicit knowledge developed from the HOT theory (Dienes and Perner 1999), i.e. the theoretical possibility of using unconscious executive control. They dub this the cold control theory of hypnosis, according to which hypnotic responses are generated by executive control without conscious intentions. They show that the cold control theory can account for why some hypnotic tasks are more difficult than others, the existence of individual differences in hypnotizability and the effects of expectation in hypnosis. Cold control theory is located in a wider conceptual framework which allows it to be compared with other possible theories of hypnotic responding. Amongst these are 'empty heat' (HOTs without first order states) and multiple selves (based on different 'I' representations). An important omission, however, is a testable model of how HOTs are implemented in the brain. It is clear that higher order monitoring and re-entrant feedback loops must be involved and that a disconnection in this network can alter the dynamics of the system. Arguably these general features are held in common by some of the more specific models presented in other chapters. This observation may provide grounds for a future rapprochement between cold control theory and some of these other theories in the field. According to HOT theory, activity in these networks must provide the basis for the neural correlates of consciousness. As with other contributions to this volume, Dienes and Perner demonstrate the fruitful interplay that is now emerging between hypnosis research and the science of conscious states.

References

Bowers KS (1990). Unconscious influences and hypnosis. In: JL Singer, ed. *Repression and dissociation: implications for personality theory, psychopathology, and health*. pp. 143–78. Chicago, University of Chicago Press.

Bowers KS (1992). Imagination and dissociation in hypnotic responding. *International Journal of Clinical and Experimental Hypnosis*, **40**, 253–75.

Dienes Z and Perner J (1999) A theory of implicit and explicit knowledge. *Behavioural and Brain Sciences*, **22**, 735–55.

Egner T, Jamieson G and Gruzelier J (2005). Hypnosis decouples cognitive control from conflict monitoring processes of the frontal lobe. *NeuroImage*, **27**, 969–78.

Faymonville ME, Roediger L, Del Fiore G, Delgueldre C, Phillips C, Lamy M, *et al.* (2003). Increased cerebral functional connectivity underlying the antinociceptive effects of hypnosis. *Cognitive Brain Research*, **17**, 255– 62.

Friston K (2002). Beyond phrenology: what can neuroimaging tell us about distributed circuitry. *Annual Review of Neuroscience*, **25**, 221–50.

Gill MM and Brenman M (1959). *Hypnosis and related states: psychoanalytical studies in regression*. New York, International Universities Press.

Gray JA (1995). The contents of consciousness—a neuropsychological conjecture. *Behavioural and Brain Sciences*, **18**, 659–76.

Jamieson GA (2005). The modified Tellegen Absorption Scale: a clearer window on the structure and meaning of absorption. *Australian Journal of Clinical and Experimental Hypnosis*, **33**, 119–39.

Jamieson GA and Sheehan PW (2004). An empirical test of Woody and Bower's dissociated control theory of hypnosis. *International Journal of Clinical and Experimental Hypnosis*, **52**, 232–49.

Jones AK, Brown WD, Friston KJ, Qi LY and Frackowiak RS (1991). Cortical and subcortical localization of response to pain in man using positron emission tomography. *Proceedings of the Royal Society B: Biological Sciences*, **244**, 39–44.

Kirsch I (2000). The response set theory of hypnosis. *American Journal of Clinical Hypnosis*, **42**, 274–93.

Norman DA and Shallice T (1986). Attention to action: willed and automatic control of behaviour. In: RJ Davidson, GE Schwartz, and D Shapiro, eds. *Consciousness and self-regulation*, Vol. 4, pp. 1–18. New York, Plenum Press.

Maquet P. Faymonville ME, Degueldre C, Delfiore G, Franck G, Luxen A, *et al.* (1999). Functional neuroanatomy of hypnotic state. *Biological Psychiatry*, **45**, 327–33.

Orne MT (1979). On the simulating subject as a quasi-control group in hypnosis research: what, why and how. In: E Fromm and RE Shor, eds. *Hypnosis: developments in research and new perspectives*. New York, Aldine.

Rainville P and Price DD (2003). Hypnosis phenomenology and the neurobiology of consciousness. *International Journal of Clinical and Experimental Hypnosis*, **51**, 105–29.

Rainville P, Hofbauer RK, Paus T, Duncan GH, Bushnell MC and Price DD (1999). Cerebral mechanisms of hypnotic induction and suggestion. *Journal of Cognitive Neuroscience*, **11**, 110–25.

Ray WJ and Tucker D (2003). Evolutionary approaches to understanding the hypnotic experience. *International Journal of Clinical and Experimental Hypnosis*, **51**, 256–81.

Raz A, Shapiro T, Fan J and Posner MI (2002). Hypnotic suggestion and the modulation of Stroop interference. *Archives of General Psychiatry*, **59**, 1155–61.

Raz A, Landzberg KS, Schweizer HR, Zephrani ZR, Shapiro T, Fan J, *et al.* (2003). Posthypnotic suggestion and the modulation of Stroop interference under cycloplegia. *Conscious Cognition* **12**, 332–46.

Raz A, Fan, J and Posner MI (2005). Hypnotic suggestion reduces conflict in the human brain. *Proceedings of the National Academy of Sciences, USA*, **102**, 9978–83.

Rosenthal DM (2002). Consciousness and higher-order thought. In: *Macmillan encyclopedia of cognitive science.* pp. 717–26. Basingstoke, UK, Macmillan Publishers Ltd.

Searle J. (1998). How to study consciousness scientifically. *Philosophical Transactions of the Royal Society B*, **353**, 1935–42.

Schilder PF (1921/1956). *The nature of hypnosis.* Translation by Gerda Corvin. New York, International Universities Press.

Searle J (2004). Mind. New York, Harvard University Press.

Sheehan PW and McConkey KM (1982). *Hypnosis and experience: a critical appraisal of contemporary paradigms of hypnosis.* Hillsdale NJ, Lawrence Erlbaum.

Sheehan PW and Perry CW (1976). *Methodologies of hypnosis: a critical appraisal of contemporary paradigms of hypnosis.* Hillsdale NJ, Lawrence Erlbaum.

Sheehan PW. Donovan PB and MacLeod CM (1988). Strategy manipulation and the Stroop effect in hypnosis. *Journal of Abnormal Psychology*, **97**, 455–60.

Spanos NP and Chaves JF (1991). History and historiography of hypnosis. In: Lynn SJ and Rhue JW, eds. *Theories of hypnosis: current models and perspectives.* pp. 43–82. New York, Guilford Press.

Shor RE (1979). The fundamental problem in hypnosis research as viewed from historical perspectives. In: E Fromm and RE Shor (eds). Hypnosis: developments in research and new perspectives, second edn. pp. 15–41. New York, Aldine.

Tart, C. (1983/2000). *States of Consciousness.* iUniverse.com: Lincoln. (Originally published by Dutton.)

Tellegen A (1981). Practicing the two disciplines for relaxation and enlightenment: comment on 'Role of the feedback signal in electromyograph biofeedback: the relevance of attention' by Qualls and Sheehan. *Journal of Experimental Psychology: General*, **110**, 217–26.

Tellegen A and Atkinson G (1974). Openness to absorbing and self-altering experiences ('absorption'), a trait related to hypnotic susceptibility. *Journal of Abnormal Psychology*, **83** 268–77.

Trippe RH, Weiss T and Miltner WHR (2004). Hypnotisch-induzierte Analgesie—Mechanismen. *Anästhesiologie & Intensivmedizin*, **45**, 642–47.

Woody E and Bowers K (1994). A frontal assault on dissociated control. In: SJ Lynn and JW Rhue, eds. *Dissociation: clinical and theoretical perspectives.* pp. 52–79. New York, Guilford.

Part I

Functional brain networks

Chapter 2

Hypnotic regulation of consciousness and the pain neuromatrix

Mélanie Boly, Marie-Elisabeth Faymonville,
Brent A Vogt, Pierre Maquet, and Steven Laureys

2.1 Introduction

Since mankind's early history, hypnosis has been used as a therapeutic tool (De Betz and Sunnen 1985). Scientific papers have aimed to demonstrate its efficacy in the treatment of pain, gastrointestinal and dermatological pathologies, depression, anxiety, stress and habit disorders, to name but a few. Unfortunately, there is not a generally accepted definition of hypnosis. For many authors, it is seen as a state of focused attention, concentration and inner absorption with a relative suspension of peripheral awareness. We have all experienced similar states many times but do not usually call it hypnosis (e.g. being so absorbed in thought while doing something that we fail to notice what is happening around us). The Executive Committee of the American Psychological Association-Division of Psychological Hypnosis (1994) has constructed a definition from the multiplicity of positions of a number of researchers advocating differing theoretical perspectives. Their definition regards hypnosis as 'a procedure during which a health professional or researcher suggests that a patient or subject experience changes in sensations, perceptions, thoughts, or behaviour …'. The hypnotic context is generally established by an induction procedure. Most hypnotic inductions include suggestions for relaxation. Our group then uses instructions to imagine or think about pleasant autobiographical experiences.

Hypnosis has three main components: absorption; dissociation; and suggestibility (Spiegel 1991). Absorption is the tendency to become fully involved in a perceptual, imaginative or ideational experience. Subjects prone to this type of cognition are more highly hypnotizable than others who never fully engage in such experience (Hilgard *et al.* 1963). Dissociation is the mental separation of components of behaviour that would ordinarily be processed together (e.g. the dream-like state of being both actor and observer when re-experiencing autobiographical memories). This may also involve a sense of involuntariness in motor functions or unusual discontinuities in the sensations of one part of the body compared with another. Suggestibility is the tendency to respond positively to hypnotic instructions. This represents not a loss of will but rather a suspension of critical judgement possibly because of the intense absorption of the hypnotic state. Hypnosis makes it easier to experience suggested events or memories as subjectively real. However, some element of the person continues to remain in contact with reality. Contrary to some depictions of hypnosis in the media, hypnotized subjects do not lose complete control over their behaviour. They typically remain aware of who they are and where they are, and, unless amnesia has been specifically suggested, they usually remember what transpired during the hypnotic state.

Since 1992, the University Hospital of Liège has used the anti-nociceptive effects of hypnosis routinely in more than 4000 surgical procedures such as thyroid and parathyroid surgery (Meurisse, et al. 1996, 1999a, b; Defechereux et al. 1998, 1999, 2000), plastic surgery (Faymonville et al. 1994, 1995, 1997, 1999) and peri-dressing change pain and anxiety in severely burned patients (Frenay et al. 2001). In patients undergoing surgery, hypnosis combined with local anaesthesia and minimal conscious sedation (a technique Faymonville et al. termed 'hypnosedation') is associated with improved intraoperative patient comfort and with reduced anxiety, pain, intraoperative requirements for anxiolytic and analgesic drugs, optimal surgical conditions and a faster recovery of the patient (for a review, see Faymonville et al. 1998). The effectiveness of incorporating hypnosis in clinical interventions has also gained positive empirical support in anxiety, depression, trauma, weight loss and eating disorders (Lynn et al. 2000).

In addition to its use in clinical settings, hypnosis can be used in scientific research, with the goal of learning more about the nature of hypnosis itself, as well as its impact on sensation, perception, learning and memory. The rapid, non-pathological and reversible changes in conscious awareness and cognitive processing encountered in hypnosis provide an intriguing domain as well as a largely unexploited tool in cognitive neuroscience (Raz et al. 2002). For instance, hypnotic manipulation of subjective experience, in conjunction with neuroimaging techniques, can help dissociate the neural basis of sensory and cognitive processes (Rainville et al. 1997; Halligan et al. 2000). Recent studies have also investigated the effect of hypnotic induction on various cognitive tasks such as Stroop interference (Egner et al. 2005; Raz et al. 2005) and cognitive control (Egner et al. 2005). However, as its acceptance by the scientific community remains limited, to date, the neural correlates of the hypnotic state remain poorly understood.

One field where the efficacy of hypnosis has been the most extensively evaluated and validated is pain control. In the present chapter, we will first try to define hypnosis, describe the hypnotic procedure and then review positron emission tomography (PET) studies led by Faymonville et al. on hypnosis in a cohort of highly hypnotizable healthy volunteers. We will do so in three steps, discussing (1) changes in regional brain function; (2) modulation of pain perception; and (3) increases in cerebral functional connectivity. Finally, we will discuss some preliminary results obtained by Boly et al. using an event-related functional magnetic resonance imaging (fMRI) paradigm to study the mechanisms of the antinociceptive effect of hypnosis at the single-subject level.

2.2 Functional neuroanatomy of the hypnotic state

Maquet et al. (1999) explored the underlying brain mechanisms of hypnosis in a cohort of healthy volunteers by determining the distribution of regional cerebral blood flow (rCBF), taken as an index of local neuronal activity, by use of the $H_2{}^{15}O$ technique.

For this study, the hypnotic procedure employed was similar to the one used in their clinical routines (Faymonville *et al.* 1995, 1997, 1999; Meurisse *et al.* 1999*b*). Hypnosis was induced using eye fixation, a 3 min muscle relaxation procedure, and permissive and indirect suggestions. Subjects were invited to re-experience very pleasant autobiographical memories. As in clinical conditions, they were continuously given cues for maintaining and deepening the hypnotic state. Just before scanning, subjects confirmed by a small foot movement that they were experiencing hypnosis. Oculographic recording showed roving eye movements sometimes intermingled with few saccades. This pattern of eye movements, in conjunction with the subject's behaviour, was used to differentiate hypnosis from other states. Electroencephalographic, electromyographic and oculographic recordings confirmed that no sleep occurred during the experimental session. Because the induction and maintenance of the hypnotic procedure relies on revivification of pleasant autobiographical memories, the most comparable control task was the evocation of autobiographical recall, in a state of normal alertness. To understand better the contrast with hypnosis, Maquet *et al.* first investigated this control condition. The results showed that listening to autobiographical material activates the anterior part of both temporal lobes, basal forebrain structures and some left mesiotemporal areas (Fig. 2.1). This pattern is in agreement with previous studies on autobiographical memory (Fink *et al.* 1996).

During hypnosis, compared with the control task, a vast network of activation was observed that involved occipital, parietal, precentral, prefrontal and cingulate cortices (Fig. 2.1). The hypnotic state seems to rely on cerebral processes different from simple evocation of episodic memory and is related to the activation of sensory and motor cortical areas, as known to occur during real perceptions or motor acts. In this respect,

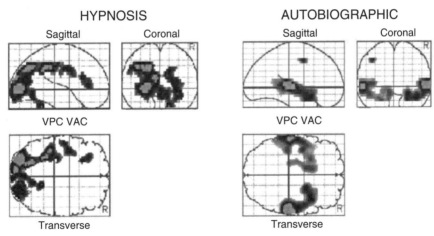

Fig. 2.1 Brain areas where regional cerebral blood flow (rCBF) is increased during hypnosis compared with mental imaging of autobiographical memories (control distraction task) (left) and brain areas where rCBF is increased during the mental imaging of autobiographical memories compared with the resting state (right). VAC and VPC identify anterior and posterior commissural planes, respectively. (Adapted with permission from Maquet *et al.* 1999.)

hypnosis is reminiscent of mental imagery (Kosslyn *et al.* 2001). Hypnotic imagery was polymodal. Although subjects predominantly reported visual impressions, somaesthetic and olfactory perceptions were also mentioned. Numerous motor images also appeared in the hypnotic experience of these subjects. In contrast, none of the subjects reported positive autobiographical auditory images. When sounds were reported, they came from the actual experimental environment (mainly, the experimenter's voice). The visual content of mental imagery is consistent with the activation observed in occipital areas. More anteriorly, the activation of precentral and premotor cortices is similar to that observed during motor imagery (Decety 1996), which could also have involved the observed parietal activation. The activation of ventrolateral prefrontal cortex has been reported in mental imagery tasks and is thought to be involved in the representation of task sets which elicit the construction of the mental image and in the maintenance of the imagery in working memory. Finally the activation in the midcingulate cortex (MCC) is closely related to the attentional effort necessary for the subject to generate mental imagery and hypnosis internally in the PET scan environment.

Prominent decreased activity during hypnosis relative to the alert state was observed in the medial parietal cortex (i.e. the precuneus). This area is hypothesized to be involved in the representation (monitoring) of the world around us (Gusnard and Raichle 2001). Indeed, the precuneus shows the highest level of glucose use (the primary fuel for the brain's energy metabolism) of any area of the cerebral cortex in the so-called 'conscious resting state'. However it is known to show decreases from this baseline during the performance of goal-directed actions. Evidence indicates that the functions to which this region of the cerebral cortex contributes include those concerned with both orientation within, and interpretation of, the environment (Vogt and Laureys 2005). Interestingly, the precuneus is one of the most dysfunctional brain regions in states of unconsciousness or altered consciousness such as coma or the vegetative state (Laureys 2005), general anaesthesia (Alkire and Miller 2005), slow wave and rapid eye movement (REM) sleep (Maquet 2000), amnesia (Aupee *et al.* 2001) and dementia (Matsuda 2001), suggesting that it is part of the critical neural network subserving conscious experience (Baars *et al.* 2003).

It remains an open question whether there is a well-determined physiological correlate of hypnosis in general, following an induction procedure and in the absence of any further specific suggestions because subjects can have a wide variety of experiences while they are in a hypnotic state. While the study of Maquet *et al.* (1999) found that their hypnosis procedure generated widespread activation of occipital, parietal, precentral, premotor and ventrolateral prefrontal cortex in the left hemisphere, and the occipital and MCC of the right hemisphere, another PET study by Rainville *et al.* (1999) reported more restricted hypnosis-related activation mainly in the occipital cortex; importantly both studies reported deactivation in the precuneus. As is so often the case in neuroimaging experiments, the difference in results may be due to differences in control conditions. While Rainville *et al.* (1999) asked their hypnotized subjects simply to relax, Maquet *et al.* (1999) asked the subjects to review a pleasant life experience. Although the concept of 'neutral' hypnosis has had its proponents (Kihlstrom and Edmonston 1971), in subjective terms this state might differ little from eyes-closed relaxation (Edmonston 1977) which bears little resemblance to the profound dissociative and hallucinatory experiences associated with specific hypnotic suggestions. As for the study of the relationship between cerebral activity during REM sleep and subsequent subjective data given by subjects awakened when dreaming (Maquet *et al.* 2005), some authors consider it unlikely that studying subjects who are merely in 'neutral hypnosis', and not responding to particular hypnotic suggestions, will tell us much about the neural correlates of hypnosis. Hence, because the experiences of hypnotic subjects are so varied, a more fruitful tack will probably involve imaging subjects while they are responding to particular hypnotic suggestions.

2.3 Hypnosis-induced analgesia

Pain is a multidimensional experience encompassing sensory-discriminative, affective-emotional, cognitive and behavioural dimensions. Its cerebral correlate is best described in terms of neural circuits or networks, referred to as the 'neuromatrix' for pain processing, and not as a localized 'pain centre' (Jones *et al.* 1991; Miltner and Weiss, Chapter 4). We have previously shown the effectiveness of hypnosis in producing analgesia in two large clinical studies. A retrospective study first showed that hypnosis as an adjunct procedure to conscious intravenous sedation provides significant peri-operative pain and anxiety relief. These benefits were obtained despite a significant reduction in drug requirements (Faymonville *et al.* 1995). A prospective randomized study confirmed these observations (Faymonville *et al.* 1997).

Faymonville *et al.* (2000) explored the brain mechanisms underlying the modulation of pain perception, proper to a validated clinical hypnotic protocol. During this procedure, hypnotized healthy volunteers and patients were invited to re-experience pleasant life episodes, without any reference to their pain perception. This technique lowered both the unpleasantness (i.e. affective component) and the perceived intensity (i.e. sensory component) of the noxious stimuli (Faymonville *et al.* 1997, 2000). Hypnosis decreased both components of pain perception by approximately 50 per cent compared with the resting state and by approximately 40 per cent compared with a distraction task (mental imagery of autobiographical events).

Our group and others (Rainville *et al.* 1997, 1999; Faymonville, *et al.* 2000 have shown that this modulatory effect of hypnosis is mediated by the MCC, in the ventral part named area 24'a. Indeed, the reduction of pain perception correlated with MCC activity distinctively in the context of hypnosis, compared with mental imagery and a resting state (Fig. 2.2). Other evidence for the involvement of the MCC during hypnosis comes from a recent study comparing different cognitive tasks in healthy volunteers. In this study, Egner *et al.* (2005) showed a hypnosis-induced modulation of conflict-related activity, known to involve the MCC, but not of cognitive control-related activity, dependent on prefrontal involvement. The anterior cingulate cortex (ACC) and MCC are functionally very heterogeneous regions thought to regulate the interaction between cognition, sensory perception and motor control in relation to changes in attentional, motivational and emotional states (Devinsky *et al.* 1995). The MCC that was shown to be

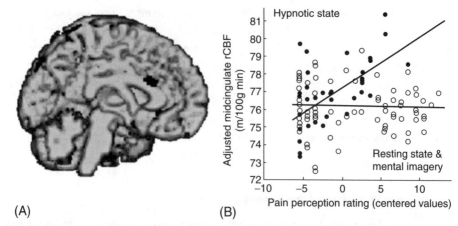

(A)   (B)

Fig. 2.2 (A) Brain area in which neural activity correlates with pain sensation ratings, in the specific context of hypnosis: the ventral part of the midcingulate cortex (area 24′a) shown in black on a 3D rendered spatially normalized MRI. (B) Plot of changes in pain perception ratings versus changes in adjusted blood flow in the midcingulate cortex, Note the difference ($P < 0.05$) in regression slopes between hypnosis (dots) and control conditions (circles). (Adapted with permission from Faymonville *et al.* 2000.)

activated in the study of Faymonville *et al.* has been related to pain perception, whereas the more anterior portions of the MCC are involved in attention-demanding tasks (Derbyshire *et al.* 1998). The location of MCC activation in this study was also more ventral and more posterior than the cingulate area reported to be associated with awareness of non-painful somatosensory stimuli (Buchel *et al.* 2002a). Anatomically speaking, the MCC is in a critical position to receive both the sensory noxious aspects from the somatosensory areas and insula, and the affective component of pain perception, encoded in the amygdaloid complexes and pregenual ACC.

Using a psychophysiological interaction analysis, assessing changes in cerebral functional connectivity, it was shown that the MCC [which mediates the hypnosis-induced reduction of pain perception (Rainville, *et al.* 1997, 1999; Faymonville *et al.* 2000)] increased its modulation of a large neural network of cortical and subcortical structures known to be involved in different aspects of pain processing, encompassing prefrontal, insular and pregenual cortices, pre-supplementary motor area (SMA), thalami, striatum and brainstem (Fig. 2.3). These findings reinforce the idea that not only pharmacological but also psychological strategies for relieving pain can modulate the interconnected network of cortical and subcortical regions that participate in the processing of noxious stimuli. The observed hypnosis-induced changes in connectivity between MCC and prefrontal areas may indicate a modification in distributed associative processes of cognitive appraisal, attention or memory of perceived noxious stimuli. Frontal increases in rCBF have previously been demonstrated in the hypnotic state (Maquet *et al.* 1999; Rainville *et al.* 1999; Faymonville *et al.* 2000). Frontal activation has also been reported in a series of studies on experimental pain, but the precise role of these regions in the central

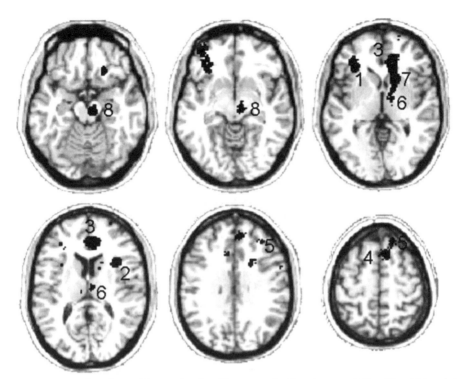

Fig. 2.3 Regions that showed hypnosis-related increased funtional connectivity with midcingulate cortex: left insula (1), right insula (2), perigenual cortex (3), pre-supplementary motor cortex (4), superior frontal gyrus (5), right thalamus (6), right caudate nucleus (7) and midbrain/brainstem (8). (Adapted with permission from Faymonville *et al*. 2003.)

processing of pain remains to be elucidated (Treede *et al*. 1999). The MCC also has a major role in motor function (Dum and Strick 1991). Its increased functional relationships with pre-SMA and striatum during hypnosis may allow the MCC to organize the most appropriate behavioural response, taking into account the affective component of pain perception. Indeed, the basal ganglia encode and initiate basic movement patterns expressed through premotor and primary motor areas, and show frequent activation to noxious stimuli (Jones *et al*. 1991; Coghill *et al*. 1994; Derbyshire *et al*. 1997, 1998). The basal ganglia are not exclusively linked to motor function but have also been proposed to support a basic attentional mechanism facilitating the calling up of motor programmes and thoughts (Brown and Marsden 1998). The insular cortex and the MCC are known to show the most consistent activation in functional imaging studies on pain perception. The insula is thought to take an intermediate position between the lateral (sensory-discriminative) and medial (affective-emotional) pain systems. It receives major input from the somatosensory system (Mesulam and Mufson 1982), has direct thalamocortical nociceptive input (Craig *et al*. 1994) and, through its projections to the amygdala, has been implicated in affective and emotional processes (Augustine 1996). Our observation of an increased midcingulate–insular modulation during hypnosis is in *can you get changed activity in a body swap experiment?*

line with its proposed role in pain affect (Rainville *et al.* 1999) and pain intensity coding (Craig *et al.* 2000). In the 'somatic marker' hypothesis of consciousness (Damasio 1994), the right insular cortex has been hypothesized to be involved in the generation of a mental image of somatic physiological states which underlies the attribution of emotional valences to external and internal stimuli. The observed increases in functional connectivity between the MCC and the thalamus and midbrain during hypnosis could be related to pain-relevant arousal or attention (Kinomura *et al.* 1996). Activation in the thalamus has recently been shown to correlate with pain threshold, whereas activation of the midbrain correlated with pain intensity (Tolle *et al.* 1999). It is tempting to hypothesize a hypnosis-related subcortical gating on cortical activation that underlies the observed decreased subjective pain perception. Previous studies have shown that different forms of defensive or emotional reactions, analgesia and autonomic regulation are represented in different regions of the midbrain's periaqueductal grey (Bandler and Shipley 1994). The perigenual cortex, insula and thalamus are also known to be implicated in autonomic regulation (Augustine 1996; Bandler and Shipley 1994). The observed modulatory role of the MCC on this network could explain the clinical finding that patients undergoing surgery during the hypnotic state show modified autonomic responses and fewer defensive reactions in response to an aversive encounter (Faymonville *et al.* 1997).

2.4 Functional magnetic resonance imaging in hypnosis

Recently, Boly *et al.* (2006) used fMRI to study the antinociceptive effect of hypnosis on pain processing. Event-related fMRI permits a more precise behavioural assessment, by allowing subjects to report their sensation immediately after each stimulus. fMRI also offers a more precise temporal and spatial resolution, and allows us to perform analyses at the single-subject level.

Our study used 3 Tesla fMRI to study the effect of hypnosis on thulium-YAG laser-induced pain in volunteers. Thulium-YAG lasers emit near-infrared radiation with a penetration depth of 360 μm into the human skin. The laser stimulation allows precise restriction of the emitted heat energy to the termination area of primary nociceptive afferents without damaging the epidermis or affecting the subcutaneous tissue (Spiegel *et al.* 2000). Additionally, the temperature rise in the superficial skin is fast enough to elicit activation of thinly myelinated Aδ- and unmyelinated C nociceptors (Buchel *et al.* 2002*b*). In this experiment, subjects underwent two separate counterbalanced fMRI sessions, one in the normal state, and one under hypnosis, in a parametric event-related design (Boly *et al.* 2005). During each session, 200 laser stimuli with intensities ranging from 300 to 600 mJ were administered on the dorsum of the subjects' left hand. After each stimulus, subjects rated their sensations as P0, no stimulus perceived; P1, warm, non-painful; P2, very mild pinprick, painful; P3, pain comparable with that evoked by a pulled hair; P4, painful sensation more important than that evoked by a pulled hair. Because of fMRI continuous background noise, the hypnotic procedure could not be continued throughout functional imaging acquisition. Subjects were instructed to interrupt the experiment if ever they returned to the normal awake state. Sleep was excluded

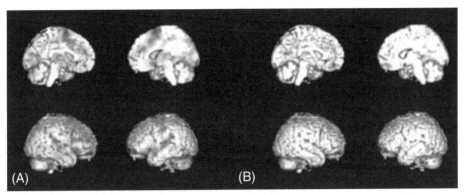

Fig. 2.4 Functional MRI results of an individual healthy volunteer showing dramatic differences in brain activity between normal and hypnotic states in response to intensity-matched noxious thulium-YAG laser stimuli. (A) In the normal awake state, presentation of noxious stimuli activates a large set of areas of the so-called 'pain matrix', including primary somatosensory cortex, insula, midcingulate cortex and fronto-parietal association cortices. (B) In the hypnotic state, the same stimuli only lead to activation of primary somatosensory cortex. The results are displayed at a threshold of $P < 0.001$ uncorrected. Please refer to Plate 1 for a colour version of this figure.

by the presence of subjects' motor responses in the context of continuous pain score monitoring during the experiment. Individual analysis compared activation induced by laser stimulation in the normal state and in the hypnotic state, for the same intensity of stimulation. Preliminary results show that a significant difference in sensation was found between the normal state and the hypnotic state for the painful intensity range of stimulation, but not for the sensorial (non-painful) range of intensity (Boly *et al.* 2006). Figure 2.4 shows a representative subject's brain activation in response to intensity-matched laser stimulati, in normal and hypnotic states. In the normal state (Fig. 2.4A), high intensity (painful) compared with low intensity (non-painful) stimuli activated bilateral thalamus, primary somatosensory cortices, insula and MCC (i.e., the pain matrix). In the hypnotic state (Fig. 2.4B), high intensity stimuli only activated primary somatosensory cortex, confirming the dramatic differences in brain processing of noxious stimuli induced by hypnotic induction.

2.5 **Concluding remarks**

Hypnosis can be seen as a particular cerebral waking state where the subject, seemingly somnolent, experiences a vivid, multimodal, coherent, memory-based mental imagery that invades and fills the subject's consciousness. The pattern of cerebral activation, measured by means of $H_2{}^{15}O$-PET, during the hypnotic state, differs from that induced by simple mental imagery. The reduced nociception during hypnosis is mediated by an increased functional connectivity between the MCC and insular, pregenual, frontal and pre-SMA regions, as well as the brainstem, thalamus and basal ganglia. These findings point to a critical role for the MCC in hypnosis-related alteration of sensory, affective, cognitive and behavioural aspects of nociception. Preliminary fMRI results also show that the hypnotic state can induce dramatic differences in brain processing of nociceptive stimuli, compared with the normal awake state. These results reinforce the idea that not only pharmacological but also psychological strategies for relieving pain can modulate the interconnected network of cortical and subcortical regions that participate in the processing of painful stimuli.

Acknowledgements

M.B., S.L. and P.M. are, respectively, Research fellow, Research Associate and Research Director at the Belgian 'Fonds National de la Recherche Scientifique' (FNRS).

References

Alkire MT and Miller J (2005). General anesthesia and the neural correlates of consciousness. *Progress in Brain Research*, **150**, 229–44.

Augustine JR (1996). Circuitry and functional aspects of the insular lobe in primates including humans. *Brain Research and Brain Research Reviews*, **22**, 229–44.

Aupee AM, Desgranges B, Eustache F, Lalevee C, de la Sayette V, Viader F and Baron JC (2001). Voxel-based mapping of brain hypometabolism in permanent amnesia with PET. *Neuroimage*, **13**, 1164–73.

Baars BJ, Ramsoy TZ and Laureys S (2003). Brain, conscious experience and the observing self. *Trends in Neuroscience*, **26**, 671–5.

Bandler R and Shipley MT (1994). Columnar organization in the midbrain periaqueductal gray: modules for emotional expression? *Trends in Neuroscience*, **17**, 379–89.

Boly M, Balteau E, Peigneux P, Faymonville ME, Schnakers C, Degueldre C, *et al.* (2005). BOLD response relates to single-trial thulium-YAG laser sensory-discriminative and pain processing without requiring subjects' subjective report. Toronto, Canada. *NeuroImage* supplement on CD-ROM.

Boly M, Balteau E, Schnakers C, Kupers R, Ngawa M, Moonen G, *et al.* (2006). Hypnosis-induced analgesia: an event-related thulium-YAG laser fMRI study. Human Brain Mapping 12th Annual Meeting. 11–15 June 2006, Florence. Neuroimage, **31**, Supplement 1.

Brown P and Marsden CD (1998). What do the basal ganglia do? *Lancet*, **351**, 1801–4.

Buchel C, Bornhovd K, Quante M, Glauche V, Bromm B and Weiller C (2002*a*). Dissociable neural responses related to pain intensity, stimulus intensity, and stimulus awareness within the anterior cingulate cortex: a parametric single-trial laser functional magnetic resonance imaging study. *Journal of Neuroscience*, **22**, 970–6.

Buchel C, Bornhovd K, Quante M, Glauche V, Bromm B and Weiller C (2002*b*). Dissociable neural responses related to pain intensity, stimulus intensity, and stimulus awareness within the anterior cingulate cortex: a parametric single-trial laser functional magnetic resonance imaging study. *Journal of Neuroscience*, **22**, 970–6.

Coghill RC, Talbot JD, Evans AC, Meyer E, Gjedde A, Bushnell MC, *et al.* (1994). Distributed processing of pain and vibration by the human brain. *Journal of Neuroscience*, **14**, 4095–108.

Craig AD, Bushnell MC, Zhang ET and Blomqvist A (1994). A thalamic nucleus specific for pain and temperature sensation. *Nature*, **372**, 770–3.

Craig AD, Chen K, Bandy D and Reiman EM (2000). Thermosensory activation of insular cortex. *Nature Neuroscience*, **3**, 184–90.

Damasio AR (1994). *Descartes' error: emotion, reason, and the human brain.* New York, G.P. Putnam.

De Betz B and Sunnen G (1985). *A primer of clinical hypnosis.* Littleton, MA, PSG Publishing.

Decety J (1996). Neural representations for action. *Reviews of Neuroscience*, **7**, 285–97.

Defechereux T, Degauque C, Fumal I, Faymonville ME, Joris J, Hamoir E, *et al.* (2000). Hypnosedation, a new method of anesthesia for cervical endocrine surgery. Prospective randomized study. *Annales de Chirurgie*, **125**, 539–46.

Defechereux T, Faymonville ME, Joris J, Hamoir E, Moscato A and Meurisse M (1998). Surgery under hypnosedation. A new therapeutic approach to hyperparathyroidism. *Annales de Chirurgie*, **52**, 439–43.

Defechereux T, Meurisse M, Hamoir E, Gollogly L, Joris J and Faymonville ME (1999). Hypnoanesthesia for endocrine cervical surgery: a statement of practice. *Journal of Alternative and Complementary Medicine*, **5**, 509–20.

Derbyshire SW, Jones AK, Gyulai F, Clark S, Townsend D and Firestone LL (1997). Pain processing during three levels of noxious stimulation produces differential patterns of central activity. *Pain*, **73**, 431–45.

Derbyshire SW, Vogt BA and Jones AK (1998). Pain and Stroop interference tasks activate separate processing modules in anterior cingulate cortex. *Experimental Brain Research*, **118**, 52–60.

Devinsky O, Morrell MJ and Vogt BA (1995). Contributions of anterior cingulate cortex to behaviour. *Brain*, **118**, 279–306.

Dum RP and Strick PL (1991). The origin of corticospinal projections from the premotor areas in the frontal lobe. *Journal of Neuroscience*, **11**, 667–89.

Edmonston WE, Jr (1977). Neutral hypnosis as relaxation. *American Journal of Clinical Hypnosis*, **20**, 69–75.

Egner T, Jamieson G and Gruzelier J (2005). Hypnosis decouples cognitive control from conflict monitoring processes of the frontal lobe. *Neuroimage*, **27**, 969–78.

Faymonville ME, Fissette J, Mambourg PH, Delchambre A and Lamy M (1994). Hypnosis, hypnotic sedation. Current concepts and their application in plastic surgery]. *Revue Médicale de Liège*, **49**, 13–22.

Faymonville ME, Fissette J, Mambourg PH, Roediger L, Joris J and Lamy M (1995). Hypnosis as adjunct therapy in conscious sedation for plastic surgery. *Regional Anesthesia*, **20**, 145–51.

Faymonville ME, Mambourg PH, Joris J, Vrijens B, Fissette J, Albert A, *et al.* (1997). Psychological approaches during conscious sedation. Hypnosis versus stress reducing strategies: a prospective randomized study. *Pain*, **73**, 361–7.

Faymonville ME, Defechereux T, Joris J, Adant JP, Hamoir E and Meurisse M (1998). Hypnosis and its application in surgery. *Revue Médicale de Liège*, **53**, 414–8.

Faymonville ME, Meurisse M and Fissette J (1999). Hypnosedation: a valuable alternative to traditional anaesthetic techniques. *Acta Chirurgica Belgica*, **99**, 141–6.

Faymonville ME, Laureys S, Degueldre C, DelFiore G, Luxen A, Franck G, *et al.* (2000). Neural mechanisms of antinociceptive effects of hypnosis. *Anesthesiology*, **92**, 1257–67.

Faymonville ME, Roediger L, Del Fiore G, Delgueldre C, Phillips C, Lamy M, *et al.* (2003). Increased cerebral functional connectivity underlying the antinociceptive effects of hypnosis. *Brain Research and Cognitive Brain Research*, **17**, 255–62.

Fink GR, Markowitsch HJ, Reinkemeier M, Bruckbauer T, Kessler J and Heiss WD (1996). Cerebral representation of one's own past: neural networks involved in autobiographical memory. *Journal of Neuroscience*, **16**, 4275–82.

Frenay MC, Faymonville ME, Devlieger S, Albert A and Vanderkelen A (2001). Psychological approaches during dressing changes of burned patients: a prospective randomised study comparing hypnosis against stress reducing strategy. *Burns*, **27**, 793–9.

Gusnard DA and Raichle ME (2001). Searching for a baseline: functional imaging and the resting human brain. *Nature Reviews Neuroscience*, **2**, 685–94.

Halligan PW, Athwal BS, Oakley DA and Frackowiak RS (2000). Imaging hypnotic paralysis: implications for conversion hysteria. *Lancet*, **355**, 986–7.

Hilgard ER, Lauer LW and Morgan AH (1963). *Manual for standard profile scales of hypnotic susceptibility, forms I and II*. Palo Alto, CA, Consulting Psychologists Press.

Jones AK, Brown WD, Friston KJ, Qi LY and Frackowiak RS (1991). Cortical and subcortical localization of response to pain in man using positron emission tomography. *Proceedings of the Royal Society B: Biological Sciences*, **244**, 39–44.

Kihlstrom JF and Edmonston WE Jr (1971). Alterations in consciousness in neutral hypnosis: distortions in semantic space. *American Journal of Clinical Hypertension*, **13**, 243–8.

Kinomura S, Larsson J, Gulyas B and Roland PE (1996). Activation by attention of the human reticular formation and thalamic intralaminar nuclei. *Science*, **271**, 512–5.

Kosslyn SM, Ganis G and Thompson WL (2001). Neural foundations of imagery. *Nature Reviews Neuroscience*, **2**, 635–42.

Laureys S (2005). The neural correlate of (un)awareness: lessons from the vegetative state. *Trends in Cognitive Science*, **9**, 556–9.

Lynn SJ, Kirsch I, Barabasz A, Cardena E and Patterson D (2000). Hypnosis as an empirically supported clinical intervention: the state of the evidence and a look to the future. *International Journal of Clinical and Experimental Hypnotism*, **48**, 239–59.

Maquet P (2000). Functional neuroimaging of normal human sleep by positron emission tomography. *Journal of Sleep Research*, **9**, 207–31. → dl in dreamless during REM

Maquet P, Faymonville ME, Degueldre C, Delfiore G, Franck G, Luxen A, *et al.* (1999). Functional neuroanatomy of hypnotic state. *Biological Psychiatry*, **45**, 327–33.

Maquet P, Ruby P, Maudoux A, Albouy G, Sterpenich V, Dang-Vu T, *et al.* (2005). Human cognition during REM sleep and the activity profile within frontal and parietal cortices: a reappraisal of functional neuroimaging data. *Progress in Brain Research*, **150**, 219–27.

Matsuda H (2001). Cerebral blood flow and metabolic abnormalities in Alzheimer's disease. *Annals of Nuclear Medicine*, **15**, 85–92.

Mesulam MM and Mufson EJ (1982). Insula of the old world monkey. III. Efferent cortical output and comments on function. *Journal of Comparative Neurology*, **212**, 38–52.

Meurisse M, Faymonville ME, Joris J, Nguyen Dang D, Defechereux T and Hamoir E (1996). Endocrine surgery by hypnosis. From fiction to daily clinical application. *Annales d'Endocrinologie*, **57**, 494–501.

Meurisse M, Defechereux T, Hamoir E, Maweja S, Marchettini P, Gollogly L, *et al.* (1999a). Hypnosis with conscious sedation instead of general anaesthesia? Applications in cervical endocrine surgery. *Acta Chirurgica Belgica*, **99**, 151–8.

Meurisse M, Hamoir E, Defechereux T, Gollogly L, Derry O, Postal A, *et al.* (1999b). Bilateral neck exploration under hypnosedation: a new standard of care in primary hyperparathyroidism? *Annals of Surgery*, **229**, 401–8.

Rainville P, Duncan GH, Price DD, Carrier B and Bushnell MC (1997). Pain affect encoded in human anterior cingulate but not somatosensory cortex. *Science*, 277, 968–71.

Rainville P, Hofbauer RK, Paus T, Duncan GH, Bushnell MC and Price DD (1999). Cerebral mechanisms of hypnotic induction and suggestion. *Journal of Cognitive Neuroscience*, **11**, 110–25.

Raz A, Shapiro T, Fan J and Posner MI (2002). Hypnotic suggestion and the modulation of Stroop interference. *Archives of General Psychiatry*, **59**, 1155–61.

Raz A, Fan J and Posner MI (2005). Hypnotic suggestion reduces conflict in the human brain. *Proceedings of the National Academy of Sciences of the USA*, **102**, 9978–83.

Spiegel D (1991). Neurophysiological correlates of hypnosis and dissociation. *Journal of Neuropsychiatry and Clinical Neurosciences*, **3**, 440–5.

Spiegel J, Hansen C and Treede RD. (2000). Clinical evaluation criteria for the assessment of impaired pain sensitivity by thulium-laser evoked potentials. *Clinical Neurophysiology*, **111**, 725–35.

The Executive Committee of the American Psychological Association, Division of Psychological Hypnosis (1994). Definition and description of hypnosis. *Contemporary Hypnosis*, **11**, 142–162.

Tolle TR, Kaufmann T, Siessmeier T, Lautenbacher S, Berthele A, Munz F, *et al.* (1999). Region-specific encoding of sensory and affective components of pain in the human brain: a positron emission tomography correlation analysis. *Annals of Neurology*, **45**, 40–7.

Treede RD, Kenshalo DR, Gracely RH and Jones AK (1999). The cortical representation of pain. *Pain*, **79**, 105–11.

Vogt BA and Laureys S (2005). Posterior cingulate, precuneal and retrosplenial cortices: cytology and components of the neural network correlates of consciousness. *Progress in Brain Research*, **150**, 205–17.

Chapter 3

Cognitive control processes and hypnosis

Tobias Egner and Amir Raz

3.1 Introduction

The striking changes in perception and conscious awareness that can be achieved with hypnotic induction have fascinated psychologists for many years. How does one account for neurologically healthy subjects who, following hypnotic induction and appropriate suggestions, report to perceive an illusory voice, or negate seeing an object placed right in front of them? To hypnosis researchers, the recent advent of cognitive neuroscience has brought forth great promise, with new techniques such as functional magnetic resonance imaging (fMRI) allowing us to take a peek into the hypnotized brain. However, the benefits of a cross-talk between the fields of hypnosis and cognitive neuroscience research are mutual, for hypnotic suggestions can serve as a rich avenue for the investigation of fundamental brain processes (Raz and Shapiro 2002). From a cognitive neuroscience perspective, the apparent dissociation between subjective experience and external stimulation observed in hypnotized subjects represents a powerful demonstration of top-down mechanisms affecting bottom-up processes, which are often thought of as automatic or involuntary. Clearly, a thorough understanding of the neural mechanisms underlying hypnosis will contribute substantially to our comprehension of human brain function *per se*.

The fact that hypnotic suggestions may help effectively to over-ride what are traditionally considered automatic or pre-potent processes is of particular intrigue to cognitive neuroscientists, because this ability is regarded as the domain of high-level 'cognitive control' processes. Cognitive control connotes a capacity-limited resource that is thought to be required when dealing with situations where mere 'automatic' processing would not suffice to produce optimal performance (or may even interfere with optimal performance), and has been closely tied to functions of the frontal lobes (Botvinick *et al.* 2001; Miller and Cohen 2001). Situations that require cognitive control include the performance of novel tasks, simultaneous tasks, task switching and, more generally, the need to over-ride pre-potent associations and responses. Does this mean that hypnotic phenomena can simply be equated to an extreme instance of normal top-down cognitive control processes? Probably not: after all, hypnotized subjects seem to be characterized by a lack of volition and control over their own actions, with the latter being dictated by the suggestions of the hypnotist. The current chapter is aimed at elucidating this apparently paradoxical relationship between cognitive control and hypnosis, and the brain processes mediating their association.

Before we commence, a few semantic and methodological pointers for the reader unfamiliar with hypnosis jargon are in order. A hypnosis session typically consists of three phases; the *hypnotic induction* (usually involving instructions to focus exclusively on the hypnotist's voice, accompanied by a progressive relaxation), followed by a number of *hypnotic suggestions* (e.g. the suggestion that there is a voice addressing the subject from a non-existent loudspeaker) and finally a *deinduction* (typically a 'countdown' for the subject to return to a normal, alert state) that finishes the session. In addition, hypnotic suggestions can be given that exhort the subjects to carry out a particular act in response to a cue given *after* the hypnotic session has concluded, a technique referred to as *post-hypnotic suggestion*. Furthermore, it is important to appreciate that subjects' susceptibility to hypnosis varies greatly. Therefore, subjects are typically pre-tested with standardized hypnotic induction scripts, such as the Harvard Group Scale of Hypnotic Susceptibility, Form A (HGSHS: A) (Shor and Orne 1962) or the Stanford Hypnotic Susceptibility Scale, Form C (SHSS: C) (Weitzenhoffer and Hilgard 1962). Obviously, for different studies to be comparable, it is important that they employ similar subject selection criteria. A typical research design in a hypnosis study compares a dependent measure (e.g. behavioural performance on an attention task) between pre-selected subjects of very low versus very high hypnotic susceptibility, outside the hypnotic context versus subsequent to hypnotic induction or in response to specific hypnotic suggestions. Hypnotic performance in this kind of design should be observed only in highly susceptible subjects in the hypnosis condition.

Finally, the discussion of cognitive control processes in relation to hypnosis and hypnotic susceptibility in the current chapter does of course take place in the context of previous theorizing, and we will interpret the literature with reference to some major currents in this field, as outlined here. Perhaps not surprisingly, theoretical models of hypnosis have traditionally emphasized the importance of attentional control processes in accounting for hypnotic phenomena (Barber 1960; Hilgard 1965; Krippner and Bindler 1974; Tellegen and Atkinson 1974; Hilgard 1977; Karlin 1979; Crawford and Gruzelier 1992; Woody and Bowers 1994; Gruzelier 1998; Raz and Shapiro 2002; Raz 2004). Two broad schools of thought have evolved around this issue. One view proposes that individuals who are highly susceptible to hypnosis possess the ability to focus their attention strongly, and that the hypnotic condition itself is characterized by a state of highly focused attention (Barber 1960; Tellegen and Atkinson 1974; Spiegel 2003). Another view argues that highly susceptible individuals may indeed be particularly adept at focusing their attention, but that once they are hypnotized, control of attention is impaired (Hilgard 1965; Hilgard 1977; Gruzelier 1990, 1998; Crawford and Gruzelier 1992; Woody and Bowers 1994; Jamieson and Sheehan 2004). At the neurophysiological level, many theoretical formulations have hypothesized a crucial involvement of frontal lobe functions in mediating hypnosis and hypnotic susceptibility (Gruzelier 1990, 1998; Crawford and Gruzelier 1992; Woody and Bowers 1994). In the following, these models will be referred to as the 'focused attention' and the 'impaired attention' views of hypnosis.

We will first review how cognitive control is measured behaviourally, focusing in particular on the use of the colour-word Stroop task (Stroop, 1935; MacLeod 1991) (Section 3.2.1). This exposition will be followed by a summary of the current literature on the functional neuroanatomy of cognitive control processes (Section 3.2.2). Then we will conduct a selective review of the behavioural and neuroimaging hypnosis literature in relation to cognitive control processes, as gauged by variants of the Stroop task (Section 3.3). This review will make an important methodological distinction between studies where the hypnotic induction procedure includes suggestions to improve Stroop task performance on the one hand (Section 3.3.2), and studies that did not incorporate such task-specific suggestions on the other hand (Section 3.3.1). Based on our discussion of this literature, we will outline a model to resolve the paradoxical relationship of hypnosis and cognitive control.

3.2 **What is cognitive control?**

In this section, we first present the concept of cognitive control and introduce psychological tasks and analysis techniques that purport to measure this construct. We then provide a brief, selective review of research into the functional neuroanatomy of cognitive control processes.

3.2.1 **Psychological concept and behavioural measures of cognitive control**

The distinction between 'controlled' and 'automatic' processing, alluded to in the Introduction, has a long tradition in theories of attention, where controlled processes have been characterized as requiring attention whereas automatic processes do not (Cattell 1886; Posner and Snyder 1975; Schneider and Shiffrin 1977). The concept of cognitive control closely resembles previous notions of attentional control, such as Shallice's supervisory attention system (Norman and Shallice 1986), or Posner's executive attention system (Posner and Petersen 1990; Posner and DiGirolamo 1998). For our current purposes, we will adopt the working definition that cognitive control describes the process or collection of processes that underpin the *flexible management of processing resources for optimal task performance*. This includes maintaining a representation of current goals in working memory, gauging the need for strategic performance adjustments, and implementing such adjustments, for example by steering attention towards task-relevant stimulus properties.

The efficiency of cognitive control functions has typically been inferred from traditional selective attention tasks, such as the Stroop task (Stroop 1935; MacLeod 1991) or the Eriksen flanker task (Eriksen and Eriksen 1974), which require subjects to attend and respond to one stimulus dimension (the 'target' dimension) while ignoring another stimulus dimension (the 'distracter' dimension). The need for controlled attention is manipulated by varying the response compatibility between target and distracter dimensions, which can either be in conflict with each other (incongruent), unrelated (neutral) or in accordance with each other (congruent). For instance, in a typical Stroop paradigm, subjects are required to name the ink colour in which a word stimulus is presented while ignoring the word meaning of the stimulus. Here, incongruent stimuli (e.g. the word RED printed in green ink) are typically associated with slower responses than neutral stimuli (e.g. XXXX in green ink), which in turn are identified more slowly than congruent stimuli (e.g. the word GREEN printed in green ink). The differential of incongruent to congruent (or neutral) reaction times constitutes the amount of interference or conflict experienced by the subject.

The amount of conflict incurred from an incongruent distracter, and by inference the degree of controlled attention required for processing the target, is determined by the *relative* strength of processing pathways (i.e. the relative 'automaticity') associated with the target and distracter dimensions, respectively, which arise from physical stimulus properties and, importantly, subjects' previous experience with the stimulus dimensions in relation to current task requirements (MacLeod and Dunbar 1988; Cohen *et al.* 1990). For instance, the fact that the word dimension of Stroop stimuli interferes substantially more with the colour dimension than the other way around is accounted for by the vastly greater experience we have with reading words compared with naming the ink colour of words (Cohen *et al.* 1990).

The Stroop task has evolved into perhaps the primary psychological measure of high-level, 'executive' cognition (MacLeod and MacDonald 2000) as well as a standard neuropsychological assessment tool of frontal lobe function (Stuss *et al.* 2001). The Stroop task has also been suggested as a potent arbitrator between models of cognitive control processes in relation to hypnosis and hypnotic susceptibility (Kirsch and Lynn 1998), and attentional control in hypnosis has indeed been investigated most extensively with variants of this paradigm (see Section 3.3 below). However, as a measure of cognitive control *per se*, the traditional Stroop interference score, gauged via the subtraction of either neutral or congruent trial reaction times from incongruent ones, is ambiguous. This is because the correct categorization of an incongruent stimulus (compared with a neutral or congruent trial) probably involves manifold processes, such as the detection of response conflict engendered by the incompatible stimulus dimensions, inhibition of the motor response associated with the distracter dimension, selection of the correct response and strategic adjustments in selective attention for the up-coming trial. Thus, behavioural and neuroimaging assays based on the standard Stroop subtraction capture an aggregate of (at least) conflict detection and control (conflict resolution) processes, and cannot unambiguously isolate the specific contribution of cognitive control.

It is possible, however, to dissociate cognitive control components of Stroop task performance from conflict detection by either manipulating conflict levels via the proportion of incongruent to congruent trials presented in a given block of trials (Logan and Zbrodoff 1979, 1982), or by analysing performance on a given trial type (congruent/incongruent) as a function of the preceding trial type (Gratton *et al.* 1992). This is because subjects appear to adjust strategically the level of control exerted in response to the level of conflict experienced or expected in a given trial or task block, such that control is upregulated following (and in anticipation of) high conflict, and downregulated following (and in anticipation of) low conflict (Botvinick *et al.* 2001), a phenomenon

how is conflict monitoring different from general monitoring? it's maybe that people have a different framework for looking at it - in the same way that Mark thinks inward attention is not the same as outward.

known as 'conflict adaptation'. For example, if subjects are presented with a Stroop task where a high proportion of trials are incongruent and a low proportion of trials are congruent, they appear to adjust to the higher level (and likelihood) of conflict by exerting more cognitive control. This is evidenced by lower interference scores in such a condition than when performing a condition where congruent trials are frequent and incongruent trials are rare (Logan and Zbrodoff 1979, 1982; Cohen *et al.* 1990; Carter *et al.* 2000). Thus, through the manipulation of the likelihood of incongruent trials occurring across blocks of trials, it is possible to distinguish between blocks where cognitive control is high and conflict is low (high proportion of incongruent to congruent trials), and blocks where cognitive control is low and conflict is high (low proportion of incongruent to congruent trials). Adjustments in cognitive control in response to varying levels of conflict can also be observed when presenting congruent and incongruent trials in equal proportions, and analysing performance on a given trial on the basis of which trial has preceded it. Here, it has been established that interference scores on current trials are reduced following high conflict (incongruent) trials compared with low conflict (congruent) trials, suggesting that conflict leads to a transient upregulation in control for the up-coming trial (Gratton *et al.* 1992; Botvinick *et al.* 1999; Kerns *et al.* 2004; Egner and Hirsch 2005a, b).

In summary, interference scores from traditional selective attention tasks have been widely employed as a *quasi* indicator of cognitive control, but they really constitute a composite measure of numerous high level processes rather than an exclusive estimate of cognitive control. More appropriate assays of the strategic control of selective attention can be obtained by gauging adaptation to varying levels of conflict in variants of the Stroop and flanker paradigms. This more direct probing of cognitive control processes, however, is under-represented in the general cognitive neuroscience research literature and to date largely unexploited within the field of hypnosis research.

Really?

3.2.2 Neural substrates of cognitive control

Not surprisingly, the classic interference tasks introduced in the previous section have formed the bedrock of neuroimaging research dedicated to outlining neural substrates of cognitive control processes. It is well established that a network of medial and lateral frontal cortices, particularly the dorsal anterior cingulate cortex (dACC) and lateral prefrontal cortex (lPFC), as well as parietal cortex, is more active when processing incongruent stimuli as compared with neutral or congruent ones (Pardo *et al.* 1990 Bench *et al.* 1993; Carter *et al.* 1995; Casey *et al.* 2000; Leung *et al.* 2000; Barch *et al.* 2001; Milham *et al.* 2001, 2003; van Veen *et al.* 2001; Durston *et al.* 2003; Fan *et al.* 2003, 2005; Hazeltine *et al.* 2003). Reliable co-activation in these regions in attentionally demanding conditions has led to the generally accepted notion of a fronto-parietal 'executive attention' network, but the delineation of the distinct functional contributions of each subregion within this network remains very much a work-in-progress, especially given that largely overlapping areas appear to be involved in a variety of other cognitive tasks as well (Duncan and Owen 2000).

As discussed previously in the context of behavioural variables, a dissociation of the neural correlates of cognitive control from other processes inherent in the processing of

incongruent trials *per se* may be achieved through the use of conflict adaptation paradigms. A number of studies have pursued this approach specifically in order to differentiate neural substrates of conflict detection from those of cognitive control. Focusing on
the role of the dACC within this context, it has been shown that activity in this region
primarily co-varies with the degree of conflict elicited by an incongruent stimulus, rather
than with strategic control processes associated with conflict resolution (Botvinick *et al.*
1999; Carter *et al.* 2000; MacDonald *et al.* 2000; Kerns *et al.* 2004). For example, dACC is
more activated by incongruent trials under conditions of low control (after a congruent
trial) than by incongruent trials under conditions of high control (after an incongruent
trial) (Botvinick *et al.* 1999; Kerns *et al.* 2004), supporting the conceptualization of the
dACC as an evaluative conflict-monitoring system (Botvinick *et al.* 2001). While a
rapidly growing body of evidence lends support to this model of dACC function
(Botvinick *et al.* 2004), it remains a possibility that other subregions of this area are
involved in more strategic (Posner and DiGirolamo 1998; Weissman *et al.* 2004) and
volitional processes (Nachev *et al.* 2005).

Neural correlates of cognitive control, on the other hand, have been localized to the
lPFC (MacDonald *et al.* 2000; Egner and Hirsch 2005*a, b*; Kerns *et al.* 2004). For instance,
when analysing conflict adaptation effects in a Stroop task, it has been shown that
regions in the lPFC exhibit an opposite activation pattern to that reported for the dACC:
activity in lPFC is higher under conditions of high control and low conflict than under
conditions of low control and high conflict (Kerns *et al.* 2004; Egner and Hirsch 2005*a, b*),
and the degree of lPFC activation is positively correlated with the degree of conflict
reduction across individuals (Egner and Hirsch 2005*a*). Furthermore, it has been
demonstrated that lPFC is particularly activated after trials on which the dACC exhibited
high activation due to conflict, and the degree of such lPFC recruitment predicts the level
of conflict reduction on the subsequent trial (Kerns *et al.* 2004). This superior conflict
resolution has recently been shown to be related to the functional interaction between
lPFC and early perceptual processing regions, resulting in an attentional amplification of
the neural representation of task-relevant stimulus properties (Egner and Hirsch 2005*b*).
In a different paradigm that sought to dissociate strategic control from conflict-monitoring processes, MacDonald and colleagues (MacDonald *et al.* 2000) found increased lPFC
activity in preparation for cued more difficult (colour naming) compared with easier
(word naming) Stroop trials, but no differential response to the actual conflict induced
by the subsequently presented stimulus (incongruent versus congruent). The dACC, on
the other hand, showed the opposite pattern of results, with more activation to incongruent than congruent stimuli, but no difference in activity with respect to the cue
period.

In conclusion, based on studies that have attempted explicitly to tease apart conflict
and control processes, it appears that the fronto-parietal executive attention network can
be broken down into a component that is primarily involved with detecting conflict
(the dACC), and another component primarily dedicated to strategic adjustments in
control (the lPFC). With reference to the well-documented role of the parietal cortex in
attentional orienting (Corbetta *et al.* 2000; Mort *et al.* 2003), one parsimonious view

would suggest that parietal regions may mediate the actual implementation of control, for example by directly biasing visual information processing in response to control signals from lPFC (Durston *et al.* 2003; Egner and Hirsch 2005*a*). However, many details of the functional interaction between components of the executive control system sketched out above remain unknown. Furthermore, performance adjustments of the type described here may arise from various sources additional to or instead of processing conflict, including lower level priming phenomena (Mayr *et al.* 2003; Hommel *et al.* 2004; Nieuwenhuis *et al.* 2006) and expectancy effects (Gratton *et al.* 1992) (cf. Egner and Hirsch 2005*b*).

3.3 Hypnosis and hypnotic susceptibility in relation to executive control processes *~ what I mean by sustained attention*

In this section, we will conduct a selective review of the hypnosis research literature that is relevant to the nature of the involvement of cognitive control processes in hypnosis and hypnotic susceptibility. Particularly, the exposition will focus on studies that have employed variants of the Stroop protocol, and highlight implications with respect to the assumptions underlying the 'focused attention' and 'impaired attention' models of hypnosis (cf. Egner *et al.* 2005) that were alluded to previously. Note that these views make opposing predictions with respect to the effects of hypnosis on Stroop task performance: The focused attention model asserts that highly susceptible subjects are characterized by focused attention during hypnosis, and should therefore predict low interference effects, compared with baseline as well as relative to subjects with low susceptibility. The impaired attention view, on the other hand, predicts that highly susceptible individuals should exhibit poorer Stroop performance in hypnosis than at baseline and in comparison with subjects of low susceptibility, due to an inhibition or dissociation of executive control functions. In discussing the research literature in this regard, an important methodological distinction will be drawn between studies where Stroop protocols were performed under conditions that included specific hypnotic instructions to promote particular cognitive strategies aimed at over-riding the Stroop effect, and studies that did not contain any task-specific hypnotic instructions.

3.3.1 Cognitive control in the absence of task-specific hypnotic suggestion

An early study that produced suggestive data on systematic differences in higher cognitive processing between individuals of low and high hypnotic susceptibility was conducted by Blum and Graef (1971). These authors sought to differentiate low susceptible 'simulators' from highly susceptible hypnotic subjects by comparing Stroop performance in response to a post-hypnotic suggestion procedure that aimed at manipulating arousal levels. Highly susceptible subjects exhibited increased Stroop interference scores with decreasing arousal, and higher interference across all levels of this manipulation than subjects with low susceptibility, suggesting less efficient attentional processing in the highly susceptible individuals. Note, however, that these results do not apply directly to cognitive processing during hypnosis, as the data were collected outside hypnosis (in response to a post-hypnotic suggestion). Furthermore, a very small sample size (five highly susceptible and two subjects with low susceptibility) precluded the use of inferential statistics. Therefore, this study may arguably serve primarily as a suggestive historical antecedent for subsequent research, rather than as strong evidence for impaired cognition in hypnotic responders.

In an influential study, Sheehan *et al.* (1988) provided the basic conceptual and empirical framework for addressing the relationship between Stroop performance and hypnotic phenomena. Their study assessed colour naming of incongruent Stroop stimuli in subjects of low and high susceptibility, once at baseline, once after hypnotic induction without task-specific suggestions and once after hypnotic induction that included task-specific suggestions to over-ride the Stroop effect. The instruction for overcoming Stroop interference consisted of exhorting the subjects to focus attention only on the bottom portion of the last letter of the colour word stimulus, so as to be aware of the ink colour only. Sheehan *et al.*'s (1988) results showed a hypnosis × susceptibility interaction effect, as reaction times slowed from baseline to hypnosis in subjects of high but not of low susceptibility. Conversely, highly susceptible individuals displayed a trend for improved performance with task-specific suggestions, which was not evident in subjects of low susceptibility (see also Section 3.3.2 below). In addition, highly susceptible subjects reported the spontaneous use of cognitive strategies for Stroop performance at baseline, but not in the hypnotic condition without task-specific instructions. Subjects of low susceptibility, on the other hand, reported consistently using spontaneous cognitive strategies across these two conditions.

In order to ascertain the reliability of these data, Jamieson and Sheehan conducted an extensive quasi-replication of the Sheehan *et al.* study, employing a large sample of 66 participants with low susceptibility and 66 highly susceptible participants (Jamieson and Sheehan 2004). Participants performed a mixed colour/word naming Stroop task, containing incongruent stimuli only, once at baseline and once following hypnotic induction. Both colour and word naming reaction times were slowed in the hypnotic condition, but this effect did not interact with hypnotic susceptibility. The amount of errors committed, on the other hand, displayed a hypnosis × susceptibility interaction effect mirroring the one reported by Sheehan *et al.* (1988) for reaction time data: highly susceptible individuals' performance deteriorated from baseline to hypnosis, but this was not the case for subjects of low susceptibility. Subsequent to the behavioural experiment, subjects were asked to report whether and how frequently they used any of three possible spontaneous strategies; subvocal rehearsal of task instructions ('word', 'colour'), an 'experiential strategy' that consisted of 'just letting responses happen' or a positional strategy that consisted of focusing on a small aspect of the overall stimulus. The use of the rehearsal strategy dropped from baseline to hypnosis, and tended to do so more in highly susceptible subjects. The use of the experiential strategy, on the other hand, increased from baseline to hypnosis, and this was more significantly the case in highly susceptible participants. The authors concluded from these data that hypnosis appears to impair both attentional control and the self-directed use of cognitive strategies (Jamieson and Sheehan 2004).

What aspect of attentional control in particular might be affected by hypnotic induction? Kaiser and colleagues (Kaiser *et al.* 1997) examined the relationship between hypnosis and performance on a Stroop-like task while measuring electric brain activity in the form of event-related potentials (ERPs). Specifically, their study assessed ERPs related to error processing, namely the error-related negativity (N_E) (Falkenstein *et al.* 1991; Gehring *et al.* 1993) and the subsequent error-related positivity (P_E) (Falkenstein *et al.* 1991), two response-locked ERP components occurring after an error has been committed. The N_E was originally interpreted as directly reflecting the detection of an error (Falkenstein *et al.* 1991; Gehring *et al.* 1993), but has since been re-conceptualized as representing the comparator process between the intended and the correct response, which precedes error detection (Falkenstein *et al.* 2000), or as reflecting post-response conflict-monitoring processes (Yeung *et al.* 2004). In either of these scenarios, the N_E is clearly proposed to constitute an important subprocess of cognitive control, namely the evaluation of a current response, which is thought to underlie strategic adjustments in performance. Modelling of the likely neural source underlying this ERP component has implicated the dACC (Dehaene *et al.* 1994; Miltner *et al.* 1997), a notion that has found corroboration in a number of fMRI studies (Carter *et al.* 1998; Kiehl *et al.* 2000; Menon *et al.* 2001; Ullsperger and von Cramon 2001). The later P_E component, also emanating from medial frontal cortex (Herrmann *et al.* 2002), is partly independent of the N_E but more reliably predicts post-error slowing (Nieuwenhuis *et al.* 2001; Hajcak *et al.* 2003), and has thus been proposed to reflect the becoming consciously aware of a committed error, which may be more directly related to performance adjustments than the N_E (Nieuwenhuis *et al.* 2001; Hajcak *et al.* 2003) (see also Jamieson and Woody, Chapter 7).

Kaiser *et al.* (1997) required subjects to push 'left' or 'right' buttons in response to arrow stimuli that pointed either to the left or right. In order to induce response conflict, the arrows could either be of green colour, requiring a response congruent with the direction of the arrow, or of red colour, requiring a response incongruent with the direction of the arrow. Error rates displayed a hypnosis × susceptibility interaction effect, as errors increased significantly from baseline to hypnosis in highly susceptible subjects but not in those with low susceptibilty. Furthermore, this effect was evident for the incongruent condition, but not the congruent one. Reaction times were slower on incongruent compared with congruent trials, but this effect did not interact with hypnosis or susceptibility variables. The ERP data disclosed no effects involving the N_E, but a marginal interaction effect with respect to the P_E component, as highly susceptible participants showed a decrease in P_E amplitude from baseline to hypnosis, which was not the case for subjects with low susceptibility. The authors interpreted the behavioural findings as supportive of the proposition that hypnosis in highly hypnotizable subjects involves the inhibition of frontal executive functions (reflected in impaired performance on incongruent trials). From the ERP results, the authors concluded that while early error processing (reflected in the N_E) appears to remain intact, hypnosis seems to attenuate consequent processes of contextual updating of the error occurrence, resulting in failed modulation of behaviour.

In a further ERP study, Nordby *et al.* (1999) employed a modified version of the colour naming Stroop task, where stimuli were presented in the left and right peripheral visual fields (rather than centrally). Behavioural and ERP data were acquired from subjects with low and high susceptibility, at baseline and following hypnotic induction. While there were no effects involving reaction times, a large increase in error rate was observed in the highly susceptible group only when going from baseline to hypnosis conditions. The authors further found that highly hypnotizable individuals displayed attenuated P3a amplitude as well as faster N2b latencies in their ERPs, compared with individuals with low susceptibility, but these differences did not interact with hypnosis. The behavioural results of this study mirror other findings of selectively impaired Stroop performance in highly susceptible subjects under hypnosis (Sheehan *et al.* 1988; Kaiser *et al.* 1997; Jamieson and Sheehan 2004). The ERP data were interpreted by the authors as reflecting a general failure in attentional orienting or disengagement of spatial attention in highly susceptible individuals (Nordby *et al.* 1999).

The data from the studies reviewed thus far are clearly in general accordance with an impaired attention view of hypnosis, in that all of them have reported performance detriments during hypnosis that were specific to highly susceptible individuals. Impairments have sometimes manifested in slowed response times (Sheehan *et al.* 1988), but more often in increased error rates (Kaiser *et al.* 1997; Nordby *et al.* 1999; Jamieson and Sheehan 2004), and appear to be accompanied by a decrease in the use of spontaneous cognitive strategies (Sheehan *et al.* 1988; Jamieson and Sheehan 2004). None of these studies have documented any evidence for Stroop performance improvements under hypnosis, a prediction of the focused attention account. A number of issues should be noted, however, that prevent the drawing of very specific conclusions with respect to the type of performance impairment that may be associated with hypnosis. After all, performance on a Stroop task may be affected by a host of processes that are not directly related to cognitive control. With respect to the methodological considerations reviewed in Section 3.2.1, none of the Stroop-type hypnosis studies reviewed above contained any manipulations aimed at parsing different aspects of executive processes during Stroop performance. Therefore, it cannot be deduced from these investigations whether the performance changes in highly susceptible subjects under hypnosis were underpinned by an impairment of conflict detection, of signalling between conflict-monitoring and cognitive control systems, of the proper maintenance and implementation of task set variables by the cognitive control system, or other attendant processes. Furthermore, in studies that exclusively employ incongruent stimuli (Sheehan *et al.* 1988; Jamieson and Sheehan 2004), it is impossible to distinguish a deficit in attentional selection of the task-relevant stimulus dimension from a generic performance decrement that may encompass processing of all stimuli, irrespective of whether they require attentional selection or not (such as neutral or congruent stimuli). This problem was avoided by Kaiser *et al.* (1997), who showed that hypnosis effects on performance were specific to the processing of incongruent trials and were not present in congruent ones. In addition, their ERP data supply evidence for the impairment of a more closely circumscribed facet of executive processing, namely the contextual updating of performance evaluation information that is necessary for successful behavioural adjustments. Regarding this latter interpretation, however, Kaiser and associates have unfortunately not provided evidence that behavioural modulation after error commission was specifically affected in highly susceptible subjects during hypnosis. Specifically, the degree of so-called 'post-error slowing', a tendency to produce slower but more accurate responses following an error trial (Rabbitt, 1966), should have been affected in the highly susceptible individuals.

Let us now turn to a small number of studies that have made some attempts at isolating strategic control processes in Stroop performance in relation to hypnotic susceptibility and hypnosis. Dixon et al. (1990) conducted an intricate experiment that employed a Stroop task variant where a colour word ('blue', 'green', 'red' or 'yellow', presented in black ink) immediately preceded the presentation of a coloured rectangle (blue, green, red or yellow), the colour of which subjects were required to name. The word primes could be congruent or incongruent with respect to the subsequent rectangle colour. Levels of conflict/control were varied in a block-wise fashion, by presenting a low congruent-to-incongruent stimulus ratio (75 per cent incongruent) in one condition of the experiment, and a high congruent-to-incongruent ratio (25 per cent incongruent) in another condition. Recall from Section 3.2.1 that a block with a high proportion of incongruent stimuli should be associated with high cognitive control, which in turn should result in low Stroop interference scores. Conversely, blocks with a low proportion of incongruent trials should be associated with low cognitive control and consequently exhibit high interference scores. The degree to which subjects employ strategic control processes to optimize performance can thus be gauged by assessing the reduction in interference between low control and high control blocks. The authors also manipulated the degree to which the distracter word information could influence colour naming. The colour words were presented either for a duration that was well above the subjects' perceptual threshold, or for a duration where subjects could not confidently identify the meaning of the word. Both conflict/control versions of the task were run at both threshold levels in subjects of low, moderate and high hypnotic susceptibility, at baseline only.

Dixon et al. (1990) found a hypnotic susceptibility × congruency interaction effect, as highly susceptible subjects exhibited significantly elevated interference scores in terms of reaction times. While there was no significant three-way interaction effect involving susceptibility, congruency and conflict/control variables, the authors present some intriguing simple effects data: with suprathreshold distracter stimuli, when going from low to high control conditions, subjects with low susceptibility displayed an abolished interference effect, whereas highly susceptible subjects still showed significant interference in the high control condition. These data can be interpreted as indicating that highly susceptible subjects were less successful at adjusting their attentional strategy than subjects with low susceptibility. (Note that the authors of the study favour a slightly different terminology and interpretation, concluding that highly susceptible subjects display a higher degree of automaticity in processing the colour word information.) Unfortunately, this study did not include hypnotic induction as an experimental factor, and therefore cannot shed light on any potential interaction between susceptibility and hypnosis variables.

In a follow-up experiment, Dixon and Laurence (1992) sought to separate automatic from strategic processing further by varying the time interval between a colour word prime ('blue' or 'red', in black ink) and a subsequent coloured rectangle (in blue or red ink) that subjects were required to categorize. The prime words were predictive of the opposite colour in the subsequent rectangle, i.e. if the prime word was 'blue', on 75 per cent of the trials the subsequent stimulus was red, and vice versa. The authors reasoned that at short prime-to-probe intervals, automatic processing would prevail and a Stroop interference effect would be evident, whereas at longer intervals, strategic processing could be implemented and the Stroop effect reversed (Logan *et al.* 1984). Subjects of low and high hypnotizability underwent testing at seven different prime-to-probe intervals. Stroop interference was reversed when going from short to long prime-to-probe intervals, attributable to the implementation of strategic processing. This effect, however, interacted with hypnotic susceptibility, as only the highly susceptible subjects displayed significant interference effects at the shortest prime-to-probe interval, and showed a reverse interference effect at a shorter prime-to-probe interval than subjects with a low susceptibility. The authors interpreted these data as indicating that highly susceptible subjects show a greater automaticity of word processing, due to greater interference at short prime-to-probe intervals, but *also* that highly susceptible individuals are better at implementing strategic adjustments than individuals with low susceptibility. Again, these data unfortunately do not address the effects of hypnotic induction, as the task was administered at baseline only.

The studies of Dixon and colleagues, while explicitly manipulating strategic control processes in Stroop performance, allow only for limited conclusions to be drawn with respect to models of attentional control and hypnosis. This is primarily because these investigations did not assess the interaction of hypnosis with hypnotic susceptibility, which is where the divergence of predictions from the focused and impaired attention models of hypnosis becomes apparent. Outside the hypnotic context, both views accommodate the assumption that highly susceptible subjects may be more adept at strongly engaging their attention compared with subjects of low susceptibility. Furthermore, with respect to the efficiency of strategic processing at baseline, results from the two studies by Dixon and associates are arguably inconsistent. The first study (Dixon *et al.* 1990) showed higher interference scores in highly susceptible subjects, and particularly so in a condition consisting of 75 per cent incongruent trials, i.e. under conditions of high strategic control, suggesting *deficient* control processes in highly susceptible subjects. In the second study (Dixon and Laurence 1992), on the other hand, strategic reversal of the Stroop effect was evident at shorter prime-to-probe intervals in individuals with high susceptibility than in those with low susceptibility, which suggests *better* strategic use of prime information in highly susceptible subjects. Therefore, on the basis of these results, it appears difficult to draw firm conclusions regarding the relationship between hypnotic susceptibility and efficient operation of cognitive control mechanisms.

A study that was specifically geared towards contrasting predictions of the focused and impaired attention models of hypnosis at the neural level was recently conducted by Egner *et al.* (2005). These authors carried out a combined fMRI and electroencephalographic (EEG) study, using a Stroop task with congruent and incongruent colour words, which were subject to either colour naming or word naming instructions, alternating between blocks of trials. Thus, there were four trial types of varying conflict; namely congruent word naming trials (low conflict), incongruent word naming and congruent colour naming trials (moderate conflict), and incongruent colour naming trials (high conflict). Based on the model of conflict-monitoring and cognitive control outlined in Section 3.2.2, it was expected that dACC activity would co-vary positively with conflict levels. Cognitive control processes, on the other hand, were expected to be more highly engaged during colour naming trials than during word naming trials (MacDonald *et al.* 2000). Egner and colleagues assessed conflict- and control-related brain activity in subjects of low and high hypnotic susceptibility, once at baseline and once after a hypnotic induction, with the order of conditions counterbalanced across groups. In addition, the same paradigm was repeated for all subjects in the EEG laboratory. Note that the focused attention model would predict that highly susceptible subjects exhibit less conflict-related dACC activation than those with low susceptibility, both at baseline and particularly during hypnosis. The impaired attention model, on the other hand, would predict that highly susceptible subjects experience more conflict in the hypnotic condition, compared both with baseline and with subjects with low susceptibility.

The authors found that, at equal behavioural performance, conflict-related dACC activity did not differ between groups at baseline, but was significantly increased in highly susceptible subjects after hypnotic induction, in comparison with baseline and in comparison with subjects with low susceptibility. This interaction corresponds precisely to the hypotheses derived from the impaired attention model of hypnosis. Next, the authors assessed how control-related activity, detected in left lPFC, varied with hypnosis and hypnotic susceptibility. In contrast to conflict-related activation in the dACC, there was no difference between groups and conditions in the control-related lPFC activation. From these data, the authors concluded that, while highly susceptible subjects experienced increased conflict in the hypnotic condition, they did not recruit additional cognitive control resources (reflected by lPFC activation) in order to resolve that conflict, which suggests a breakdown in communication between conflict detection and control processes. In support of this interpretation, EEG coherence data, reflecting functional connectivity between neuronal populations underlying different scalp sites (Miltner *et al.* 1999; Tallon-Baudry and Bertrand 1999), showed that coherence between the mid-frontal electrode site (overlying the dACC) and the left lateral frontal site (overlying lPFC) in the high-frequency gamma range was reduced in highly susceptible subjects after hypnotic induction, but not in subjects with low susceptibility. These data were interpreted as further corroboration of a possible disruption of functional interaction between medial frontal conflict-monitoring and lateral frontal control functions in hypnosis (Egner *et al.* 2005).

In summary, studies examining behavioural and neural correlates of Stroop-type task performance with respect to hypnosis and hypnotic susceptibility in the absence of task-specific hypnotic instructions have produced some consistent and many convergent findings. The most replicable finding is that highly susceptible subjects suffer performance decrements after hypnotic induction, while subjects of low susceptibility do not

(Sheehan *et al.* 1988; Kaiser *et al.* 1997; Nordby *et al.* 1999; Jamieson and Sheehan 2004). The precise nature of impaired attention performance under hypnosis, however, remains an intriguing issue for future empirical investigation. For instance, no study as of yet has assessed performance on a conflict adaptation Stroop protocol, arguably the most appropriate measure of cognitive control processes (as outlined in Section 3.2.1), as a function of hypnosis and hypnotic susceptibility. Nevertheless, the evidence reviewed here unequivocally supports an impaired attention view over a focused attention view of hypnosis, thus lending credence to models that postulate the hypnotic condition to be characterized by an inhibition (Gruzelier 1990, 1998; Crawford and Gruzelier 1992) or dissociation (Woody and Bowers 1994) of frontal lobe cognitive control functions. Two convergent findings from Kaiser *et al.* (1997) and Egner *et al.* (2005) provide grounds for some interesting speculation regarding a possible mechanism for such a deficit in frontal control. Both of these studies have shown that the mechanism underlying the detection of conflict or errors appears to remain intact in hypnosis. However, it may be the case that a later processing stage, which underlies conscious awareness of error commission and/or the communication of the detected processing conflict to cortical regions implementing performance adjustments, is affected during hypnosis. This conjecture is based on the finding that in highly susceptible subjects under hypnosis, the error-related positivity (P_E) is diminished (Kaiser *et al.* 1997), and the functional interaction between medial frontal and lateral frontal sites is disrupted (Egner *et al.* 2005). Consequently, even though the conflict-monitoring system may detect high conflict levels, there is no resultant strategic adjustment in cognitive control processes (Egner *et al.* 2005). This suggested refinement of the dissociated control view of hypnosis (see also Jamieson and Woody, Chapter 7) may serve to guide and constrain future rigorous empirical testing of the psychological and neural substrates of hypnotic phenomena.

3.3.2 Cognitive control in response to task-specific hypnotic instructions

In the previous section, we have reviewed evidence to suggest that cognitive control processes are specifically impaired in highly susceptible individuals after a generic hypnotic induction. Recall, however, that when Sheehan and colleagues instructed subjects to employ a specific cognitive strategy aimed at over-riding the Stroop effect, it was the highly susceptible subjects who benefited significantly from this intervention (Sheehan *et al.* 1988). This would suggest that, while cognitive control may be generally suppressed or dissociated during instruction-free hypnosis, this condition does nevertheless lend itself to the efficient implementation of an externally instructed strategy. In the following, a number of studies will be reviewed where task-specific instructions to overcome Stroop interference have been employed. Note that here, hypnosis is employed in the attempt to over-ride what is considered a highly automatic process (word reading). In this way, these hypnotic suggestions serve precisely the kind of function that usually is associated with cognitive control processes.

In a series of studies, Raz and colleagues (2002, 2003, 2005) have assessed Stroop performance in response to task-specific post-hypnotic suggestions. In these studies, performance by subjects of high and low hypnotic susceptibility was compared at baseline and in response to a post-hypnotic trigger. The hypnotic suggestion that was supposed to be recalled by the post-hypnotic trigger (e.g. a handclap) was to treat the word stimuli as if they were presented in an unfamiliar foreign language. This manipulation was aimed at preventing the 'automatic' processing of the word meaning, and thus to reduce Stroop interference. In an initial study, subjects of high and low susceptibility were required to indicate the ink colour of congruent or incongruent colour words, or neutral word stimuli (Raz *et al.* 2002). Raz and colleagues found that, in terms of reaction time data, highly susceptible subjects experienced Stroop interference at baseline, but that both Stroop interference and facilitation effects were successfully abolished in response to the post-hypnotic suggestion, whereas participants with low susceptibility exhibited comparable Stroop interference and facilitation effects between the two conditions. The authors concluded that post-hypnotic suggestion, presumably operating via a top-down mechanism, can effectively overcome the highly automatic word reading process. The authors further emphasized that the nature of the post-hypnotic suggestion did not reflect an overtly attentional strategy, such as only focusing on a single letter of the word stimuli.

In a follow-up investigation, Raz and associates endeavoured to substantiate these results while excluding the possibility that highly susceptible subjects may have achieved the reduction of Stroop interference by alternative means, other than by implementation of the post-hypnotic instruction (Raz *et al.* 2003). Specifically, the authors precluded the possibility of intentional visual blurring by pharmacologically inducing cycloplegia, the paralysis of the ocular muscles subserving visual accommodation. Furthermore, gaze orientation was monitored via video surveillance. Performance on a Stroop task identical to that in the previous study (Raz *et al.* 2002) was compared between conditions of a fixed crisp visual focus and a fixed blurred visual focus, at baseline. Performance was also assessed in response to a post-hypnotic suggestion (as above), given to highly susceptible subjects only, and an instruction to avert the gaze from the central stimulus, given to subjects with low susceptibility only. The reaction time data showed that significant Stroop effects were evident under clear vision and to a lesser extent under blurred vision conditions, but were abolished in highly susceptible subjects under post-hypnotic suggestions and in subjects with low susceptibility that had been instructed to 'look away' from the stimulus. From these data, the authors concluded that the abolition of Stroop interference in highly susceptible subjects under post-hypnotic suggestions could not be attributed to intentional blurring of visual focus, but rather appears to represent a genuine suppression of lexical word processing (Raz *et al.* 2003).

Finally, Raz *et al.* (2005) conducted a combined fMRI and EEG investigation in order to elucidate the neural correlates of post-hypnotic elimination of Stroop interference. A colour naming Stroop task was administered to subjects of high and low susceptibility while undergoing fMRI scanning. Subsequently, ERP data were acquired from the highly susceptible subjects only. The task was broken down into blocks, and half of the blocks were preceded by a post-hypnotic trigger (recalling the same type of instructions as in the previous studies), while the other half were not. Reaction time data showed that highly susceptible individuals had a significantly reduced interference effect during the fMRI session, while there was no effect of suggestion on the performance of individuals of low susceptibility. In addition, highly susceptible subjects abolished Stroop interference after post-hypnotic suggestion during the EEG session. Both of these findings were accompanied by corresponding improvements in accuracy. Regarding the fMRI data, the authors reported an interaction effect in a rostral portion of the ACC, as activation in this region was significantly reduced with suggestion in the highly susceptible individuals only. Highly susceptible participants furthermore displayed a concurrent reduction in activity in extrastriate visual cortex. ERP data from mid-occipital and mid-frontal electrode sites indicated that relatively early components of the stimulus-locked response (P100, N100) were suppressed and delayed under post-hypnotic suggestion, for both congruent and incongruent trials. Raz and associates interpreted these data as showing that post-hypnotic suggestion leads to decreased conflict in highly susceptible participants (as reflected in reduced ACC activity and behavioural interference), and that this effect may be mediated by top-down suppression of the visual processing stream, even though this dampening of visual processing appears to be generic rather than specific to word processing (Raz et al. 2005).

In summary, studies that have employed task-specific instructions aimed at overcoming Stroop interference have shown that such externally instructed cognitive strategies are more successfully implemented by highly susceptible subjects than by subjects with low susceptibility. These data have stemmed partly from a hypnotic context (Sheehan et al. 1988), but mostly from responses to post-hypnotic suggestions (Raz et al. 2002, 2003, 2005). A general concern when comparing some of these data with the results reviewed previously (Section 3.3.1) is that it is not entirely clear how exactly post-hypnotic responses correspond to responses after induction, i.e. 'during' hypnosis. Keeping this caveat in mind, these data nevertheless appear to pose a conundrum: why would highly susceptible subjects exhibit impaired cognitive control after an instruction-free hypnotic induction, but also display superior ability at implementing a suggested strategic instruction to improve task performance? One way in which these data may be reconciled is the proposition that hypnosis constitutes a state of dissociated attentional control that impairs the *internal* generation and implementation of strategic performance adjustments, but at the same time makes the hypnotized individual highly amenable to carrying out *externally* suggested task strategies. Recall that impaired performance after hypnotic induction has been characterized by a lack in the use of self-generated task strategies (Sheehan et al. 1988; Jamieson and Sheehan 2004). During hypnosis, the cognitive control system may lack the internal input signals from the conflict-monitoring system and thus fail to implement strategic performance adjustments (Kaiser et al. 1997; Egner et al. 2005). However, when furnished with a specific task strategy externally (i.e. at the hands of the hypnotist), the cognitive control system can implement this strategy in a highly efficient manner (Sheehan et al. 1988; Raz et al. 2002, 2003, 2005). It is an intriguing conjecture that the high efficiency in implementing external hypnotic instructions is precisely due to the fact that task processing is unencumbered by signals from internal performance-monitoring mechanisms, and may consequently be performed in a more automatic manner, akin to a 'contention scheduling' system (Norman and Shallice 1986) (see also Woody and Bowers 1994; Jamieson and Woody, Chapter 7).

This proposal can easily be tested empirically. Specifically, in order to integrate the seemingly disparate findings from instruction-free versus task-specific instruction studies, it would be desirable to assess both instruction-free and externally suggested strategy conditions in the same study, and to combine this manipulation with a Stroop task variant that explicitly isolates on-task cognitive control processes. In this context, the view advocated here would first predict that instruction-free performance would be inferior, but instructed performance would be superior in highly susceptible individuals (as in Sheehan *et al.* 1988). Secondly, this view would suggest that while overall Stroop interference may be reduced in highly susceptible individuals subsequent to external strategic task instructions, their performance should nevertheless be relatively immune to conflict-driven sequential performance effects (i.e. conflict adaptation) that arise from the ongoing interaction between the subjects and the stimulus history. Similarly, highly susceptible subjects would in this context be expected to show a failure in post-error slowing of their responses. Thus, while highly susceptible subjects may be superior at implementing an externally suggested strategy on a cognitive task, such as the Stroop protocol, their performance should also be highly inflexible, so that they would perform very poorly when task contingencies change. This could alternatively be tested in a variety of task-switching paradigms, which also offer a rich set of low- and high-level cognitive variables for manipulation (Monsell 2003), but have to our knowledge not been much exploited in hypnosis research.

3.4 **Conclusions**

In this chapter we have selectively reviewed the research literature pertaining to cognitive control processes and their neural instantiation in relation to hypnosis and hypnotic susceptibility. A discussion of commonly employed measures of cognitive control, particularly the Stroop task, has highlighted shortcomings of the traditional interference effect measure. We have concluded that the application of recent advances in the dissociation of various subcomponents of Stroop task performance, specifically the fractionation into conflict-monitoring and strategic control processes, would be highly informative to the hypnosis research enterprise. The hypnosis literature as it stands to date is concordant with an 'impaired attention' view of hypnosis, as highly susceptible individuals exhibit replicable attention performance detriments after generic hypnotic induction, which are accompanied by a lack of self-generated task strategies. However, if hypnotic induction is combined with task-specific strategic suggestions, highly susceptible individuals can perform exceptionally well. This has been demonstrated both with hypnotic, and particularly with post-hypnotic suggestions. We have interpreted these findings as indicating that hypnosis impairs the internal generation and implementation of strategic performance adjustments, but permits for very efficient implementation of externally suggested strategies. Neurophysiological data suggest that conflict and errors are detected normally in hypnosis, but that their detection apparently does not result in appropriate subsequent performance adjustments. The costs and benefits of hypnotic performance could be related to a breakdown in communication between a medial frontal performance-monitoring system and a lateral frontal cognitive control system. On the one hand, a lack of input from an internal conflict-monitoring system to top-down control regions results in inflexible, and therefore often poor performance. On the other hand, implementation of an externally suggested task strategy may proceed in an automatic fashion, unencumbered by signals from ongoing internal performance monitoring.

References

Barber TX (1960). The necessary and sufficient conditions for hypnotic behavior. *American Journal of Clinical Hypnotism*, **3**, 31–42.

Barch DM, Braver TS, Akbudak E, Conturo T, Ollinger J and Snyder A (2001). Anterior cingulate cortex and response conflict: effects of response modality and processing domain. *Cerebral Cortex*, **11**, 837–48.

Bench CJ, Frith CD, Grasby, PM, Friston KJ, Paulesu E, Frackowiak RS, *et al.* (1993). Investigations of the functional anatomy of attention using the Stroop test. *Neuropsychologia*, **31**, 907–22.

Blum GS and Graef JR (1971). The detection over time of subjects simulating hypnosis. *International Journal of Clinical and Experimental Hypnosis*, **19**, 211–24.

Botvinick M, Nystrom LE, Fissell K, Carter CS and Cohen JD (1999). Conflict monitoring versus selection-for-action in anterior cingulate cortex. *Nature*, **402**, 179–81.

Botvinick MM, Braver TS, Barch DM, Carter CS and Cohen JD (2001). Conflict monitoring and cognitive control. *Psychological Review*, **108**, 624–52.

Botvinick MM, Cohen JD and Carter CS (2004). Conflict monitoring and anterior cingulate cortex: an update. *Trends in Cognitive Sciences*, **8**, 539–46.

Carter CS, Mintun M, and Cohen JD (1995). Interference and facilitation effects during selective attention: an H215O PET study of Stroop task performance. *Neuroimage*, **2**, 264–72.

Carter CS, Braver TS, Barch DM, Botvinick MM, Noll D and Cohen JD (1998). Anterior cingulate cortex, error detection, and the online monitoring of performance. *Science*, **280**, 747–9.

Carter CS, Macdonald AM, Botvinick M, Ross LL, Stenger VA, Noll D, *et al.* (2000). Parsing executive processes: strategic vs. evaluative functions of the anterior cingulate cortex. *Proceedings of the National Academy of Sciences of the USA*, **97**, 1944–48.

Casey BJ, Thomas KM, Welsh TF, Badgaiyan RD, Eccard CH, Jennings JR, *et al.* (2000). Dissociation of response conflict, attentional selection, and expectancy with functional magnetic resonance imaging. *Proceedings of the National Academy of Sciences of the USA*, **97**, 8728–33.

Cattell JM (1886). The time it takes to see and name objects. *Mind*, **11**, 63–5.

Cohen JD, Dunbar K and McClelland JL (1990). On the control of automatic processes: a parallel distributed processing account of the Stroop effect. *Psychological Review*, **97**, 332–61.

Corbetta M, Kincade JM, Ollinger JM, McAvoy, MP and Shulman GL (2000). Voluntary orienting is dissociated from target detection in human posterior parietal cortex. *Nature Neuroscience*, **3**, 292–7.

Crawford HJ and Gruzelier JH (1992). A midstream view of the neuropsychophysiology of hypnosis: recent research and future directions. In: E Fromm and M Nash, eds. *Contemporary hypnosis research*. pp. 227–266. New York, Guilford Press.

Dehaene S, Posner MI and Tucker DC (1994). Localization of a neural system for error detection and compensation. *Psychological Science*, **5**, 303–5.

Dixon M and Laurence JR (1992). Hypnotic susceptibility and verbal automaticity: automatic and strategic processing differences in the Stroop color-naming task. *Journal of Abnormal Psychology*, **101**, 344–47.

Dixon M, Brunet A and Laurence JR (1990). Hypnotizability and automaticity: toward a parallel distributed processing model of hypnotic responding. *Journal of Abnormal Psychology*, **99**, 336–43.

Duncan J and Owen AM (2000). Common regions of the human frontal lobe recruited by diverse cognitive demands. *Trends in Neuroscience*, **23**, 475–83.

Durston S, Davidson MC, Thomas KM, Worden MS, Tottenham N, Martinez A, *et al.* (2003). Parametric manipulation of conflict and response competition using rapid mixed-trial event-related fMRI. *Neuroimage*, **20**, 2135–41.

Egner T and Hirsch J (2005*a*). The neural correlates and functional integration of cognitive control in a Stroop task. *Neuroimage*, **24**, 539–47.

Egner T and Hirsch J (2005*b*). Cognitive control mechanisms resolve conflict through cortical amplification of task-relevant information. *Nature Neuroscience*, **8**, 1784–90.

Egner T, Jamieson GA, and Gruzelier J (2005). Hypnosis decouples cognitive control from conflict monitoring processes of the frontal lobes. *Neuroimage*, **27**, 969–78.

Eriksen BA and Eriksen CW (1974). Effects of noise letters upon the identification of a target letter in a nonsearch task. *Perception and Psychophysics*, **16**, 143–49.

Falkenstein M, Hohnsbein J, Hoormann J and Blanke L (1991). Effects of crossmodal divided attention on late ERP components. II. Error processing in choice reaction tasks. *Electroencephalogric and Clinical Neurophysiology*, **78**, 447–55.

Falkenstein M, Hoormann J, Christ S and Hohnsbein J (2000). ERP components on reaction errors and their functional significance: a tutorial. *Biological Psychology*, **51**, 87–107.

Fan J, Flombaum JI, McCandliss BD, Thomas KM and Posner MI (2003). Cognitive and brain consequences of conflict. *Neuroimage*, **18**, 42–57.

Fan J, McCandliss BD, Fossella J, Flombaum JI and Posner MI (2005). The activation of attentional networks. *Neuroimage*, **26**, 471–79.

Gehring WJ, Gross B, Coles MGH, Meyer DE and Donchin E (1993). A neural system for error detection and compensation. *Psychological Science*, **4**, 385–90.

Gratton G, Coles MG and Donchin E (1992). Optimizing the use of information: strategic control of activation of responses. *Journal of Experimental Psychology-General*, **121**, 480–506.

Gruzelier JH (1990). Neurophysiological investigations of hypnosis: cerebral laterality, and beyond. In: R Van Dyck, PH Spinhoven and AJW Van der Does, eds. *Hypnosis: theory, research, and clinical practice*. pp. 38–51. Amsterdam, Free University Press.

Gruzelier JH (1998). A working model of the neurophysiology of hypnosis: a review of the evidence. *Contemporary Hypnosis*, **15**, 3–21.

Hajcak G, McDonald N and Simons RF (2003). To err is autonomic: error-related brain potentials, ANS activity, and post-error compensatory behavior. *Psychophysiology*, **40**, 895–903.

Hazeltine E, Bunge SA, Scanlon MD and Gabrieli JD (2003). Material-dependent and material-independent selection processes in the frontal and parietal lobes: an event-related fMRI investigation of response competition. *Neuropsychologia*, **41**, 1208–17.

Herrmann MJ, Rommler J, Ehlis AC, Heidrich A and Fallgatter AJ (2004). Source localization (LORETA) of the error-related-negativity (ERN/Ne) and positivity (Pe). *Brain Research Cognitive Brain Research*, **20**, 294–99.

Hilgard ER (1965). *Hypnotic susceptibility*. New York, Harcourt Brace and World.

Hilgard ER (1977). *Divided consciousness: multiple controls in human thought and action*. New York, Wiley Interscience.

Hommel B, Proctor RW and Vu KP (2004). A feature-integration account of sequential effects in the Simon task. *Psychological Research*, **68**, 1–17.

Jamieson GA and Sheehan PW (2004). An empirical test of Woody and Bowers's dissociated-control theory of hypnosis. *International Journal of Clinical and Experimental Hypnosis*, **52**, 232–49.

Kaiser J, Barker R, Haenschel C, Baldeweg T and Gruzelier JH (1997). Hypnosis and event-related potential correlates of error processing in a stroop-type paradigm: a test of the frontal hypothesis. *International Journal of Psychophysiology*, **27**, 215–22.

Karlin RA (1979). Hypnotizability and attention. *Journal of Abnormal Psychology*, **88**, 92–5.

Kerns JG, Cohen JD, MacDonald AW 3rd, Cho RY, Stenger VA and Carter CS (2004). Anterior cingulate conflict monitoring and adjustments in control. *Science*, **303**, 1023–26.

Kiehl KA, Liddle PF and Hopfinger JB (2000). Error processing and the rostral anterior cingulate: an event-related fMRI study. *Psychophysiology*, **37**, 216–23.

Kirsch I and Lynn SJ (1998). Dissociation theories of hypnosis. *Psychological Bulletin*, **123**, 100–15.

Krippner S and Bindler PR (1974). Hypnosis and attention: a review. *American Journal of Clinical Hypnosis*, **16**, 166–77.

Leung HC, Skudlarski P, Gatenby JC, Peterson BS and Gore JC (2000). An event-related functional MRI study of the stroop color word interference task. *Cerebral Cortex*, **10**, 552–60.

Logan GD and Zbrodoff NJ (1979). When it helps to be misled: facilitative effects of increasing the frequency of conflicting stimuli in a Stroop-like task. *Memory and Cognition*, **7**, 166–74.

Logan GD and Zbrodoff NJ (1982). Constraints on strategy construction in a speeded discrimination task. *Journal of Experimental Psychology-Human Perception and Performance*, **8**, 502–20.

Logan GD, Zbrodoff NJ and Williamson, J (1984). Strategies in the color-word Stroop task. *Bulletin of the Psychonomic Society*, **22**, 135–8.

MacDonald AW 3rd, Cohen JD, Stenger VA and Carter CS (2000). Dissociating the role of the dorsolateral prefrontal and anterior cingulate cortex in cognitive control. *Science*, **288**, 1835–38.

MacLeod CM (1991). Half a century of research on the Stroop effect: an integrative review. *Psychogical Bulletin*, **109**, 163–203.

MacLeod CM and Dunbar K (1988). Training and Stroop-like interference: evidence for a continuum of automaticity. *Journal of Experimental Psychology-Learning, Memory and Cognition*, **14**, 126–35.

MacLeod CM and MacDonald PA (2000). Interdimensional interference in the Stroop effect: uncovering the cognitive and neural anatomy of attention. *Trends in Cogn Science*, **4**, 383–91.

Mayr U, Awh E and Laurey P (2003). Conflict adaptation effects in the absence of executive control. *Nature Neuroscience*, **6**, 450–52.

Menon V, Adleman NE, White CD, Glover GH and Reiss AL (2001). Error-related brain activation during a Go/NoGo response inhibition task. *Human Brain Mapping*, **12**, 131–43.

Milham MP, Banich MT, Webb A, Barad V, Cohen NJ, Wszalek T, *et al.* (2001). The relative involvement of anterior cingulate and prefrontal cortex in attentional control depends on nature of conflict. *Brain Research Cognitive Brain Research*, **12**, 467–73.

Milham MP, Banich MT, Claus ED and Cohen NJ (2003). Practice-related effects demonstrate complementary roles of anterior cingulate and prefrontal cortices in attentional control. *Neuroimage*, **18**, 483–93.

Miller EK and Cohen JD (2001). An integrative theory of prefrontal cortex function. *Annual Review of Neuroscience*, **24**, 167–202.

Miltner WHR, Braun CH and Coles MGH (1997). Event-related brain potentials following incorrect feedback in a time estimation task: evidence for a generic neural system for error detection. *Journal of Cognitive Neuroscience*, **9**, 788–98.

Miltner WH, Braun C, Arnold M, Witte H and Taub E (1999). Coherence of gamma-band EEG activity as a basis for associative learning. *Nature*, **397**, 434–6.

Monsell S (2003). Task switching. *Trends in Cognitive Science*, **7**, 134–40.

Mort DJ, Malhotra P, Mannan SK, Rorden C, Pambakian A, Kennard C, *et al.* (2003). The anatomy of visual neglect. *Brain*, **126**, 1986–97.

Nachev P, Rees G, Parton A, Kennard C and Husain M (2005). Volition and conflict in human medial frontal cortex. *Current Biology*, **15**, 122–28.

Nieuwenhuis S, Ridderinkhof KR, Blom JB, Blom GP, and Kok A (2001). Error-related brain potentials are differentially related to awareness of response errors: evidence from an antisaccade task. *Psychophysiology*, **38**, 752–60.

Nieuwenhuis S, Stins JF, Posthuma D, Polderman TJC, Boomsma DI and de Geus EJ (2006). Accounting for sequential effects in the flanker task: conflict adaptation or associative priming? *Memory and Cognition*, in press.

Nordby H. Hugdahl K, Jasiukaitis P and Spiegel D (1999). Effects of hypnotizability on performance of a Stroop task and event-related potentials. *Perceptual and Motor Skills*, **88**, 819–30.

Norman DA and Shallice T (1986). Attention to action: willed and automatic control of behavior. In: GE Schwarz and D Shapiro, eds. *Consciousness and self-regulation*, Vol. 4. pp. 1–18. New York, Plenum Press.

Pardo JV, Pardo PJ, Janer KW and Raichle ME (1990). The anterior cingulate cortex mediates processing selection in the Stroop attentional conflict paradigm. *Proceedings of the National Academy of Sciences of the USA*, **87**, 256–59.

Posner MI and DiGirolamo GJ (1998). Executive attention: conflict, target detection, and cognitive control. In: R Parasuraman, ed. *The attentive brain*, pp. 401–423. Cambridge MA, MIT Press.

Posner MI and Petersen SE (1990). The attention system of the human brain. *Annual Review of Neuroscience*, **13**, 25–42.

Posner MI and Snyder CR (1975). Attention and cognitive control. In: RL Solso, ed. *Information processing and cognition*. pp. 55–85. Hillsdale NJ, Erlbaum.

Rabbitt PM (1966). Errors and error correction in choice-response tasks. *Journal of Experimental Psychology*, **71**, 264–72.

Raz, A. (2004). Atypical attention: hypnosis and conflict reduction. In: MI Posner, ed. *Cognitive neuroscience of attention*. pp. 420–29. New York, Guilford Press.

Raz A and Shapiro T (2002). Hypnosis and neuroscience: a cross talk between clinical and cognitive research. *Archives of General Psychiatry*, **59**, 85–90.

Raz A, Shapiro T, Fan J and Posner MI (2002). Hypnotic suggestion and the modulation of Stroop interference. *Archives of General Psychiatry*, **59**, 1155–61.

Raz A, Landzberg KS, Schweizer HR, Zephrani ZR, Shapiro T, Fan J, *et al.* (2003). Posthypnotic suggestion and the modulation of Stroop interference under cycloplegia. *Conscious Cognition*, **12**, 332–46.

Raz A, Fan, J and Posner MI (2005). Hypnotic suggestion reduces conflict in the human brain. *Proceedings of the National Academy of Sciences of the USA*, **102**, 9978–83.

Schneider W and Shiffrin RM (1977). Controlled and automatic human information processing: I, detection, search, and attention. *Psychological Review*, **84**, 1–66.

Sheehan PW, Donovan P and MacLeod CM (1988). Strategy manipulation and the Stroop effect in hypnosis. *Journal of Abnormal Psychology*, **97**, 455–60.

Shor RE and Orne EC (1962). *The Harvard Group Scale of Hypnotic Susceptibility, form A*. Palo Alto, CA, Consulting Psychologists Press.

Spiegel D (2003). Negative and positive visual hypnotic hallucinations: attending inside and out. *International Journal of Clinical and Experimental Hypnosis*, **51**, 130–46.

Stroop JR (1935). Studies of interference in serial verbal reactions. *Journal of Experimental Psychology*, **18**, 643–62.

Stuss DT, Floden D, Alexander MP, Levine B and Katz D (2001). Stroop performance in focal lesion patients: dissociation of processes and frontal lobe lesion location. *Neuropsychologia*, **39**, 771–86.

Tallon-Baudry C and Bertrand O (1999). Oscillatory gamma activity in humans and its role in object representation. *Trends in Cognitive Science*, **3**, 151–62.

Tellegen A and Atkinson G (1974). Openness to absorbing and self-altering experiences ('absorption'), a trait related to hypnotic susceptibility. *Journal of Abnormal Psychology*, **83**, 268–77.

Ullsperger M and von Cramon DY (2001). Subprocesses of performance monitoring: a dissociation of error processing and response competition revealed by event-related fMRI and ERPs. *Neuroimage*, **14**, 1387–401.

van Veen V, Cohen JD, Botvinick MM, Stenger VA and Carter CS (2001). Anterior cingulate cortex, conflict monitoring, and levels of processing. *Neuroimage*, **14**, 1302–8.

Weissman DH, Warner LM and Woldorff MG (2004). The neural mechanisms for minimizing cross-modal distraction. *Journal of Neuroscience*, **24**, 10941–49.

Weitzenhoffer AM and Hilgard ER (1962). *Stanford Hypnotic Susceptibility Scale, form C*. Palo Alto, CA, Consulting Psychologists Press.

Woody E and Bowers K. (1994). A frontal assault on dissociated control. In: SJ Lynn and JW Rhue, eds. *Dissociation: clinical and theoretical perspectives*. pp. 52–79. New York, Guilford Press.

Yeung N, Cohen JD and Botvinick MM (2004). The neural basis of error detection: conflict monitoring and the error-related negativity. *Psychological Review*, **111**, 931–59.

Chapter 4

Cortical mechanisms of hypnotic pain control

Wolfgang HR Miltner and Thomas Weiss

4.1 Introduction

Hypnosis has been known for centuries to modify significantly subjects' perceptions and other psychological processes. Thus, several studies have shown that colourful visual stimuli can lose their brightness and colour, and physically strong auditory stimuli can become almost inaudible when subjects are exposed to corresponding hypnotic suggestions of colour blindness or deafness (Revenstorf 1993). Furthermore, the skin of fakirs can become deeply penetrated by knives, daggers or swords without pain and without negative emotions while being in a hypnotic-like trance, whereas the same physical event would be perceived as terribly painful by the same persons outside the trance state (Larbig 1988; Larbig and Miltner 1990).

The reduction or even obviation of pain by specific hypnotic suggestions—called hypnotic analgesia—is a powerful tool of pain control and, perhaps, one of the most striking phenomena of hypnosis. The induction of hypnotic analgesia represents one of the most effective non-pharmacological methods for the control of acute pain that has been used in clinical practice for pain relief during different syndromes of disease and in different disciplines (Crasilneck and Hall 1973; Hilgard and Hilgard, 1983; for meta-analyses, see Montgomery et al. 2000; Bongartz et al. 2002). However, despite its successful application, we still do not understand how hypnotic analgesia affects the processing of noxious stimuli within the human nervous system and how the brain organizes the alleviation of pain by hypnotic analgesia. While the literature is full of speculative conceptions, only a few theories exist whose assumptions are based on current neurobiological foundations about the role of brain structures subserving the feeling of pain and whose central hypotheses were tested experimentally by modern neuroscientific methods. In this chapter, we will first introduce some of these brain structures and mechanisms and address some specific theories on hypnotic analgesia, and then summarize some current experimental evidence that supports or dismisses these theories.

4.2 Brain structures and mechanisms subserving the perception of pain—a short introduction

Nociception consists of the translation of physical properties of noxious stimuli into a code that can be understood by neurons and its transformation from peripheral/visceral receptors along the neuraxis to the central nervous system. Nociceptors are the end-points of neurons of the peripheral nervous system, whose cell bodies lie in the dorsal root ganglia. Nociceptors are sensitive to thermal, mechanical, chemical and electrical stimuli (for details, see e.g. Loeser *et al.* 2001, Weiss and Schaible 2003). When activated by noxious stimulation, action potentials are generated and transmitted to the spinal cord via C- and Aδ-fibres. Within the dorsal root of the spinal cord, these fibres are synaptically linked to one of two types of neurons, i.e. nociceptive-specific neurons (NS) which are activated exclusively by noxious stimuli, and wide-dynamic range neurons (WDR) which can become activated by, weak, innoxious and noxious stimuli. The activity of NS and WDR neurons passes through the spinal cord along several pathways to different subcortical and cortical structures. The most prominent efferent pathway is the spino-thalamo-cortical pathway which has, at least, two important subsystems. One sub-system, called the lateral system, innervates lateral nuclei of the thalamus, e.g. the ventral posterior lateral nucleus (VPL) whose nuclei innervate the primary somatosensory cortex, secondary somatosensory cortices and posterior parietal cortices of both cerebral hemispheres. This subsystem is thought to be responsible for the sensory-discriminative analysis of noxious stimuli, i.e. it is responsible for the perception of its location, intensity, duration, etc. The second subsystem, called the medial system, innervates medial nuclei of the thalamus, e.g. the posterior part of the ventromedial nucleus (VMpo) whose neurons primarily innervate the insula, the anterior cingulate cortex (ACC) and the prefrontal cortex. This subsystem is thought to be responsible for the affective-motivational analysis of noxious input. Besides the spino-thalamo-cortical projections, additional pathways exist that give input into the reticular formation, the midbrain and the hypothalamus. From these structures, different pathways reach cortical regions most of which are implemented in the affective-motivational analysis of stimuli. Within and between all these structures, noxious information is processed in parallel, serial and reciprocal ways. Previous psychophysical research has emphasized the importance of separating the experience of pain into sensory-discriminative and affective-motivational components. The sensory-discriminative component of pain can be considered as the sensory modality of pain similar to vision or olfaction. The affective-motivational component includes all aspects associated with suffering and is clearly related to aspects of emotion, arousal and the programming of behaviour. This dichotomy, however, has turned out to be too simple a concept for the functional significance and complexity of nociceptive cortical networks. Recent progress in imaging technology has, therefore, provided considerable new insights into the multiple dimensions of pain and evidenced that the experience of pain is mediated by the activity of different cortical and subcortical structures.

By means of positron emission tomography (PET), functional magnetic resonance imaging (fMRI) and different experimental methods with animals, it has been shown that several spatially distributed subcortical and cortical areas participate in the processing of nociceptive input and the generation of pain (for a review, see Apkarian *et al.* 2005) including primary and secondary somatosensory cortical areas, the insulae, prefrontal cortex, anterior parts of the gyrus cinguli, the thalamus and the periaquaductal grey (PAG).

Besides these afferent systems, recent research has also shown that the central nervous system of most vertebrates also includes several nocifensive systems for the control of pain. Since Descartes, the experience of pain has been conceived as a direct function of the extent of peripheral nerve activation. However, pain goes far beyond nociception in so far as the degree of general arousal, the amount of autobiographical experience and memory, the actual and general emotional state and aspects of subjective coping modulate the processing of nociceptive information and the generation of pain. These processes can at least partially be independent of nociception (Miltner 1998). These considerations are supposed to have significant clinical consequences: *pain should be defined as a private experience* whose individual qualia depends on each individual's capacity of cognition and emotion, its previous experience, the socio-cultural context and the individual behavioural capacities of pain control (Miltner and Weiss 1998, 2000).

Another aspect that contributes significantly to the experience of pain is the modular organization of spatially and temporally distributed neural networks of the brain and its mutual communication by which the quality and intensity of the pain experience is organized. Recent research has indicated that the experience of pain is the result of synchronized activities of spatially distributed cortical and subcortical areas including primary and secondary somatosensory cortical areas, the insulae, prefrontal cortex, anterior and medial parts of the gyrus cinguli, the reticular formation, thalamus and PAG, the amygdala, the hippocampal system and the hypothalamus. In order to constitute the experience of pain, all these structures must be activated in a temporally correlated manner. With regard to our main topic, disturbances of this synchronized activity should change the perception and experience of pain, as will be shown in the following sections.

4.3 Neuroscientific accounts of hypnotic analgesia

Recent neuroscientific accounts of hypnotic analgesia have mainly argued that it represents either (1) a specific kind of distraction or (2) a phenomenon during which normal information processing becomes disrupted or disorganized due to a significant dissociation of neural communication between brain areas.

4.3.1 Hypnotic analgesia—a specific form of distraction?

From an information processing viewpoint, hypnotic analgesia has been conceptualized as a specific form of attention modulation, i.e. as a state of divided attention where subjects become distracted from pain by simultaneously allocating all attentional resources to the ongoing suggestions of hypnotic analgesia (Crawford *et al.* 1993, 1998; Crawford 1994). This manipulation of attention was thought of as dynamically changing the neural interactions between subcortical and prefrontal areas of the brain (Crawford 1994). While the fronto-limbic attentional system was conceived to attenuate the processing of noxious input transmitted from thalamic relay nuclei to cerebral structures, the prefrontal cortex was implicated to inhibit thalamo-cortical neural projections (Birbaumer *et al.* 1990). A further crucial role of thalamo-cortical structures in attention was also emphasized by models on the existence of a central attentional capacity system

(Posner and Petersen 1990). According to this idea, hypnotic suggestions are thought to act as verbal stimuli that pull subject's attention towards the auditory input and its processing and apart from the processing of noxious input. This shift of attention from the somatosensory input channel to the auditory channel is thought to be one of the most significant and crucial mechanisms of hypnosis-induced pain control (Hilgard and Hilgard 1983). Based on these considerations, it was suggested that hypnotic analgesia and distraction of attention might share similar, if not the same, brain mechanisms.

However, recent studies on brain electrical neural activities in humans during hypnotic analgesia and distraction from painful stimulation have shown that this conception might be misleading. In two studies, the effects of distraction and hypnotic analgesia on pain ratings and the information processing of the brain to noxious stimulation were investigated by recording subjects' pain ratings to several hundred noxious stimuli and somatosensory evoked potentials (SEPs) of the brain in response to these stimuli. The analysis of SEPs represents a well-established method for the investigation of noxious information processing and the identification of brain mechanisms associated with the experience of pain. Late components of SEPs in response to noxious electrical, mechanical, thermal or laser heat stimuli normally show biphasic waveforms with a negative deflection of about 150 ms in response to an electrical stimulus, called N150 or N200 in the case of laser heat stimulation (also called laser-evoked potentials, LEPs). With electrical stimulation, this negative waveform is immediately followed by a positive deflection at about 260 ms post-stimulation, whereas a similar positive waveform occurs at about 320 ms (P320) in the case of the LEP. This shift of peak amplitudes indicates that the latencies of most SEP amplitudes are sensitive to the stimulus modality used and to the speed by which the afferent neural fibres conduct the information from the stimulus site to the brain. The magnitude of peak-to-peak-measures of these late SEP components, i.e. the N150/P260 or the N200/P320, was found to be significantly correlated with the physical intensity of the stimulus applied (Bromm and Scharein 1983) and even more with subjects' reports on the intensity and aversiveness of stimulation (e.g. Flor et al. 1992). The stronger the physical stimulus was perceived, the larger were these peak-to-peak magnitudes. Similar positive correlations between peak-to-peak measures and both physical stimulus intensity and pain report were reported for noxious electrical tooth-pulp stimulation, laser stimulation and electrical intracutaneous stimulation. Partial correlation analysis between event-related potential (ERP) measures (peak-to-peak amplitudes or baseline-to-peak of SEP components), physical stimulus intensity and pain report furthermore confirmed that the magnitude of the ERP measures is more closely related to the subjective experience of pain than to the physical intensity of stimulation (Chen et al. 1979). Due to this observation, it was suggested that these late ERP components primarily represent correlates of cognitive and evaluative stimulus processing and less probably reflect physical properties of the stimulus input (Miltner and Weiss 1998). Due to this reason, a number of studies have used these ERP measures for the evaluation of different methods of pain control. In many studies, it was demonstrated that these ERP amplitudes were significantly smaller when the pain treatment in question significantly affected a subject's pain as compared with placebo methods that had no effect on a subject's pain (e.g. for pharmacological treatments, see Bromm and Lorenz 1998; for psychological interventions such as distraction of attention, see Miltner et al. 1989; Friederich et al. 2001; for hypnotic analgesia, see Sommer 1966; Arendt-Nielsen et al. 1990; Miltner et al. 1992; Friederich et al. 2001).

In the first study of our group on the effects of hypnotic analgesia as compared with distraction, a group of 26 high suggestible subjects was selected from 200 undergraduate students according to their hypnotic suggestibility assessed by the Barber Suggestibility Scale (BSS) and the Harvard Group Scale of Hypnotic Susceptibility (HGSHS: A). Additionally, subjects were tested in a cold pressure test before and after receiving a glove analgesia induction. Subjects were accepted for the experiment proper where they were able to maintain their hands for at least 100 s in ice water with a constant temperature of about $+4°C$ while being exposed to hypnotic glove analgesia. Twelve subjects fulfilled this criterion and volunteered to take part in this experiment. After being familiarized with the experimental setting and determination of each individual's pain threshold to electrical intracutaneous stimuli (IES; Bromm and Meier 1984), subjects were exposed in a counterbalanced sequence to three experimental conditions during each of which they received three series of 20 painful IES. The three experimental conditions included a control condition without any intervention (CC), a condition with suggestions of hypnotic analgesia (HA) and a distraction of attention (DA) condition where the subject's attention was distracted away from the stimulation. After each block of stimulus presentations, subjects were requested to rate the intensity and aversiveness of pain on a visual analogue scale (VAS). During the control condition, subjects were asked to sit silently in their experimental chair and stay in a relaxed state. In condition HA, hypnotic suggestions were given by an experienced hypnotherapist. After the induction of hypnosis, subjects received suggestions that they would wear anaesthetic gloves that cause the sensations of their middle finger tip to become absolutely numb and totally insensitive to any kind of pain. During the DA condition, subjects received a word puzzle task. They had to find words from a conglomerate of letters organized in crossword puzzle style. During all conditions, subjects sat in a reclining chair in an electrically shielded, sound-attenuated room, and brain electrical activities to ICE were recorded from a dense array of electrodes. When subjects were exposed to suggestions of hypnotic analgesia as compared with the control condition without intervention, subjects' pain intensity ratings were significantly reduced, with values partially below the pain threshold. Similarly, pain ratings were also significantly lower during the distraction instruction as compared with the control condition. No significant difference for pain intensity ratings was found between the hypnosis and the distraction condition, indicating that both instructions affected subjects' pain intensity similarly. Also, the aversiveness of stimuli was significantly affected by hypnotic analgesia, with stimuli being rated as less aversive during hypnotic analgesia and distraction as compared with the control condition (see Fig. 4.1)

During all three conditions, the SEP showed three major components at the vertex of the subject's head (see Fig. 4.2): a positive component at 60–100 ms post-stimulus (P80), a negative component at 100–180 ms (N150) post-stimulus and a positive component at 150–300 ms (P260) post-stimulus. Additionally, a positive component at 300–400 ms

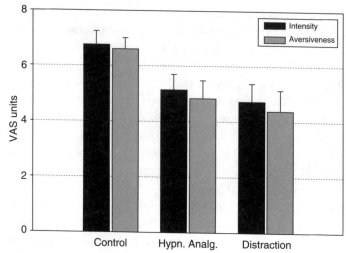

Fig. 4.1 Pain intensity and pain aversiveness ratings on a visual analogue scale (VAS) in response to intracutaneous electrical stimulation during a control situation, suggestions of hypnotic analgesia and distraction of attention.

post-stimulus (P300) was detected at Pz. While comparisons of latencies of these components and for the magnitude or topography of earlier components of the SEP (~80 ms) showed no significant differences between conditions, the comparisons of late SEP amplitudes revealed significant differences between the three experimental conditions. The most relevant finding was that the peak amplitude of the positive brain electrical activity at around 260 ms post-stimulus was significantly lower during distraction as

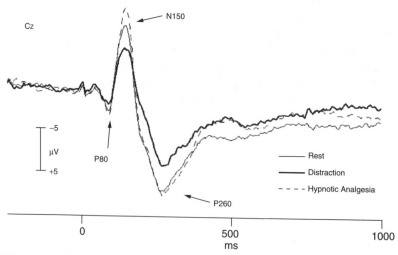

Fig. 4.2 Event-related potentials at electrode Cz in response to intracutaneous electrical stimulation during a control situation, suggestions of hypnotic analgesia, and distraction of attention. The components investigated are marked.

compared with hypnotic analgesia and the control condition, but no significant differ-ences were found for the magnitude of this component between hypnotic analgesia and the control condition. Similar results were also seen for components at around 300 ms post-stimulus and thereafter.

Results from this study clearly indicate that suggestions of hypnotic analgesia and dis-traction of attention significantly affect subjects' feelings of pain when stimulated painfully with electrical stimuli. Stimuli rated as painful and aversive during a control condition turn into stimuli rated as less painful and less aversive during both hypnotic analgesia and distraction from stimulation. This difference between hypnotic analge-sia/distraction and the control condition occurred in spite of the fact that the physical strength of stimuli was kept constant throughout all three experimental conditions. Therefore, the present investigation confirms earlier reports that hypnotic analgesia (Halliday and Mason 1964; Hilgard and Hilgard 1983; Miltner *et al.* 1992; Peter, 1998; Friederich *et al.* 2001) and distraction of attention (Miltner *et al.* 1989; Johnson *et al.* 1991; Friederich *et al.* 2001) represent effective methods for the control of acute experi-mentally induced pain.

In this second study (Friederich *et al.* 2001), these observations were further tested with 220 young healthy student volunteers. Prior to the experiment proper, subjects again were examined for hypnotic susceptibility using a German version of the Harvard Group Scale of Hypnotic Susceptibility: Form A (HGSHS: A) and the German version of the Stanford Hypnotic Susceptibility Scale: Form C (SHSS: C). From this sample, 15 highly hypnotizable subjects aged 19–30 years with high HGSHS scores (9–12) and additional high scores in the SHSS (9–12) participated in the experiment proper. Its main session again consisted of three experimental conditions counterbalanced across subjects: (1) a control condition where subjects were instructed to rest; (2) a condition of hypnotic analgesia where subjects received hypnotic induction and then suggestions for glove analgesia and instructions for relaxation imagery (i.e. walking on a beach); and (3) a con-dition where subjects' attention was distracted by listening to a tape recording of a short crime story. Subjects were told that they would have to recall as many details of this story in a subsequent memory test and that a bonus will be paid for good recall. During each condition, subjects were stimulated with noxious heat laser stimuli. After each block of 10 stimuli, the subjects were requested to rate the average intensity and aversiveness of the 10 preceding stimuli. During each experimental condition, 70 stimuli were applied with a constant laser energy evoking a subjective perception of moderate pain (for more methodical details, see Weiss *et al.* 1997; Weiss and Miltner 2006). During the whole experiment proper, LEPs were obtained from 62 electroencephalography (EEG) electrode sites.

Results of the behavioural data were similar to those of study 1. Ratings of pain intensity and pain aversiveness were significantly reduced, with values below the pain threshold when subjects were exposed to suggestions of hypnotic analgesia or to the distraction condition as compared with the control condition. During all three conditions, LEPs showed two major components, i.e. the N200 and P320, respectively. Again, the N200 magnitude to laser heat stimuli was significantly reduced while subjects were requested to distract their attention from stimulation as compared with hypnotic analgesia, while no significant differences were found between hypnotic analgesia and the control condition and between the control and distraction condition. The P320 amplitude was significantly reduced during distraction as compared with the control condition and with hypnotic analgesia, while no significant difference was found when hypnotic analgesia was compared with the control condition. The same pattern of results was obtained when the analysis was based on peak-to-peak measures representing the magnitude of the N200–P320 complex.

Like the previous study, this study also clearly reveals that suggestions of hypnotic analgesia significantly affected subjects' feelings of pain when they were stimulated with moderately painful stimuli. These remarkable subjective effects of distraction are also confirmed by the observations of late ERP amplitudes that again were significantly reduced as compared with the control condition. This finding confirms earlier studies by Miltner *et al.* (1989) and Yamasaki *et al.* (1999). When the brain electrical activities and its SEP amplitudes to the experimental stimulation are considered as additional indicators for the effectiveness of analgesic procedures, the data of this study confirm that distraction represents an effective method of pain control. During distraction, we found significantly reduced magnitudes of the N150–P260 complex as well as of the P260 and P300 components as compared with hypnotic analgesia and, in part, as compared with the control condition. This finding confirms earlier studies (e.g. Miltner *et al.* 1990, Yamasaki *et al.* 1999; Friederich *et al.* 2001) and points to the option that filters at thalamic and thalamo-cortical levels are activated during distraction so as to prevent or to protect the somatosensory cortices from noxious input. In contrast, our analyses of ERP components did not reveal similar results on the size of the late ERP components for hypnotic analgesia. When highly suggestible subjects were exposed to suggestions of hypnotic analgesia, late ERP amplitudes in both studies were not reduced but actually tended to show even larger magnitudes than during the control condition. This difference clearly indicates that hypnotic analgesia acts on the brain in a different manner than distraction. According to these observations, it appears as if the somatosensory cortex and associated cortical areas still receive full information about the noxious input and that this processing of information is not affected by the suggestions of analgesia. However, our subjects reported that the laser stimulation was perceived as less painful during hypnotic analgesia than the stimulation during the control condition, although in both conditions the stimulus type and its physical intensity were kept constant. This observation is consistent with suggestions by Hilgard and Hilgard (1983) that hypnotic analgesia is characterized by a dissociation of the processing of somatosensory stimulus features and cognitive and motor processes related to the organization of appropriate behaviours (i.e. flight/fight responses, complex behavioural reflexes, changes of motivational responses and other fronto-cortical control manoeuvres). From our data, it appears that the somatosensory features of noxious stimuli are still evaluated properly during hypnotic analgesia, as they are in the non-hypnotic control condition, but the output of this processing is not communicated appropriately to other brain areas that complete the evaluation of these stimuli as being painful and which are responsible for the organization of proper behaviours to pain. Such a hypothesis can be tested by means of an analysis of the coupling between different brain areas. An adequate method is the analysis of coherences. We will report on such analyses in one of the following sections.

4.3.2 The role of hypnotic suggestibility on the effects of hypnotic analgesia and distraction of attention

In the previous section, it has been postulated that one of the possible reasons for the different results found for the effects of hypnotic analgesia and distraction on the perception and feelings of pain might lie in the difference in hypnotic suggestibility. In a third study that used the same procedure as study 2 with 15 highly suggestible subjects and 15 subjects with a low level of susceptibility, these questions were addressed. In this study, 256 young healthy student volunteers were tested for hypnotic susceptibility using a German version of HGSHS: A and the German version of the SHSS: C. From this sample, 15 highly suggestible subjects and 15 subjects with a low degree of suggestibility with HGSHS scores or 9–12 (high) or 0–3 (low) and SHSS scores of either 9–12 (high) or 0–3 (low) participated in the experiment proper.

Results of the behavioural data demonstrated that pain intensity and pain aversiveness ratings were significantly reduced below the pain threshold for both groups of subjects when subjects were exposed to the distraction of attention as compared with the control condition. However, only highly suggestible subjects showed a reduction of pain ratings during hypnotic analgesia as compared with the control condition. In contrast, subjects with a low degree of suggestibility showed even a slight increase of pain ratings during hypnotic analgesia as compared with the control condition. LEP components were not different between groups.

Taken together, our recent studies and data from earlier investigations clearly demonstrate that hypnotic analgesia represents an effective strategy for highly suggestible subjects to control acute experimentally induced pain. One hypothesis put forward to explain the effect as well as the observed changes in ERPs was that the effects of hypnotic analgesia are based on dissociation of neural activities of brain areas responsible for the analysis of somatosensory features of noxious stimuli and the final evaluation of these stimuli. Such a hypothesis can be tested by means of coherence analysis of neural activities in different brain areas.

4.3.3 The breakdown in the communication between neural modules

That hypnotic analgesia might be based on a breakdown of neural communication between neural structures involved in the processing of pain was derived from recent studies on the effects of anaesthesia. A series of studies by Schwender and his group (Schwender et al. 1993, 1994, 1997; Daunderer and Schwender 2000) and suggestions by Kulli and Koch (1991) indicated that midlatency neural activity in response to auditory or visual stimulation became significantly smaller or completely suppressed as a function of the anaesthetic dose when subjects were treated by volatile anaesthetics or general anaesthetic agents as compared with placebo. Further analyses revealed that most of these midlatency responses were characterized by fast oscillatory activities within the gamma band for which several research groups have postulated a putative role in consciousness (for hypnosis, see, for example, de Pascalis *et al.* 2004, de Pascalis, Chapter 5). A recent study by our group further evaluated the putative role of gamma activity by investigating the coherence of neural oscillations between different areas of the brain when subjects were exposed to hypnotic analgesia as compared with a control condition. While as in the studies of our group mentioned above, ERP amplitudes to painful stimuli applied to the tip of the middle finger were still unaffected during hypnotic analgesia and were of about a similar magnitude to during a non-hypnotic control condition, the results of an additional coherence analysis of brain activity indicated a significant decrease of coherence within the gamma band between somatosensory and frontal sites of the brain while subjects were hypnotized as compared with the control condition. This loss of coherence between somatosensory and frontal brain areas during hypnotic analgesia was hypothesized to reflect a similar breakdown of functional connectivity between the brain areas involved in the analysis of the somatosensory aspects of the noxious input and areas organizing the emotional and behavioural responses to pain as during states of anaesthesia. Based on this study, we suggested that hypnosis affects integrative functions of the brain and induces an alteration or even a breakdown of communication between subunits within the brain responsible for the formation of conscious experience (Trippe *et al.* 2004).

Additional analysis of these data further revealed that this breakdown of functional connectivity might have been controlled by frontal brain areas for which Gruzelier and co-workers have consistently advocated the view of hypnosis as a form of frontal inhibition. Replicated neuropsychological findings (Gruzelier and Warren 1993; Kallio *et al.* 2001) show impaired letter fluency (left frontal) but not category fluency (left temporal) performance during hypnosis for subjects with high but not low levels of hypnotic susceptibility. This suggests that for hypnotizable subjects, hypnosis is associated with inhibition of the left dorsolateral prefrontal cortex (Gruzelier 1998). Selective influences within the cingulate have also been inferred from evidence of the maintenance of the error-related negativity wave in concert with an abolition of the ensuing positivity wave in highly hypnotizable subjects during hypnosis (Kaiser *et al.* 1997). Some recent studies investigated hypnotic analgesia to test the hypothesis that at least part of the phenomena occurring under hypnosis might also be explained by a dissociation between functional subunits organizing conscious behaviour. Thus, Croft *et al.* (2002) analysed EEG component frequencies in the period following painful electrical stimulation of the right hand in a control condition, during hypnosis and after hypnotic analgesia suggestion. Prefrontal gamma EEG activity localized in the ACC predicted the intensity of subjects' pain ratings in the control condition. This relationship remained unchanged by hypnosis for the subjects with low susceptibility but was abolished in highly hypnotizable subjects following instructions of hypnosis.

4.3.4 Frontal control of cortical activities

Several accounts of the effects of hypnotic analgesia have hypothesized that the control of pain by hypnotic analgesia is also based on activities in frontal cortical areas (for a review, see Vaitl *et al.* 2005). This hypothesis was recently tested by a study on the activation of frontal cortices and other areas involved in the processing of noxious information in 20 highly suggestible subjects during hypnotic analgesia by means of fMRI techniques. The experiment proper consisted of two experimental conditions: a control condition and a condition where suggestions of hypnotic analgesia were applied. Suggestions included relaxation, glove analgesia and the use of an anaesthetic cream. During each condition, subjects were stimulated by heat stimuli applied to the dorsum of their right hand using a skin Peltier thermode. Three different temperatures were used in blocks of 45 s: neutral temperature; warm stimulation; and painful heat, with blocks of warm or painful heat followed by a block of neutral temperature. Subjects rated the intensity and aversiveness of the whole stimulation after each condition on a standardized scale from 0 (no pain) to 6 (unbearable pain).

Result show that hypnotic analgesia significantly affected subjects' pain. During hypnotic analgesia, heat stimuli were rated as significantly less painful and aversive than during the control condition. Contrasting painful heat with warm temperature in the control condition, we found significant activations in the contralateral primary somatosensory cortex (S1), the primary motor cortex (M1) and the ACC. Furthermore, significant activations were found bilaterally in the secondary somatosensory cortex (S2) thalamus and insula, as well as ipsilaterally in the posterior cingulate cortex (PCC). Contrasting painful heat with warm temperature under hypnotic analgesia, significant activations were found contralaterally in S2, ACC, insula, and superior and inferior frontal gyrus. Significant ipsilateral activations were found in the supplementary motor area (SMA), caudate nucleus and pons. Furthermore, the direct contrast of painful heat stimulations during hypnotic analgesia versus the control condition revealed significant activations ipsilaterally in the prefrontal cortex (Brodmann area BA 9), S1, BA 19, and contralaterally in the cerebellum and hippocampus (see Fig. 4.3). Contrasting the painful heat stimulation of the control condition versus hypnotic analgesia, significant activations were found bilaterally in the thalamus, S2, insula, in the contralateral ACC, and the ipsilateral cerebellum.

These observations demonstrate some common and some different activation patterns during control and hypnotic analgesia in response to heat pain. During the control condition, significant activations were found in well-known structures of both the lateral (e.g. contralateral S1, bilateral S2) and the medial system (e.g. insula, ACC) of pain processing (e.g. Rainville *et al.* 1997, 1999, 2002; Casey 1996; Davis *et al.* 1998; Chapter 12). In the condition of hypnotic analgesia, our pre-selected, highly susceptible subjects perceived the thermal stimulation less intensively and aversively than during the control condition. Moreover, activation of the central nervous system was not as distributed across the brain as under the control condition. While some regions that usually were activated during heat stimulation were not significantly activated during hypnotic analgesia, additional areas normally not activated by heat stimulation became significantly activated during hypnotic analgesia, for example especially those at frontal cortices. Furthermore, the inverse contrast revealed that a number of regions usually activated when painful stimuli are processed showed significantly stronger BOLD (blood oxygen

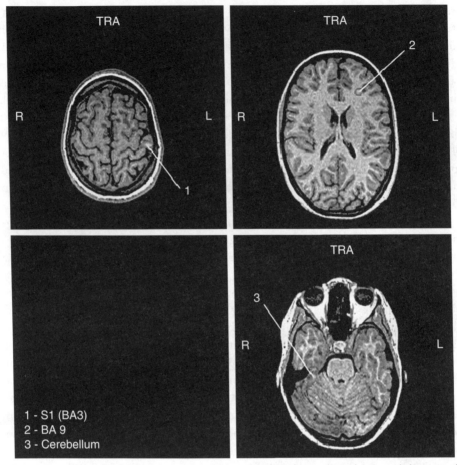

Fig. 4.3 Contrast of fMRI signal during painful heat between hypnotic analgesia and the control condition. Significantly higher activations were found in the prefrontal cortex (BA 9), the primary somatosensory cortex S1 and the cerebellum contralateral to the stimulation (all *P* < 0.001). Please see Plate 2 for a colour version of this image.

level-dependent) responses under the control condition as compared with hypnotic analgesia. Based on these observations, we propose that these additional prefrontal activations during hypnotic analgesia might have affected the processing of noxious input so that this input became perceived as less painful.

By use of brain electrical cortical source analysis in combination with structural MRIs of subjects' brain, the role of frontal areas in controlling pain during hypnotic analgesia was further investigated in a group of high suggestible subjects and compared with brain electrical sources of pain processing during a control condition. Source analysis revealed that 3–4 sources explained more than 80 per cent of the variance of brain electrical activity in response to painful stimulation during both conditions. All subject showed a dipole in the ACC that explained a considerable part of the activity for the P2 component. However, a striking difference in the distribution of the remaining dipoles was found

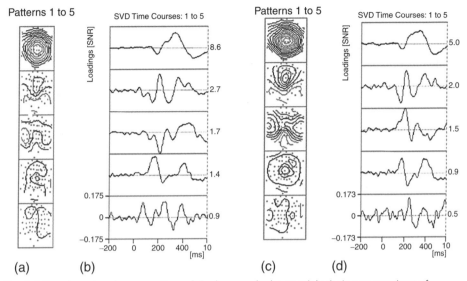

Fig. 4.4 Singular value decomposition of the laser-evoked potentials during suggestions of hypnotic analgesia and the control situation with the spatial patterns (a and c, respectively) and the time courses (b and d, respectively). Please see Plate 3 for a colour version of this image.

between the control condition and hypnotic analgesia. For the control condition, additional dipoles were found bilaterally in S2 and insula, S1, and in the PCC. In contrast, subjects under suggestion of hypnotic analgesia never showed sources in the contralateral S2 or in S1 but a dipole in the right lateral prefrontal area. In all cases with this prefrontal dipole, no dipole in S2 was observed (see Figs 4.4 and 4.5).

These data demonstrate that the effect of hypnotic analgesia on pain might at least in part be associated with less activation of the S2/insula complex during hypnotic analgesia

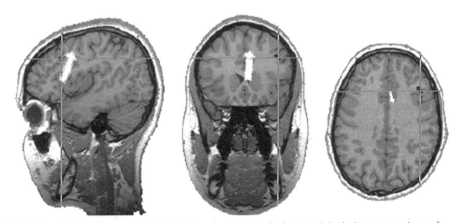

Fig. 4.5 Typical example of localized dipoles for laser-evoked potentials during suggestions of hypnotic analgesia. The figure shows two dipoles, the first and stronger in the anterior cingulate cortex, and a second in the right prefrontal cortex. Further explanations, see text.

and by an additional dipole of maximal activity around 160 ms and stable activity for the following 50 ms in the right lateral prefrontal cortex. Based on these observations and the coherence data reported above, we postulate the effects of hypnotic analgesia to be based on the inhibitory control of S2 activities by inhibitory input from neural sources in prefrontal cortex.

Recent research on the question of how the brain binds together different features of internal or external stimuli into meaningful representations has suggested that such binding might be organized by synchronous neural activation within groups of cells with specialized functional properties. Whereas stimuli with low complexity are assumed to be represented by only a few such cell assemblies with restricted topographical distribution, stimuli composed of many complex features are hypothesized to be represented by larger cell assemblies with widespread topographical organization. Since Hebb (1949), who first suggested such functional cell assemblies, a number of studies have shown that the assembly of each cell can be characterized by its own high-frequency oscillations. Among the carrier frequencies identified for such oscillations, activities within the gamma band have become the most prominent, and were demonstrated to be critical for normal conditions of attention, the ability for learning and memory formation, language and meaningful motor behaviours. In contrast, a breakdown of the connectivity between large groups of cell assemblies was suggested to be a basis for the emergence of hypnotic states, and the loss of consciousness induced by anaesthesia. Such a breakdown of coherent oscillations, very probably organized and controlled by frontal brain areas, turns complex groups of cell assemblies into functionally independent units and seems to be associated with serious disturbances of stimulus representations and other cognitive and behavioural functions.

Acknowledgements

We thank Dr Christoph Braun, Dr Marc Friederich, Holger Hecht, Mustafa Öczan, Professor Dirk Revenstorf, Dr Ralf Trippe, Gertrud Schuler and Professor Vaitl for their support during the performance of the studies. We are grateful for the financial support for these studies from the Institut für Grenzgebiete der Psychologie und Psychohygiene, Freiburg im Breisgau.

References

Apkarian AV, Bushnell MC, Treede R-D and Zubieta J-K (2005). Human brain mechanisms of pain perception and regulation in health and disease. *European Journal of Pain*, **9**, 463–84.

Arendt Nielsen L, Zachariae R and Bjerring P (1990). Quantitative evaluation of hypnotically suggested hyperaesthesia and analgesia by painful laser stimulation. *Pain*, **42**, 243–51.

Birbaumer N, Elbert T, Canavan AG and Rockstroh B (1990). Slow potentials of the cerebral cortex and behavior. *Physiological Reviews*, **70**, 1–41.

Bongartz W, Flammer E and Schwonke R (2002). Die Effektivität der Hypnose. Eine meta-analytische Studie. *Psychotherapeut*, **47**, 67–76.

Bromm B and Lorenz J (1998). Neurophysiological evaluation of pain. *Electroencephalography and Clinical Neurophysiology*, **107**, 227–53.

Bromm B and Meier W (1984). The intracutaneous stimulus: a new pain model for algesimetric studies. *Methods and Findings in Experimental and Clinical Pharmacology*, **6**, 405–10.

Bromm B and Scharein E (1983). A sensitive method to evaluate effects of analgesics in man. *Methods and Findings in Experimental and Clinical Pharmacology*, **5**, 545–51.

Casey KL (1996). Resolving a paradox of pain. *Nature*, **384**, 217–18.

Chen ACN, Chapman CR and Harkins SW (1979). Brain evoked potentials are functional correlates of induced pain in man. *Pain*, **6**, 365–74.

Crasilneck HB and Hall JA (1973). Clinical hypnosis in problems of pain. *American Journal of Clinical Hypnosis*, **15**, 153–61.

Crawford HJ (1994). Brain dynamics and hypnosis: attentional and disattentional processes. *International Journal of Clinical and Experimental Hypnosis*, **42**, 204–32.

Crawford HJ, Brown AM and Moon CE (1993). Sustained attentional and disattentional abilities: differences between low and highly hypnotizable persons. *Journal of Abnormal Psychology*, **102**, 534–43.

Crawford HJ, Knebel T and Vendemia JMC (1998). The nature of hypnotic analgesia: neurophysiological foundation and evidence. *Contemporary Hypnosis*, **15**, 22–33.

Croft RJ, Williams JD, Haenschel C and Gruzelier JH (2002). Pain perception, hypnosis and 40 Hz oscillations. *International Journal of Psychophysiology*, **46**, 101–08.

Daunderer M and Schwender D (2000). Awareness during general anaesthesia—extent of the problem and approaches to prevention. *CNS Drugs*, **14**, 173–90.

Davis KD, Kwan CL, Crawley AP and Mikulis DJ (1998). Functional MRI study of thalamic and cortical activations evoked by cutaneous heat, cold, and tactile stimuli. *Journal of Neurophysiology*, **80**, 1533–46.

De Pascalis V, Cacace I and Massicolle F (2004). Perception and modulation of pain in waking and hypnosis: functional significance of phase-ordered gamma oscillations. *Pain*, **112**, 27–36.

Flor H, Miltner W and Birbaumer N (1992). Psychophysiological recording methods. In: DC Turk and R Melzack, eds. *Handbook of Pain Assessment*. pp. 169–90. The Guilford Press, New York.

Friederich M, Trippe RH, Ozcan M, Weiss T, Hecht H, and Miltner WHR (2001). Laser-evoked potentials to noxious stimulation during hypnotic analgesia and distraction of attention suggest different mechanisms of pain control. *Psychophysiology*, **38**, 768–76.

Gruzelier J (1998). A working model of the neurophysiology of hypnosis: a review of evidence. *Contemporary Hypnosis*, **15**, 3–21.

Gruzelier J and Warren K (1993). Neuropsychological evidence of reductions on left frontal tests with hypnosis. *Psychological Medicine*, **23**, 93–101.

Halliday AM and Mason AA (1964). Cortical evoked potentials during hypnotic anaesthesia. *Electroencephalography and Clinical Neurophysiology*, **16**, 312–14.

Hebb DO (1949). *The organization of behavior*. Wiley, New York.

Hilgard ER and Hilgard JR (1983). *Hypnosis in the relief of pain*. Kaufmann, Los Altos.

Johnson R, Miltner W and Braun C (1991). Auditory and somatosensory event-related potentials: I. Effects of attention. *Journal of Psychophysiology*, **5**, 11–25.

Kaiser J, Barker R, Haenschel C, Baldeweg T and Gruzelier JH (1997). Hypnosis and event-related potential correlates of error processing in a stroop-type paradigm: a test of the frontal hypothesis. *International Journal of Psychophysiology*, **27**, 215–22.

Kallio S, Revonsuo A, Hämäläinen H, Markela J and Gruzelier J (2001). Anterior brain functions and hypnosis: a test of the frontal hypothesis. *International Journal of Clinical and Experimental Hypnosis*, **49**, 95–108.

Kulli J and Koch C (1991). Does anesthesia cause loss of consciousness. *Trends in Neuroscience*, **14**, 6–10.

Larbig W (1988). Transkulturelle und laborexperimentelle Untersuchungen zur zentralnervösen Schmerzverarbeitung: Empirische Befunde und klinische Konsequenzen. In: W Miltner, W Larbig and JC Brengelmann, eds. *Therapieforschung für die Praxis 8. Psychologische Schmerzbehandlung*. pp. 1–18. Röttger Verlag, München.

Larbig W and Miltner W (1990). Hirnelektrische Korrelate der Hypnose. In: D Revenstorf, ed. *Klinische Hypnose*. pp. 100–15. Springer-Verlag, Berlin.

Loeser JD, Butler SH, Chapman RS and Turk DC, eds. (2001). *Bonica's management of pain*. Lippincott Williams & Wilkins, Philadelphia.

Miltner WHR (1998). Psychophysiologie des Schmerzes. In: F Rösler, ed. *Enzyklopädie der Psychologie*. pp. 479–538. Hogrefe, Göttingen.

Miltner WHR and Weiss T (1998). Brain electrical correlates of pain processing. *Zeitschrift für Rheumatologie*, **57** Suppl. 2, 14–18.

Miltner WHR and Weiss T (2000). Korrelate der kortikalen Schmerzverarbeitung—ine ‹bersicht. *Zeitschrift für Neuropsychologie*, **11**, 97–106.

Miltner W, Johnson R, Braun C and Larbig W (1989). Somatosensory event-related potentials to painful and non-painful stimuli—effects of attention. *Pain*, **38**, 303–12.

Miltner W, Braun C and Revenstorf D (1992). Nociception ist nicht gleich Schmerz. Eine Studie Über schmerzreizkorrelierte hirnelektrische Potentiale unter Hypnose. *Hypnose und Kognition*, **10**, 22–34.

Miltner W, Johnson RJ and Braun C (1990). Effects of attention on the late components of somatosensory event-related potentials. In: CHM Braunia, AWK Gaillard, A Kok, G Mulder and NN Verbaten, eds. *Proceedings of the IXth International Conference on Event-Related Potential Research*. pp. 212–217. Tilbourg University Press, Tilbourg.

Montgomery GH, DuHamel KN and Redd WH (2000). A meta-analysis of hypnotically induced analgesia: how effective is hypnosis? *International Journal of Clinical and Experimental Hypnosis*, **48**, 138–53.

Peter B (1998). Möglichkeiten und Grenzen der Hypnose in der Schmerzbehandlung. *Der Schmerz*, **3**, 179–86.

Posner MI and Petersen SE (1990). The attention system of the human brain. *Annual Reviews of Neuroscience*, **13**, 25–42.

Rainville P (2002). Brain mechanisms of pain affect and pain modulation. *Current Opinion in Neurobiology*, **12**, 195–204.

Rainville P, Duncan GH, Price DD, Carrier B and Bushnell MC (1997). Pain affect encoded in human anterior cingulate but not somatosensory cortex. *Science*, **277**, 968–71.

Rainville P, Carrier B, Hofbauer RK, Bushnell MC and Duncan GH (1999). Dissociation of sensory and affective dimensions of pain using hypnotic modulation. *Pain*, **82**, 159–71.

Revenstorf D (1993). *Klinische Hypnose*. Springer Verlag, Berlin.

Schwender D, Klasing S, Madler C, Pöppel E and Peter K (1993). Mid-latency auditory evoked potentials during ketamine anaesthesia in humans. *British Journal of Anaesthesia*, **71**, 629–32.

Schwender D, Klasing S, Madler C, Pöppel E and Peter K (1994). Midlatency auditory evoked potentials and purposeful movements after thiopentone bolus injection. *Anaesthesia*, **49**, 99–104.

Schwender D, Daunderer M and Poppel E (1997). Central anaesthetic effects and suppression of auditory information processing during general anaesthesia. *Theory in Biosciences*, **116**, 284–89.

Sommer H (1966). Hirnelektrische Reizantworten bei suggerierter Anästhesie. *Psychotherapy and Psychosomatics*, **14**, 379–86.

Trippe RH, Weiss T and Miltner WHR (2004). Hypnotisch-induzierte Analgesie—Mechanismen. *Anästhesiologie & Intensivmedizin*, **45**, 642–47.

Vaitl D, Birbaumer N, Gruzelier J, Jamieson GA, Kotchoubev B. Kubler A, *et al.* (2005). Psychobiology of altered states of consciousness. *Psychological Bulletin*, **131**, 98–127.

Weiss T and Miltner WHR (2006). Selektive C-Faser-Stimulation durch Stimulation winziger Hautareale. *Der Schmerz*, **20**, 238–44.

Weiss T and Schaible H-G (2003). Physiologie des Schmerzes und der Nozizeption. Strukturen der Nozizeption und der Schmerzverarbeitung. In: F van den Berg, ed. *Schmerzen verstehen und beeinflussen*. pp. 6–32. Thieme, Stuttgart.

Weiss T, Kumpf K, Ehrhardt J, Gutberlet I and Miltner WHR (1997). A bioadaptive approach for experimental pain research in humans using laser-evoked brain potentials. *Neuroscience Letters*, **227**, 95–98.

Yamasaki H, Kakigi R, Watanabe S and Naka D (1999). Effects of distraction on pain perception: magneto- and electro-encephalographic studies. *Cognitive Brain Research*, **8**, 73–76.

Chapter 5

Phase-ordered gamma oscillations and the modulation of hypnotic experience

Vilfredo De Pascalis

5.1 Introduction

Neuroscience has begun to open up a whole new perspective on the nature and causes of hypnosis that promises to transform the field over the next few years. This has occurred for three main reasons. First, a number of theories of brain functioning and attentional control in hypnosis have been elaborated that can be explicitly tested using neurophysiological methods (Woody and Bowers 1994; Ray 1997; Gruzelier 1998, 2000; Oakley 1999; Crawford 2001). Secondly, researchers have moved from studying passive resting states to experimental designs that assess brain function while participants respond to hypnotic suggestions such as hypnosis-induced analgesia (De Pascalis and Perrone 1996; Rainville *et al.* 1997) and hallucinations (Szechtman *et al.* 1998; Kosslyn *et al.* 2000). Thirdly, but by no means least, developments in electroencephalography (EEG) analysis and functional imaging methods have made it possible to track changes in brain functioning in greater detail than ever before.

One of the most important recent developments has been the growing appreciation of the role of cortical oscillations for normal brain functioning. Of particular note in this regard is the gamma frequency range (~40 Hz) some aspects of which have been proposed as a neural correlate of consciousness. It is my belief that the role of gamma oscillations will be a necessary feature in any complete explanation of how suggestions operate to change conscious experience during hypnosis. However, before I describe current research on the links between gamma activity and hypnosis, I think it will be helpful to the reader to review briefly the account of the significance of gamma oscillations for mental activity which has driven this programme of research.

5.2 Gamma band activity

5.2.1 Measurement and classification

The original designation of '40 Hz EEG' has been used as a curtail notation for different narrow frequency bands in the broad gamma frequency range (35–85 Hz). Highly synchronous bursts of 40 Hz EEG activity can be recorded from the olfactory bulb and other rhinencephalic nuclei in a number of species from catfish to man (Sheer and Grandstaff 1970; Bressler and Freeman 1980). The bands of gamma oscillations and specific coherent frequencies may vary among species and for different neural structures in the same species (e.g. 46 Hz in the visual system and 38 Hz in the olfactory system of the cat). These variations are thought to be dependent upon the different time constants of their relevant recurrent neural networks. It is clear that oscillations at maximal amplitude occur, within the limit of stability for optimal synaptic efficiency, in a narrow high-frequency band within the gamma range. According to Sheer (1989), amplitude bursts of 40 Hz EEG are synchronized with sniffing behaviour in quadruped animals, since olfaction is an important distance receptor and sniffing is a highly adaptive orienting response for food, sex and exploratory behaviour. In humans, the 40 Hz event-related potential (ERP) has been thought of as a measure of focused arousal in specific sensory circuitry and that synchronization of this activity may reflect the manner in which the brain integrates our thoughts and perceptions into a coherent output (Phillips and Singer 1997; Engel and Singer 2001). For these reasons, gamma activity emerges as an obvious choice with which to test predicted changes in attention-related brain functioning during hypnosis.

EEG gamma activity has been recorded at different levels of the brain either using microscopic recordings (intracellular or extracellular) or using non-invasive macroscopic recordings. Whichever recording method is used, however, the measures that are obtained are most usually (1) amplitude or power of the signal and (2) measures of synchrony. The first measures the magnitude of gamma activity whereas the latter measures refer to the extent in which gamma oscillations are in phase between pairs of recording sites or between stimulus-dependent EEG responses (Engel *et al.* 1991).

There is an unfortunate terminological confusion around the word 'synchrony', and many studies that claim to detect gamma synchrony actually refer to spectral amplitude or power. The origins of this usage go back to the early days of EEG when a reduction in alpha power at a given electrode site was referred to as desynchronization, and an increase in power as synchronization, and the terminology arose from the assumption that an increase in scalp EEG occurs as a result of a local increase in the synchronization of neuronal firing. The second meaning of synchrony refers to a consistent phase relationship between the EEG recorded at distal sensor positions, and may be thought of as a measure of functional connectivity. It is in this second sense that the term 'synchrony' most accurately aligns with the hypothesized role of gamma activity in the binding of mental representations (see below) and so is most important for the study of changes in the organization of cognitive control within hypnosis.

A useful classification of EEG gamma rhythms is given by Galambos (1992). He distinguished four types of gamma responses: (1) spontaneous gamma waves which are present at any given moment in the EEG; (2) evoked gamma responses which are induced by, and precisely time-locked to, the onset of a stimulus; (3) the induced gamma oscillations which are initiated but not tightly time-locked to a stimulus (e.g. the enhancement of gamma activity induced by olfactory stimuli; Freeman 1975); and (4) the emitted gamma oscillations which represent an enhancement of gamma oscillation amplitude or power time-locked to a stimulus that has not been presented (Basar *et al.* 1989 for humans; Basar-Eroglu and Basar 1991 for hippocampal recordings in cat).

A number of methodological approaches have been employed in the study of synchronous oscillations. Foremost among the traditional methods of detecting dependency between two signals is the calculation of the coherence function. This method is obtained by calculating the cross-spectral density function from the Fourier components of each of the two individual time series. The coherence is obtained by dividing (normalizing) the cross-spectral density function with the product of each individual spectra and may be thought of as a frequency-specific index of phase consistency. When two time series are completely independent and show a random phase relationship, coherence is equal to 0. When the two signals show a constant phase relationship, the coherence value equals 1. The coherence function has proved to be a useful tool to evaluate the degree of interdependence between two time series of EEG rhythms. The coherence function obtained for the EEG gamma band, usually termed as gamma band coherence, has been widely used in electrophysiological recordings (Bullock *et al.* 1995; Pfurtscheller and Andrew 1999).

However, there are several methodological limitations of coherence as an index of functional connectivity. Coherence values depend upon the choice of reference electrode and the phenomenon of volume conduction, by which neural sources can affect distal recording sites (Fein *et al.* 1988). Coherence, as with all Fourier-based methods, is also not suitable for use with non-stationary signals. Furthermore, coherence does not make it possible to distinguish unambiguously between the relative contributions of phase and amplitude covariance. Fortunately, this limit has been overcome by the development of alternative methods which make it possible to evaluate phase relationships between signals without the confounding influence of amplitude. These two main methods include: (1) Hilbert transform; and (2) wavelet analysis.

The Hilbert transform is a Fourier-based method that provides an estimate of the instantaneous amplitude and phase in a given frequency band (Clochon *et al.* 1996). The main alternative, wavelet analysis, permits a time–frequency decomposition of the EEG signal that has numerous advantages over conventional Fourier analysis. Among these are the facts that (1) it is applicable to non-stationary time series and is suitable for detecting transients in the time series; and (2) its does not require the *a priori* definition of specific frequency bands. Like the Hilbert transform, it is possible to obtain instantaneous estimates of phase and amplitude from wavelet analysis. Once estimates of instantaneous phase have been obtained, there are several methods that permit an estimate of phase synchrony (Lachaux *et al.* 1999; Miltner *et al.* 1999). The enormous flexibility of wavelet analysis makes it a very powerful tool for time series analysis but, because of its greater complexity, it may lead some to prefer the simplicity and speed of the Hilbert transform for calculating instantaneous amplitude and phase. In practice, the two methods are broadly equivalent (Le van Quyen 2001)

5.2.2 Gamma activity and the binding problem

One of the basic questions that neuroscience has to explain is how the brain codes, represents and integrates its complex and disparate neural processes such as perception, memory, cognition and sensory awareness. The core means by which these basic processes are integrated has been labelled the 'binding mechanism'. Two main 'binding' theories have been put forward to explain sensory awareness: the 'grandmother cell' and 'distributed coding'. The first theory (see Gross and Sergent 1992; Bauer and Dicke 1997) assumes that each unitary percept is the product of the activity of a pool of single cells (i.e. 'grand-mother neurons') that respond to specific conjunctions of features that identify a partic-ular object and whose firing triggers a set of synapses related to that specific perception. Such a mechanism implies a rigid and hard-wired neural network in which the flow of the information is channelled in a pre-determined network for that specific perception (Barlow 1972; Singer 1995). For example, one of these cells will become active when a person sees his/her grandmother, but not when he/she sees his/her grandfather or some other elderly person.

A number of objections have been raised to the view that there are neurons that respond to specific individuals, yet such cells do exist. Kreiman *et al.* (2000a, b, 2002) recorded spiking activity from a neuron in the amygdala of neurological patients who were presented pictures of actors, politicians and other known persons, buildings, animals and other figures. The neuron fired selectively to three out of 50 pictures. The three pictures were all images of the former President of the USA, Bill Clinton. This neuron in the amygdala was highly responsive to a pencil drawing, an official portrait and a group photo of Bill Clinton, and remained relatively silent to images of other US Presidents.

The second theory about how the binding mechanism works is the 'distributed coding' or 'distributed representation' theory, supported by von der Malsburg and Schneider (1986), which suggests that information is encoded by the spiking activity of a large, dis-tributed group of neurons. Neurons involved in the processing of a single object will tend to synchronize their firing with each other while they, at the same time, will simultane-ously desynchronize from neurons not involved in the representation of that object. In this way, different sensory contexts can involve the same neurons in different combina-tions such that a single neuron may be involved in the representation of many different sensory objects. In this way, the theory of 'distributed representation' implies a 'flexible capacity' for the brain rather than the 'limited capacity' account of its functioning implied by the grandmother cell theory. Studies recording EEG gamma activity in the visual cortex of cats and primates in response to moving stimuli provide experimental evidence for a distributed coding account of visual perception. In these animals, neurons spatially located in different cortical columns and in the two hemispheres were seen to synchronize their activity to the stimuli within the gamma frequency range with time lag near to zero (Singer and Gray 1995; Engel *et al.* 1997).

These two theoretical views of grandmother cell versus distributed representations have not yet been reconciled. Recently, Koch (2004) in reviewing the findings of Kreiman *et al.* (2000a, b, 2002) concluded that the hypothesis that one single cell constitutes the entire neural correlate of the percept ('President Bill Clinton') is not tenable since the firing of one cortical cell is too weak strongly to activate, by itself, the other neurons to which it is connected. For this reason, many cells are needed for a coding scheme of objects, animals or known people. A study examining thousand of neurons in the infero-temporal cortex of the monkey concluded that cells devoted to face selection are effec-tively widely distributed throughout the area (Baylis *et al.* 1987). Other studies have shown that information about face identity is carried by populations of face-selective neurons rather than by individual grandmother cells acting as feature detectors (Gross and Sergent 1992; Rolls 1992).

It has been suggested that gamma oscillation may be the modulator for the integration of information that is associated through synchronous neuronal firing in the gamma frequency range (Von der Melsburg 1981; Desmedt and Tomberg 1994; Buzsaki and Chrobak 1995), i.e. oscillations within the gamma frequency range act as a 'carrier signal' that establish synchronization and hence binding among widely distributed neurons. In this way, neurons that represent the same object or event can align their firing in synchrony with a precision of milliseconds (Konig *et al.* 1995). At the same time, there should be no synchronization between cells that are not part of the same representation. Such context-dependent synchrony has been proposed as an elegant solution to explain the binding mechanisms for sensory awareness.

Many authors share the view that sensory awareness is one of the facets of consciousness that is most easily subjected to theoretical explanation (Crick and Koch 1990; Delacour 1997; Young and Pigott 1999). There is general agreement that the physiological expression of sensory awareness includes all the processes necessary for sensory intake (arousal, feature detection, differentiation or segmentation, and working memory). In this respect, Engel and Singer (2001) proposed that all these processes either require or modify the operation of neuronal binding and for this reason these authors proposed neuronal synchrony in the gamma frequency range as a necessary mechanism to enable sensory awareness. This binding process is manifested in the time domain by transient and precise synchronization of the widely distributed neuronal activities.

5.2.3 Gamma activity and states of consciousness

Gamma oscillations not related to any specific stimulus have been observed in studies with anaesthetized animals (Sil'kis and Bogdanova 1999) and in the electrocortigram of humans recorded in the medial temporal lobe during the resting waking state (Hirai *et al.* 1999). Spontaneous gamma activity has been found in many studies to correlate with changing stages of the sleep/wake cycle (Llinas and Ribary 1993; Achermann and Borbély 1998; Gross and Gotman 1999; Ferri *et al.* 2000). The most robust associations are found with rapid eye movement (REM) sleep and the alert awake state. These findings indicate that spontaneous gamma oscillations may play a role in conscious processing, most plausibly in object representation, since both waking and dreaming conditions require the representation of objects. The association of gamma activity amongst distant regions in the cortex with brain states characterized by conscious awareness such as REM sleep and waking is consistent with the idea that gamma oscillations serve the function of integration or binding the diverse elements of unified phenomenal representations, i.e. the objects of awareness. In particular, Singer has suggested that conscious awareness itself might be unified by means of spatially distributed synchronous oscillations (Singer 1998). This hypothesis was advanced as an extrapolation of the binding account of perceptual representations to the wider phenomenal awareness of those objects, including components of awareness such as arousal, segmentation, selection and working memory

(Engel and Singer 2001). Engel *et al.* (1999) cite binocular rivalry studies in which perception of an object is associated with gamma synchronization.

Though plausible claims linking gamma oscillation with changes in consciousness (which inform the approach taken here) must be made cautiously because there is no method of directly measuring subjective awareness, and external input and output cues are not present in the recorded spontaneous activity. For these reasons, the extension of the binding hypothesis from object representations to states of conscious awareness has been considered by Hardcastle (1997) as a weak hypothesis. Hardcastle argues that the gamma synchrony–binding–consciousness hypothesis is a very different proposal from the gamma synchrony–binding–object representation hypothesis, although they are often confused. The binding hypothesis is plausible in relation to object representation because the brain processes being bound all have in common the representation of the attributes of one object; however, it remains logically possible that the brain processes underlying consciousness *per se* remain distinct from the representations which they take as their objects.

Despite this caveat, recent studies using EEG gamma activity during different types of meditation provide clear evidence that gamma activity and the location of activated brain regions parallels self-induced alterations in conscious states. In particular, Lehmann *et al.* (2001) studied the EEG activity of an experienced meditator in order to test whether subjectively different meditations are associated with the activity of different neuronal ensembles working at the gamma (35–44 Hz) frequency band. The analyses yielded converging results, describing significantly different brain regions as active during the different meditations that the subject described as clearly different subjective states. Moreover, two of the spatial patterns of activation associated with the phenomenologically distinct, volitionally induced meditative states were consistent with known functional anatomy. The authors suggested that their findings confirm a key role for brain electric activity of the gamma frequency band in the mechanisms implementing states of consciousness, and they emphasized that gamma activity may reflect a 'focused arousal' in task-relevant neural circuitries. This conclusion is in line with the assumption that rhythmic synchronization of neuronal discharges may act as a link between and within areas involved in a given network.

In a more recent study, Lutz *et al.* (2004) found that long-term Buddhist practitioners self-induced sustained high-amplitude EEG gamma band oscillations and phase synchrony during meditation. These gamma patterns over lateral frontoparietal electrodes were found to be different from those of controls. Moreover, the ratio of gamma band activity (25–42 Hz) to slow oscillatory activity (4–13 Hz) over medial frontoparietal electrodes, which was initially higher in the resting baseline before meditation for the practitioners than the controls, was found to increase sharply during meditation over most of the scalp electrodes and also remains higher than the initial baseline during a baseline period after meditation. Robust gamma band oscillation and long-distance phase synchrony were also reported during the generation of a 'non-referential compassion' meditative state. These phenomenological differences suggest that these various meditative states (those that involve focus on an object and those that are objectless) may be associated with different EEG oscillatory signatures.

5.3 Gamma band activity and hypnosis

5.3.1 Hypnotizability

The hypothesis for a link of gamma (40 Hz) activity with individual hypnotic respon-siveness (hypnotizability) was first proposed by De Pascalis *et al.* (1987; see also De Pascalis *et al.* 1989). The rationale for this hypothesis was based on two earlier propos-als. First, according to Hilgard's (1977) neodissociation theory, a high level of hypnotic susceptibility was mainly attributed to the high absorption abilities of these people in eliminating sources of irrelevant stimulations and to focus on relevant information. Secondly, the 40 Hz EEG signal was suggested as the physiological marker of *focused arousal* (Sheer, 1970, 1976, 1984; Makeig and Inlow 1993; Steriade *et al.* 1993; Tiitinen *et al.* 1993). Sheer (1976, 1989) developed the psychophysiological construct of 'focused arousal' as a first-order functional component in attention, specifying its brain circuitry and its direct electrical measurement operationalized on spontaneous 40 Hz EEG activity. De Pascalis (1999) argued that if gamma synchronization serves as an operator which links or binds otherwise scattered activity in the central nervous system into coherent functional states and if highly hypnotizable people, during hypnosis, are characterized by a greater ability to shut off irrelevant stimuli and to focus their attentional resources on the most relevant of information then, after hypnotic induction, an increased level of synchronized gamma activity should be observed in highly hypnotizable people in response to hypnotic suggestions.

Thus, in one of the first studies of gamma activity and hypnosis (De Pascalis *et al.* 1987), it was predicted that highly hypnotizable individuals, both inside and outside of hypnosis, should exhibit more pronounced spontaneous gamma activity as compared with individuals with a low susceptibility to hypnosis. A further hypothesis of this study was that highly hypnotizable subjects have a greater capacity to recollect positive and negative emotional life events and to access affect in a waking condition. Moreover, if this hypothesis was confirmed, we expected to find more affect-related hemispheric asymme-tries of gamma activity in highly hypnotizable individuals during affective recall. This study disclosed a lower overall gamma density in highly hypnotizable individuals, as compared with those with a low susceptibility. This finding was in the opposite direction of the hypothesis. However, highly hypnotizable subjects, in comparison with those with a low susceptibility, were found more able to access memories of emotional events, and this finding was paralleled, in highly hypnotizable subjects, by an increase of gamma density over both left and right hemispheres during recollection of positive emotional events, whereas they showed reduced gamma activity over the left and increased activity over the right hemisphere during recall of negative emotions. These findings were also confirmed in a later study carried out in our laboratory (De Pascalis *et al.* 1989) with subjects asked to recall in the hypnosis condition. In particular, highly hypnotizable sub-jects, who were more able to access affects during hypnosis, reported greater emotional feeling than did those with a low susceptibility. After hypnotic induction, highly hypno-tizable subjects displayed significantly lower gamma density than did those who were not highly hypnotizable. Finally, more pronounced gamma hemispheric asymmetries during recollection of emotional events were found during hypnosis, as compared with the waking condition, in highly hypnotizable subjects. For these subjects, there was an increase of gamma density over both left and right temporo-parietal–occipital junctions for recall of events with positive affect, whereas for events with negative affect these subjects showed a density increase in the right with a density decrease in the left hemisphere regions. These results appear to contradict those obtained in an early study by Akpinar *et al.* (1971) and Schnyer and Allen (1995) who found greater 40 Hz spectral amplitudes in subjects who were highly hypnotizable as compared with those with a low susceptibility. However, our findings appear in line with an account of hypnosis that proposes impaired attentional control after a generic hypnotic induction that does not entail specific suggestions devoted at focusing attention on specific mental imagery tasks (Gruzelier 1990; Crawford and Gruzelier 1992; Hilgard 1992; Woody and Bowers 1994). In cases where specific instructions are given, the suggested experience is better able to be focused on by highly hypnotizable subjects, and the concomitant gamma EEG activity increases or decreases, respectively, in the more engaged or less engaged hemisphere according to task requirements.

The dual attentional model of Tucker and Williamson (1984) adopted by Gruzelier (Gruzelier *et al.* 1984; Gruzelier and Warren 1993) to account for changes in neuropsychological test performance observed in hypnosis may also be able to explain the task-related hemispheric asymmetries observed in the study of De Pascalis *et al.* (1989). According to this model, the left hemisphere is more involved in selective or focal attention and the right in 'sustained' attention. Our results can be explained assuming that the memories of positive affects may require the enhancement of activity in both hemispheres: the left to recall from memory and to analyse the positive emotional material and the right to monitor if the left has received information. The recollection of negative emotional experiences may produce a decrease in the left hemisphere activity because the negative connotation of the recollected material *per se* tends to reduce the focus of attention that is mainly under the control of the left hemisphere. It may be noteworthy that differences in hypnotic ability are associated with the patterning of EEG hemispheric response to negative and positive affect.

5.3.2 Hypnotic induction and dissociation

The theory of dissociated control (Bowers 1990, 1992) explains hypnotic behaviour as arising from a disruption in the functioning of the supervisory attentional system, drawing parallels with explanatory models of frontal lobe disorders. This suggests that hypnosis will be characterized by changes in the functional engagement of frontal lobe regions. Other researchers examined neuropsychological tests to assess left and right hemispheric activity during hypnosis (e.g. Cikurel and Gruzelier 1990; Gruzelier and Warren 1993; Gruzelier 1996). Gruzelier and co-workers reported that parallel with left frontal inhibition, right posterior brain functions may become enhanced as the subject enters a condition of receptivity and vivid imagery (e.g. Crawford 1990; Gruzelier 1990; Jutai *et al.* 1993; McCormack and Gruzelier 1993). Guided by these neurophysiological and dissociated control models of hypnosis, I carried out hypnosis studies first to evaluate EEG concomitants of generic hypnosis induction and then to validate the assumption that highly hypnotizable subjects have a greater cognitive and physiological flexibility in the allocation of processing resources (e.g. highly hypnotizable individuals exhibiting a greater ability to shift from one strategy to another in response to task requirements).

The association of hypnotic induction and hypnotizability on left and right hemisphere 40 Hz EEG activity was evaluated in our laboratory in two separate investigations (De Pascalis and Penna 1990; De Pascalis 1993). In the first study (De Pascalis and Penna 1990), changes in gamma EEG density production during hypnotic induction and during the administration of Stanford Hypnotic Susceptibility Scale, Form C (SHSS: C; Weitzenhoffer and Hilgard 1962) items were examined in subjects highly susceptible or not to hypnosis. Highly hypnotizable subjects showed an increase of gamma activity across both hemispheres at the beginning of the hypnotic induction as compared with a baseline resting condition. Moreover, they then showed a decrease of gamma activity over the left and an increase over the right hemisphere during the end of hypnotic induction. A reduction of gamma density in both hemispheres characterized the subjects with low susceptibility. These findings were seen by the authors as in agreement with Gruzelier's (1986, 1988) neuropsychological model of hypnosis, where the inhibition of the initially dominant left hemisphere activity and the release of right hemisphere processes characterize the hypnosis condition.

In a later study by De Pascalis (1993), EEG spectral amplitude changes across high and low divisions within theta, alpha, beta and gamma frequency bands were examined during hypnotic induction and hypnotic testing. In waking eyes-open and eyes-closed conditions preceding hypnotic induction and during hypnotic induction, highly hypnotizable subjects displayed a 40 Hz EEG activity of greater amplitude compared with those subjects with a low susceptibility at frontal, central and posterior locations. Highly hypnotizable subjects, during the hypnotic dream instruction, displayed greater 40 Hz EEG amplitude in the right hemisphere with respect to the left hemisphere. This difference was even more pronounced over posterior scalp recordings.

Finally, one of the most interesting findings of this study was that among highly hypnotizable individuals, beta2 amplitude in the early hypnotic induction was greater in the left hemisphere as compared with the right and, as the induction proceeded, the activity of this hemisphere was inhibited, resulting in the hemispheres becoming similar. Beta2 (20–30 Hz) is a high-frequency band lying immediately below the start of the gamma band. The temporal dynamics of beta and gamma have been shown to be intrinsically linked in the 'encoding' of active perceptual representations into longer term memory structures (Haenschel et al. 2000). This significant, although post hoc, finding appears to be in agreement with the frontal inhibition model proposed by Gruzelier et al. (1984). In general, our findings support those of other researchers who posit a relationship between hypnosis and frontal inhibition (Gruzelier and Warren 1993; Jutai et al. 1993; Gruzelier 1996) as well as other studies in which beta activity was found to discriminate task performance between subjects with high and low susceptibility to hypnosis (Meszaros et al. 1986, 1989; Sabourin et al. 1990; Sebastiani et al. 2003). In particular, changes in activity in the gamma band and the closely related high beta band have

...strated their importance as a window on the changing organization of brain
...cs in hypnosis.

5.3.3 Perceptual alterations in hypnosis

Another important hypnotic phenomenon in which gamma band dynamics may be
expected to play a crucial role is that of negative hallucination. Highly hypnotized individuals can be presented with noxious stimuli such as pain or the smell of ammonia and,
upon suggestion, abolish characteristic aversive reactions including subjective negative
experiences. It is of great practical and theoretical importance to understand the manner
in which an individual can create experiences such as positive and negative hallucinations. In other words, how does hypnosis modulate perceptual processing within the
brain? According to Spiegel and Vermutten (1994), when subjects in hypnosis are fully
'absorbed' in perceptual imaginative or ideational experiences, cognitive resources are
fully allocated to the central task, while information out of the attentional focus is dissociated from conscious awareness. Spiegel and Vermutten (1994) have defined hypnosis as
a controlled and structured dissociation that provides a model for exploring neurophysiological correlates of dissociative processes.

Electrophysiological studies have repeatedly demonstrated changes in the amplitude of
ERPs consistent with hypnotically suggested alterations in perception. Examples can be
found in the studies on hypnotic modulation of ERPs to visual perceptual stimuli
(Spiegel et al. 1985; Spiegel and Barabasz 1988; De Pascalis 1994; Jasiukaitis et al. 1996)
and somatosensory stimuli (Spiegel et al. 1989; De Pascalis and Carboni 1997; De Pascalis
et al. 1999, 2001). Spiegel et al. (1985) reported that highly hypnotizable individuals
produced significant amplitude reductions in the P100 and P300 components of the
visual ERP in response to a hypnotic suggestion of an obstructive hallucination blocking
view of the stimulus. P300 reduction was also reported to somatosensory stimulation
after a suggestion of hypnotic numbness (Spiegel and Barabasz 1988; Spiegel et al. 1989).

In recent years, a number of studies have reported coherent oscillatory gamma band
responses to auditory stimuli (Pantev et al. 1991; Basar et al. 1999) appearing shortly
after stimulus onset, as well as in the P300 latency range (Basar-Eroglu and Basar 1991;
Gurtubay et al. 2001). Unfortunately, due to the different stimulation, recording and
analysis methods used, the time evolution and distribution of gamma activities is not as
clear as they should be. However, using the time–frequency analysis in the gamma band
during auditory oddball paradigms, Gurtubay et al. (2004) found, only after target auditory stimuli, a later (250–400 ms) phase-locked gamma response (33–45 Hz) range, with
maximal scalp projection over midline electrodes. This oscillatory burst had similar
latencies to the P300, and was suggested to reflect later stimulus context processing. This
conclusion was derived from a positive correlation between this phase-locked gamma
response and the latency of the P300 wave. This relationship was mediated by attention
since it was only significant during a counting targets condition.

In a study by Haig et al. (1999), a significant positive correlation between peak gamma
latency (37–41 Hz, occurring at about the same time as the P300 component of the
ERPs) and reaction time was obtained in a conventional cognitive ERP paradigm.

A potential link between arousal, information processing and integrative network activity was observed by Gordon and Haig (2001) and by Haig *et al.* (2000*a*). Using a new method quantifying phase synchronization of gamma oscillations, these authors found that responses to oddball target stimuli consisted of two bursts of synchronous gamma oscillations, an early and a late response, the first being elicited by only the background stimuli. Early and late gamma synchrony was found to correlate with the amplitude of the N100 and P300 ERP components, indicating a potential link between arousal, information processing and integrative network activity.

It has been reported for the auditory modality that gamma activity occurs after but not during the P300 (Marshall *et al.* 1996; Fell *et al.* 1997). A relative independence was observed between a phase-locked oscillatory activity (20–35 Hz) to visual grating oddball stimuli and P300 by Sannita *et al.* (2001). Gamma activity phase-locked to the stimulus was recorded at occipital locations with time dynamics anticipating the visual evoked potentials The low-frequency components (8–10 Hz) of the P300 recorded at central sites were almost totally phase-locked to the stimulus, while gamma activity at the central location did not vary over time in amplitude and was mostly non-locked to the target stimulus. These findings were seen as indicating a role for the gamma band oscillatory responses in visual information processing

In a very recent study by Kranczioch *et al.* (2006), gamma band responses to target and standard stimuli were investigated in two experiments using a rapid serial visual presentation oddball paradigm. Significant target modulations were observed for the P300 of the ERP, and a later increase of induced (i.e. not phase-locked) gamma activity occurred at a time when the P300 was already descending. Thus, the expected significant correlation between the P300 amplitude and the magnitude of the induced gamma band response was not obtained. However, the coincidence of the induced gamma response with the P300 decay is consistent with the notion that gamma band activity might be suppressed by the P300 (Fell *et al.* 2002). Conceptually, the induced gamma band response was thought to reflect utilization of information derived from previous processing steps for future performance or memory storage, as suggested in the 'match and utilization' model of gamma activity. From the perspective of this chapter, it will be an important goal of future work to address the relationship between the functional and physiological processes underlying the P300 evoked potential and gamma band cortical oscillations in order to grasp the broader picture of hypnosis-related brain dynamics.

Another line of EEG research is oriented towards understanding how suggestions of analgesia in hypnosis modulate the perception of pain. Croft *et al.* (2002) conducted a study in which EEG spectral power (8–100 Hz range) was measured to painful electric stimuli delivered using an oddball paradigm. Gamma activity (32–100 Hz) over prefrontal scalp sites predicted subject pain ratings in the control condition. Source analysis with LORETA indicated that this pain-linked gamma activity was generated in the region of the anterior cingulate cortex (ACC). This pain–gamma relationship was not altered by hypnosis in subjects with a low susceptibility to hypnosis but disappeared during hypnosis and hypnotic analgesia in the highly hypnotizable subjects. This pattern of findings was interpreted supporting the view that hypnosis disrupts a high-order frontal attention system involving the ACC. This interpretation is in line with findings showing that highly hypnotizable subjects, but not those with low susceptibility, exhibit impaired attentional control (i.e. deteriorated error performance on the Stroop task) after hypnotic induction (Kaiser *et al.* 1997; Nordby *et al.* 1999; Jamieson and Sheehan 2004).

In recent studies carried out in our laboratory (De Pascalis *et al.* 2004; De Pascalis and Cacace 2005), a new method for evaluating phase-ordered gamma patterns in the time domain was used (Maltseva *et al.* 2000). Somatosensory event-related phase-ordered gamma oscillations (38–42 Hz) to painful electric stimuli using an oddball paradigm were analysed in 13 subjects with high, 13 with medium and 12 with low susceptibility to hypnosis during waking, hypnosis and post-hypnosis conditions. In each of these conditions, subjects received a suggestion of focused analgesia directed to produce an obstructive hallucination of stimulus perception. A no-analgesia treatment served as a control. After hypnosis, a post-hypnotic suggestion was given to draw waking subjects into a deep hypnosis with eyes opened. Correlational analysis of EEG sweeps of each individual revealed brief intervals of phase-ordered gamma patterns, preceding and following stimulus onset. Highly hypnotizable subjects, but not those with medium or low susceptibilty, produced significant reductions of phase-ordered gamma activity over both frontal and central scalp sites during focused analgesia in both hypnosis and post-hypnosis conditions, as compared with a painful control condition. The reductions in highly hypnotizable individuals were paralleled by significant reductions in pain and distress ratings. The significant reduction of fronto-central gamma synchrony during suggested analgesia in hypnosis is consistent with earlier electrophysiological studies reporting the blocking of visual stimulus perception (Spiegel *et al.* 1985; Spiegel and Barabasz 1988; De Pascalis 1994) or the perception of noxious somatic stimulation due to suggestions of obstructive hallucination (Spiegel *et al.* 1989; De Pascalis *et al.* 1999, 2001; Ray *et al.* 2002). Obstructive hallucination may evoke an inhibitory process in the brain capable of modulating early perceptual processing. The precise nature of these inhibitory processes (e.g. whether they are global or specific) and the identification of the underlying cortical networks remain an important focus for future research.

5.3.4 Schizotypy and hypnotizability

Experimental evidence for dysfunctional gamma activity in other conditions in which perceptual experience may be disturbed also has the potential to provide insights into the dynamics of gamma activity during hypnosis. Llinas *et al.* (1999), using magnetoencephalography (MEG) recording during an eyes-closed relaxation period in a heterogeneous group of neurological and psychiatric patients, observed that psychotic 'positive symptoms' were associated with increased gamma activity compared with controls. These authors proposed that in these patients, dysfunctional gamma activity is the product of an underlying thalamo-cortical dysfunction. According to this view, positive symptoms may reflect the generation of cognitive experiences out of context with the external world and/or unintentional motor behaviour. Although there has been relatively little research to date on gamma activity and psychopathology, the findings suggest that, depending on the content, dysfunctional mental states can be associated with either increased or decreased gamma activity. In particular, disturbances of integration of sensory input with stored information have been implicated in schizophrenia (Hemsley 1996; Gray 1998; Andreasen *et al.* 1999; Gruzelier 2003). If gamma synchrony plays a key role in the 'binding' or integration of brain functions, such as perception and action (Phillips and Singer 1997), then it may be hypothesized that schizophrenia will involve a disruption in synchronous gamma activity entailing multiple 'binding errors' in the integration of cognitive activities across engaged brain regions. Haig *et al.* (2000*b*) reported reduced gamma activity in response to target stimuli in an auditory oddball paradigm in patients with schizophrenia. In this study, a significant decrease was observed in the amplitude of late gamma across frontal and left hemisphere sites and an increase over parieto-occipital and right hemisphere sites in patients with schizophrenia. In a later study, Lee *et al.* (2001) observed that reductions in early gamma power, in schizophrenic patients, were most pronounced in the right hemisphere in response to novel stimuli that are associated with increased phasic arousal.

Although studies of gamma activity in schizophrenia have mainly revealed a reduction in gamma activity, intense hallucinations have been associated with even higher (rather than decreased) gamma power (Baldeweg *et al.* 1998). Gordon *et al.* (2001), using the Positive and Negative Syndrome Scale (PANSS; Kay *et al.* 1986) reported that 'reality distortion' (hallucinations and delusions) was also associated with increased gamma activity, whereas 'psychomotor poverty' (deficit negative symptoms) was related to reduced gamma activity. Thus heterogeneous symptoms of schizophrenia may be accounted for by abnormal increases in bindings ('binding errors') or exorbitant information processing underlying 'reality distortion' and positive symptoms of 'disorganization' or distinct reductions in binding (minimum cognitive activity underlying 'psychomotor poverty' and negative symptoms of 'disorganization'). The gamma findings reported by Baldeweg *et al.* (1998) led Vernon *et al.* (2005) to examine fast frequency EEG oscillations including gamma in relation to unreality experiences in normal subjects. These authors found that a non-clinical group of participants exhibiting high scores on the unreality subscale of the Personality Syndrome Questionnaire (PSQ; Gruzelier 1996; Gruzelier *et al.* 2006) show delayed habituation of non-phase-locked gamma and slow beta activity, relative to those with low scores. The initial gamma burst is believed to reflect a comparator process activating associative memories of the stimulus (Miltner *et al.* 1999; Rodriguez *et al.* 1999; Haenschel *et al.* 2000), with the subsequent slow beta activity reflecting the activation of short-term memory and habituation processes (Tallon-Baudry *et al.* 2001). This has led to the suggestion that abnormal habituation may represent a trait marker of psychotic vulnerability.

The concept of schizotypy was proposed as a continuum of emotional and cognitive–behavioural tendencies across the ordinary population corresponding to personality dimension traits paralleling the main symptoms of schizophrenia (Claridge 1985). A generally recognized dimension amongst the different measures of schizotypy is the factor labelled 'unreality experience' (Gruzelier 1996; Gruzelier and Doig 1996) which describes symptom-like cognitive and perceptual experiences such as perceptual distortions and magical thinking. A phenotypic similarity between hypnotizability and unreality experience may be observed in the experience of parapsychological phenomena or aberrant distortions in the sense of self (Wilson and Barber 1983). A reliable finding among studies is that individuals with high hypnotizability or perceptual suggestibility, as compared with those with low susceptibilty, also display higher frequency, faster latency and greater intensity of a number of perceptual illusions. Perceptual illusions related to hypnotizability include autokinetic movement (Wallace *et al.* 1974), the Ponzo illusion (Miller 1975) and the Necker Cube and Schroeder Staircase illusions (Wallace *et al.* 1976; Wallace 1986; Kruse and Gheorghiu 1992; De Pascalis *et al.* 1995; De Pascalis 2000). Similar findings were also obtained by Crawford *et al.* (1993), Spanos *et al.* (1989) and Nadon *et al.* (1987). These important and reliable findings must be incorporated within any comprehensive theory of hypnosis.

Kruse and Gheorghiu (1992) reported significant and positive correlations between the rate of apparent perceptual change measured both by stroboscopic alternative movement and by binocular rivalry with a measure of sensory suggestibility [Sensory Suggestibility Test (SST) by Gheorghiu and Rehyer 1982]. The amount of hysteresis (i.e. the tendency to persist in one stable state) was also found to be negatively correlated with SST scores. A link between perceptual multistability and sensory suggestibility, cognitive flexibility and schizophrenia has been proposed by Kruse and Staedler (1995). In a study by De Pascalis *et al.* (1995), direct evidence of the hypothesized link between an individual level of inner systemic instability and SST was found by using EEG gamma (40 Hz) recordings during visual perception of multistable patterns (Thièry Blocks, Necker Cube and Schröder Staircase). Subjects with high SST scores, while they experienced perceptual reversal phenomenon, exhibited a 40 Hz amplitude reduction in the left frontal lead during the 500–250 ms time interval that preceded the subject's signal of the experienced reversal ($t = 0$). These subjects also displayed a significant left hemisphere increase in gamma over temporo-parietal leads. This last effect was found to be significant for Thièry Blocks during the 500–250 and 250–0 ms pre-response signal time intervals. The Schröder Staircase task showed a similar effect during the 250–0 ms pre-response signal time interval. Subjects with low SST scores did not show reliable hemispheric asymmetries across pre-response signal time intervals that were associated with the perceptual reversal phenomenon.

Experimental evidence has also been given suggesting a link between hypnotizability and cognitive flexibility or creativity as consequences of schizotypy (Crawford and Gruzelier 1992; De Pascalis 1999, 2000). Jamieson and Gruzelier (2001), using a modified form of the Harvard Group Scale of Hypnotic Susceptibility (HGSHS; Shor and Orne 1962) and the schizotypy items of the PSQ, hypothesized that responses to positive attributes of schizotypy, in the direction of perceptual and cognitive reality distortion, would be positively associated with hypnotic susceptibility. A subset of 15 schizotypy items was found to be significantly correlated with hypnotic susceptibility. These items formed a subscale which was found to correlate 0.43 with the modified HGSHS: A. Among the three PSQ component syndromes, activation, withdrawal and unreality, those described as 'positive' features of schizotypy, i.e. the activated or unreality components, were the items significantly correlated with hypnotic susceptibility. However, in an

Italian sample of women psychology students (Gruzelier *et al.* 2004), a different pattern of correlation coefficients was obtained between PSQ items and the more cognitively loaded SHSS: C. In the Italian study, the presence of significant correlations with unreality cognitive items, and the absence of a significant correlation with withdrawn scale items, suggested heterogeneity in both schizotypy and hypnotizability constructs. Future electrophysiological research is required in order to unravel the intriguing possibility that the 'unreality experience' dimension of schizotypy and the various objective measures of susceptibility to perceptual illusions may be linked to hypnotizability through common factors in the organization of fast frequency (gamma) cortical oscillations.

5.4 **Summary and conclusions**

This chapter provided experimental evidence suggesting that synchronization in EEG gamma band oscillations (40 Hz EEG) play an essential role in the neural correlates of consciousness. Within this context, a number of methodological approaches employed in the study of synchronous oscillations have been described, briefly, in addition to some terminological issues and limitations of EEG gamma measures of consciousness.

In broad outline, neuronal synchrony in the gamma frequency range has been proposed as a *binding* mechanism enabling sensory awareness. The association of gamma activity amongst distant regions across the cortex with conscious awareness is consistent with the assumption that gamma oscillations are related to focal arousal, subserving the integration or 'binding' perceptual elements into unified representations (Singer 1998).

The central hypothesis advanced in this chapter assumes a link of synchronized gamma (40 Hz) activity with individual hypnotic responsiveness (De Pascalis *et al.* 1987; see also De Pascalis *et al.* 1989). This hypothesis has been discussed in relation to the role of hemispheric functioning and the recollection of positive and negative emotional events vis-à-vis individual differences in hypnotic ability. More specifically, findings regarding the P300 component of the ERP and the gamma band response have been discussed, suggesting that obstructive hallucination in hypnosis clearly affects the organization of higher brain functions. This conclusion is derived from findings showing a more pronounced P300 peak reduction during obstructive hallucination in hypnosis and from the evidence that the pain–gamma relationship found in the waking state disappeared during hypnotic analgesia in the highly hypnotizable subjects. This pattern of findings was seen as indicating that hypnosis disrupts a high-order attention system regulated by frontal lobe networks. The results of pain studies, in particular, indicated that the attentional demands required by hypnotic suggestions play a critical role in evoking altered brain states. The focused attention mechanisms involved in producing obstructive hallucination induce functional changes in specific regions of the brain consisting of the activation of cognitive systems and the reduction of perceptual-emotional systems. The evidence reviewed in this chapter suggested an inhibitory process associated with hypnotic analgesia in highly hypnotizable subjects. This inhibitory process is assumed to be of a global rather than specific nature, considering the variety of conditions and range of suggestions that produce hypnotic analgesia. The inhibitory process associated with hypnotic analgesia is consistent with the dissociated control model proposed by Bowers (1990, 1994). Thus, the obstructive hallucination of tonic painful stimulation may prime dissociated control in hypnosis, since it requires less cognitive effort for pain reduction. Several recent findings from our laboratory are consistent with this view by showing a significant reduction in fronto-central gamma synchrony during suggested analgesia in hypnosis. This reduction is likely to indicate that obstructive hallucination in hypnosis primes an inhibitory process in the brain capable of modulating early perceptual processing. How this is done remains an important issue for future research that should highlight the relationship between the functional processes underlying the P300 component of the ERP and those underlying EEG gamma band cortical oscillations

A final tentative proposal was advanced based on the relationship between changes in EEG gamma synchrony associated with positive or negative symptoms in schizophrenia and changes in normal subjects reporting high unreality experiences on the PSQ questionnaire. In conjunction with recent results from studies examining the relationship between hypnotizability and cognitive flexibility or creativity, as consequences of schizotypy, it was proposed that further electrophysiological research should seek to identify the broader system which modulates fast frequency (gamma) cortical oscillations which may in turn be playing a principal role in regulating the experiences associated with both the 'unreality experience' dimension of schizotypy and hypnotizability.

References

Achermann P and Borbély AA (1998). Coherence analysis of the human sleep electroencephalogram. *Neuroscience*, **85**, 1195–208.

Akpinar S, Ulett GA and Itil M (1971). Hypnotizability predicted by digital computer-analyzed EEG pattern. *Biological Psychiatry*, **3**, 387–92.

Andreasen NC, Nopoulos P, O'Leary DS, Miller DD, Wassink T and Flaum M (1999). Defining the phenotype of schizophrenia: cognitive dysmetria and its neural mechanisms. *Biological Psychiatry*, **46**, 908–20.

Baldeweg T, Spence S, Hirsch SR and Gruzelier J (1998). γ-band electroencephalographic oscillations in a patient with somatic hallucinations. *Lancet*, **352**, 620–21.

Barlow HB (1972). Single units and sensation: a neuron doctrine for perceptual psychology? *Perception*, **1**, 371–94.

Basar E, Basar-Eroglu C, Röschke J and Schütt A (1989). The EEG is a quasi deterministic signal anticipating sensory-cognitive tasks. In: E Basar and TH Bullock, eds. *Brain dynamics. Progress and perspectives.* pp. 43–71. Heidelberg, Springer.

Basar E, Basar Eroglu C, Karakas S and Schürmann M (1999). Are cognitive processes manifested in event-related gamma, alpha, theta and delta oscillations in the EEG? *Neuroscience Letters*, **259**, 165–68.

Basar-Eroglu C and Basar E (1991). A compound P300–40 Hz response of the cat in hippocampus. *International Journal of Neuroscience*, **60**, 227–37.

Bauer R. and Dicke P (1997). Fast cortical selection: a principle of neuronal self-organization for perception? *Biological Cybernetics*, **77**, 207–15.

Baylis GC, Rolls ET and Leonard CM (1987). Functional subdivisions of the temporal lobe neocortex. *Journal of Neuroscience*, **7**, 330–42.

Bowers KS (1990). Unconscious influences and hypnosis. In: JL Singer, ed. *Repression and dissociation: implications for personality theory, psychopathology and health.* pp. 143–78. Chicago, University of Chicago Press.

Bowers KS (1992). Imagination and dissociation in hypnotic responding. *International Journal of Clinical and Experimental Hypnosis*, **40**, 253–75.

Bowers KS (1994). Dissociated control, imagination, and the phenomenology of dissociation. In: D Spiegel, ed. *Dissociation—culture, mind and body*. pp. 21–38. Washington, DC, American Psychiatric Press, Inc.

Bressler SJ and Freeman WJ (1980). Frequency analysis of olfactory system EEG in cat, rabbit and rat. *Electroencephalography and Clinical Neurophysiology*, **50**, 19–24.

Bullock T, McClune MC, Achimowicz JZ, Iragui-Madoz VJ, Duckrow RB and Spencer SS (1995). EEG coherence has structures in the millimeter domain: subdural and hippocampal recordings from epileptic patients. *Electroencephalography and Clinical Neurophysiology*, **95**, 161–77.

Buzsaki G. and Chrobak JJ (1995). Temporal structure in spatially organized neuronal ensembles: a role for interneuronal networks. *Current Opinion in Neurobiology*, **5**, 504–10.

Cikurel K. and Gruzelier J (1990). The effect of an active-alert hypnotic induction on lateral asymmetry in haptic processing. *British Journal of Experimental and Clinical Hypnosis*, **7**, 17–25.

Claridge GS (1985). *Origin of mental illness*. Oxford, Blackwell.

Clochon P, Fontbonne J-M, Lebrun N and Etevenon P (1996). A new method for quantifying EEG event-related desynchronization: amplitude envelope analysis. *Electroencephalography and Clinical Neurophysiology*, **98**, 126–29.

Crawford HJ (1990). Cognitive and psychophysiological correlates of hypnotic responsiveness and hypnosis. In: ML Fass and DP Brown, eds. *Creative mastery in hypnosis and hypnoanalysis: a festschrift for Erika Fromm*. pp. 155–68. Hillsdale, NJ, Lawrence Erlbaum.

Crawford HJ (2001). Neuropsychophysiology of hypnosis: towards an understanding of how hypnotic interventions work. In: DG Burrows, RO Stanley and PB Bloom, eds. *International handbook of clinical hypnosis*. pp. 61–84. New York, Wiley.

Crawford HJ and Gruzelier JH (1992). A midstream view of the neuro-psychophysiology of hypnosis: recent research and future directions. In: E Fromm and M Nash, eds. *Contemporary Hypnosis Research*. pp. 227–66. New York, Guilford Press.

Crawford HJ, Brown A and Moon C (1993). Sustained attentional and disattentional abilities: differences between low and highly hypnotizable persons. *Journal of Abnormal Psychology*, **102**, 534–43.

Crick F and Koch C (1990). Some reflections on visual awareness. *Cold Spring Harbor Symposia on Quantitative Biology*, **55**, 953–62.

Croft RJ, Williams JD, Haenschel C and Gruzelier JH (2002). Pain perception, hypnosis and 40 Hz oscillations. *International Journal of Psychophysiology*, **46**, 101–08.

Delacour J (1997). Neurobiology of consciousness: an overview. *Behavioral Brain Research*, **85**, 127–41.

De Pascalis V (1993). EEG spectral analysis during hypnotic induction, hypnotic dream and age-regression. *International Journal of Psychophysiology*, **15**, 153–66.

De Pascalis V (1994). Event-related potentials during hypnotic hallucination. *International Journal of Clinical and Experimental Hypnosis*, **1**, 39–55.

De Pascalis V (1999). Psychophysiological correlates of hypnosis and hypnotic susceptibility. *International Journal of Clinical and Experimental Hypnosis*, **47**, 117–43.

De Pascalis V (2000). Suggestion and suggestibility: theoretical and psychophysiological aspects. In: V De Pascalis, VA Gheorghiu, PW Sheehan and I Kirsch, eds. *Suggestion and suggestibility—theory and research*. pp. 29–62. Munich, M.E.G.

De Pascalis V and Cacace I (2005). Pain perception, obstructive imagery and phase-ordered gamma oscillations. *International Journal of Psychophysiology*, **56**, 157–69.

De Pascalis V and Carboni G (1997). P300 event-related-potential amplitudes and evoked cardiac responses during hypnotic alteration of somatosensory perception. *International Journal of Neuroscience*, **92**, 187–208.

De Pascalis V and Penna PM (1990). 40-Hz EEG activity during hypnotic induction and hypnotic testing. *International Journal of Clinical and Experimental Hypnosis*, **2**, 125–38.

De Pascalis V and Perrone M (1996). EEG asymmetry and heart rate during experience of hypnotic analgesia in high and low hypnotizables. *International Journal of Psychophysiology*, 21, 163–75.

De Pascalis V, Marucci FS and Penna PM (1987). Hemispheric activity of 40 Hz during recall of emotional events in waking and hypnosis: differences between low and high hypnotizables. *International Journal of Psychophysiology*, 5, 167–180.

De Pascalis V, Marucci FS and Penna PM (1989). 40 Hz EEG asymmetry during recall of emotional events in waking and hypnosis: differences between low and high hypnotizables. *International Journal of Psychophysiology*, 7, 85–96.

De Pascalis V, Gheorghiu V, Marucci FS and Geissler HG (1995). The influence of suggestibility on 40-Hz EEG activity during depth reversal phenomenon. In: E Bolcs, G Guttmann, M Martin, M Mende, H Kanitschar and H Walter, eds. *6th European Congress of Hypnosis in Psychotherapy and Psychosomatic Medicine*. August 14–20, 1993, Vienna, pp. 143–47. Wien, Medizinisch-pharmazeutische Verlagsgesellschaft m.b.H.

De Pascalis V, Magurano M and Bellusci A (1999). Pain perception, somatosensory event-related potentials and skin conductance responses to painful stimuli in high, mid, and low hypnotizable subjects: effects of differential pain reduction strategies. *Pain*, 83, 499–508.

De Pascalis V, Magurano M, Bellusci A and Chen A (2001). Somatosensory event-related potential and autonomic activity to varying pain reduction cognitive strategies in hypnosis. *Clinical Neurophysiology*, 112, 1475–85.

De Pascalis V, Cacace I and Massicolle F (2004). Perception and modulation of pain in waking and hypnosis: functional significance of phase-ordered gamma oscillations. *Pain*, 112, 27–36.

Desmedt JE and Tomberg C (1994). Transient phase-locking of 40 Hz electrical oscillations in prefrontal and parietal human cortex reflects the process of conscious somatic perception. *Neuroscience Letters*, 168, 126–29.

Engel AK, Fries P, König P, Brecht M and Singer W (1999). Temporal binding, binocular rivalry and consciousness. *Consciousness and Cognition*, 8, 128–51.

Engel AK, Konig P, Kreiter AK and Singer W (1991). Interhemispheric synchronization of oscillatory neuronal responses in cat visual cortex. *Science*, 252, 1177–79.

Engel AK, Roelfsema PR, Fries P, Brecht M and Singer W (1997). Role of the temporal domain for response selection and perceptual binding. *Cerebral Cortex*, 7, 571–82.

Engel AK and Singer W (2001). Temporal binding and the neural correlates of sensory awareness. *Trends in Cognitive Sciences*, 5, 16–25.

Fein G, Raz J, Brown FF and Merrin EL (1988). Common reference coherence data are confounded by power and phase effects. *Electroencephalography and Clinical Neurophysiology*, 69, 581–84.

Fell J, Hinrichs H and Röschke J (1997). Time course of human 40 Hz EEG activity accompanying P3 responses in an auditory oddball paradigm. *Neuroscience Letters*, 235, 121–24.

Fell J, Klaver P, Elger CE and Fernandez G (2002). Suppression of EEG gamma activity may cause the attentional blink. *Consciousness and Cognition*, 11, 114–22

Ferri R, Elia M, Musumeci SA and Pettinato S (2000). The time course of high-frequency bands (15–45 Hz) in all-night spectral analysis of sleep EEG. *Clinical Neurophysiology*, 111, 1258–65.

Freeman WJ (1975). *Mass action in the nervous system*. New York, Academic Press.

Galambos R (1992). A comparison of certain gamma band (40-Hz) brain rhythms in cat and man. In: E Basar and TH Bullock, eds. *Induced rhythms in the brain*. pp. 201–16. Berlin, Birkhauser.

Gheorghiu V and Rehyer J (1982). The effect of different types of influence of an 'indirect–direct' form of a scale of sensory suggestibility. *American Journal of Clinical Hypnosis*, 24, 191–99.

Gordon E and Haig A (2001). Links accross EEG, ERP, and synchronous gamma activity. *Neuroimage*, 13, Supplement, June 2001, p. 635.

Gordon E, Williams L, Haig AR, Wright J and Meares RA (2001). Symptom profile and 'gamma' processing in schizophrenia. *Cognitive Neuropsychiatry*, 6, 7–19.

Gray JA (1998). Integrating schizophrenia. *Schizophrenia Bulletin*, **24**, 249–66.

Gross CG and Sergent J (1992). Face recognition. *Current Opinion in Neurobiology*, **2**, 156–61.

Gross DW and Gotman J (1999). Correlation of high-frequency oscillations with the sleep–wake cycle and cognitive activity in humans. *Neuroscience*, **94**, 1005–18.

Gruzelier JH (1986). *Left and right hemisphere dynamics in the induction of hypnosis.* Paper presented at the Third International Conference of the International Organization of Psychophysiology, Vienna, Austria, July 1986.

Gruzelier JH (1988). The neuropsychology of hypnosis. In: M Heap, ed. *Hypnosis: current clinical, experimental and forensic practices.* pp. 68–76. London, Croom Helm.

Gruzelier JH (1990). Neurophysiological investigations of hypnosis: cerebral laterality, and beyond. In: R Van Dyck, PH Spinhoven and AJW Van der Does, eds. *Hypnosis: theory, research, and clinical practice.* pp. 38–51. Amsterdam, Free University Press.

Gruzelier JH (1996). The factorial structure of schizotypy: part I. Affinities with syndromes of schizophrenia. *Schizophrenia Bulletin*, **22**, 611–20.

Gruzelier JH (1998). A working model of the neurophysiology of hypnosis: a review of evidence. *Contemporary Hypnosis*, **15**, 3–21.

Gruzelier JH (2000). The relevance of neuro-psychophysiological evidence to cognitive, social and phenomenological theories of hypnosis. *International Journal of Psychophysiology*, **35**, 40–40.

Gruzelier JH (2003). Theory, methods and new directions in the psychophysiology of the schizophrenic process and schizotypy. *International Journal of Psychophysiology*, **48**, 221–45.

Gruzelier JH and Doig A (1996). The factorial structure of schizotypy: part II. Cognitive asymmetry, arousal, handedness, and sex. *Schizophrenia Bulletin*, **22**, 621–34.

Gruzelier JH and Warren K (1993). Neuropsychological evidence for reductions on left frontal tests with hypnosis. *Psychological Medicine*, **23**, 93–101.

Gruzelier JH, Brow TD, Perry A, Rhonder J and Thomas M (1984). Hypnotic susceptibility: a lateral predisposition and altered cerebral asymmetry under hypnosis. *International Journal of Psychophysiology*, **2**, 131–39.

Gruzelier JH, De Pascalis V, Jamieson G, Laidlaw T, Naito A, Bennett B, *et al.* (2004). Relations between hypnotizability and psychopathology revisited. *Contemporary Hypnosis*, **21**, 169–175.

Gruzelier JH, Jamieson GA, Croft RJ, Kaiser J, Burgess AF, Ettinger U, *et al.* (2006). Personality Syndrome Questionnaire: reliability, validity, and experimental evidence. *International Journal of Psychophysiology*, submitted for publication.

Gurtubay IG, Alegre M, Labarga A, Malanda A, Iriarte J and Artieda J (2001). Gamma band activity in an auditory oddball paradigm studied with the wavelet transform. *Clinical Neurophysiology*, **112**, 1219–28.

Gurtubay IG, Alegre M, Labarga A, Malanda J and Artieda J (2004). Gamma band responses to target and non-target auditory stimuli in humans. *Neuroscience Letters*, **367**, 6–9.

Haenschel C, Baldeweg T, Croft RJ, Whittington M and Gruzelier J (2000). Gamma and beta frequency oscillations in response to novel auditory stimuli: a comparison of human electroencephalogram (EEG) data with in vitro models. *Proceedings of the National Academy of Sciences of the USA*, **97**, 7645–50.

Haig AR, De Pascalis V, and Gordon E (1999). Peak gamma latency correlated with reaction time in a conventional oddball paradigm. *Clinical Neurophysiology*, **110**, 158–65.

Haig AR, Gordon E, Wright JJ, Meares RA and Bahramali H (2000*a*). Synchronous cortical gamma-band activity in task-relevant cognition. *Neuroreport*, **11**, 669–75.

Haig AR, Gordon E, De Pascalis V, Meares RA, Bahramali H and Harris A (2000*b*). Gamma activity in schizophrenia: evidence of impaired network binding? *Clinical Neurophysiology*, **111**, 1461–68.

Hardcastle VG (1997). Consciousness and the neurobiology of perceptual binding. *Seminars in Neurology*, **17**, 163–70.

Hemsley DR (1996). Schizophrenia. A cognitive model and its implications for psychological intervention. *Behavior Modification*, **20**, 139–69.

Hilgard ER (1977). *Divided consciousness: multiple controls in human thought and action*. New York, Wiley Interscience.

Hilgard E (1992). Dissociation and theories of hypnosis. In: E Fromm and M Nash, eds. *Contemporary hypnosis research*. pp. 69–101. New York, Guilford.

Hirai N, Uchida S, Maehara T, Okubo Y and Shimizu H (1999). Enhanced gamma (30–150 Hz) frequency in the human medial temporal lobe. *Neuroscience*, **90**, 1149–55.

Jamieson GA and Gruzelier JH (2001). Hypnotic susceptibility is positively related to a subset of schizotypy items. *Contemporary Hypnosis*, **18**, 32–37.

Jamieson GA and Sheehan PW (2004). An empirical test of Woody and Bower's dissociated control theory of hypnosis. *International Journal of Clinical and Experimental Hypnosis*, **52**, 232–49.

Jasiukaitis P, Nouriani B and Spiegel D (1996). Left hemisphere superiority for event-related potential effects of hypnotic obstruction. *Neuropsychologia*, **34**, 661–68.

Jutai J, Gruzelier JH, Golds J and Thomas M (1993). Bilateral auditory-evoked potentials in conditions of hypnosis and focused attention. *International Journal of Psychophysiology*, **15**, 167–76.

Kaiser J, Barker R, Haenschel C, Baldeweg T and Gruzelier JH (1997). Hypnosis and event-related potential correlates of error processing in a Stroop-type paradigm: a test of the frontal hypothesis. *International Journal of Psychophysiology*, **27**, 215–22.

Kay SR., Opler RA and Fiszbein A (1986). *Positive and negative syndrome scale (PANSS)*. North Tonawanda, NY, Multi-Health Systems Inc.

Koch C (2004). *The quest for consciousness. A neurobiological approach*. Englewood, CO, Roberts & Company Publishers.

Konig P, Engel AK, Roelfsema PR and Singer W (1995). How precise is neuronal synchronization? *Neural Computation*, **7**, 469–85.

Kosslyn SM, Thompson WL, Costantini-Ferrando MF, Alpert NM and Spiegel D (2000). Hypnotic visual illusion alters color processing in the brain. *American Journal of Psychiatry*, **157**, 1279–84.

Kranczioch C, Debener S, Herrmann CS, Engel AK (2006). EEG gamma-band activity in rapid serial visual presentation. *Experimental Brain Research*, **169**, 246–54.

Kreiman G, Koch C and Fried I (2000a). Category-specific visual responses of single neurons in the human medial temporal lobe. *Nature Neuroscience*, **3**, 946–53.

Kreiman G, Koch C and Fried I (2000b). Imagery neurons in the human brain. *Nature*, **408**, 357–61.

Kreiman G, Fried I and Koch C (2002). Single-neuron correlates of subjective vision in the human medial temporal lobe. *Proceedings of the National Academy of Sciences of the USA*, **99**, 8387–83.

Kruse P and Gheorghiu V (1992). Self-organization theory and radical constructivism: a new concept for understanding hypnosis, suggestion, and suggestibility. In: W Bongartz, VA Gheorghiu and B Bongartz, eds. *Hypnosis: 175 years after Mesmer*. pp. 161–71. Konstanz, Universitas Verlag.

Kruse P and Stadler M (1995). Ambiguity in mind and nature. Multistable cognitive phenomena. Berlin, Springer Verlag.

Lachaux JP, Rodriguez E, Martinerie J and Varela FJ (1999). Measuring phase synchrony in brain signals. *Human Brain Mapping*, **8**, 194–208.

Le Van Quyen M, Foucher J, Lachaux J, Rodriguez E, Lutz A, Martinerie J, *et al.* (2001). Comparison of Hilbert transform and wavelet methods for the analysis of neuronal synchrony. *Journal of Neuroscience Methods*, **111**, 83–98.

Lee KH, Williams LM, Loughland CM, Davidson DJ and Gordon E (2001). Syndromes of schizophrenia and smooth-pursuit eye movement dysfunction. *Psychiatry Research*, **101**, 11–21.

Lehmann D, Faber PL, Achermann P, Jeanmonod D, Gianotti LRR and Pizzagalli D (2001). Brain sources of EEG gamma frequency during volitionally meditation-induced, altered states of consciousness, and experience of the self. *Psychiatry Research Neuroimaging*, **108**, 11–121.

Llinas R and Ribary U (1993). Coherent 40-Hz oscillation characterises dream state in humans. *Proceedings of the National Academy of Sciences of the USA*, **90**, 2078–81.

Llinas RR, Ribary U, Jeanmonod D, Kronberg E and Mitra PP (1999). Thalamocortical dysrhythmia: a neurological and neuropsychiatric syndrome characterized by magnetoencephalography. *Proceedings of the National Academy of Sciences of the USA*, **96**, 15222–27.

Lutz A, Greischar LL, Rawlings NB, Ricard M and Davidson RJ (2004). Long-term meditators self-induce high-amplitude gamma synchrony during mental practice. *Proceedings of the National Academy of Sciences of the USA*, **101**, 16369–73.

Makeig S and Inlow M (1993). Lapses in alertness: coherence of fluctuations in performance and EEG spectrum. *Electroencephalography and Clinical Neurophysiology*, **86**, 23–35.

Maltseva I, Geissler HG and Basar E (2000). Alpha oscillations as an indicator of dynamic memory operations—anticipation of omitted stimuli. *International Journal of Psychophysiology*, **36**, 185–97.

Marshall L, Molle M and Bartsch P (1996) Event-related gamma band activity during passive and active oddball tasks. *Neuroreport*, **7**, 1517–20.

McCormack K and Gruzelier JH (1993). Cerebral asymmetry and hypnosis: a signal detection analysis of divided visual field stimulation. *Journal of Abnormal Psychology*, **102**, 352–57.

Meszaros I, Banyai E and Greguss AC (1986). *Enhanced right hemisphere activation during hypnosis: EEG and behavioral task performance evidence.* Paper presented at the meeting of the Third International Conference of the International Organization of Psychophysiology, Vienna, Austria.

Meszaros I, Crawford HJ, Szabo C, Nagy-Kovacs A and Revesz MA (1989). Hypnotic susceptibility and cerebral hemisphere preponderance: verbal–imaginal discrimination task. In: V Gheorghiu, P Netter, H Eysenck and R Rosenthal eds. *Suggestion and suggestibility: theory and research.* pp. 191–204. Heidelberg, Springer-Verlag.

Miller RJ (1975). Response to the Ponzo illusion as reflection of hypnotic susceptibility. *International Journal of Clinical and Experimental Hypnosis*, **23**, 148–57.

Miltner WH, Braun C, Arnold M, Witte H and Taub E (1999). Coherence of gamma-band EEG activity as a basis for associative learning. *Nature*, **397**, 434–36.

Nadon D, Laurence JR and Perry C (1987). Multiple predictors of hypnotic susceptibility. *Journal of Personality and Social Psychology*, **53**, 948–60.

Nordby H, Hugdahl K, Jasiukaitis P and Spiegel D (1999). Effects of hypnotizability on performance of a Stroop task and event-related potentials. *Perceptual and Motor Skills*, **88**, 819–30.

Oakley DA (1999). Hypnosis and consciousness: a structural model. *Contemporary Hypnosis*, **16**, 215–23.

Pantev C, Makeig S, Hoke M, Galambos R, Hampson SA and Gallen CC (1991). Human auditory evoked gamma-band magnetic fields. *Proceedings of the National Academy of Sciences of the USA*, **88**, 8996–9000.

Pfurtscheller G and Andrew C (1999). Event-related changes of band power and coherence: methodology and interpretation. *Journal of Clinical Neurophysiology*, **16**, 512–19.

Phillips WA and Singer W (1997). In search of common foundations for cortical computation. *Behavioral and Brain Sciences*, **20**, 657–83.

Rainville P, Duncan GH, Price DD, Carrier B and Bushnell MC (1997). Pain affect encoded in human anterior cingulate but not somatosensory cortex. *Science*, **277**, 968–70.

Ray WJ (1997). EEG concomitants of hypnotic susceptibility. *International Journal of Clinical and Experimental Hypnosis*, **45**, 301–13.

Ray WJ, Keil A, Mikuteit A, Bongartz W and Elbert T (2002). High resolution EEG indicators of pain responses in relation to hypnotic susceptibility and suggestion. *Biological Psychology*, **60**, 17–36.

Rodriguez E, George N, Lachaux JP, Martinerie J, Renault B and Varela FJ (1999). Perception's shadow: long distance synchronization of human brain activity. *Nature*, **397**, 430–33.

Rolls ET (1992). Neurophysiological mechanisms underlying face processing within and beyond the temporal cortical visual areas. *Philosophical Transactions of the Royal Society B: Biological Sciences*, **335**, 11–20.

Sabourin ME, Cutcomb SD, Crawford HJ and Pribram K (1990). EEG correlates of hypnotic susceptibility and hypnotic trance: spectral analysis and coherence. *International Journal of Psychophysiology*, **10**, 125–42.

Sannita WG, Bandini F, Beelke M, De Carli F, Carozzo S, Gesino D, *et al.* (2001). Time dynamics of stimulus- and event-related gamma band activity: contrast-VEPs and the visual P300 in man. *Clinical Neurophysiology*, **112**, 2241–49.

Schnyer DM and Allen JJ (1995). Attention related electroencephalographic and event-related potential predictors of responsiveness to suggested posthypnotic amnesia. *International Journal of Clinical and Experimental Hypnosis*, **43**, 295–315.

Sebastiani L, Simoni A, Gemignani A, Ghelarducci B and Santarcangelo EL (2003). Autonomic and EEG correlates of emotional imagery in subjects with different hypnotic susceptibility. *Brain Research Bulletin*, **60**, 151–60.

Sheer DE (1970). Electrophysiological correlates in memory consolidation. In: G Ungar, ed. *Molecular mechanisms in memory and learning.* pp. 177–211. Plenum, New York.

Sheer DE (1976). Focused arousal and 40-Hz EEG. In: RM Knight and DJ Bakker, eds. *The neuropsychology of learning disorders.* pp. 71–87. Baltimore, University Park Press.

Sheer DE (1984). Focused arousal, 40 Hz EEG and dysfunction. In: T Elbert, B Rockstroh, W Lutzenberger and N Birbaumer, eds. *Self-regulation of the brain and behavior.* pp. 63–84. Springer, New York.

Sheer DE (1989). Sensory and cognitive 40-Hz event-related potentials: behavioral correlates, brain function, and clinical application. In: E Basar and TH Bullock, eds. *Brain dynamics 2.* pp. 339–74. Berlin, Springer-Verlag.

Sheer DE and Grandstaff N (1970). Computer-analysis of electrical activity in the brain and its relation to behavior. In: HT Wycis, ed. *Current research in neurosciences: topical problems in psychiatry and neurology.* pp. 160–72. Basel, Karger.

Shor RE and Orne EC (1962). *Harvard Group Scale of Hypnotic Susceptibility, form A.* Palo Alto, CA, Consulting Psychologists Press.

Sil'kis IG and Bogdanova OG (1999). The properties and possible mechanisms of interhemisphere synchronization of the motor cortex of the rat. *Neuroscience and Behavioral Physiology*, **29**, 523–30.

Singer W (1995). Development and plasticity of cortical processing architectures. *Science*, **270**, 758–64.

Singer W (1998). Consciousness and the structure of neuronal representations. *Philosophical Transactions of the Royal Society B: Biological Sciences*, **353**, 1829–40.

Singer, W and Gray CM (1995). Visual feature integration and the temporal correlation hypothesis. *Annual Review of Neuroscience*, **18**, 555–86.

Spanos NP, Dèon JL, Pawlak AE, Mah CD and Ritchie G (1989). A multivariate study of hypnotic susceptibility. *Imagination, Cognition and Personality*, **9**, 33–48.

Spiegel D and Barabasz AF (1988). Effects of hypnotic instructions on P300 event-related-potential amplitudes: research and clinical implications. *American Journal of Clinical Hypnosis*, **31**, 11–17.

Spiegel D and Vermutten E (1994). Physiological correlates of hypnosis and dissociation. In: D Spiegel, ed. *Dissociation—culture, mind and body.* pp. 185–209. Washington, DC, American Psychiatric Press, Inc.

Spiegel D, Cutcomb S, Ren C and Pribram K (1985). Hypnotic hallucination alters evoked potentials. *Journal of Abnormal Psychology*, **94**, 249–55.

Spiegel D, Bierre P and Rootenberg J (1989). Hypnotic alteration of somatosensory perception. *American Journal of Psychiatry*, **146**, 749–54.

Steriade M, McCormick DA and Sejnowski TJ (1993). Thalamocortical oscillations in the sleeping and aroused brain. *Science*, **262**, 679–85.

Szechtman H, Woody E, Bowers KS and Nahmias C (1998). Where the imaginal appears real: a positron emission tomography study of auditory hallucinations. *Proceedings of the National Academy of Sciences of the USA*, **95**, 1956–60.

Tallon-Baudry C, Bertrand O and Fischer C (2001). Oscillatory synchrony between human extrastriate areas during visual short-term memory maintenance. *Journal of Neuroscience*, **21**, RC177.

Tiitinen H, Sinkkonen J, Reinikainen K, Alho K, Lavikainen J and Näätänen R (1993). Selective attention enhances the auditory 40-Hz transient response in humans. *Nature*, **364**, 59–60.

Tucker DM and Williamson PA (1984). Asymmetric neural control systems in human self-regulation. *Psychological Review*, **91**, 185–215.

Vernon D, Haenschel C, Dwivedi P and Gruzelier J (2005). Slow habituation of induced gamma and beta oscillations in association with unreality experiences in schizotypy. *International Journal of Psychophysiology*, **56**, 15–24.

von der Malsburg C (1981). The correlation theory of brain function. (Internal Report 81–2). Max Planck Institute for Biophysical Chemistry. Reprinted (1994). In: E Domany, JL van Hemmen, and K Schulten (eds). *Models of neural networks*. Vol. II, pp. 95–119. Berlin, Springer.

von der Malsburg C and Schneider W (1986). A neural cocktail-party processor. *Biological Cybernetics*, **54**, 29–40.

Wallace B (1986). Latency and frequency reports to Necker cube illusion: effects of hypnotic susceptibility and mental arithmetic. *Journal of General Psychology*, **113**, 187–94.

Wallace B, Garrett J and Anstadt SP (1974). Hypnotic susceptibility, suggestion, and reports of autokinetic movement. *American Journal of Psychology*, **87**, 117–23.

Wallace B, Knight TA and Garrett JB (1976). Hypnotic susceptibility and frequency reports to illusory stimuli. *Journal of Abnormal Psychology*, **85**, 558–63.

Weitzenhoffer AM and Hilgard ER (1962). *Stanford Hypnotic Susceptibility Scale: form C*. Palo Alto, CA, Consulting Psychologist Press.

Wilson SC and Barber TX (1983). The fantasy prone personality: implications for understanding imagery, hypnosis and parapsychological phenomena. In: AA. Sheikh, ed. *Imagery: current theory research and application*. pp. 349–90. New York, Wiley.

Woody EZ and Bowers KS (1994). A frontal assault on dissociated control. In: SJ Lynn and JW Rhue, eds. *Dissociation: clinical and theoretical perspectives*. pp. 52–79. New York, Guilford Press.

Young GB and Pigott SE (1999). Neurobiological basis of consciousness. *Archives of Neurology*, **56**, 153–57.

Part II

Dissociation

Chapter 6

Hypnosis and the unity of consciousness

Tim Bayne

6.1 Introduction

Hypnosis appears to generate unusual—and sometimes even astonishing—changes in the contents of consciousness. Hypnotic subjects report perceiving things that are not there, they report not perceiving things that are there, and they report unusual alterations in the phenomenology of agency. In addition to apparent alterations in the contents of consciousness, hypnosis also appears to involve alterations in the structure of consciousness. According to many theorists—most notably Hilgard—hypnosis demonstrates that the unity of consciousness is an illusion (Hilgard 1977).

The hypnotic phenomenon that bears most directly on the unity of consciousness is known as the 'hidden observer' (Knox et al. 1974; Hilgard et al. 1975, 1978; Crawford et al. 1979; Spanos and Hewitt 1980; Laurence and Perry 1981; Nogrady et al. 1983; Spanos 1983; Spanos et al. 1983, 1985a; Zamansky and Bartis 1985). In a typical hidden observer experiment, the subject is hypnotized and informed that he or she will be amnesic for some stimulus, typically pain produced by immersion in icy water (cold-pressor pain). The subject is then given a 'hidden observer' induction, on the model of the following:

> When I place my hand on your shoulder, I shall be able to talk to a hidden part of you that knows things that are going on in your body, things that are unknown to the part of you to which I am now talking. The part of you to which I am now talking will not know what you are telling me or even that you are talking.

(Knox et al. 1974, p. 842)

A common finding is that highly hypnotizable subjects appear to be amnesic for the target stimulus when required to report via normal methods, but when given the hidden observer cue their reports are akin to those they give in conditions of hypnosis without amnesia. Such subjects appear to have a hidden part of them that is aware of the stimulus, just as the hidden observer induction suggests! This is a tempting conclusion, but we will find that there are reasons to resist drawing it.

6.2 Two models of the hidden observer

Although Hilgard was the first to use the term, the hidden observer phenomenon pre-dates his work by some considerable time. Alfred Binet discussed automatic writing in his

Double consciousness (1889–1900), as did William James in his *Principles of psychology* (1890). James took the phenomenon to demonstrate that 'in certain persons, at least, the total possible consciousness may be split into parts which coexist but mutually ignore each other, and share the objects of knowledge between them' (James 1890, p. 206). Morton Prince (1909) used the term 'co-consciousness' to refer to the relationship that experiences have when they are split off from each other and no longer occur within a single stream of consciousness.[1]

It is not hard to have some sympathy with these conclusions. The hidden observer phenomenon does tempt one to think that the subject has a divided or split consciousness—that he or she has lost the normal unity of consciousness. But what exactly might it mean to talk of consciousness being 'split into parts'? Indeed, what do we mean here by 'consciousness'?

It is notoriously difficult to provide an illuminating and non-question-begging explication of the notion of consciousness. Perhaps the best that one can do is to say that there is 'something it is like' to have a (phenomenally) conscious mental state (Nagel 1974). Conscious states differ from unconscious states in that there is something it is like to have the former but there is nothing it is like to have the latter. Conscious states also differ from each other in terms of their phenomenal character. What it is like to hear a sound differs from what it is like to see a dog, and both of these states differ from what it is like to feel pain.

Just as 'consciousness' is variously understood in the literature, so too is the 'unity of consciousness'. Some authors use the term to refer to the thesis that the contents of consciousness must be consistent at a time. Other authors use the term to refer to a sense of self-consciousness—the sense that all of our experiences are our own. Still other authors use the term to refer to the availability of the contents of consciousness to a wide range of consuming systems. I use the term to refer to the thesis that the simultaneous conscious states of a person occur as parts (components, aspects) of a single field of consciousness (Dainton 2000; Bayne and Chalmers 2003). My visual, auditory, tactile, cognitive, emotional and agentive experiences do not occur as phenomenal atoms but are unified in a single global field of consciousness; they are mutually phenomenally unified.

The proponent of what I will call the 'two-streams model' argues that this global unity is lost in the hidden observer context, and perhaps in hypnosis more generally. According to this model, hypnotic subjects manifesting a hidden observer enjoy two streams of consciousness at once—a 'central' stream and a 'hidden observer' stream. The subject's overt reports are guided by conscious states in their central stream of consciousness, while their hidden observer reports are guided by those conscious states in their hidden observer stream.

The two-streams model is neutral as to the nature of those conscious states within the subject's hidden observer stream. To fix ideas, consider a hidden observer experiment involving cold-pressor pain. One possibility is that the subject is reporting conscious

---

[1] Within the philosophical literature on the unity of consciousness, the term 'co-consciousness' is typically employed to refer to a very different relationship—the relationship that experiences have when they are components of a larger experiential whole. In an attempt to stave off confusion, I use the term 'phenomenal unity' for this relationship (see immediately below).

states of pain that are caused by immersion in the icy water. This would be a 'bottom-up' account of the aetiology of hidden observer experiences. Another possibility is that the subject is indeed reporting conscious states of pain, but these conscious states are not caused by the icy water but by the subject's imaginative involvement in the experiment. Roughly speaking, the subject expects to have a sensation of pain, and so she does. Call this a 'top-down' account of the aetiology of hidden observer experiences. Although the bottom-up theorist and the top-down theorist have very different accounts of how hidden observer states are formed, they agree that these states are experiences, i.e. conscious states.

Opposed to the two-streams model is what I call the 'zombie model'.[2] According to this model, hidden observer responses are made on the basis of unconscious representations of the stimulus. The subject perceives the stimulus in question (the 'pain', for example), but neither this perception nor the subject's report of it is conscious. The zombie theorist holds that those representations involved in hidden observer behaviours are no more conscious than are subliminal perceptions involved in priming experiments. Note, importantly, that the zombie theorist is not committed to the claim that the hypnotic *subject* is unconscious while engaged in hidden observer reports. The claim is that the mental states that generate such reports are unconscious, not that the subject of those mental states is unconscious.

The difference between these two models is of some importance for theories of consciousness. The truth of the two-streams model would show that the unity of consciousness is a contingent feature of consciousness that can be disrupted with relative ease. It is widely granted that distinct streams of mental processing can proceed in parallel, but few would grant that such streams could be separately conscious, at least in the absence of major brain injury.

The truth of the zombie model would also have important ramifications for accounts of consciousness. While it is widely acknowledged that unconscious states can have cognitive effects, it is typically thought that only conscious states can generate the kind of intentional and goal-directed behaviours seen in the hidden observer context.

The zombie and two-streams models are both represented in the hypnosis literature, sometimes within the work of a single author. Hilgard frequently refers to hypnosis as involving a 'division' or a 'split' in consciousness, and in an early paper he and collaborators say of the painful experience that it is 'diverted from the normal open consciousness, but is processed by a hidden consciousness' (Knox *et al.* 1974, p. 847). Hilgard's more considered comments, however, seem to side with the zombie model. He writes: '... the "hidden observer" is a metaphor for something occurring at an intellectual level but not available to the consciousness of the hypnotized person' (1977, p. 188; see also 1992, p. 21). Hilgard does go on to say that the hidden observer had a 'covert experience of pain', but it is clear from the context that he is using the term 'experience' in such a way that an experience need not be conscious, for he says that this experience was

---

2 My use of the term 'zombie' draws on recent discussions of consciousness rather than voodoo practices as portrayed in B-grade films. A philosophical zombie is a creature who can carry out the normal cognitive operations of consciousness but lacks phenomenally conscious states.

'masked by the amnesia-like process before it ever became conscious' (1977, p. 191). Hilgard is not the only hypnosis theorist to argue that hypnosis involves a division of consciousness without being entirely clear about the nature of the division in question. Kihlstrom seems to endorse the two-streams model when he says that dissociation involves 'a division of consciousness into multiple, simultaneous streams of mental activity', but in the very next sentence he appears to side with the zombie model, writing that 'dissociation proper occurs when one or more of these streams influences experience, thought, and action *outside phenomenal awareness* and voluntary control' (1985, p. 406; my emphasis).

6.3 **The zombie model**

Although the central thrust of Hilgard's account of the hidden observer is suggestive of the zombie account, there is surprisingly little argument in his work for the view. His central motivation for the claim that hidden observer states are not conscious is that hidden observer 'reports' are produced by a subpersonal part of the subject: '… the experimenter makes contact with a cognitive system that is hidden from the subject himself as well as from the experimenter' (1973, p. 406; see also Hilgard 1977, p. 244). If hidden observer 'reports' are not made by the subject then they can provide no direct evidence for claims about the subject's conscious states—indeed, they can hardly qualify as *reports*.

I find the argument unconvincing. Contrary to Hilgard, hidden observer behaviours appear to be reports, and it is not clear who produces them if not the hypnotic subject. In fact, there is a nasty little problem for hidden observer studies here. What is it that distinguishes hidden observer reports from standard reports? The literature provides no clear answer to this question. One cannot define hidden observer reports in terms of the motor systems employed, for there is considerable variety in the motor systems that have been taken to convey hidden observer reports. Hilgard and collaborators have elicited hidden observer reports via automatic writing, button pressing and even 'automatic talking' (Hilgard *et al.* 1975). Nor can hidden observer reports be distinguished from overt reports by reference to temporal factors, for in some experiments hidden observer reports and overt reports have been given roughly simultaneously, while in other experiments hidden observer reports have followed overt reports. The literature has treated any report that is made under the conditions specified by the experimenter as hidden observer conditions as a hidden observer report.[3] Theorists sometimes note

---

[3] This is not to say that there have not been debates over what qualifies as a genuine hidden observer paradigm. Kihlstrom and Barnier (2005) criticize the hidden observer study of Green *et al.* (2005) on the grounds that Green *et al.* substituted Hilgard's 'prosaic touch on the shoulder' probe for the sound of 'Ohm in a slow, deep, mantra-like voice'. But why should altering the nature of the probe in this way prevent this study from being a hidden observer study? Laurence *et al.* (1983) detail what they describe as a canonical method for eliciting the hidden observer effect, but they do not say why the method that they outline is canonical. [They also misrepresent the hidden observer procedure used by Hilgard, as Spanos (1983) points out.] If the hidden observer has a robust existence, then it should be possible to study it by means of a variety of experimental tasks.

that hidden observer reports do not occur spontaneously, as if this is an empirical observation (see, for example, Spanos 1983, p. 71), but if the account of hidden observer reports just offered is correct, then reports given spontaneously simply would not be coded as hidden observer reports. In light of all this, it seems uncontroversial that hidden observer behaviours qualify as genuine reports.[4] The question is whether these reports are indicative of conscious states or whether—as the proponent of the zombie model asserts—they are indicative only of unconscious states.

The answer given by the zombie model is prima facie implausible: if—as I have suggested—hidden observer behaviours are reports of bodily and perceptual states, then we ought to treat them as we treat other reports of perceptual and bodily states, i.e. as representations of the subject's conscious states.

In response to this objection, the zombie theorist might say that the real criterion of consciousness is *global availability* (Baars 1988, 2002; Dehaene and Naccache 2001; Dennett 2001). The contents of consciousness differ from those of unconscious states in that all and only the former are available for the global control of thought and behaviour. We can unpack the notion of global availability in terms of what Ned Block calls 'consuming systems'—systems that are involved in the voluntary allocation of attention, memory consolidation, categorization, motor responses, and so on. On this model, reportability is a guide to consciousness only insofar as it is a guide to global availability. Since hidden observer content is not globally available to the subject, we have good reason to think that it is not conscious *even when verbally reportable*.

A first response to this argument concerns the status of global availability accounts of consciousness. Although such accounts are often advanced as (well-confirmed) empirical theories of consciousness, they are in fact nothing of the sort. Rather, they are methodological posits: the theorist assumes that all and only globally available content is conscious. Content that is not globally available is deemed by methodological fiat not to be conscious. These theorists use global availability as their criterion of consciousness, and hence could have no evidence that consciousness is identical to, or even correlated with, global availability.

A second issue concerns the characterization of global availability. What exactly does it take for content to be globally available? We can put the issue confronting the zombie theorist here as a dilemma.

On the one hand, the theorist might work with a very broad conception of global availability, according to which content must be available to a wide range of consuming systems in order to be globally available. On this conception of global availability, it may well follow that hidden observer content is not globally available, but there is good reason to think that conscious content need not be globally available in this sense.

---

4 I suppose that one could allow that hidden observer reports are the action of a subject, but insist that the subject who produces the hidden observer reports is distinct from that which produces the normal reports. However, not only is this move unappealing in its own right, it is also of no help to the proponent of the zombie model, because a homunculus is a subject and as such is the kind of thing that could have conscious states.

Subjects who are delirious or who are in a dream state appear to have states of consciousness whose content is not available to each of their consuming systems. The strangest events occur in delirium and dreaming—a dog turns into an elephant, one's aged grandmother eats a hamster on toast, and the Queen gets married to Lenny Bruce—without the subject registering any awareness of the incongruity. Those systems involved in belief-revision, introspection and (in at least some cases) memory consolidation appear to be off-line (Lipowski 1990; Gill and Mayou 2000; Fleminger 2002). So if dreaming and delirium involve conscious states—as they seem to—then global availability cannot be a necessary feature of consciousness.

On the other hand, the zombie theorist might work with a more restricted conception of 'global availability', according to which content need be available only to a restricted pool of systems—perhaps only working memory—in order to count as globally available. This conception of global availability shores up the connection between global availability and unconsciousness, but there is now no reason to think that hidden observer content fails to be globally available.[5]

A third problem with the zombie account concerns the conception of non-conscious states that the zombie theorist is committed to. The zombie model attempts to assimilate hidden observer behaviours to syndromes in which non-conscious (or 'implicit') states exert physiological effects, influence categorization and trigger motor routines (Rossetti 1998; Koch and Crick 2001; Koch 2004). The assimilation is troublesome, because hidden observer behaviours appear to involve more cognitive sophistication and flexibility than those seen in those syndromes in which we are most inclined to invoke zombie systems. Attempts to explain more sophisticated behavioural routines—such as those that occur in the complex partial seizures of epilepsy—in terms of zombie systems (see, for example, Koch 2004) are highly tendentious precisely because we think that consciousness is necessary for high-level flexible behaviour.

6.4 The two-streams model

If the zombie model is wrong, then the states that generate hidden observer reports must be conscious. Are these states of consciousness unified with the subject's other conscious states in a single stream of consciousness, or does the hidden observer subject have two streams of consciousness, as the two-streams theorist claims?

The first point to note here is that if the two-streams model is right, then hypnosis involves a departure—a quite *radical* departure—from the normal structure of consciousness. Consciousness is typically unified, in the sense that the simultaneous experiences of a single subject occur within a single state of consciousness—a unified

---

[5] One way to think about global availability is in terms of access to whatever consuming systems are active at the time in question. It might be that the hypnotic context has the effect of 'shutting down' some of the subject's consuming systems, such that although the content is not available to all of the subject's consuming systems, it is available to each of the consuming systems that are 'on-line' at the time in question.

phenomenal field. It is the content of this field that determines what it is like to be the subject in question. Assuming that consciousness is normally unified, the question arises as to how the hidden observer context might bring about its division. The most powerful evidence for the claim that a human being can have two streams of consciousness comes from data deriving from persons who have undergone a callosotomy (a section of the corpus callosum)—so-called 'split-brain' patients (Zaidel *et al.* 2003; Gazzaniga 2005). However, hypnotic subjects have undergone no such operation, and it is unclear what feature of the hypnotic context in general—or the hidden observer paradigm in particular—might change the structure of consciousness.[6]

One might challenge the claim that consciousness is normally unified, as Hilgard himself does (1977, p. 185). Hilgard does not elaborate on what he takes a division in consciousness to involve, and the only example he gives of an everyday division of consciousness—involving the participation in a conversation—is unpersuasive. 'Person A, while listening to Person B, is simultaneously planning his reply, and even while replying he may monitor how well he is doing by watching the facial expression of person B, perhaps changing the direction of his argument if he appears to be unconvincing' (1977, p. 1f.). In what sense does this scenario involve a division in consciousness? There might be two (or more) thoughts proceeding in parallel here, but it seems clear that these thoughts could be phenomenally unified—they could occur as components of a single stream of experience.

A similar account can be given of so-called trance logic, in which both the actual and suggested states of affairs appear to be simultaneously represented in consciousness (Orne 1959). Orne described trance logic as the 'apparently simultaneous perception and response to both hallucinations and reality without any apparent attempts to satisfy a need for logical consistency' (1959, p. 295). One might argue that subjects fail to appreciate the need to resolve the tensions between the perceptual and imaginative experiences because these two sets of representations are not phenomenally unified—they involve not only different streams of mental activity, but different streams of *consciousness*. Indeed, one might argue that representational consistency is a constraint on phenomenal unity, such that experiences with inconsistent contents cannot be phenomenally unified.

Although there may be something to this line of argument, it is not adequate as stated, for experiences with representationally inconsistent contents can be phenomenally unified. Consider the fact that one can perceive the lines of the Müller–Lyre illusion as differing in length, even while one believes that they are of the same length. These two conscious states can be phenomenally unified, despite the representational conflict between them. Similarly, it is possible that the perceptual and imaginative experiences of subjects exhibiting trance logic might also be phenomenally unified, despite the fact that the contents of these states are at odds with each other.

------

6 One might argue that our inability to conceive of how the hypnotic context could generate changes in the structure of consciousness is no reason to think that it does not. After all, we have good reason to think that hypnosis operations generate changes in the contents of consciousness even though we have no good model of how this occurs. Nonetheless, it seems more plausible to suppose that features of the hypnotic context might alter the contents of consciousness than to suppose that they might alter the structure of consciousness.

The following line of thought, which Kirsch and Lynn ascribe to the neo-dissociationist, suggests a second argument for the two-streams view:

> Responses to suggestion are produced by a division of the executive ego into two parts, separated by an amnesiac barrier. On one side of the barrier is a small hidden part of consciousness that initiates suggested actions and perceives the self and the external world accurately. On the other side is the hypnotized part of consciousness that experiences suggested actions as involuntary and is not aware of blocked memories or perceptions to which only the hidden part has access.
>
> (Kirsch and Lynn 1998, p. 67)[7]

We might develop this 'phenomenology of agency' argument as follows. A common component of the phenomenology of hypnosis is the experience that certain actions are non-voluntary.[8] When given suitable instructions, subjects exhibiting arm levitation report a diminished sense of agency with respect to the movement of their arm (Spanos and Barber 1972; Bowers et al. 1988; Comey and Kirsch 1999). Why do such subjects lack the normal experience of agency? The two-streams theorist has a neat answer to this question: the subject has not lost the experience of agency, it is merely relegated to the 'hidden part of consciousness'. Hypnosis has split the subject's central executive, together with their stream of consciousness, into two. We should not expect the subject to report a normal phenomenology of agency, for the subject's reports are guided by the main part of their central executive, and it is the 'hidden' part of the central executive that initiated the actions in question.

Dissociated control theorists reject the phenomenology of agency argument on the grounds that hypnotic actions involve only non-executive mechanisms. They hold that the experience of non-executive agency in hypnosis is veridical, for hypnotic actions are produced by automatic action systems rather than executive systems (Bowers 1990, 1991; Bowers and Davidson 1991; Miller and Bowers 1993). The problem with this response, I think, is that subjects can lose the experience of agency for actions that appear to be executive, such as eliminating the concept of the number 4 from their mathematical operations (Evans 1980).

I think the phenomenology of agency argument fails for quite different reasons. The argument assumes that actions must be accompanied by an experience of agency—or at least that actions cannot be accompanied by an experience of automaticity. I see no reason to grant either assumption. There is no reason to think that the phenomenology of agency is a necessary concomitant of agency itself, even when the actions in question are 'executive'. It seems possible that hypnosis could remove the experience of agency—what we might call the experience of willing—without impairing the exercise of agency itself (Bayne 2006; Bayne and Levy 2006).

....

[7] However, note that in their diagram of the neo-dissociation model, Kirsch and Lynn label the contents of the hidden part as *unavailable* to consciousness (p. 67)!

[8] It is sometimes suggested that this experience of a lack of normal agency is a typical component of the phenomenology of hypnosis—that it is a feature of the hypnotic state as such. However, in fact, such experiences appear to attach to particular actions as a result of the hypnotist suggesting that the subject will lose the sense of agency for an action. Thanks to Graham Jamieson for this point.

Another argument for the two-streams model appeals to the restricted availability of hidden observer content. Consider the hidden observer subject in an analgesic experiment. If her experience of pain were unified with her other experiences (visual experiences, auditory experiences, and so on), why does she not report them when asked? After all, she can report her visual and auditory experiences, why should her pain experiences be unreportable? Why, instead, does she report levels of pain that approximate those reported by hypnotic subjects in non-analgesic conditions? Ruling out dishonesty, we must conclude that she is unable to report them. If she is unable to report them, then it seems to follow that they must occur in a stream of consciousness that is inaccessible to the subject's report modalities (prior to the hidden observer prompt, at least).

The problem with this argument is that hidden observer subjects *can* report their hidden observer experiences.

> I felt … that I was hypnotized but that there really was a clear side of me. … it felt like a division, a division in myself.
>
> (Laurence and Perry 1981, p. 339)

> After you put your hand on my shoulder I felt much lighter, as though I was floating … It is as though you were contacting someone else outside of me but part of me at the same time; as though I had a twin 'me' and in a way I could not immediately communicate with each part at the same time.
>
> (Spanos *et al.* 1985a, p. 1161)

> A sort of numbness—detachment—came over me, almost as if I were two entities, but still I as one … When the [experimenter's] hand touched my shoulder I did indeed feel as if there were two parts to myself. My left hand was supposed to tap out numbers corresponding to the pain it felt, and it was much less sensitive than my real hypnotized self.
>
> (Spanos 1983, p. 174)

These reports also indicate that there are some consuming systems that have access to both normal and hidden observer experiences. How else would subjects be able to report both normal and hidden observer experiences? These facts are difficult to reconcile with the two-streams model.

6.5 The switch model

Rejecting the zombie and two-streams models leaves us with one option: the hidden observer states must be conscious, and they must be unified with the rest of the subject's conscious states. In this final section, I examine two versions of this model.

We might gain a hint for how to develop a 'unity' model of the hidden observer by considering the so-called 'duality reports' of age-regressed subjects (Perry and Walsh 1978; Laurence and Perry 1981). Whereas some age-regressed hypnotic subjects report having experienced themselves as solely age-regressed, others report the feeling of having been both an adult and a child:

> Subject 21: I became small again, small, small. Physically, … I saw myself again with my curls at school. … I felt 5, and I felt 23 also … I knew I was 5 years old at school, but I knew I was 23 years old, also, that I was an adult …. I really felt 5 years old. I would not be able to say that I was solely 23 years old.

Subject 17 (Did you really feel you were 5 years old?): I felt … you know, I was two people, one standing off looking at the other, and the other that was standing was saying, you idiot, you can write your name, why are you taking so long? Yet the one that's writing it is struggling away, to form these letters ….can't.

(Laurence and Perry 1981, p. 338)

These subjects appear to experience two contents at once: the feeling of being an adult and the feeling of being a child. Nonetheless, these contents appear to occur as components of a single phenomenal state, what I have been calling a 'stream of consciousness'.

Now, if age-regressed subjects can maintain two separate identities within a single stream of consciousness, then it might also be possible for hidden observer subjects to do likewise. Perhaps hidden observer subjects have two clusters of content, each of which occur within a single unified stream of phenomenology. The connection between duality reports and the hidden observer is supported by the fact that Laurence and Perry (1981) found a correlation between the two: subjects who produced duality reports in age regression tended to show significant differences between levels of pain as reported by the hidden observer and as reported normally.[9] Might hidden observer and normal experiences co-exist as simultaneous components of a single phenomenal state?

I think not. The problem is this. Consider a hidden observer subject (HO) who produces 'overt' reports in line with hypnotic analgesia but produces hidden observer reports of high levels of cold-pressor pain. Applying the model just examined to this case generates the result that HO has, at a single time, an experience of pain and an experience of no pain. It is unclear that this is a phenomenal state that one could be in. Arguably, one could experience an absence of pain only by not experiencing pain; but, by hypothesis, HO *is* experiencing pain. Whereas the experience of being a child is not inconsistent with the experience of being an adult, some hidden observer experiences do appear to be inconsistent with the subject's corresponding 'overt' experiences. If we are to develop a 'full unity' account of the hidden observer, we need look elsewhere.

Let us take a step back. An account of the hidden observer needs to explain why the subject's reports differ depending on whether or not they are subject to a normal or a hidden observer probe. Both the zombie and two-streams models explain this by reference to the fact that the normal and hidden observer probes are tapping independent streams of information (which may or may not be conscious). Perhaps the subject has but one stream of consciousness, the content of which depends on how it is probed. As Spanos and Hewitt (1980) suggest, the hidden observer probe might change the patient's phenomenology by directing his or her attention to the previously neglected stimulus. The probe ('hand on the shoulder') functions as an alarm bell, bringing into consciousness previously unconscious content. I will call this the 'switch model' model, for it conceives of hidden observer reports as tracking a switch in the contents of the subject's consciousness.[10]

---

[9] Note that this finding is contested. Nogrady *et al.* (1983) replicated the correlation, but Spanos *et al.* (1985*b*) failed to find a significant relationship between hidden observer responses and duality reports.

[10] There are also hints of this model in Oakley and Eames (1985).

Although Spanos and Hewitt were the first to endorse the switch model, Hilgard had considered and rejected it some years earlier (Hilgard 1977). Hilgard begins his criticisms of the switch model by pointing out that in some hidden observer experiments the hidden observer probe occurs *after* the trial has been completed (1977, p. 238f.). Since only the memory of the stimulus is accessed, it follows that the information must have been stored while the analgesia or deafness persisted, and thus that the availability of the target information could not depend on the presence of a probe, as the switch model demands.

In making this objection, Hilgard adopts what I earlier called a bottom-up account of the hidden observer: hidden observer reports are primarily responsive to the perceptual stimulus rather than the subject's expectations or imaginative states. Hilgard argues for the bottom-up approach by pointing to the fact that the levels of hidden observer pain reported by his subjects were in rough agreement with the levels of pain reported by control subjects, i.e. hypnotized subjects who had not been given analgesia suggestions. As I understand Hilgard's view, the hidden observer probe makes the hidden stimulus *reportable*, but it does not make the stimulus *conscious*, because it was already conscious.

In an important series of studies, Spanos and collaborators cast doubt on the claim that the content of hidden observer reports is controlled by the stimulus administered to the subject. Spanos and Hewitt (1980) were able to elicit hidden reports of high levels of pain or low levels of pain depending on the wording of the hidden observer instructions, a finding replicated in Spanos *et al.* (1983). Spanos *et al.* (1985a) provided additional evidence of top-down effects on hidden observer responses by showing that hidden observers could be led to breach hypnotic amnesia according to whether or not the possibility of such breaches was implicated in the hidden observer instructions. In a delightful variant on this approach, Spanos *et al.* (1985a) gave subjects a hidden observer induction in which they were informed that concrete words were stored in one half of the brain and abstract words in the other half, and were led to believe that each half of the brain had its own hidden part. Breaching was now category specific, with subjects able to remember only concrete or abstract words depending on which hidden part the experimenter contacted.

In response to these studies, Kihlstrom and colleagues have argued that although hidden observer behaviours might be influenced by the content of the induction, it does not follow that the hidden self is an experimental creation, as Spanos puts it (Laurence *et al.* 1983; Kihlstrom and Barnier 2005). Kihlstrom and Barnier (2005) point out that nobody would conclude from the results of Sherif's or Asch's experiments on social influence (Sherif 1935; Asch 1956) that the autokinetic phenomenon is not genuine or that subjects do not really perceive the length of lines. True, but the analogy is not a fair one.[11] The results that Spanos and collaborators report do not merely show that the contents of hidden observer reports are subject to top-down *modulation*, rather, they suggest that such contents can be *fully accounted for* in terms of such influences. Consider the first experiment reported in Spanos *et al.* (1983), in which subjects were told that they had a hidden observer, but were not given *any* cues about how much access the hidden self had to the pain. If, as Hilgard and Kihlstrom hold,

---

[11] For a full response to Laurence *et al.* (1983) see Spanos (1983).

the hidden observer induction enables the subject to access previously inaccessible representations of pain, one would expect subjects in this experiment to spontaneously report a higher level of pain than in the hypnotic condition. However, this was not the case: subjects did not report higher levels of hidden observer pain than they did during hypnotic analgesia, and in fact the majority reported equal levels of hidden and hypnotic pain. The work of Spanos undermines Hilgard's response to the switch objection, for even when hidden observer reports of the stimulus in question are veridical, it is possible that such reports are veridical only because the experimental context contains the appropriate cues, and that the reports are grounded in top-down expectations rather than bottom-up sensory processing.

Note, as an aside, that there is nothing in the results of Spanos that demonstrates that hidden observer subjects deliberately misrepresent their experiential states (as Spanos and colleagues sometimes suggest). It is quite possible that the experimental context— the hidden observer instructions together with the prompt—leads subjects to imagine that they are (say) in pain, which in turn leads them to be in pain. Presumably this sort of top-down modulation of experiential content occurs in typical hypnotic contexts, with the subject (say) forming a visual experience of a rabbit in her lap on the basis of the hypnotist's suggestions. Alternatively, it could be that the experimental situation leads the subject to form the (false) belief that they are in the target phenomenal state. Deciding between these possibilities can be done only in the context of a general account of how hypnosis brings about changes in the contents of consciousness, and this is too ambitious a project to be tackled in this chapter.

However, although Hilgard's objection cannot be sustained on the basis of his own hidden observer studies, there may be something to it nonetheless. Zamansky and Bartis (1985) gave subjects a battery of hypnotic suggestions, one of which was an anosmia suggestion and another one of which was a negative visual hallucination. After each of these suggestions, the stimulus was removed and the suggestion cancelled. Subjects were then quizzed on their ability to identify the stimuli, with a pass being awarded only if at least one of the two stimuli could be identified. Those subjects who passed the first stage were then given a hidden observer induction, and were told that after a count of three the previously hidden information 'will no longer be hidden and you will be aware of things that you were not aware of or did not know before' (1985, p. 245). Of the 11 subjects who passed the first stage, 10 identified the previously unidentified stimulus or stimuli successfully. The switch model has no account of these findings ready to hand.

Hilgard's second objection to the switch model is that hypnotic subjects do report the occasional intrusion of the stimulus in question, but 'these reports are not given when the covert experience is accounted for' (Hilgard 1977, p. 238). I am not completely sure what Hilgard has in mind here, but I think his point is this: if the switch model were right, hidden observer subjects would describe hidden observer experiences in the way that normal subjects report their experiences of spontaneous intrusions into conscious-ness of suppressed stimuli, but in fact hidden observer reports are easy to distinguish from such reports.

The objection underestimates the resources of the switch model. There are two ways in which a previously suppressed stimulus might intrude into the subject's consciousness: spontaneously, or via a hidden observer probe. The subject's phenomenology will be similar in the two conditions in that the subject will be aware of the stimulus, but the manner of the subject's awareness may well differ. When the subject's attention is sponta-neously drawn to the stimulus, the subject will be inclined to describe the stimulus as intruding into consciousness but, when the subject's attention is drawn to the stimulus by the hidden observer trigger, they will probably be inclined to describe themselves as accessing what they have been told by the hypnotist are the experiences of a 'hidden part of them'. It is not surprising that some subjects are drawn to report their experiences in homuncular terms because, in giving the hidden observer induction, the experimenter contrasts 'the hidden part of you' with 'the part of the subject to which I am now talking'! Those administering the hidden observer induction may not endorse homuncular conceptions of the hidden observer, the induction that they administer to the subjects suggests that they do.

That the contents of consciousness can seamlessly and rapidly switch between contents—often without the subject realizing that such a switch has occurred—is suggested by a series of studies conducted by Levy and Trevarthen on split-brain subjects (Trevarthen 1974; Levy and Trevarthen 1976; Levy 1977, 1990). Levy and Trevarthen pre-sented their subjects with stimuli created by conjoining two similar stimuli at the vertical midline. Since each hemisphere received a different stimulus, one would expect subjects to have produced conflicting motor responses if representations of both stimuli were conscious. Such responses were vanishingly rare ...

> For all patients examined, and for tasks including the perception of faces, nonsense shapes, pictures of common objects, patterns of Xs and squares, words, word meaning, phonetic images of rhyming pictures, and outline drawings to be matched to colours, patients gave one response on the vast majority of competitive trials. Further, the nonresponding hemisphere gave no evidence that it had any perception at all. Thus, if the right hemisphere responded there was no indication, by words or facial expression, that the left hemisphere had any argument with the choice made, and, similarly, if the left hemisphere responded, no behavior on the part of the patient suggested a disagreement by the right hemisphere.
>
> (Levy 1990, p. 235)

Of course, even if the switch model accounts for the split-brain data, it might not account for the hidden observer data. Nevertheless, I think it is instructive to note that a syndrome which is often presented as involving two streams of consciousness in a single human being might be best accounted for in terms of the switch model.

It is also instructive to note that the switch model has been given for another experi-mental result that has shades of the hidden observer about it. Miller and Bowers (1993) asked subjects engaged in a cold-pressor task to report on their levels of pain intensity by means of two report modalities: verbally, and via a foot-pedal mechanism that used pressure to indicate pain intensity. The subjects' verbal reports were retrospective, while their foot-pedal reports were concurrent with the stimulus. The pedal-pressure reports of hypnotized highly hypnotizable individuals indicated increasing levels of pain over the duration of the task, while no equivalent increase of pain over time was indicated via retrospective verbal report. Miller and Bowers themselves suggest that changes in the focus of the subjects' attention might account for the discrepancies between their verbal reports and their foot-pedal reports.

It might be objected that in at least one hidden observer experiment subjects were said to have produced simultaneous overt and covert reports (Hilgard *et al.* 1975). If the covert and overt reports were simultaneous, then it is hard to see how one could explain the difference between them in terms of alterations in the focus of the subject's attention. However, I am sceptical that these reports really were produced simultaneously. Hilgard's reports contain no quantitative data about the timing of reports, and when hidden observer studies have specified simultaneity measures they have operationalized it to within 500 ms (Spanos and Hewitt 1980), which is certainly long enough for the subject's attention to change its focus.

There is another objection lurking in these waters. Even if subjects do not produce overt and 'hidden observer' reports simultaneously, they do report having been simultaneously aware of normal and 'hidden observer' experiences 'from the inside', as we might say. I think this is the toughest objection facing the switch model, and I am not entirely sure what to say in response to it. It is possible that subjects are remembering (and thus reporting) sequential experiences as having been simultaneous. Here, as elsewhere, further research on the phenomenology of hypnosis is vital.

6.6 Conclusion

I have argued that hypnosis does not involve a breakdown in the unity of consciousness. By far and away the most suggestive data in this regard are provided by the hidden observer paradigm, and for the most part these data are best accounted for in terms of switches in the contents of consciousness rather than simultaneous (but disunified) streams of consciousness, or in terms of two streams of mental activity, only one of which is conscious. I have not examined the question of whether hypnotic subjects really undergo the radical changes in the content of consciousness that they seem to, and, if so, how these changes might come about. However, those seeking to develop an account of consciousness would do well to address these questions. Hypnosis provides students of consciousness with an intriguing data set, one that it would be as foolish to ignore as the data sets deriving from the study of dreaming, psychosis or indeed ordinary waking consciousness.

Acknowledgements

My thanks to Barry Dainton, Graham Jamieson and John Kihlstrom for very helpful comments on previous drafts of this chapter.

References

Asch SE (1956). Studies of independence and conformity: I. A minority of one against a unanimous majority. *Psychological Monographs* 70 (416).

Baars B (1988). *A cognitive theory of consciousness*. Cambridge, Cambridge University Press.

Baars B (2002). The conscious access hypothesis: origins and recent evidence. *Trends in Cognitive Sciences*, **6**, 47–52.

Bayne T (2006). Phenomenology and the feeling of doing: Wegner on the conscious will. In: S Pockett, WP Banks and S Gallagher, eds. *Does consciousness cause behavior? An investigation of the nature of volition*. Cambridge, MA, MIT Press, pp. 169–186.

Bayne T and Chalmers D (2003). What is the unity of consciousness? In: A Cleeremans, ed. *The unity of consciousness*. pp. 23–58. Oxford, Oxford University Press.

Bayne T and Levy N (2006). The feeling of doing: deconstructing the phenomenology of agency. In: W Prinz and N Sebanz, eds. *Disorders of volition*. Cambridge, MA, MIT Press, pp. 49–68.

Binet A (1889–1900). *On double consciousness*. Chicago, Open Court Publishing Co.

Bowers KS (1990). Unconscious influences and hypnosis. In: JL Singer, ed. *Repression and dissociation: implications for personality theory, psychopathology and health*. pp. 143–78. Chicago, University of Chicago Press.

Bowers KS (1991). Dissociation in hypnosis and multiple personality disorder. *International Journal of Clinical and Experimental Hypnosis*, **39**, 155–76.

Bowers KS and Davidson TM (1991). A neo-dissociative critique of Spanos's social psychological model of hypnosis. In: SJ Lynn and JW Rhue, eds. *Theories of hypnosis: Current models and perspectives*, pp. 105–43. New York, Guilford Press

Bowers P, Laurence JR and Hart D (1988). The experience of hypnotic suggestions. *International Journal of Clinical and Experimental Hypnosis*, **36**, 336–49.

Comey G and Kirsch I (1999). Intentional and spontaneous imagery in hypnosis: the phenomenology of hypnotic responding. *International Journal of Clinical and Experimental Hypnosis*, **47**, 65–85.

Crawford JH, Macdonald H and Hilgard ER (1979). Hypnotic deafness—psychophysical study of responses to tone intensity as modified by hypnosis. *American Journal of Psychology*, **92**, 193–214.

Dainton B (2000). *Stream of consciousness: unity and continuity in experience*. London, Routledge.

Dehaene S and Naccache L (2001). Towards a cognitive neuroscience of consciousness: basic evidence and a workspace framework. *Cognition*, **79**, 1–37.

Dennett D (2001). Are we explaining consciousness yet? *Cognition*, **21**, 221–37.

Evans FJ (1980). Posthypnotic amnesia. In: GD Burrows and L Dennerstein, eds. *Handbook of hypnosis and psychosomatic medicine*. pp. 85–103. Amsterdamn, Elsevier/North-Holland.

Fleminger S (2002). Remembering delirium. *British Journal of Psychiatry*, **180**, 4–5.

Gazzaniga MS (2005). Forty-five years of split-brain research and still going strong. *Nature Reviews Neuroscience*, **6**, 653–59.

Gill D and Mayou R (2000). Delirium. In: Gelder MG, López-Ibor Jr. JJ, Andreasen N (eds), *The New Oxford Textbook of Psychiatry*. pp. 382–387. Oxford, Oxford University Press.

Green JP, Page RA, Handley GW and Rasekhy R (2005). The 'Hidden Observer' and ideomotor responding: a real–simulator comparison. *Contemporary Hypnosis*, **22**, 123–37.

Hilgard ER (1973). A neodissociation interpretation of pain reduction in hypnosis. *Psychological Review*, **80**, 396–411.

Hilgard ER (1977). *Divided consciousness: multiple controls in human thought and action*. New York, John Wiley and Sons.

Hilgard ER (1992). Divided consciousness and dissociation. *Consciousness and Cognition*, **1**, 16–31.

Hilgard ER, Morgan AH, Macdonald H (1975). Pain and dissociation in the cold pressor test: a study of hypnotic analgesia with 'hidden reports' through automatic key pressing and automatic talking. *Journal of Abnormal Psychology*, **84**, 280–89.

Hilgard ER, Hilgard JR, Macdonald H, Morgan AH and Johnson LS (1978). Covert pain in hypnotic analgesia: its reality as tested by the real-simulator design. *Journal of Abnormal Psychology*, **87**, 655–663.

James W (1890). *Principles of psychology*. New York, Holt.

Kihlstrom JF (1985). Hypnosis. *Annual Review of Psychology*, **35**, 385–418.

Kihlstrom JF and Barnier A (2005). The hidden observer: a straw horse, undeservedly flogged. *Contemporary Hypnosis*, **22**, 144–151.

Kirsch I and Lynn SJ (1998). Social-cognitive alternatives to dissociation theories of hypnotic involuntariness. *Review of General Psychology*, **2**, 66–80.

Knox VJ, Morgan AH and Hilgard ER (1974). Pain and suffering in ischemia: the paradox of hypnotically suggested anesthesia as contradicted by reports from the hidden observer. *Archives of General Psychiatry*, **30**, 840–847.

Koch C (2004). *The quest for consciousness*. Englewood, CO, Roberts and Co.

Koch C and Crick F (2001). On the zombie within. *Nature*, **411**, 893.

Laurence J.-R. and Perry C (1981). The 'hidden observer' phenomenon in hypnosis: some additional findings. *Journal of Abnormal Psychology*, **90**, 334–44.

Laurence J.-R, Perry C and Kihlstrom JF (1983). 'Hidden observer' phenomena in hypnosis: an experimental creation? *Journal of Personality and Social Psychology*, **44**, 163–169.

Levy J (1977). Manifestations and implications of shifting hemi-inattention in commissurotomy patients. *Advances in Neurology*, **18**, 83–92.

Levy J (1990). Regulation and generation of perception in the asymmetric brain. In: C Trevarthen, ed. *Brain circuits and functions of the mind: essays in honour of Roger W. Sperry*. pp. 231–48. Cambridge, Cambridge University Press.

Levy J and Trevarthen C (1976). Metacontrol of hemispheric function in human split-brain patients. *Journal of Experimental Psychology: Human Perception and Performance*, **2**, 299–312.

Lipowski ZJ (1990). *Delirium: acute confusional states*. New York, Oxford University Press.

Miller ME and Bowers KS (1993). Hypnotic analgesia: dissociated experience or dissociated control? *Journal of Abnormal Psychology*, **102**, 29–38.

Nagel T (1974). What is it like to be a bat? *Philosophical Review*, LXXXIII, **4**, 435–50.

Nogrady H, McConkey KM, Laurence J-R and Perry C (1983). Dissociation, duality, and demand characteristics in hypnosis. *Journal of Abnormal Psychology*, **92**, 223–35.

Oakley DA and Eames LC (1985). The plurality of consciousness. In: DA Oakley, ed. *Brain and mind*. London, Metheun, pp. 217–251.

Orne MT (1959). The nature of hypnosis: artifact and essence. *Journal of Abnormal and Social Psychology*, **58**, 277–99.

Perry C and Walsh B (1978). Inconsistencies and anomalies of response as a defining characteristic of hypnosis, *Journal of Abnormal Psychology* **87**, 547–577.

Prince M (1909). Experiments to determine co-conscious (subconscious) ideation. *Journal of Abnormal Psychology*, **3**, 33–42.

Rossetti Y (1998). Implicit short-lived motor representations of space in brain damaged and healthy subjects, *Consciousness and Cognition*, **7**, 520–57.

Sherif M (1935). A study of some social factors in perception. *Archives of Psychology*, **27**, 1–60.

Spanos NP (1983). The hidden observer as an experimental creation. *Journal of Personality and Social Psychology*, **44**, 170–76.

Spanos NP and Barber TX (1972). Cognitive activity during 'hypnotic' suggestibility: goal-directed fantasy and the experience of nonvolition. *Journal of Personality*, **40**, 510–24.

Spanos NP and Hewitt EC (1980). The hidden observer in hypnotic analgesia: discovery or experimental creation? *Journal of Personality and Social Psychology*, **39**, 1201–14.

Spanos NP, Gwynn MI and Stam HJ (1983). Instructional demands and ratings of overt and hidden pain during hypnotic analgesia. *Journal of Abnormal Psychology*, **92**, 479–88.

Spanos NP, Radtke HL and Bertrand LD (1985*a*). Hypnotic amnesia as a strategic enactment: breaching amnesia in highly susceptible subjects. *Journal of Personality and Social Psychology*, **47**, 1155–1169.

Spanos NP, de Groot HP, Tiller DK, Weekes JR and Bertrand LD (1985*b*). 'Trance logic' duality and hidden observer responding in hypnotic, imagination control, and simulating subjects. *Journal of Abnormal Psychology*, **94**, 611–23.

Trevarthen C (1974). Functional relations of disconnected hemispheres with the brain stem, and with each other: monkey and man. In: M Kinsbourne and W Lynn Smith, eds. *Hemispheric disconnection and cerebral function*. pp. 187–207. Springfield, IL, Charles C. Thomas.

Zaidel E, Iacoboni M, Zaidel DW, Bogen JE (2003). The Cattosel Syndromes. In: Heilman KH and Valenstein E (eds.). *Clinical Neuropsychology*, fourth edition, 347–403. Oxford: Oxford University Press.

Zamansky HS and Bartis SP (1985). The dissociation of an experience: the hidden observer observed. *Journal of Abnormal Psychology*, **94**, 243–48.

Chapter 7

Dissociated control as a paradigm for cognitive neuroscience research and theorizing in hypnosis

Graham A Jamieson and Erik Woody

7.1 Introduction

For much of its history, hypnosis has tended to be somewhat of a rogue topic, difficult to connect with the main body of psychological understanding. Hilgard's (1977) neodissociation theory of hypnosis represented an attempt to integrate a scientific understanding of hypnosis into the broader landscape of psychology. He commented, 'Any satisfactory theory of hypnosis should also be a theory bearing on psychology at large' (Hilgard 1991, p. 101).

Accordingly, he attempted to explain hypnotic phenomena in terms of underlying cognitive control mechanisms and the alteration of their function in hypnosis (Hilgard 1991, 1992). He posited a system of multiple cognitive control subsystems that can operate somewhat autonomously, but which are ordinarily subordinate to a higher order executive system that monitors and coordinates the interaction among them. He hypothesized that hypnosis somehow alters the executive functions and their hierarchical relationship to the subsystems of control. For example, he indicated that the hypnotist may take over some of the executive control functions that would otherwise be managed autonomously by the subject.

Hilgard's attempts to develop and clarify these ideas took two rather distinct directions, relying on different conceptions of dissociation, the idea at the centre of his theory. On one hand, the term 'dissociation' can be taken to mean a 'disassociation' or 'disaggregation' of mental processes, whereby processes that are normally closely related become functionally more separate. Along these lines, Hilgard remarked, 'If dissociation is conceived broadly to imply an interference with or loss of familiar associative processes, most phenomena of hypnosis can be conceived as dissociative' (Hilgard 1991, p. 84). One of Hilgard's most important speculations about such disassociation of processes concerned the possible loss of integration of the monitoring and control functions of the executive system. For example, in hypnotic age regression, when the hypnotic subject experiences himself or herself as a child, 'all available information is not used by the activated subsystem, and the monitor does not offer a correction; hence imagination may be confused with external reality' (Hilgard 1992, p. 97).

On the other hand, a contrasting conception of dissociation is one that stems more directly from Janet (1901, 1907/1965) and his emphasis on conscious versus unconscious processes. Specifically, the term 'dissociation' can be taken to mean 'the splitting off of certain mental processes from the main body of consciousness with various degrees of autonomy' (Hilgard 1992, p. 69). This is the conception of dissociation that Hilgard pursued more vigorously, partly because of the great importance he attached to the discovery of the 'hidden observer' (Hilgard 1977). The finding that a 'hidden observer' could report the presence of pain in an otherwise hypnotically analgesic subject implied to Hilgard that there is a split in consciousness, in which two parallel streams of consciousness co-exist. He hypothesized that the split in consciousness is effected by an amnesia-like barrier, which divides perceptions into separate, co-existing channels. This conception of dissociation, instead of focusing on the relationship of monitoring to control, focused on division within the monitoring function: 'some fraction of it exists behind an amnesia-like barrier' (Hilgard 1992, p. 99).

In hindsight, so closely yoking neodissociation theory to the hidden observer phenomenon may have been a mistake. Not only is the empirical basis of the hidden observer open to telling lines of criticism (Spanos and Hewitt 1980; Bayne, Chapter 6), but so is the amnesic barrier conception of dissociation in hypnosis (e.g. Kirsch and Lynn 1998). Indeed, the postulation of multiple co-existing channels of consciousness in order to explain the partial reversal of analgesia with the suggestion of a hidden observer has struck many commentators as gratuitous and unconvincing (e.g. Kallio and Revonsuo 2003).

Perhaps the most generative line of criticism of Hilgard's theory came from Bowers (1990, 1992). He pointed out that amnesic barriers were not a plausible mechanism for most hypnotic effects. Spontaneous amnesias (ones not directly suggested) are very rare in hypnosis; hence, the amnesic barrier concept was perversely attempting to explain relatively common hypnotic effects in terms of a very rare one. In addition, the theory required these barriers to be implausibly and arbitrarily selective: 'The pain and cognitive effort to reduce it is hidden behind an amnesic barrier, but not the original suggestions for analgesia, nor the goal-directed fantasies that typically accompany the reductions in pain' (Bowers 1992, pp. 261–262). Furthermore, Bowers pointed out that the concept of amnesic barriers implied, in contradiction to the rest of Hilgard's theory, that in hypnosis there need not be any change in the cognitive control of behaviour, but only a distortion in its self-perception. Specifically, the amnesic barrier concept implied that the hypnotic subject would simply enact suggestions voluntarily and effortfully in the usual fashion, but this fact would be occluded from his or her awareness by an amnesic barrier. Hence, the subject's perception of his or her hypnotic behaviour as involuntary and effortless would be an illusion, rather than a reflection of a true underlying alteration in the control of behaviour (see also Shor 1979; Kihlstrom 1992).

To salvage what Bowers (1990, 1992) perceived to be the viable aspects of neodissociation theory, he jettisoned the amnesic barrier concept of dissociation, which he termed a theory of 'dissociated experience', and refocused attention on the concept of hypnotically altered control of behaviour, which he termed a theory of 'dissociated control.' He argued that 'dissociation is not intrinsically a matter of keeping things out of consciousness—whether by amnesia, or any other means' (Bowers 1992, p. 267). Instead, he argued that 'dissociation is primarily concerned with the fact that subsystems of control can be directly and automatically activated, instead of being governed by high level executive control' (Bowers 1992, p. 267). That is, the dissociation at work in hypnosis was between subsystems of control and the higher, executive level of control. This revised statement of Hilgard's neodissociation theory then served as the beginning proposition of dissociated control theory, which we review in the next section.

To set the stage for the rest of this chapter, we wish to draw out two major themes from the foregoing discussion of neodissociation theory. First, Hilgard's attempts to devise a cognitive control model of hypnosis remained frustratingly incomplete and vague. Indeed, he was eventually quite apologetic for its promissory nature: 'I regret to leave the theory in this incomplete form, so that it is more of a promise than a finished theory' (Hilgard 1991, p. 98). Even Bowers' reformulation mainly trimmed away some of what he perceived to be the theory's excesses. A major problem is that the implied model was always, to use a technical term, 'underidentified'—within the theory, it was not straightforward to disambiguate what its multiple hypothetical entities (subsystems of control, monitors, and so forth) really referred to and how to measure them. Dixon and Laurence (1992) made a closely related comment: 'As elegant as Hilgard's rendition of Janet's dissociation theory may be, it is and will remain an exercise in metaphors' (p. 42).

The problem with the theory has always been, in a sense, how to get beyond the level of metaphor. What was needed for this purpose, in our view, is an additional level of analysis, which is provided by cognitive neuroscience. Woody and McConkey (2003) described such a combination of levels as follows:

> The exciting prospect of a bridge to the underlying biology of hypnosis encourages us to reformulate some basic themes in hypnosis research, so as to ask more sophisticated and differentiated questions .... In addition, ... the challenge of connecting our psychological understanding to underlying biology can reveal important gaps in our psychological understanding, which serve a vital role in stimulating future research (p. 332).

We believe the work to be reviewed in this chapter demonstrates the creative interplay between two levels of analysis—the careful functional analysis of behaviour, on one hand, and the detailed mapping of neural underpinnings, on the other. In this interplay, we see the application of powerful new tools which are quite different from anything that was available to Hilgard, just a few years ago.

Secondly, the strong distinction between dissociated experience and dissociated control, proposed by Bowers, was important rhetorically for re-emphasizing that hypnosis may alter the control of behaviour, rather than simply its self-perception. However, as Woody and Sadler (1998) pointed out, the concepts of dissociated experience and dissociated control are not at all incompatible, and the sharp distinction between them may have been somewhat premature. As mentioned previously, before Hilgard's thinking became dominated by the hidden observer, his focus was on changes in the relationship between the monitoring and control functions of the executive system. As we will detail shortly, recent work breathes rich new life into this old idea.

7.2 **Dissociated control theory**

Woody and Bowers' (1994) formulation of dissociated control theory (DCT) may be considered the first of a new generation of hypnosis theories based within the emerging perspective of cognitive neuroscience. Of course, other, alternative approaches may also be taken within a cognitive neuroscience framework; the further development and testing of these competing accounts is a task for the readers of this volume. DCT in its initial formulation is a theory which integrates findings across three domains of data and explanation: phenomenological; functional (behavioural); and neurophysiological. DCT applies an early and influential cognitive neuroscience account of cognitive control systems in the human brain to one of the principal phenomenological characteristics of hypnosis—the sense of involuntariness in response to hypnotic suggestions (Weitzenhoffer 1953).

Norman and Shallice (1986) sought to account for the pattern of functional deficits observed in neuropsychological testing with frontal lesion patients. They proposed two distinct but interacting systems of cognitive control, which they labelled contention scheduling (CS) and the supervisory attentional system (SAS). For well-learned habitual tasks, unconscious, automatic, modular neural processing structures (schemata) control the required actions. CS controls the selection of specific schemata through a decentralized process of competitive and cooperative activation of schemata by sensory input and the input of other active schemata. When a specific schema reaches its required activation threshold, the corresponding action or cognitive operation is performed. However, when the task is novel or complex or requires a strong habitual response to be overcome, a higher level control system, the SAS, is engaged to assist CS.

The SAS incorporates representations of goals and intentions, and monitors contention scheduling. The SAS does not implement actions directly, but instead biases the selection of particular schemata by CS through modulating their activation levels. As elaborated by Shallice (1988), SAS modulation of the selection of schemata corresponds to the phenomenal experience of will. In contrast, when the SAS is neither monitoring nor modulating CS, action is experienced as automatic. The SAS is mediated by frontal cortical structures, and the classic functional impairments associated with frontal lesions may be understood as a consequence of the disruptions of SAS regulation of the largely posterior cortically mediated process of CS.

Woody and Bowers (1994) applied the Norman and Shallice model to explain the range of dissociations observed in hypnosis. In response to the suggestions of the hypnotist, motor and cognitive processes normally experienced as under willed, volitional control seem to occur independently of the conscious will of the hypnotized person. According to DCT, hypnosis, in susceptible individuals, produces a temporary functional dissociation of CS from SAS control, similar in some respects to the effect of frontal lesions. For highly susceptible individuals, hypnosis partly disables the higher level control system associated with the experience of will, resulting in a lack of spontaneous self-generated action. This leaves the hypnotized person especially dependent on CS-like, automatic control processes.

In the non-hypnotic condition, SAS control allows for a greater degree of autonomy from contextual influences and prior expectations. When frontally mediated executive control is diminished in the hypnosis condition, subjects' expectancies and interpretations exert influence via the intrinsic linkages of activated representations rather than the monitored execution of plans and strategies. Contextual cues and the communications of the hypnotist then become the major factors structuring the content of cognitive processes and phenomenal experience, as they emerge in hypnosis ('hypersuggestibility'). An additional consequence of the release of some cognitive processes from the constraints of SAS control may be the wider activation of loose associations idiosyncratic to that individual. More generally, the framework of cognitive control which regulates the influence of information from contextual sources and prior expectations on hypnotic responses—what Orne (1959) labelled the 'demand characteristics' of the hypnotic situation—is different from that which normally regulates the non-hypnosis condition. Consequently these processes are even more salient for hypnotized, as compared with non-hypnotized, responses.

7.3 Testing dissociated control

DCT predicts a disruption of frontally mediated cognitive processes requiring executive (supervisory) attentional control in highly susceptible individuals during hypnosis. Alternatively, it might be expected that individual differences in hypnotic susceptibility would be positively correlated with disruptions in executive cognitive control even in non-hypnotic contexts. Several attempts have been made recently to test these predictions explicitly with a range of behavioural neuropsychological measures. Kallio *et al.* (2001) administered a battery of neuropsychological frontal lobe measures to eight individuals who were highly susceptible and nine individuals with a low susceptibility both at baseline and during hypnosis. Letter fluency, a test highly sensitive to Broca's area (left frontal) lesions, was found to decline in hypnosis for highly susceptible individuals but not for those with a low susceptibility, a result reported previously by Gruzelier and Warren (1993). Aikens and Ray (2001), using a different battery, found that a group of nine highly susceptible individuals performed significantly better than a group of seven individuals with low susceptibility on the Wisconsin Card Sorting Task, a finding contrary to DCT.

These studies utilized relatively small samples, and lack of statistical power may therefore have been a factor. Farvolden and Woody (2004) administered a battery of memory tasks sensitive to frontal lobe functioning to 30 individuals who were highly susceptible and 30 individuals with low susceptibility both at baseline and in hypnosis. Highly susceptible individuals generally had more difficulty with frontally mediated memory tasks (but not with non-frontal control tasks) than those with low susceptility in both hypnotized and non-hypnotized conditions, thus supporting the prediction of greater vulnerability to disruptions in frontal control amongst highly hypnotically susceptible individuals. However, no differences were observed between hypnotized and non-hypnotized conditions in the highly susceptible individuals, inconsistent with the state predictions of DCT.

Jamieson and Sheehan (2004) sought to contrast directly the prediction of DCT that SAS control is compromised in hypnosis versus the alternative prediction that hypnosis is a state of enhanced SAS control (e.g. Horton and Crawford 2004). Following Sheehan *et al.* (1988), they adopted a version of the classic Stroop task, which required participants to name either the colour or the colour word of a stimulus which comprises a colour word presented in a colour which is incongruent to the colour named. Successful colour naming requires overcoming the strong conflicting response tendency produced by the colour word. The conscious selection of correct responses against competition from stronger automatic response tendencies is one of the most fundamental functions of the SAS or indeed any account of anterior-mediated cognitive control. If SAS control is enhanced in hypnosis, then Stroop performance should be enhanced in hypnotized highly susceptible individuals. However, if DCT is correct, Stroop performance should be impaired in hypnotized highly susceptible individuals.

As predicted by DCT, Stroop task errors increased significantly for highly susceptible individuals in hypnosis, but not for those with low susceptibility. This study had high power, with 66 participants in each group. It also utilized a particularly difficult version of the Stroop task with fast-paced incongruent stimuli and rapid changes between colour naming and word naming requirements. Thus, the considerable demands of the task required high levels of SAS control; in contrast, less rigorous paradigms may not result in overt behavioural differences. However, two previous studies have reported similar results using response conflict paradigms in hypnosis or hypnosis-like conditions (Kaiser *et al.* 1997; Nordby *et al.* 1999). In addition to power, both the precise nature of the task demands and the appropriate setting of task parameters governing difficulty level may be important in obtaining positive results in these investigations.

The wider body of neuropsychological studies of hypnosis in relation to frontal functioning are mixed. Some results seem to suggest enhanced attentional control in highly susceptible individuals (Horton and Crawford 2004), whilst others suggest just the opposite (Gruzelier 1998). Methodological issues, sample size and lack of replication make firm conclusions from much of this literature difficult to reach (there is a great need for some of these intriguing findings to be revisited by current investigators). In summary, carefully designed studies with appropriate power do provide support for disruptions in specific aspects of frontally mediated cognitive control in relation to both hypnotic susceptibility and the hypnotic condition. However, it is fair to say that current neuropsychological data do not support a simple global shutdown of frontal functioning during hypnosis.

7.4 **Conceptual problems for dissociated control**

Brown and Oakley (2004) and Dienes and Perner (Chapter 16) make the important criticism that DCT leaves cognitive control in hypnosis entirely dependent on CS, which normally controls only routine overlearned behaviours. This, they argue, cannot account for either the novel responses required by some hypnotic suggestions or the apparent requirement for classic (frontal) executive control in producing some hypnotic responses.

Dienes and Perner (Chapter 16) point out that response to the hypnotic suggestion 'forget the number 4' and then to count the fingers on one's hand requires both active monitoring for the occurrence of 'the number 4' and the inhibition of the overlearned response to count in sequence 1, 2, 3, 4. Both are classic examples of SAS-controlled functions.

DCT does not offer a detailed account of the mechanisms producing the explicit content of (negative or positive) hypnotic hallucinations. Nor does it give an obvious account for other arguably core features of hypnotic experience such as tolerance for logical incongruity (Orne 1959, 1979) or loss of generalized reality orientation (Shor 1959, 1979). Sophisticated phenomenological analysis of hypnotic experience demonstrates that while some participants experience suggestions in a passive, involuntary way (the classic suggestion effect), some highly responsive participants experience a complex and fluidly shifting mix of reality and hallucination (Sheehan and McConkey 1982; McConkey and Barnier 2004). McConkey (1991) highlighted the active (rather than passive) nature of the cognitive processes needed to resolve the conflicting demands of reality and suggestion. A full account of the phenomenological aspects of hypnosis must be able to explain these diverse features. It could be argued that DCT is a successful account of hypnotic involuntariness and many of the dissociations which occur in hypnotic consciousness without being a complete theory of hypnosis. However, successful extension of DCT will ultimately need to address these additional features of hypnotic consciousness.

7.5 Lessons from the neuroscience of voluntary motor control

A detailed account of the discrimination of self- and non-self-generated movement—which is closely related to the experience of movement as volitional or non-volitional—has emerged from the neuroscience of motor control. This work highlights the role of the cerebellum and inferior parietal operculum, as well as frontal cortical regions, in this process (Miall and Wolpert 1996; Weiller et al. 1996). It also emphasizes the role of an 'efference copy', a neural representation of motor commands produced by or in conjunction with the 'motor intentions' that trigger the commands (Blakemore et al. 1999). The efference copy is the basis for generating a predictive model of the immediate sensory consequences of those motor commands, which is then matched against the actual sensory feedback from the movement. Forward output model generation and comparison with sensory input is believed to be mediated by the cerebellum (Wolpert et al. 1998). A match (indicating self-produced movement) leads to an inhibition of these sensory representations in the parietal cortex (Blakemore et al. 1999). Thus, these parietal representations are more active in the case of involuntary than voluntary movements.

According to this account, activity in the cerebellum and parietal cortex plays an essential role in producing the feeling that a movement is occurring involuntarily. This hypothesis was tested in relation to hypnotic involuntariness in a recent positron emission tomography (PET) study by Blakemore et al. (2003). During hypnosis, six highly susceptible individuals were scanned whilst voluntarily raising their left hand and forearm, performing hypnotic arm levitation of the left hand and forearm, having their left hand and forearm raised by a mechanical device, and at rest. As predicted, hypnotic arm levitation (which was perceived as involuntary) was associated both with greater bilateral cerebellar activation and with greater bilateral parietal operculum and left inferior parietal cortex than voluntary arm movement (Blakemore *et al.* 2003). Blakemore and colleagues propose that when hypnotic subjects responded to the arm levitation suggestion, motor intentions were unavailable to inform the generation of an accurate forward output model, leading to a mismatch between predicted and actual sensory feedback (corresponding to increased cerebellar activation). This mismatch resulted in a lack of inhibition of the sensory feedback (corresponding to greater parietal activation), which formed the basis of the experience of the movement as not generated by the self.

The model put forward by Blakemore and colleagues is an important advance in our understanding of some aspects of hypnotic behaviour. However, it leaves unaddressed why an efference copy either does not result from the motor preparation for hypnotic arm levitation (an activity orchestrated by the frontal premotor cortex in conjunction with other frontal regions) or is not available to the cerebellum. This itself points to a fundamental difference in core aspects of frontal cortical involvement in the control of voluntary arm raising versus that of hypnotic arm levitation. Neither does their model obviously generalize to account for the non-volitional quality of cognitive, rather than motor, responses to hypnotic suggestion (e.g. hypnotic amnesia). Nonetheless, this important application of a contemporary neuroscience paradigm to the experience of non-volition in hypnosis has clear implications for the extension of DCT.

Higher order cognitive controls involve wide networks of functional interactions between specialized frontal, posterior and subcortical regions (see, for example, Friston 2002; Makeig *et al.* 2004; Egner and Hirsch 2005). Frontal regions play distinctive roles within such processes, but those roles can best be understood by examining these regions within their wider context of functional interactions. This broader framework was implicit but undeveloped in the Norman and Shallice SAS model. The availability of modern imaging technologies and consequent rapid development of cognitive neuroscience make possible the detailed analysis of such relationships. The challenge for DCT is to locate its account of frontal cortical regions and higher order cognitive control within a broader understanding of functional relationships between various brain regions. This new level of detail should permit the formulation of specific predictions about the changes in cognitive control that underlie hypnosis, predictions which will be testable with the newly available technologies.

7.6 The role of the anterior cortex in cognitive control

According to the SAS model and many subsequent accounts, cognitive control is implemented by top-down biasing of task-relevant processes (Miller and Cohen 2000). Specific task or goal representations, which are the source of these biasing influences, are localized within various regions of the prefrontal cortex (PFC). However, Cohen *et al.* (2004), in their conflict-monitoring model, argued that flexible cognitive control, sensitive to changes in task demands, requires an additional element to monitor the effectiveness of existing control and to provide feedback for appropriate control adjustments. They proposed that a specific region of the frontal cortex, the anterior cingulate cortex (ACC), performs the function of monitoring for processing conflicts between operations under the active control of PFC task representations (Botvinick *et al.* 2001). Conflict-related activation in the ACC then signals the need for greater activation in PFC representations to strengthen further the bias toward task-relevant processing pathways in frontal motor areas, posterior cortex and related subcortical structures. Thus, monitoring and control, both core elements of the original SAS formulation, are functionally and anatomically fractionated in this conflict-monitoring model of cognitive control.

In one earlier event-related functional magnetic resonance imaging (fMRI) study of this model, MacDonald *et al.* (2000) utilized a version of the Stroop task to produce a dissociation between demands for cognitive control task preparation and levels of response conflict during stimulus response. For each Stroop stimulus, the colour and word were either congruent (low conflict) or incongruent (high conflict). Before each trial, participants received an instruction to either name the word (low demand for cognitive control) or name the colour (high demand for cognitive control) of the stimulus. Consistent with the predictions of the model, the contrast between high and low demands for control in the preparation period showed activation in the left dorsolateral prefrontal cortex (lDLPFC) corresponding to the recruitment of control resources. However, the contrast between high and low response conflict stimuli in the stimulus response period showed activation in the ACC corresponding to the detection of increased response conflict. Predictions from this model have since received further empirical support by results from a wide range of behavioural, electroencephalographic (EEG) and imaging studies (Botvinick *et al.* 2004).

7.7 DCT and the cognitive neuroscience of cognitive control

Key insights of DCT are that disruptions to the process of cognitive control play a central role in the generation of hypnotic phenomena, and that these disruptions stem from a fundamental shift in the organization of executive functions within the brain. From the perspective of the conflict-monitoring model, it would be expected that such disruptions in cognitive control would result in greater cognitive interference, particularly during tasks eliciting response conflict such as the Stroop paradigm. This greater interference should elicit greater activation from conflict-sensitive monitoring processes in the ACC of highly susceptible individuals in hypnosis. Egner *et al.* (2005) set out to test this novel prediction of DCT and the conflict-monitoring model. Using an adaptation of the MacDonald *et al.* (2000) paradigm, they administered an event-related fMRI paradigm consisting of congruent and incongruent Stroop stimuli, requiring either word naming or colour naming responses to individuals of high and low susceptibility in baseline and hypnosis conditions (see also Egner and Raz, Chapter 3). Similarly to MacDonald *et al.*, they were able to identify regions of conflict-related activation within the ACC by contrasting conditions of high response conflict (colour naming incongruent trials) and medium response conflict (colour naming congruent and word naming incongruent) with the low conflict condition (word naming congruent trials). Regions that were identified in both contrasts were selected as the most conflict-sensitive ACC regions for further analysis of response conflict effects. Prefrontal regions sensitive to differences in task demands for cognitive control were identified by contrasting colour naming (higher control) with word naming (lower control) trials. This contrast identified a control-related region of activation within the left lateral PFC.

In this paradigm, the activation of ACC regions most sensitive to response conflict showed a classic interaction between hypnotic susceptibility and the hypnotic condition. As predicted by the contemporary interpretation of DCT advanced above, conflict-related ACC activation increased for highly susceptible individuals in hypnosis (but not for those with low susceptibility). There were no behavioural differences between individuals with high and low susceptibility in either baseline or hypnosis conditions due to the very long (12 s) interstimulus interval in this experiment. This is a stringent methodological safeguard adopted (where possible) in imaging studies to rule out differences in task difficulty as an alternative explanation for obtained differences between conditions. Recall that Jamieson and Sheehan (2004) demonstrated a decrease in the efficiency of the cognitive control in the face of sufficiently demanding response conflict, through increased error commission in hypnotized highly susceptible individuals. Egner et al. (2005) demonstrated a similar decrease in the efficiency of this cognitive control system, through increased activation in the cortical regions maximally sensitive to the level of response conflict. Taken together, these two studies constitute strong evidence in favour of one of the principal predictions of DCT.

In the study by Egner and colleagues (2005), the anterior system of rapid, flexible cognitive control sketched by Norman and Shallice (1986) and carefully fractionated by Cohen and his associates (Cohen et al. 2004) appears to have been disrupted by hypnosis. However, the individuals with high and low susceptibility continued to perform the task with comparable levels of speed and accuracy even in the hypnotized condition. There were no significant differences between individuals with high and low susceptibility in the activation of left frontal regions identified as corresponding to the demand for cognitive control in either baseline or hypnotized conditions. These results are not consistent with a simple shift from SAS to CS control in the highly susceptible individuals in hypnosis. Rather, components of the SAS (prefrontal representations of task requirements) appear to continue to be involved in task performance (which still requires response selection in the presence of competing response tendencies), but without flexible regulation to carefully match changing cognitive demands.

The conflict-monitoring function of the ACC component of anterior cognitive control appears to be undiminished in hypnosis, as indicated by the increase in conflict-related activation observed by Egner et al. (2005). This conclusion is also supported by the findings of Kaiser et al. (1997). Using a response conflict paradigm, they showed that although error rates increased for individuals with higher susceptibility in hypnosis, there was no change in the error-related negativity (N_E), an event-related potential component generated by the ACC when a response error occurs. Although there is some controversy about the role of the N_E (Holroyd *et al.* 2004), the N_E is plausibly explained as a post-response consequence of conflict between the error response and continued processing of the correct response (Yeung *et al.* 2004). How, then, is cognitive control impaired if ACC error and conflict monitoring remain intact and PFC representations of task-relevant goals and rules continue to exert an active influence?

The conflict-monitoring model provides a plausible answer to this question. However, it is important to distinguish between two different levels of cognitive control within the model. The first level of SAS control is implemented by active task or rule representations in the PFC, which facilitate non-routine cognitive and motor responses. A second-order level of cognitive control within the SAS is the flexible modulation of the implementation of control in response to changing cognitive requirements. This level of attentional control emerges from the ability to detect interference or conflict (in processes influenced by currently active PFC representations) by the regions within the ACC. This conflict detection, in turn, signals appropriate changes in the activation of concurrent task-relevant goal representations in specific regions of the PFC. For example, working within this paradigm, Kerns *et al.* (2004) demonstrated that increases in ACC conflict-related activation on a preceding trial led to increases in the activation of PFC task-related representations on subsequent trials, corresponding in turn to improved behavioural performance on those trials. Similarly, Ridderinkoff *et al.* (2003) demonstrated that, in comparison with correct trials, response errors (failures of control) were preceded by lower levels of ACC activation in the previous (correct) response. If conflict-related ACC activation increases in hypnosis, then cognitive control is being less appropriately matched with task demands. Because the PFC representations implementing the primary level of attentional control remain active (indeed unchanged), it follows that on the basis of this model, it must be the second level of cognitive control, rather than the first, that is impaired. Therefore, it may be the functional integration of ACC and PFC components that is being disrupted in hypnosis.

This interpretation garnered further support in the EEG results obtained by Egner *et al.* (2005). These authors also found an interaction in the coherence of the gamma (30–50 Hz) frequency band between left frontal and frontal midline recording sites. These sites largely reflect electrophysiological activity in left lateral PFC and ACC regions, respectively. This result was observed in the same participants performing the same task and conditions when outside the scanner environment. Coherence is a measure of linear statistical dependence in the amplitude and timing of cortical oscillations at different recording sites in the same time slice (Nunez *et al.* 1997). It can be considered to represent the functional connectivity (i.e. shared or mutual information) between oscillatory activities in separate cortical regions, in response to functional changes in task demands (see, for example, Edelman and Tononi 2000; Friston 2002). Synchronization in fast frequency (gamma band) EEG activity has been associated both theoretically and in numerous empirical studies with the binding of activity in separate cortical locations into a single unified perceptual or cognitive representation (see De Pascalis, Chapter 5; see also Kaiser and Lutzenberger 2003; Tallon-Baudry 2004).

Gamma coherence between these regions decreased in hypnosis for highly susceptible individuals, whereas for individuals with low susceptibility it increased. This pattern is clearly consistent with a breakdown in highly susceptible individuals under hypnosis in the integration of processing in ACC and left PFC during ongoing cognitive control.

This modification of DCT maintains the key insights of Woody and Bowers' original version while specifying precisely those forms of control that are dissociated in hypnosis and those which are not. It also entails an extension of the understanding of forms of control available in hypnosis beyond the strict limitations of CS proposed in the initial formulation. As Brown and Oakley (2004) and Dienes and Perner (Chapter 16) point out, hypnotic suggestions do not appear to call only for routine or overlearned responses, implying at least some degree of SAS involvement. Consistent with recent advances in cognitive neuroscience, the revised DCT model incorporates the further distinction within the SAS between a first-order level of cognitive control and a second-order level of cognitive control based on higher order monitoring. It is the latter rather than the former level of control that appears to be dissociated in hypnosis. This dissociation alters the fundamental functioning of the SAS as a whole. PFC representations of task-related goals and rules are still able to regulate cognitive processes; however, both the flexibility and complexity of the cognitive processes able to be managed in this way remain much more limited than those normally available to the SAS.

7.8 Signalling the adjustment of cognitive control

The revisions of DCT proposed so far, in addition to offering specific details on many aspects of the neural implementation of functional aspects of the model, raise further specific questions that address not only unresolved aspects of the model but also fundamental issues in the cognitive neuroscience of cognitive control. In particular, how does ACC conflict monitoring signal appropriate adjustments in cognitive control, and how does this signalling process break down in hypnosis? Aston-Jones and Cohen (2005) proposed that ACC projections trigger phasic changes in the neuromodulatory noradrenergic activity of the locus coeruleus, which brings about an adjustment in activity of current prefrontal task representations. Nieuwenhuis et al. (2005) further proposed that this neuromodulatory response is the cause of the time-locked increase in frontal and posterior EEG activity in response to motivationally salient sensory stimuli observed in the P3 component of averaged waveforms. If these proposals are correct, one testable implication for the revised model of DCT advanced here would be a general weakening of the P3 responses (or similar novelty or error detection responses) in hypnotized highly susceptible individuals.

Though there is considerable evidence for attenuation of P3 responses in the context of specific hypnotic suggestions, e.g. analgesia (DePascalis et al. 1999) and obstructive hallucination (Spiegel et al. 1985), these are not necessarily equivalent to the broader effects of the hypnotized condition. Interestingly, in the study by Kaiser et al. (1997), although N_E was unaffected by hypnosis, the later error-related positivity (P_E) was diminished by hypnosis in the more highly susceptible participants. Even though much more work is needed to identify clearly the distinct functional role of the P_E, there is evidence for a distinct role for the P_E in affective evaluation, behavioural adaptation and error awareness processes (Falkenstein 2004). In a recent review of experimental literature contrasting the P_E with the N_E, Overbeek et al. (2005) concluded that different responses to a range of experimental manipulations demonstrate that the P_E and N_E must correspond to distinct aspects of the error response process. They argued that in view of its latency, topography and context, the most promising interpretation of the P_E was that of a P3 to an emotionally salient error response (an interpretation not inconsistent with any of those listed by Falkenstein). A replication and further investigation of the findings of Kaiser et al., correcting the methodological limitations of that study, may open an important avenue for the investigation of the neural processes underlying the dissociation of conflict monitoring from adaptive change in cognitive control observed in hypnosis.

7.9 Differing roles of rostral versus dorsal ACC in hypnotic experience

Increases in the activation of various regions within the ACC have been a common denominator in almost all imaging studies of the effects of hypnosis or various specific hypnotic suggestions. One possible interpretation is that this simply reflects ACC response to increased response conflict as a general feature of the hypnotic condition. However, the ACC is a functionally heterogeneous region with roles extending well beyond conflict monitoring. Single-cell recording studies in monkeys have identified different cells within the ACC that fire differentially in response to distinct events, such as a reduction in anticipated rewards, the occurrence of response errors and the adjustment of behaviour following feedback (Ridderinkhof et al. 2004). Bush et al. (2000) conducted a meta-analysis of human imaging studies of cognitive and emotional tasks which supported a division between sensitivity to affective versus cognitive task demands along the rostral to caudal axis of the ACC. Ridderinkhof et al. (2004) also conducted a meta-analysis of feedback, error and conflict-related fMRI studies, and concluded that despite considerable overlap, ACC foci activated by response conflict tend to cluster more dorsally than those activated by error or response feedback (i.e. response evaluation). Yeung (2004) has proposed that ACC conflict monitoring (as evident in the N_E) forms the basis of cognitive input into further ACC evaluative, affective processing, which then recruits adjustments in cognitive control.

PET studies of hypnotic hallucinations have identified changes in activation common to both hallucinated and real sensory stimuli (but not to imagined stimuli) in both more rostral (Szechtman et al. 1998; utilizing auditory experience) and caudal/dorsal (Derbyshire et al. 2004; utilizing pain experience) regions of the ACC. Rainville et al. (2002) carried out a PET study that contrasted activation before and after hypnotic induction. In addition to other regions, the results identified multiple regions of the ACC along the caudal–rostral axis from midcingulate ACC to rostral ACC, and, further along this axis, to perigenual ACC. Rainville et al. (2002) then carried out a regression analysis of changes in regional cerebral blood flow on self-ratings of mental relaxation and absorption taken after each scan. Relaxation during hypnosis was associated with activation in mid-ingulate and perigenual ACC, whereas ratings of absorption in hypnosis were associated with activations in rostral ACC (a relationship further accentuated by removal of relaxation-related variance from the absorption scores). In another PET study, Faymonville *et al.* (2000) found the analgesic effects of pleasant hypnotic suggestions were related to changes in activity in the midcingulate region of the ACC. Faymonville *et al.* (2003; see also Boly *et al.*, Chapter 2) then conducted a psychophysiological interaction analysis to determine which brain regions were modulated by midcingulate activity in their response to noxious stimuli during the pleasant hypnotic suggestions. Amongst the network of regions identified was the perigenual ACC. In summary, these studies highlight multiple regions of ACC involvement in hypnosis as part of wider cortical and subcortical networks regulating conscious experience.

In addition to regions of the ACC selectively sensitive to response conflict, other regions engaged by hypnotic suggestions include both more rostral and, arguably, higher order evaluative regions of the ACC. For example, ACC activations corresponding to experiences of pain and 'reality' in the studies above may also be considered to reflect evaluations of the corresponding sensory representations. In these experiments, different ACC regions appear to be playing distinct but connected roles in the generation of hypnotic experiences. We interpret these findings by first elaborating on the proposal by Yeung (2004) for unifying conflict monitoring and motivational accounts of the N_E. We suggest that the activity of specialized conflict-sensitive regions within dorsal and midcingulate ACC (which in the case of errors generates the N_E) is subsequently monitored and evaluated in relation to affectively and motivationally relevant performance outcomes in more rostral regions of the ACC. This process (which may include interactions with other cortical and subcortical regions) occurs later than the initial conflict-monitoring response and requires strong functional connectivity between dorsal and rostral regions of the ACC. It is the outcome of this evaluative monitoring process which then either directly or indirectly (through the modulation of phasic locus coeruleus activity) triggers adaptive changes in cognitive control. In the case of error responses, it is this system that triggers the conscious correction processes associated with the P_E.

7.10 Further development of DCT

In an important sense, the revised DCT turns out to be a theory about the control of control. We suggest that the crucial breakdown in the flexible (and, in particular, the conscious intentional) adjustment of cognitive control occurs as a result of the disruption, not of the unconscious detection of conflict, but rather of the further evaluative monitoring of that conflict detection. This evaluative process probably engages more rostral regions of the ACC and is subsequently responsible for signals triggering adaptive change. In the results obtained by Egner *et al.* (2005), conflict-related activations to colour naming incongruent stimuli were more extensive than to, for example, colour naming congruent stimuli. This greater activation occurred particularly in more rostral regions of the ACC. We suggest that this was due not only to ACC detection of greater levels of response conflict, but also to the engagement of processes that evaluate and signal the greater demands for cognitive control engendered by this conflict. Due to their specificity, these further proposals for the neural implementation of dissociated control are readily testable in a variety of available behavioural, EEG and imaging paradigms.

We conclude by summarizing the two related proposals we have advanced for the extension of DCT. The first is based upon the cognitive neuropsychological model of cognitive control developed and tested by Cohen and associates, and applied in studies such as Jamieson and Sheehan (2004) and Egner *et al.* (2005) to examine the effects of hypnosis and hypnotic susceptibility on the resolution of Stroop interference conflict. This proposal incorporates, as did Hilgard's earlier formulations of dissociation in hypnosis (e.g. Hilgard 1977), the critical distinction between monitoring and the implementation of control in the flexible regulation of cognitive systems. According to this, top-down biasing by prefrontal representations is able to play an important role in facilitating responses in hypnosis that would not be possible by CS alone. However, although information from conflict monitoring, mediated by regions within the ACC, continues to be processed during hypnosis, it is (to varying degrees) unavailable to guide the adjustment of active control of PFC representations.

The second proposed extension of DCT is more speculative. It seeks to specify more closely how the neural implementation of higher order control breaks down in hypnosis by drawing on recent attempts to integrate the affective and evaluative functions of the ACC with its conflict-monitoring functions. In so doing, it also seeks to explain the varied findings with respect to activation of differing regions within the ACC in a number of diverse imaging studies of hypnotic consciousness.

Both proposals are sufficiently clear to yield results that will show where and how they fail to fit the phenomena and in what way they will need to be modified and developed to achieve a more adequate theory. We hope they offer fruitful bases for the development of our understanding of the altered relationship between consciousness and control that DCT sees at the heart of hypnosis. In addition, this work should contribute to a wider understanding of the nature of consciousness and control, and the variety of possible relationships between them, which lie at the core of human experience.

References

Aikens D and Ray WJ (2001). Frontal lobe contributions to hypnotic susceptibility: a neuropsychological screening of executive functioning. *International Journal of Clinical and Experimental Hypnosis*, **49**, 320–9.

Aston-Jones G and Cohen JD (2005). Adaptive gain and the role of the locus coeruleus-norepinephrine system in optimal performance. *Journal of Comparative Neurology*, **493**, 99–110.

Blakemore S-J, Frith CD and Wolpert DW (1999). Spatiotemporal prediction modulates the perception of self-produced stimuli. *Journal of Cognitive Neuroscience*, **11**, 551–9.

Blakemore S-J, Oakley DA and Frith CD (2003). Delusions of alien control in the normal brain. *Neuropsychologia*, **41**, 1058–67.

Botvinick MM, Braver TS, Barch DM, Carter CS and Cohen JD (2001). Conflict monitoring and cognitive control. *Psychological Review*, **108**, 624–52.

Botvinick MM, Cohen JD and Carter CS (2004). Conflict monitoring and anterior cingulate cortex: an update. *Trends in Cognitive Science*, **8**, 539–46.

Bowers KS (1990). Unconscious influences and hypnosis. In: JL Singer, ed. *Repression and dissociation: implications for personality theory, psychopathology, and health*. pp. 143–78. Chicago, University of Chicago Press.

Bowers KS (1992). Imagination and dissociation in hypnotic responding. *International Journal of Clinical and Experimental Hypnosis*, **40**, 253–75.

Brown RJ and Oakley DA (2004). An integrative cognitive theory of hypnosis and high hypnotizability. In: M Heap, RJ Brown and DA Oakley, eds. *The highly hypnotizable person: theoretical, experimental and clinical issues*. pp. 152–86. Hove, UK, Bruner-Routledge.

Bush G, Luu P and Posner M (2000). Cognitive and emotional influences in the anterior cingulate cortex. *Trends in Cognitive Sciences*, **4**, 215–22.

Cohen JD, Aston-Jones G and Gilzenrat MS (2004). A systems level theory of attention and cognitive control. In: MI Posner, ed. *Cognitive neuroscience of attention*. pp. 71–90. New York, Guilford Press

De Pascalis V, Magurano M and Bellusci A (1999). Pain perception, somatosensory event-related potentials and skin conductance responses to painful stimuli in high, mid, and low hypnotizable subjects: effects of differential pain reduction strategies. *Pain*, **83**, 499–508.

Derbyshire SWG, Whalley MG, Stenger VA and Oakley DA (2004). Cerebral activation during hypnotically induced and imagined pain. *NeuroImage*, **23**, 392– 401.

Dixon M and Laurence J-R (1992). Two hundred years of hypnosis research: questions resolved? Questions unanswered! In: E Fromm and MR Nash, eds. *Contemporary hypnosis research*. pp. 34–66. New York, Guilford Press.

Edelman GM and Tononi G (2000). *Consciousness: how matter becomes imagination*. London, Allen Lane.

Egner T and Hirsch J (2005). Cognitive control mechanisms resolve conflict through cortical amplification of task-relevant information. *Nature Neuroscience*, **8**, 1784–90.

Egner T, Jamieson G and Gruzelier JH (2005). Hypnosis decouples conflict monitoring and cognitive control functions of the frontal lobe. *NeuroImage*, **27**, 969–78.

Falkenstein M (2004). ERP correlates of erroneous performance. In: M Ullsperger and M Falkenstein, eds. *Errors, conflicts, and the brain. Current opinions on performance monitoring*. pp. 5–14. Leipzig, Max Planck Institute for Cognitive Neuroscience.

Farvolden P and Woody EZ (2004). Hypnosis, memory and frontal executive functioning. *International Journal of Clinical and Experimental Hypnosis*, **52**, 3–26.

Faymonville ME, Laureys S, Degueldre C, DelFiore G, Luxen A, Franck G, *et al.* (2000). Neural mechanisms of antinociceptive effects of hypnosis. *Anesthesiology*, **92**, 1257–67.

Faymonville ME Roediger L, Del Fiore G, Delgueldre C, Phillips C, Lamy M, *et al.* (2003). Increased cerebral functional connectivity underlying the antinociceptive effects of hypnosis. *Cognitive Brain Research*, **17**, 255 – 62.

Friston K (2002). Beyond phrenology: what can neuroimaging tell us about distributed circuitry? *Annual Review of Neuroscience*, **25**, 221–50.

Gruzelier J (1998). A working model of the neurophysiology of hypnosis: a review of evidence. *Contemporary Hypnosis*, **15**, 5–23.

Gruzelier J and Warren K (1993). Neuropsychological evidence of reductions on left frontal tests with hypnosis. *Psychological Medicine*, **23**, 93–101.

Hilgard ER (1977). *Divided consciousness: multiple controls in human thought and action*. New York, Wiley.

Hilgard ER (1991). A neodissociation interpretation of hypnosis. In: SJ Lynn and JW Rhue, eds. *Theories of hypnosis: current models and perspectives*. pp. 83–104. New York, Guilford Press.

Hilgard ER (1992). Dissociation and theories of hypnosis. In: E Fromm and MR Nash, eds. *Contemporary hypnosis research*. pp. 69–101. New York, Guilford Press.

Holroyd CB, Nieuwenhuis S, Mars RB and Coles MGH (2004). Anterior cingulate cortex, selection for action, and error processing. In: MI Posner, ed. *Cognitive neuroscience of attention*. pp. 219–31. New York, Guilford Press.

Horton JE and Crawford, HJ (2004). Neurophysiological and genetic determinants of high hypnotizability. In: M Heap, RJ Brown and DA Oakley, eds. *The highly hypnotizable person: theoretical, experimental and clinical issues*. pp. 133–151. Hove, UK, Brunner-Routledge.

Janet (1901). *The mental state of hystericals*. New York, Putnam.

Janet (1965). *The major symptoms of hysteria*. New York, Hafner. (Original work published 1907.)

Jamieson GA and Sheehan, PW (2004). An empirical test of Woody and Bower's dissociated control theory of hypnosis. *International Journal of Clinical and Experimental Hypnosis*, **52**, 232–49.

Kaiser J and Lutzenberger W (2003). Induced gamma band activity and human brain function. *The Neuroscientist*, **9**, 475 – 84.

Kaiser J, Barker R, Haenschel C, Baldeweg T and Gruzelier JH (1997). Hypnosis and event related potential correlates of error processing in a stroop-type paradigm: a test of the frontal hypothesis. *International Journal of Psychophysiology*, **27**, 215–2.

Kallio S and Revonsuo A (2003). Hypnotic phenomena and altered states of consciousness: a multilevel framework of description and explanation. *Contemporary Hypnosis*, **20**, 111–64.

Kallio S, Revonsuo A, Hamalainen H, Markela J and Gruzelier J (2001). Anterior brain functions and hypnosis: a test of the frontal hypothesis. *International Journal of Clinical and Experimental Hypnosis* **49**, 95–108.

Kerns JG, Cohen JD, MacDonald AW, Cho RY, Stenger VA and Carter CS (2004). Anterior cingulate conflict monitoring and adjustments in control. *Science*, **303**, 1023–26.

Kihlstrom JF (1992). Hypnosis: a sesquicentennial essay. *International Journal of Clinical and Experimental Hypnosis*, **40**, 301–14.

Kirsch I and Lynn S J (1998). Dissociation theories of hypnosis. *Psychological Bulletin*, **123**, 100–15.

MacDonald AW, Cohen JD, Stenger VA and Carter CS (2000). Dissociating the role of dorso-lateral prefrontal cortex and anterior cingulate cortex in cognitive control. *Science*, **288**, 1835–8.

McConkey KM (1991). The construction and resolution of experience and behaviour in hypnosis. In: SJ Lynn and JW Rhue, eds. *Theories of hypnosis: current models and perspectives*. pp. 542–63. New York, Guilford Press.

McConkey KM and Barnier A (2004). High hypnotisability: unity and diversity in behaviour and experience. In: M Heap, RJ Brown and DA Oakley, eds. *The highly hypnotizable person: theoretical, experimental, and clinical issues*. pp. 61–84. Hove, UK, Bruner-Routledge.

Makeig S, Delorme A, Westerfield M, Jung TP, Townsend J, Courchesne E, *et al.* (2004). Electroencephalographic brain dynamics following manually responded visual targets. *Public Library of Science Biology*, **2**, 747–62.

Miall RC and Wolpert DM (1996). Forward models for physiological motor control. *Neural Networks*, **9**, 1265–79.

Miller EK and Cohen, JD (2001). An integrative theory of prefrontal cortex function. *Annual Review of Neuroscience*, **24**, 167–202.

Nieuwenhuis S, Aston-Jones G and Cohen JD (2005). Decision making, the P3, and the locus coeruleus–norepinephrine system. *Psychological Bulletin*, **131**, 510–32.

Nordby H, Hugdhal K, Jasiukaitis P and Spiegel D (1999). Effects of hypnotizability on performance of a Stroop task and event-related potentials. *Perceptual and Motor Skills*, **88**, 819–30.

Norman DA and Shallice T (1986). Attention to action: willed and automatic control of behaviour. In: RJ Davidson, GE Schwartz and D Shapiro, eds. *Consciousness and self-regulation*, Vol. 4. pp. 1–18. New York, Plenum Press.

Nunez PL, Srinivasan R, Westdrop AF, Wijesinghe RS, Tucker DM, Silberstein RB, *et al.* (1997). EEG coherency. I: Statistics, reference electrode, volume conduction, Laplacians, cortical imaging, and interpretation at multiple scales. *Electroencephalography and Clinical Neurophysiology*, **103**, 499–515.

Orne MT (1959). The nature of hypnosis: artifact and essence. *Journal of Abnormal Psychology*, **58**, 277–99.

Orne MT (1979). On the simulating subject as a quasi-control group in hypnosis research: what, why and how. In: E Fromm and RE Shor, eds. *Hypnosis: developments in research and new perspectives*, second edn. pp. 519–65. New York, Aldine.

Overbeek TJM, Nieuwenhuis S and Ridderinkhof KR (2005). Dissociable components of error processing: on the functional significance of the Pe vs. the ERN/Ne. *Journal of Psychophysiology*, **19**, 319–29.

Rainville P, Hofbauer RK, Bushnell MC, Duncan GH and Price DD (2002). Hypnosis modulates activity in brain structures involved in the regulation of consciousness. *Journal of Cognitive Neuroscience*, **14**, 887–901.

Ridderinkhof KR, Nieuwenhuis S and Bashore TR (2003). Errors are foreshadowed in brain potentials associated with action monitoring in cingulate cortex in humans. *Neuroscience Letters*, **348**, 1–4.

Ridderinkhof KR, Ullsperger M, Crone EA and Nieuwenhuis S (2004). The role of the medial frontal cortex in cognitive control. *Science*, **306**, 443–7.

Shallice T (1988). *From neuropsychology to mental structure*. Cambridge, Cambridge University Press.

Sheehan PW and McConkey KM (1982). *Hypnosis and experience: the exploration of phenomena and process*. Hillsdale, NJ, Erlbaum.

Sheehan PW. Donovan PB and MacLeod CM (1988). Strategy manipulation and the stroop effect in hypnosis. *Journal of Abnormal Psychology*, **97**, 455–60.

Shor RE (1959). Hypnosis and the concept of generalized reality orientation. *American Journal of Psychotherapy*, **13**, 582–602.

Shor RE (1979). The fundamental problem in hypnosis research as viewed from historical perspectives. In: E Fromm and RE Shor, eds. *Hypnosis: developments in research and new perspectives*, 2nd edn. pp. 15–41. New York, Aldine.

Spanos NP and Hewitt EC (1980). The hidden observer in hypnotic analgesia: discovery or experimental creation? *Journal of Personality and Social Psychology*, **39**, 1201–14.

Spiegel D, Cutcomb S, Ren C and Pribram K (1985). Hypnotic hallucination alters evoked potentials. *Journal of Abnormal Psychology*, **94**, 249–55.

Szechtman H, Woody E, Bowers KS and Nahmias C (1998). Where the imaginal appears real: a positron emission tomography study of auditory hallucinations. *Proceedings of the National Academy of Sciences of the USA*, **95**, 1956–60.

Tallon-Baudry C (2004). Attention and awareness in synchrony. *Trends in Cognitive Science*, **8**, 523–5.

Weiller C, Juptner M, Fellows S, Rijntjes M, Leonhardt G, Kiebel S, *et al.* (1996). Brain representation of active and passive movements. *NeuroImage*, **4**, 105–10.

Weitzenhoffer AM (1953). *Hypnotism: an objective study in suggestibility*. New York, Grune and Stratton.

Wolpert DM, Miall RC and Kawato M (1998). Internal models in the cerebellum. *Trends in Cognitive Science*, **2**, 338–47.

Woody E and Bowers K (1994). A frontal assault on dissociated control. In: SJ Lynn and JW Rhue, eds. *Dissociation: clinical and theoretical perspectives*. pp. 52–79. New York, Guilford Press.

Woody EZ and McConkey KM (2003). What we don't know about the brain and hypnosis, but need to: a view from the Buckhorn Inn. *International Journal of Clinical and Experimental Hypnosis*, **51**, 309–38.

Woody E and Sadler P (1998). On reintegrating dissociated theories: comment on Kirsch and Lynn. *Psychological Bulletin*, **123**, 192–7.

Yeung N (2004). Relating cognitive and affective theories of the error-related negativity. In: M Ullsperger and M Falkenstein, eds. *Errors, conflicts, and the brain. Current opinions on performance monitoring.* pp. 63–70. Leipzig, Max Planck Institute for Cognitive Neuroscience.

Yeung N, Botvinick MM and Cohen JD (2004). The neural basis of error detection: conflict monitoring and the error-related negativity. *Psychological Review,* 111, 931–59.

Part III

States of consciousness

Chapter 8

New paradigms of hypnosis research

Graham A Jamieson and Harutomo Hasegawa

8.1 Introduction

In hypnosis, verbal suggestions, in responsive individuals, can lead to remarkable alterations in subjective experiences. These include atypical changes in perception (positive and negative hallucinations), pain (analgesia), memory (amnesia) and the experience of volition. Some behaviours may appear to occur without volitional control (ideomotor suggestion) whilst others occur despite volitional control (challenge suggestion). The considerable effects of hypnotic suggestion on somatic physiology have been successfully applied to the treatment of a variety of medical disorders, i.e. the effects of hypnosis may be observed in phenomenological, behavioural and physiological data. Historically, research paradigms in hypnosis have emphasized methodologies largely restricted to one or another of these possible data sets.

Hypnotic suggestions do not ask subjects simply to imagine the suggested state of affairs. Rather, the hypnotized person is required to experience, *as if real*, circumstances which would permit responses consistent with the hypnotist's suggestions (White 1941; Sarbin and Coe 1972). However, if the hypnotized person were to operate only within this framework, they would lose contact with the changing demands of the hypnotist's communications, the actual social reality with which they are engaged. Such a response is neither imagination nor hallucination in the usual sense of these terms. Rather, it calls for a complex and fluidly shifting set of relationships between the subject and hypnotist, subject and reality; and subject and their own sense of self (McConkey and Barnier 2004). Hypnotized persons are required to cooperate but not to comply, in the literal sense with the hypnotist's suggestions. This instills a particular motivation to adopt a mental framework consistent with the suggestions of the hypnotist (Shor 1962). This important motivational component of hypnotic response has traditionally been termed rapport. A theory of hypnosis is therefore a theory of phenomena in which the interplay of social, affective and cognitive elements is inextricably bound. At the same time, it is a theory of phenomena with essential expressions in phenomenological, behavioural and physiological domains.

8.2 The need for convergent inquiry

These complex social, motivational and cognitive elements within the hypnotic context have been the subject of careful behavioural and phenomenological investigation by the last wave of hypnosis researchers. Sheehan and Perry (1976) carefully document and contrast many of the specialized methodologies that emerged in that generation of hypnosis research. They observe the close relationships between the methodologies adopted by different groups of researchers and the theoretical frameworks within which they operate. Each methodological paradigm makes possible a certain set of observations, but in doing so necessarily excludes the possibility of observations lying outside that framework. Thus the methodological paradigms developed by researchers from radically differing theoretical perspectives may serve to act as a hermetic seal preventing data from one such paradigm from challenging the internal logic linking observation and theories within alternative paradigms. Sheehan and Perry called for, and presented a detailed example of, systematic cross-paradigm enquiry to address this issue. Alas, that call fell on largely deaf ears. A generation later it is perhaps even more relevant to emerging cognitive affective and social neuroscience research programmes in hypnosis and consciousness. *Methodologies of hypnosis* (Sheehan and Perry 1976) remains essential reading if this generation of hypnosis researchers is to build upon the lessons of the past rather than repeat its mistakes.

8.3 Levels of explanation

A widely influential account of the relationship between various *types* of scientific explanation is that they mirror the division of the physical world into a nested series of organized systems. This view has its roots in nineteenth century studies of the physiology of homoeostasis and later in the development of cybernetics in the early twentieth century. In this framework, a system refers to a set of processes forming a functional unit, the properties of which depend on the relationships between its parts. Nature may be illustrated as a hierarchy of systems, extending from subatomic particles to ecosystems and perhaps beyond (see Fig. 8.1). A structure on one level of organization in this scheme is a function of processes on a lower level, and a structure does not exist independently of the sum of its components and their interactions (Wimsatt 1976). For example, Wagstaff (2000, p. 155) uses the notion of levels of explanation to locate psychological explanations in the physical world without reducing them to physiological explanations, 'In psychology there are many complex explanatory models that are not based on physiology ... However, the argument that such models cannot ultimately explain anything because they do not refer to physiology is mistaken: instead, it is more accurate to say that the processes described by such theories represent a different level of explanation.'

In a recent attempt to apply this framework to the divisions within hypnosis research, Kallio and Revonsuo (2003, p. 137) first suggest that there is a 'correct level' for the explanation of any phenomena, 'Determining the correct level of description of any phenomenon is absolutely vital, for otherwise the details of the explanatory task will remain unclear ... It should be noted that the complete description and explanation usually crosses several levels of description. Still, a particular phenomenon resides at a particular level of description, and as long as it is unclear what the proper level of description is, the explanatory task cannot be completed'. Kallio and Revonsuo (2003) then develop the thesis that the state/non-state debate in hypnosis research may be interpreted as a

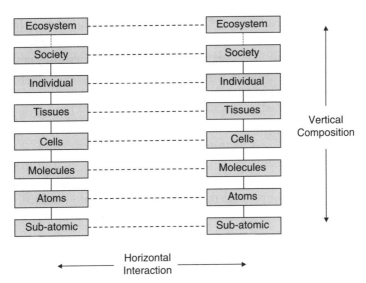

Fig. 8.1 Hierarchy of systems.

disagreement about the level of description on which hypnosis should be conceptualized. However, Wagstaff and Cole (2005) have argued that the differences between (for example) Hilgard's neodissociation (state) theory and Spanos' social–psychological (non-state) theory arise not primarily because they involve different levels of explanation, but because the postulated mechanisms are different. As they state (Wagstaff and Cole 2005, p. 15), 'Hilgard's (1977, 1986) theory assumes that there exist dissociated and fairly autonomous control subsystems, whereas Spanos (1991) argues that, at a cognitive level, there are no such autonomous systems, and Kirsch and Lynn (1997) argue that control in hypnosis should best be viewed in terms of the sort of cognitive supervisory attentional system postulated by Shallice and others'. Wagstaff himself believes that the pursuit of a unifying theory of hypnosis is misguided. As he states (Wagstaff 1991, p. 362), 'If we have not been able to find *the* explanation for hypnotic phenomena, it is not because we lack the technology; it is because there is no single explanation for all hypnotic phenomena'.

8.4 **Domains of explanation**

Psychological phenomena play an important role in many physiological explanations. For example, a physician might conclude in a case of aggravated rheumatoid arthritis that inflammation in the joints resulted from 'anger'. One approach is simply to regard these psychological explanations as metaphors for dynamic physiological states. However, the subjective experiences which lie at the core of these psychological phenomena possess properties (qualia) that, despite ingenious arguments to the contrary, remain resistant to interlevel reduction (Chalmers 1995, 2000). This has important implications for any scientific methodology seeking to understand psychological phenomena as part of a unified natural order. 'Biological naturalism', which acknowledges the fundamental, irreducible nature of subjective experiences as well as its neurobiological basis, should now be considered as an alternative to either functionalism or reductionist materialism by the cognitive neuroscience community (Searle, 1998, 2004). Consistent with this framework, we propose approaching psychological phenomena (and hence hypnosis) not as a level of explanation but as an expression of a unified underlying reality requiring distinct forms of description but spanning multiple levels of physical organization.

We introduced the concept of *domains of explanation* in order to construct integrated explanations of psychological processes (Hasegawa and Jamieson 2002). Whilst levels of organization refer to divisions within a specific explanatory domain (the physical), domains of explanation distinguish descriptions (comprising both theories and data) of irreducible but interdependent facets of a single underlying reality. We identify three domains of explanation: the physical, the experiential and the informational, where these divisions correspond to currently understood ontological boundaries (Fig. 8.2).

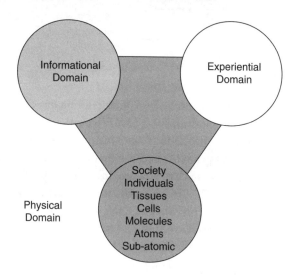

Fig. 8.2 Domains of explanation.

- The physical domain of explanation concerns the structures and processes traditionally described by the natural sciences, which may be considered on multiple levels of organization.

- The experiential domain of explanation concerns the qualities, content and meaning of subjective experiences.

- The informational domain of explanation concerns the content and transformation of *information* embodied in physical processes, which are inferred through their observable behaviour.

Psychological phenomena such as hypnosis may be investigated from within each of the three domains of explanation. Although the domains may be ontologically irreducible, they are interdependent. The relationships across domains for particular phenomena must be specified through actual research. Data from the three domains may be applied to constrain unified theoretical accounts of the reality underlying the phenomena. This approach builds upon the call by Sheehan and Perry (1976) for the development of strategic experimental

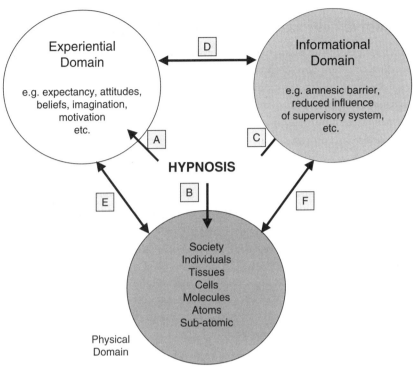

Fig. 8.3 Hypnosis research in perspective.

Table 8.1 Research agendas for hypnosis

Fig. 8.3	Research question
A	Which experiences are associated with hypnosis?
B	Which behaviours and neurophysiology are associated with hypnosis?
C	Which information processing functions are associated with hypnosis?
D	How does experience relate to information processing functions?
E	How does experience relate to observed behaviour and neurophysiology?
F	How does information processing relate to observed behaviour and neurophysiology?

programmes of convergent enquiry across divergent methodological paradigms. Unlike previous proposals, it mandates active cooperation in ongoing research (rather than peaceful co-existence) to achieve integration between existing research programmes.

Figure 8.3 is a diagrammatic representation of our view. It shows how the study of hypnosis can be approached from different perspectives, which may be related to each other. It directly suggests specific research agendas, as shown in Table 8.1. Until recently A, B and C largely described the approaches available for hypnosis research. However, the emergence of systems-level neuroscience now enables the development of D, E and F, which represent research programmes across the boundaries of previous scientific disciplines.

8.5 **Cognitive neuroscience and integrated explanation**

The practical possibility of such a programme of convergent inquiry has emerged as a consequence of recent developments in technology and signal processing that enable the study of patterns of dynamic physiological activity in the living human brain as it engages in specific behavioural tasks, mental activities and experiences. Electroencephalography (EEG) and magnetoencephalography (MEG) provide millisecond temporal resolution snapshots of patterns of electrocortical activity, while imaging modalities such as functional magnetic resonance imaging (fMRI) and positron emission tomography (PET) are capable of providing a high level of spatial resolution on other aspects of physiological brain activity. These data may be integrated with concurrent behavioural and phenomenological data obtained during experimentally manipulated cognitive, affective, social or other psychological states. An important additional element of this revolution in research technologies is that it enables us to study patterns of interconnected activity across many elements of a system, rather than isolated data from individual elements. Furthermore, the transformation of these patterns can be mapped as they evolve in time in specific functional contexts. The application of new mathematical tools from the field of signal processing to the analysis of complex patterns of linear and non-linear functional connectivity in such data sets (Stam 2005; Burgess, Chapter 11) is crucial to the development of a new generation of psychological explanation. It is now possible to develop *and test* hypothetical constructs with logical and empirical links across physiological, behavioural and phenomenological data sets.

Cognitive and social psychologists working within existing behavioural experimental paradigms provide important criticisms of earlier physiological theory and experimentation in hypnosis research. For example, there are many reports of isolated physiological measures, purported to be correlates of hypnosis or hypnotizability, which have been observed to vary in relation to either hypnotic susceptibility or a particular hypnotic manipulation. These results have frequently been interpreted in association with reports of relationships between the same measure and other psychological constructs. Whilst this is a legitimate heuristic for generating hypotheses for further investigation, it cannot provide a deductively valid inference to underlying theoretical models (Wagstaff 2000). The logic of such an inference is analogous to:

'Rover' has 4 legs

A chair has 4 legs

Therefore, 'Rover' is a chair.

For example, it is reported that hypnosis is associated with increased power in the theta band of EEG frequencies (see Ray, Chapter 12). These findings are of genuine interest. However, theta power has been observed to be associated with relaxation in some studies and cognitive effort in others, so relying on this common logic, theta in hypnosis may be (and has been) interpreted as a marker of focused concentration and mental relaxation. Further observational studies employing such loose inductive inference will be able to match almost any psychophysiological observation to fit their desired interpretation.

What is instead required is self-critical research based on explicit theoretical models specifying the precise role of physiological variables in implementing psychological processes.

8.6 **Hypnosis and altered states of consciousness**

The differences between the paradigm advocated here and existing alternatives is clearly illustrated in its strategic approach to the unresolved question dominating hypnosis research for the last 50 years, that is whether or not hypnosis constitutes an altered state of consciousness (ASC). The basis on which an ASC has been inferred in hypnosis is the occurrence of apparently striking changes in the subjective experience of hypnotized subjects. As Kihlstrom puts it:

> There *is* a state of altered consciousness in hypnosis: amnesic subjects cannot remember things they should be able to remember; analgesic subjects do not feel pain that they should feel; subjects asked to be 'blind' and 'deaf' do not see and hear things that they should be able to see and hear … These are alterations in conscious experience observed in hypnosis, and it does not matter if they can also occur in the absence of a hypnotic induction, and it does not matter if there are no physiological markers of hypnosis. These alterations in consciousness are what make hypnosis interesting, and they remain to be described and explained.
>
> (Kihlstrom 1997, p. 326)

There is broad agreement between both state and non-state theorists that marked qualitative changes do occur in the experience of hypnotized subjects. The key area of disagreement is on how these changes in experience are to be explained. State theorists believe such phenomena require the presence of an alteration in the structure, not merely the content, of consciousness. Non-state theorists, such as Barber (1969), object that in so doing state theorists are merely substituting one unknown for another. As an alternative, non-state theorists refer to a range of mundane cognitive and social psychological processes which may account for hypnotic responses. Kirsch, a non-state theorist, offers the following useful definition of the state/non-state debate:

> The questions dividing state from non-state theorists are: (1) is there a uniquely hypnotic background state (trance) produced by hypnotic inductions (2) if so, are the experiences produced by suggestion in any way dependent on this trance state.
>
> (Kirsch 2000, p. 277)

According to the logic of the non-state position, if an ASC is playing a causal role then a hypnotic induction ritual, which presumably induces the ASC, should play a critical role in enabling hypnotic responses (Sheehan and Perry 1976). In order to test this logic, non-state theorists have devised a number of suggestion scales that can be administered with or without a hypnotic induction. Work with these scales has demonstrated that responsiveness to suggestions in hypnosis is closely correlated with responsiveness to the same suggestions without a hypnotic induction (Barber 2000). Indeed, Braffman and Kirsch (1999) have even argued that hypnotic susceptibility should be redefined not as response to suggestion in hypnosis but as the increase in responsiveness to these suggestions that results from the administration of a hypnotic induction ritual. This non-state logic is hotly contested by state theorists who maintain that the hypnotic state may be (and often is) spontaneously elicited by highly susceptible subjects in their daily life outside of the hypnotic context (Barabasz 2005/2006).

The empirical question of the causal role of an ASC in the production of hypnotic phenomena raises a series of important conceptual questions. Is it possible to define an ASC in a meaningful way? How is it possible for an ASC to cause or explain anything? Finally, how can an ASC be represented in scientific measurements?

Tart (1983/2000) proposes the useful definition that a state of consciousness may be considered as a discrete pattern of interactions amongst, what he terms, psychological structures:

> The terms state of consciousness and altered state of consciousness have come to be used too loosely, to mean whatever is on one's mind at the moment. The new term discrete state of consciousness (d-SoC) is proposed for greater precision. A d-SoC is a unique, dynamic pattern or configuration of psychological structures, an active system of psychological subsystems. Although the component structures/subsystems show some variation within a d-SoC, the overall pattern, the overall system properties remain recognisably the same. If, as you sit reading, you think, 'I am dreaming' instead of 'I am awake,' you have changed a small cognitive element in your consciousness but not affected at all the basic pattern we call your waking state. In spite of subsystem variation and environmental variation, a d-SoC is stabilized by a number of processes so that it retains its identity and function …. A discrete *altered* state of consciousness (d-ASC) refers to a d-SoC that is different from some baseline state of consciousness (b-SoC). Usually the ordinary state is taken as the baseline state. A d-ASC is a new system with unique properties of its own, a restructuring of consciousness. Altered is intended as a purely descriptive term, carrying no values.

(Tart 1983/2000, p. 5)

This definition requires the use of appropriate phenomenological measures capable of reflecting just such changes in the organization of experience as a first step in identifying the presence of an ASC. Current methodologies which may contribute to this requirement include the Experiential Analysis Technique (Sheehan and McConkey 1982), the Experiential Method (Price and Barrell 1990) and the Phenomenology of Consciousness Inventory (Pekala and Kumar, Chapter 10). Whilst phenomenology can identify and describe many important features of an ASC such a description is not in itself an explanatory construct. Determining the nature of what Tart describes as 'psychological structures' will be crucial to any causal explanation. The psychological structures referred to above must be further specified as those which regulate the basic parameters of consciousness (Rainville and Price 2003). Only in this way can changes in the operation of these structures correspond to changes in the organizational framework of experience over and above the specific objects of consciousness (Shor 1959). These structures therefore overlap, but extend beyond, the domain of consciousness. From the perspective of biological naturalism we would expect to find:

1. their expression in the physiological dynamics of the systems involved and;

2. a recognizable isomorphism (not merely a correlation) between the phenomenological dynamics and physiological dynamics of such overlapping structures.

8.7 Altered states of consciousness and altered states of brain networks

Available methods for the analysis of brain imaging data readily permit the identification of networks of interaction and communication between multiple brain regions engaged in specific functional contexts (Boly *et al.*, Chapter 2). Distinct networks of brain regions have been reported in relation to aspects of the state of consciousness and in relation to aspects of the representational objects of consciousness (Rainville and Price 2003). The meta-analysis of functional brain imaging studies has identified an important network of functionally interacting brain regions characteristic of the waking baseline condition which frequently forms the control condition of such studies (Gusnard and Raichle 2001; Greicius *et al.* 2003). This waking baseline network has important implications for the concept of the waking state in hypnosis research. This pattern of activation and functional connectivity is typically suppressed when the subject begins to perform an active cognitive task, i.e. waking consciousness does not consist of a single discrete state but occurs in different modes each with its characteristic state of brain organization. The concept of discrete states of brain organization is emerging as a critical theoretical tool both for systems-level neuroscience and for the scientific study of consciousness.

Our framework predicts that a discrete ASC must also be expressed in a discrete altered state of brain networks (ASB). A discrete *altered* state of the conscious brain is present when the dominant network of functional connectivity between local brain regions and its oscillatory dynamics have changed from a defined baseline state. Whilst the former is best approached employing the spatial resolution of brain imaging technologies (such as fMRI), the latter is best approached through the temporal resolution of EEG/MEG. Both approaches must be combined for critical elements of this picture to emerge. While something like the concept of an ASB is necessary for the description of brain dynamics, the ASBs corresponding to ASCs are a subset of possible and actual ASBs. If identified and described, they will constitute a core component of what has been called the neural correlates of consciousness (NCC). As such, they make definite claims about what kind of thing can be a candidate NCC and focus our efforts on where and how to look for such candidates.

Consider, for example, when an alert wakeful baseline state of consciousness changes to an ASC in the transition from wakefulness to sleep. The alert wakeful state, in which conscious awareness is largely preoccupied with external reality, is replaced by an apparent loss of consciousness first in non-REM (rapid eye movement) sleep in which perception is dull or absent, then proceeding to REM sleep in which there can be vivid internally generated imagery. As Hobson (2005, p. 1254) states, '… sleep should be regarded as a reorganisation of neuronal activity rather than a cessation of activity'. The cellular and molecular mechanisms that underlie these transitions in states of consciousness have been demonstrated in animal models and have been shown to involve the complex interplay of thalamic and cortical neurons (Steriade *et al.* 1993; Hobson and Pace-Schott 2002; Massimini *et al.* 2005). Another example of an ASC is the absence seizure, in which there is an isolated loss of consciousness whilst the subject appears to be awake. The cellular and molecular derangements in this disorder have been found to resemble closely those that occur during the transition from waking to non-REM sleep (Kostopoulos 2000; Steriade 2005).

8.8 Testing for altered states of brain consciousness

The flow of consciousness from one experience to another (e.g. now I see a tree, next I hear a bird) does not in itself constitute a change in d-SoC. Neither does the constant flux of brain activity from one moment to another in itself qualify as the sort of ASB hypothesized as a conjoint condition of a phenomenological ASC. Rather an ASB corresponds to a discrete change in the dynamics which regulate the spatial and temporal flux of physiological brain states. In this way, an ASB is not immediately identifiable with the changes in individual physiological measures reported in many psychophysiological studies of hypnosis. It remains extremely important to study the relationship of individual psychophysiological measures to specific hypnotic phenomena. Such observations may provide clues to the influence of an ASB relevant to hypnosis; however, such an ASB must in principle be identifiable beyond the dynamics either of isolated physiological measures or of specific hypnotic phenomena (cf. Kirsch 2000). In order to confirm the presence of either a baseline or altered state of brain functioning, we require the application of tools specifically developed to describe and identify discrete patterns of higher order dynamics in the spatial and temporal transformations of more localized neurophysiological measures. Whilst they remain important traditional measures, such as averaged event-related potentials and spectral band power in EEG or simple subtraction contrasts to identify regions of activation in imaging studies, they are not *in themselves* adequate for this task. The development of appropriate tools is currently the subject of an intensive effort by some of the leading contributors to EEG/MEG and imaging research methods (see, for example, the work of, Dietrich Lehman, Karl Friston, Walter Freeman, Cornelius Stam, Michael Breakspear, Olaf Sporns and their associates). Whilst much work remains to be done a substantial tool kit is already available for researchers to apply to the question of the role of ASCs in hypnosis (see Burgess, Chapter 11).

Different experiences (with or without an ASC) entail different patterns of brain activity readily detectable in many measures. By itself, demonstrating that changes in a measure of brain activity occur in conjunction with the changes in experience which occur in hypnosis is insufficient to establish the role of an ASC in the production of hypnotic phenomena. In contrast to this approach, we predict that a major change in the organizational framework controlling conscious experience will be reflected in a major change in brain dynamics (the pattern of integration and interaction amongst specific ongoing brain processes). This is a testable proposition within the scope of contemporary cognitive neuroscience. However, it is necessary to employ methodologies which allow the identification and description of discrete states of brain dynamics. If there is no change in the organizational dynamics (as distinct from highly specific brain events) that map onto the changes in the organizational framework of conscious experience (as distinct from the specific elements within conscious experience) associated with highly susceptible individuals in hypnotic contexts, then there is no state of hypnosis.

This is now ultimately an empirical question. Empirical questions are, however, rarely if ever resolved by a single study. Rather, they require sustained programmes of mutually critical research amongst a community of scientists. Although a number of studies have taken important steps in this direction, we do not believe the issue to be resolved. For example, the serendipitous discovery of characteristic states of the brain within waking consciousness strongly suggests that the concept of a single waking state, so often assumed in the state–non-state debate, simply does not correspond to reality. Instead it raises the intriguing possibility that what has been called the state of hypnosis will correspond to a variant of one (or more) of the states otherwise found in waking awareness. Such an outcome would require deep revisions in current state and non-state positions alike. We are clearly at the beginning of a new phase of discovery and exploration, and we invite the reader to join us.

References

Barabasz AF (2005/2006). Whither spontaneous hypnosis: a critical issue for practitioners and researchers. *American Journal of Clinical Hypnosis*, **48**, 2–3.

Barber TX (1969). *Hypnosis: a scientific approach*. New York, Van Nostrand Reinhold.

Barber TX (2000). A deeper understanding of hypnosis: its secrets, its nature, its essence. *American Journal of Clinical Hypnosis*, **42**, 208–72.

Braffman W and Kirsch I (1999). Imaginative suggestibility and hypnotizability: an empirical analysis. *Journal of Personality and Social Psychology*, **77**, 578–87.

Chalmers DJ (1995). Facing up to the problem of consciousness. *Journal of Consciousness Studies*, **2**, 200–19.

Chalmers DJ (2000). What is a neural correlate of consciousness? In: T Metzinger, ed. *Neural correlates of consciousness, empirical and conceptual question*. pp. 17–39. Cambridge, MA, MIT Press.

Greicius MD, Krasnow B, Reiss AL and Menon V (2003). Functional connectivity in the resting brain: a network analysis of the default mode hypothesis. *Proceedings of the National Academy of Sciences of the USA*, **100**, 253–58.

Gusnard DA and Raichle ME. (2001). Searching for a baseline: functional imaging and the resting human brain. *Nature Reviews Neuroscience*, **2**, 685–94.

Hasegawa H and Jamieson GA (2002). Conceptual issues in hypnosis research: explanations, definitions and the state/non-state debate. *Contemporary Hypnosis*, **19**, 103–17.

Hilgard ER (1977). *Divided consciousness: multiple controls in human thought and action*. New York, Wiley Interscience.

Hilgard ER (1986). Neodissociation theory of multiple cognitive control systems. In: Shapiro GE and Schwartz D, eds. *Consciousness and self-regulation*. pp. 137–71. New York, Plenum Press.

Hobson JA (2005). Sleep is of the brain, by the brain and for the brain. *Nature*, **437**, 1254–56.

Hobson JA and Pace-Schott EF (2002). The cognitive neuroscience of sleep: neuronal systems, consciousness and learning. *Nature Reviews Neuroscience*, **3**, 679–93.

Kallio S and Revonsuo A (2003). Hypnotic phenomena and altered states of consciousness: a multilevel framework of description and explanation. *Contemporary Hypnosis*, **20**, 111–64.

Kihlstrom JF (1997). Convergence in understanding hypnosis? Perhaps, but perhaps not quite so fast. *International Journal of Clinical and Experimental Hypnosis*, **35**, 324–32.

Kirsch I (2000). The response set theory of hypnosis. *American Journal of Clinical Hypnosis*, **42**, 274–88.

Kirsch I and Lynn SJ (1997). Hypnotic involuntariness and the automaticity of everyday life. *American Journal of Clinical Hypnosis*, **40**, 329–48.

Kostopoulos GK (2000). Spike-and-wave discharges of absence seizures as a transformation of sleep spindles: the continuing development of a hypothesis. *Clinical Neurophysiology*, 111 (S2), S27–38.

Massimini M, Ferrarelli F, Huber R, Esser SK, Singh H and Tononi G (2005). Breakdown of cortical effective connectivity during sleep. *Science*, 309, 2228–32.

McConkey KM and Barnier AJ (2004). High hypnotizability: unity and diversity in behaviour and experience. In: M Heap RJ Brown and DA Oakley, eds. *The highly hypnotizable person: theoretical, experimental and clinical issues.* pp. 61–84. Hove, UK, Brunner-Routledge.

Price DD and Barrell JJ (1990). The structure of the hypnotic state: a self directed experiential study. In: JJ Barrell, ed. *The experiential method: exploring the human experience.* pp. 85–97. Acton, MA, Copely Publishing Group.

Rainville P and Price DD (2003). Hypnosis phenomenology and the neurobiology of consciousness. *International Journal of Clinical and Experimental Hypnosis*, 51, 105–29.

Sarbin TR and Coe WC (1972). *Hypnosis: a social psychological analysis of influence communication.* New York, Holt Rinehart and Winston.

Searle J. (1998). How to study consciousness scientifically. *Philosophical Transactions of the Royal Society B: Biological Science* 353, 1935–42.

Searle J. (2004). *Mind.* New York, Harvard University Press.

Sheehan PW and McConkey KM (1982). *Hypnosis and experience: the exploration of phenomena and process.* Hillsdale, NJ, Laurence Earlbaum Associates.

Sheehan PW and Perry CW (1976). *Methodologies of hypnosis: a critical appraisal of contemporary paradigms of hypnosis.* Hillsdale NJ, Laurence Earlbaum Associates.

Shor RE (1959). Hypnosis and the concept of generalized reality orientation. *American Journal of Psychotherapy*, 13, 582–602.

Shor RE (1962). Three dimensions of hypnotic depth. *International Journal of Clinical and Experimental Hypnosis*, 10, 23–8.

Spanos NP (1991). A sociocognitive approach to hypnosis. In: SJ Lynn and JW Rhue, eds. *Theories of hypnosis: current models and perspectives.* pp. 324–61. New York, Guilford Press.

Stam CJ (2005). Nonlinear dynamical analysis of EEG and MEG: review of an emerging field. *Clinical Neurophysiology*, 116, 2266–301.

Steriade M (2005). Sleep, epilepsy and thalamic reticular inhibitory neurons. *Trends in Neuroscience*, 28, 317–24.

Steirade M, McCormick DA and Sejonowski TJ (1993). Thalamocortical oscillations in the sleeping and aroused brain. *Science*, 262, 679–85.

Tart C. (1983/2000). *States of consciousness.* iUniverse.com: Lincoln. (Originally published by Dutton.)

Wagstaff G (1991). Compliance belief and semantics in hypnosis: a nonstate sociocognitive perspective. In: Lynn SJ, Rhue JW, eds. *Theories of hypnosis: current models and perspectives.* pp. 362–96. New York, Guilford Press.

Wagstaff GF (2000). On the physiological redefinition of hypnosis: a reply to Gruzelier. *Contemporary Hypnosis*, 17, 154–62.

Wagstaff G and Cole J (2005). Levels of explanation and the concept of a hypnotic state. *Contemporary Hypnosis*, 22, 14–7.

White RW (1941). A preface to a theory of hypnotism. *Journal of Abnormal and Social Psychology*, 36, 477–506.

Wimsatt WC (1976). Reductionism, levels of organization, and the mind–body problem. In: GG Globus, G Maxwell, I Savodnik, eds. *Consciousness and the brain.* pp. 205–67. New York, Plenum.

Chapter 9

Hypnosis and neuroscience: implications for the altered state debate

Steven Jay Lynn, Irving Kirsch, Josh Knox, Oliver Fassler, and Scott O Lilienfeld

For more than 200 years, the phenomena of hypnosis have intrigued the scientific community and the general public. During hypnosis, many people appear to lose control over normally voluntary behaviour; some exhibit temporary, selective amnesia; they report seeing and hearing things that are not present and not seeing or hearing things that are present. Additionally, suggested responses often have an involuntary or automatic quality. Behaviour and reported experiences of this sort seem so extraordinary that it is not surprising that both laypersons and workers in the field of hypnosis have assumed they were due to an altered state of consciousness or 'trance' (e.g. Hilgard 1965; Spiegel and Spiegel 1978; Erickson 1980; Edmonston 1981; Spiegel 1998). According to Kallio and Revonsuo (2003), the central question regarding hypnosis as an altered state of consciousness (ASC) is whether a special hypnotic state gives rise to altered experiences produced by suggestion. Many altered state proponents also believe that enhanced suggestibility is one of the features of trance.

In contrast to these views, non-state theorists (e.g. Barber 1969; Spanos 1986; Kirsch 1991; Lynn and Rhue 1991; Sarbin 1991; Wagstaff 1991) hold that the feeling of an altered state is merely one of the many subjective effects of suggestion, and that it is not required for the experience of any other suggested effects (Kirsch and Lynn 1995). According to non-state theorists, variables including motivation, expectancies, responsiveness to imaginative suggestions, demand characteristics, rapport and how participants interpret suggestions account for differences in suggestibility and shape hypnotic experiences.

Theories that are difficult to classify as either state or non-state generally posit what has been referred to as a weak interpretation of the altered state hypothesis (Kihlstrom 1985). From this perspective, altered state is merely a descriptive term denoting changes in consciousness, rather than a causal factor in the production of hypnotic experiences. These theories (McConkey 1991; Sheehan 1991; Brown and Oakley 2004) acknowledge the importance of the social cues, participants' motivated commitment to experience hypnosis, and cognitive skills and strategies.

During the 1960s and 1970s, the altered state issue was acknowledged to be the most contentious issue in the field (Sheehan and Perry 1976). Despite various pronouncements of convergence in the altered state debate (Spanos and Barber 1974; Kirsch and Lynn 1995), the controversy has continued. Some proponents of the altered state view have claimed to find more or less definitive evidence for the neurological underpinnings of the hypothesized 'trance' or altered state. De Benedittis and Sironi (1988) stated, 'the trance state is associated with the hippocampal activity, concomitant with a partial amydaloid (sic) complex functional inhibition' (p. 104). Gruzelier's (1996) review of the psychophysiological concomitants of hypnosis concluded, 'We can now acknowledge that hypnosis is indeed a "state" and redirect energies earlier spent on the "state–non state debate".' Maquet and his colleagues (Maquet *et al.* 1999) claimed to have determined the 'functional neuroanatomy of hypnotic state' (p. 327). Woody and Szechtman (2003) observed that brain imaging work has breathed new life into the state issue by providing a detailed 'psychophysiological window' (Rainville *et al.* 1999, 2002). Killeen and Nash (2003) stated, 'It has become clear … that the operation of the brain is different in important ways for subjects in the hypnotic state engaged in hypnotic responses versus those engaged in the same responses absent the hypnotic protocol' (pp. 220–221).

The debate has sometimes been obscured by mischaracterizations of non-state theorists' positions. Gruzelier (2000) proposed that an integration of neurobiological and socio-cognitive perspectives could promote the understanding of hypnosis and its humanistic applications. He further stated, '… hypnosis is an altered state of brain functional organization …' (p. 51). Under a heading 'The death knell of neurobiological investigation: the rush to judgment', Gruzelier (2000) states, 'Kirsch and Lynn (1998) and Wagstaff (1998) claim that no marker of a hypnotic state has been discovered after decades of investigation, and that the search for one should be discontinued. A neurobiological explanation does not exist. Neurobiologists may rightly wonder how such an unworldly view exists' (p. 52). However, contrary to Gruzelier's accusation of a 'rush to judgment', we never implied any such thing. In fact, in the article Gruzelier cited, we made no mention of the role of neurobiological investigations in the domain of hypnosis research.

Here is what we actually said about the issue at hand. In our 1995 review (Kirsch and Lynn 1995), we did state that after the failure to find reliable markers of trance after 50 years of careful research, 'most researchers have concluded that this hypothesis has outlived its usefulness' (p. 853). However, we went on to say that this state of affairs did not preclude the possibility that such indicators would eventually be discovered, and we underscored the importance of identifying the physiological substrates of hypnosis. Far from declaring the issue dead, we identified three ways in which scientists could usefully approach the question of identifying the physiological substrates of hypnosis: (1) identify the physiological substrate of the hypothesized hypnotic state; (2) identify the physiological correlates of differences in hypnotic suggestibility; and (3) determine the physiological substrates of responses to suggestions.

More recently, we (Lynn and Kirsch 2006) observed that the search for a discrete state of hypnosis '… is arguably one of the most fascinating and important endeavors in the field of hypnosis, which will no doubt be abetted by increasingly sophisticated brain imaging methodologies (Ray and Oathies 2003). Research on the neurophysiological concomitants of both hypnotic and nonhypnotic experiences promises to illuminate many important aspects of human consciousness (see Hasegawa and Jamieson 2002)' (p. 200).

The present chapter is written in the spirit of fostering a congenial dialogue between state and non-state theorists (Kihlstrom 2003). We will review studies relevant to each of the three ways we proposed to address the question of the physiological substrates of hypnosis, including studies that Christensen (2005, p. 286) identified as representing 'replicated research over the past 2 decades supporting state-based theories of hypnosis'.

9.1 The effects of suggestions

Non-state theorists contend that there is no need to infer the existence of a special hypnotic state or trance to account for responsiveness to suggestions. However, non-state theorists do not deny that hypnosis reflects genuine alterations in consciousness. Based on findings that changes in brain activation in a number of regions can be observed during hypnosis (Faymonville *et al.* 2000; Rainville *et al.* 2000), Peter Bloom (2004) declared 'We now have the proof: Words change physiology!' We agree with this assessment (e.g. see also Kirsch and Lynn 1995). However, the power of words, much less the power of imagination, is not under dispute. Finding physiological concomitants of a hypnotic induction and suggestions would be consistent with all theories, including non-state theories. All subjective experiences are assumed to have physiological substrates or correlates that are potentially localizable or detectable (Hyland 1985; Wagstaff 2000; Willlingham and Dunn 2003). According to non-state theorists, psychophysiological correlates of hypnosis are inevitable and expected by-products of 'the various activities engaged in by the subject as he or she responds to the demands of hypnotic suggestions by variously relaxing, sifting attention, concentrating, "drifting", imagining, "letting go", thinking, complying and so on, depending on the suggestion' (Wagstaff 2000, p. 156).

There is a surprising degree of consensus, among researchers identified with both a non-state and weak interpretation of the altered state position, that hypnosis is not a uniform state, but rather reflects what participants 'do' during hypnosis (see Kihlstrom 2003), which varies as a function of the suggestions they receive. As Kihlstrom (2003) observed, 'At one moment, the hypnotic subject is experiencing a direct motor suggestion; at another, a challenge suggestion; at another, suggestion for a positive or negative hallucination; at yet another, a suggestion for amnesia or posthypnotic response. Each of these hypnotic activities and experiences is likely to be mediated by a different brain module or system, and it is not clear that they will have anything in common' (p. 181). Kihlstrom (2003) further noted that Crawford and Gruzelier's proposal 'that hypnosis selectively activates a variety of cortical and subcortical structures and systems, depending on the task required of the subject (Crawford 2001; Gruzelier 1998) ... marks the abandonment of the search for unique correlates of hypnosis or hypnotizability, because it predicts quantitative, but not qualitative differences between hypnosis and control conditions' (p. 181).

In a similar vein, Horton and Crawford (2004) recently concluded that different patterns of electroencephalographic (EEG) activity depend upon the task being experienced because hypnosis is not a unitary state. They point to hypnosis studies showing that enhanced theta is observed 'when there is task performance or concentrative hypnosis' (e.g. Crawford 1990; Sabourin et al. 1990; Graffin et al. 1995), but not when the highly hypnotizable individuals are passively relaxed, somewhat sleepy and/or more diffuse in their attention (Graffin et al. 1995; Williams and Gruzelier 2001)' (p. 140). Jasiukaitis et al. (1997) also underlined the importance of the task in determining hemispheric activation during hypnosis. Woody and McConkey (2003) imply that different patterns of brain activation will correspond to different suggestions insofar as disparate abilities, presumably related to different cortical activation patterns, may be required to respond to suggestions, say for hand levitation versus hypnotic analgesia. They also proposed that people with different abilities may produce the same response in different ways, presumably via different cortical structures or mechanisms.

Research from a variety of quarters supports the suggestion-bound nature of psychophysiological activity. Barabasz et al. (1999) found that participants responded very differently depending on the suggestion they received for hypnotic blindness. In all cases, subjects reported that they could not perceive the target stimulus. When subjects received suggestions to produce blindness by creating a hypnotically obstructed hallucination, their P300 component of the event-related potential (ERP) in response to the visual stimulus was reduced, as expected. The authors suggested that this occurred because the suggestion conveyed the demand that perception of the stimulus would diminish. However, when subjects received suggestions that they would not see or hear anything at all, the amplitude of the P300 component increased, contrary to expectations. The authors attributed the unexpected finding as due to participants' surprise that they could still perceive the stimulus to some extent, despite suggestions to mask perception of the stimulus.

Wagstaff (1998) proffered a non-state, strategy-based account of the findings. More specifically, he contended that the results make sense if subjects strategically concentrate on the stimulus to 'obliterate it', but are unsuccessful in doing so. The fact that cognitive strategies did come into play is suggested by the following example cited by Barabasz et al. (1999): 'One [participant], showing only a moderate ERP amplitude attenuation in the obstructive condition, noted she pictured a cardboard box in front of the computer monitor, but "I pictured a rather small box that didn't block the entire screen!"' De Pascalis and Carboni (1997) asked subjects to imagine a glove that covered a wrist that was exposed to electric stimuli of mild intensity. The authors interpreted a reduction of P300 peak in the posterior region of the left hemisphere as 'the product of a competing effect between the hallucinated obstructive mental image and the processing of somatosensory stimulation' (Ray and De Pascalis 2003, pp. 151–152). These results are consistent with strategic attempts to reconcile suggestion and reality rather than an unvarying altered state that is produced by hypnosis across subjects.

The modulating effects of suggestions are likewise evident in other studies of hypnotic analgesia. DePascalis et al. (1999) determined that a focused analgesia suggestion (focus on hand and produce an obstructive hallucination of a glove covering it) produced more pronounced task-related changes in evoked potential responses (P300 and N2) than both suggestions for dissociated imagery (i.e. imagine oneself floating out of the body and 'up in the air') and deep relaxation. The study showed that the nature of the suggestion does affect brain activity; however, it is difficult to conclude much beyond this, insofar as the nature of the suggestion is conflated with task difficulty. That is, the dissociative imagery may have been more difficult to produce than the obstructive imagery, as implied by the authors, who argued that the latter condition might have required more processing capacity. Moreover, relaxation-based strategies may not promote distraction and may therefore be less effective in diminishing pain in general. However, what is clear is that if hypnosis produces an altered state that yields a consistent biological marker of trance, then this marker should be apparent regardless of how suggestions are worded or what strategies are used.

Two studies conducted by Rainville and his associates' underline this conclusion. In their first study (Rainville et al. 1997) using positron emission tomography (PET), they used hypnotic suggestions to alter the affective dimension of pain sensation. This resulted in changes in ratings of the *unpleasantness* of painful heat stimuli, and modulation in activity in the anterior cingulate cortex (ACC). However, the suggestions did not alter ratings of stimulus intensity, and did not affect somatosensory brain structures (S1 or S2). In their second study (Hofbauer et al. 2001), when participants received suggestions that modulated pain *sensation* (see also Rainville et al. 1999a), one of the somatosensory structures (S1) was activated, but no changes were observed in the ACC. In summary, consistent with a non-state view (and therefore also with a 'weak' state view), the physiological correlates of hypnotic responses depend heavily on the task, the participants' cognitive activities and the specific suggestions presented, rather than the production of a singular, fixed, or unique altered state following an induction (Wagstaff 1998; Ray and DePascalis 2003).

Participants' responses to suggestions for altered perceptions are correlated with physiological responses. For example, Spiegel's (2003) review indicates that hypnotic suggestions can modulate ERP amplitude changes in the sensory association cortex with respect to: (1) visual stimuli (Spiegel 1985; Spiegel and Barabasz 1988; Jasiukaitis et al. 1996; DePascalis and Carboni 1997); (2) olfactory stimuli (Barabasz and Lonsdale 1983); (3) somatosensory perceptual stimuli (Spiegel et al. 1989; De Pascalis et al. 1999, 2001); and (iv) suggestions for hypnotic numbness (Spiegel et al. 1989). Changes in the somatosensory cortex have also been observed, as a function of hypnotic analgesia suggestions for ischaemic pain (Crawford et al. 1993).

Hypnotic suggestions can produce impressive changes in brain activation that closely resemble those produced by actual perceptual experiences. Szechtman et al. (1998) demonstrated that highly suggestible subjects exhibited increased regional blood flow in the right ACC, as assessed by PET, in response to suggestions to hallucinate a person's voice during hypnosis (Szechtman et al. 1998; Woody and Szechtman 2000), in contrast to imagining and baseline. In the hallucinating group, a strong positive correlation was found between activation (as measured by regional blood flow by PET) in this region and the participants' ratings of their experience (match with external reality $r = 0.95$; clarity $r = 0.85$). Woody and Szechtman (2000) are clear that the intent of their study was to use hypnosis to study the nature of hallucinations, rather than to study the nature of hypnosis itself. Indeed, their study did not evaluate subjects who were not hypnotized but received the identical suggestion to hallucinate a person's voice.

Kosslyn et al. (2000) found that hypnotic suggestions produce changes in blood flow in the brain similar to those that occur in the actual perception of colour. During PET scanning, highly suggestible subjects who received suggestions to see a grey scale pattern in colour showed activation in their left and right hemispheres, regardless of whether they were shown the stimuli in colour or grey scale. In contrast, when the subjects received a suggestion to see the colour pattern as grey scale, the same brain regions exhibited decreased activation, regardless of whether the stimuli were in colour or grey scale. The authors reported that the results were obtained only during hypnosis in the left hemisphere. In contrast, in the right hemisphere, blood flow changes reflected instructions to perceive colour versus grey scale, regardless of whether subjects had been hypnotized.

Kosslyn et al. (2000) concluded that their findings 'support the claim that hypnosis is a psychological state with distinct neural correlates and is not just the result of adopting a role' (p. 1297). This conclusion is problematic. First, it betrays the common misconception that non-state theories reduce hypnotic response to conscious role-playing (or simulation) and are not genuinely experienced. Secondly, definitive conclusions regarding hypnosis are not warranted in that subjects in the hypnosis and mental imagery control received very different instructions with different task demands. Subjects in the hypnosis group were asked to alter their perception of the stimuli as much as possible and to let the investigators know when they had successfully added or drained the colour. However, in the no-hypnosis condition, when subjects were asked to perceive the grey scale stimulus in colour or vice versa, they were asked to try to 'remember and visualize' the stimulus in its other form. By telling hypnotized subjects that they will see something, and telling visualizing subjects to remember something, suggestion is confounded with induction. This precludes any conclusions about the altered state hypothesis. As Kosslyn (1999; see also Kosslyn 1994) aptly noted, 'it has long been known that changing one aspect of a task can lead subjects to adopt qualitatively different strategies' (p. 1286), in which case different structures and processes might be used, and hence different areas activated.

Lacking appropriate controls, it is tempting to interpret a hypnotically suggested effect as an indicator of a trance. Raz et al. (2002) reported that a hypnotic suggestion to see words as if they were in a foreign language reduced Stroop interference in highly suggestible subjects. Because Stroop inhibition is widely regarded as automatic, some readers might interpret this as a major shift in information processing and hence as an altered state (although Raz et al., to their credit, did not make this claim). Raz et al. (2006) have since replicated these results with unhypnotized as well as hypnotized subjects, although they used a post-hypnotic suggestion in their initial study. Their data confirm that suggestion can modulate the Stroop effect, but they also indicate that this does not require the induction of hypnosis. Altered Stroop inhibition may be an altered state, but it is not necessarily a hypnotic state and does not reveal the presence of a trance.

9.2 **Individual differences in hypnotic suggestibility**

Differences in suggestibility have been described for centuries, and must be explained by state and non-state theorists alike. State theorists generally account for these differences in terms of abilities or predispositions to enter an altered state of consciousness, whereas non-state theorists attribute such differences to socio-cognitive variables (e.g. beliefs, expectancies, cognitive strategies or imaginative abilities). Finding baseline individual differences in physiological response as a function of suggestibility has the potential of illuminating the trait-like character of hypnotic responsiveness. For example, Graffin *et al.* (1995) found indications of greater theta power in the frontal cortex during baseline in highly suggestible versus participants with a low level of suggestibility (see also Sabourin *et al.* 1990). Whereas EEG differences surfaced during baseline, no such differences were apparent during hypnosis: the theta power of participants with both high and low levels of suggestibility increased in the posterior areas of the cortex, whereas alpha increased over all areas measured.

The baseline findings are consistent with both state and non-state theories. According to a non-state, social psychological model, subjects who have a low suggestibility are not necessarily lacking in the ability to respond to suggestions, but are instead more resistant or anxiously focused on the task than highly suggestible participants before hypnosis. In short, participants with high and low suggestibility are different subject populations that in turn exhibit different sets toward the task. In addition, non-state theorists have posited individual differences in the capacity for role involvement (Sarbin 1950) including fantasy proneness (Lynn and Rhue 1988), which may underlie differences in hypnotic responsiveness. Kirsch (1991, p. 461) proposed 'a personal factor that is not entirely determined by expectancy' underlying individual differences in hypnotic suggestibility.

Studies have revealed differences in theta activity during hypnosis as a function of suggestibility across a wide range of sites (Graffin 1995; Ray *et al.* 1997; De Pascalis *et al.* 1998). These studies prompted Killeen and Nash (2003) to comment that theta activity '… seems to be one of the rare individual differences that correlates with hypnotizability' (p. 214). However, questions can be raised about the meaning of increased theta in highly suggestible subjects. As Graffin *et al.* stated, 'Because our overall understanding of EEG theta activity is limited, it is difficult to state clearly whether the increase in theta activity seen during the actual hypnotic induction was related to depth of hypnotic trance or the accompanying relaxation and absorption, or was more related to the process of cognitively focusing on the instructions verbally presented' (p. 128). Indeed, Williams and Gruzelier (2001) found effects only for a narrow sub-band within theta which they interpret as relaxation rather than concentration. Accordingly, it is problematic to use an index of brain activity to distinguish between state and non-state accounts of hypnosis.

A similar issue crops up in studies of hemispheric asymmetries. Horton and Crawford (2004) concluded that highly suggestible participants often display greater EEG hemispheric asymmetries and hemispheric specificity for tasks than subjects with low suggestibility (see also De Pascalis and Palumbo 1986). The authors interpreted these findings as evidence for differences in interhemispheric communication, cognitive flexibility or both. Although Horton and Crawford (2004) may be correct, a definitive interpretation is highly problematic insofar as frontal asymmetries are associated with a hodge-podge of variables (see Cacioppo 2004) including socio-economic status (Tomarken *et al.* 2004), basal cortisol levels (Kalin *et al.* 1998), immune function (e.g. Kang *et al.* 1991), self-report measures of affect and personality (e.g. Tomarken and Davidson 1994), shyness and social anxiety (Schmidt 1999), and memory for sad narratives (Nitschke *et al.* 2004). In any case, many of these variables are correlated with responses to suggestions. As Kirsch and Lynn (1995) noted, there ought to be correlations between brain activity and the performance of suggested activities, just as there should be brain activity correlates of the successful performance of any cognitive task. Accordingly, it is not altogether clear what hemispheric differences mean in terms of support for state versus non-state theories.

EEG asymmetry is not itself a mechanism, but rather a marker of underlying neural processes. The fact that responses to hypnotic suggestions are associated or correlated with EEG asymmetries or increased theta in highly suggestible individuals does not warrant the conclusion that hypnosis causes the EEG patterns. Other variables that potentially co-vary with hypnotic responses and differences in suggestibility (e.g. expectancies, motivation, fantasy proneness, etc.; see Braffman and Kirsch 1995) may be responsible for the differences in asymmetries observed. As Hasewgawa and Jamieson (2002) have pointed out: (1) the functional significance of differences in neurophysiology are not clearly established; (2) the measurements only provide a limited picture of the brain's functional organization; and (3) the extent to which local markers contribute to hypnotic experience is uncertain (p. 113).

The lack of consistency in findings is another problem in interpreting the physiological underpinnings of individual differences in suggestibility (Perlini and Spanos 1991; Crawford and Gruzelier 1992; Ray 1997; Gruzelier 1998; De Pascalis 1999; Rainville *et al.* 1999b; Williams and Gruzelier 2001). For instance, Crawford (1990) found that asymmetries of high theta were observed in highly suggestible subjects when attending to (left greater than right) and ignoring pain (right greater than left), whereas no such asymmetries or differences between conditions were observed in participants with low suggestibility. DePascalis and Perrone (1996), in contrast to Crawford (1990), used a between-group design (waking, hypnosis with no analgesia and hypnosis with analgesia) to examine hemispheric asymmetries. Although the researchers did not assess theta in the temporal region, where Crawford identified hemispheric shifts, DePascalis and Perrone (1996) observed no differences in theta across multiple brain sites (mid-frontal, central and posterior regions). Whereas Graffin *et al.* (1995) found no individual differences in theta activity during hypnosis, Sabourin *et al.* (1990) found increases in theta during hypnosis for highly suggestible subjects, but not for those with a low suggestibility. Additionally, Sabourin *et al.* (1990) observed that theta increased during hypnosis across both hemispheres of the frontal, central, and occipital regions, but Graffin *et al.* observed theta increases only in the posterior regions of the brain. Horton and Crawford (2004) contend that research that encompasses functional magnetic resonance imaging (fMRI) studies (e.g. Crawford *et al.* 1998, Crawford *et al.* 1998, 2000), PET studies (Rainville *et al.* 1997; Maquet *et al.* 1999; Wik *et al.* 1999; Faymonville *et al.* 2000), regional blood flow studies (Crawford *et al.* 1993) and electrophysiological research (e.g. Spiegel *et al.* 1989; De Pascalis and Perrone 1996; Crawford *et al.* 1998*a, b, d*) points to a singular conclusion regarding hypnotic analgesia: 'highly hypnotizable individuals have more physiological flexibility involving an active inhibitory process of supervisory executive control by the anterior frontal cortex ...' (pp. 137–138).

Horton and Crawford's (2004) conclusion might be correct. However, it bears no relevance for the state–non-state issue, as all mind–body monists agree that there should be neurophysiological correlates of hypnotic suggestibility and of responses to particular suggestions (Kirsch and Lynn 1995), including the suggestion to experience an altered state (i.e. a hypnotic induction; see Wagstaff 1998). However, a key impediment to evaluating mechanisms proposed to account for the effects of hypnosis or particular suggestions is that the findings from which they are derived are, virtually without exception, based on comparisons between exceptionally good and exceptionally poor hypnotic subjects. We suspect that the 'extreme group' strategy that is typically used in the literature may be as limited in the domain of hypnosis as attempts to understand gifted children by comparing them with profoundly retarded children, or by comparing schizophrenic patients with the best adjusted, most highly functioning individuals in the population. To understand the neurophysiology of hypnosis, it is important to assess subjects with a medium level of suggestibility, as well as those with high and low suggestibility.

Even though we (Kirsch and Lynn 1995) raised the issue regarding difficulties in interpreting comparisons between individuals who test at the extremes of suggestibility more than a decade ago, it has only recently been revived by psychophysiologically oriented researchers. More specifically, Horton and Crawford (2004) stated 'it is crucial that future research into the neurophysiological correlates of hypnotizability include the highly hypnotizable virtuosos as well as moderate and low hypnotizable individuals' (p. 142).

The inclusion of participants with a medium level of suggestibility is essential for at least three reasons tied to an 'extreme group' design. According to Preacher *et al.* (2005), extreme group designs have numerous disadvantages, including: (1) artificially increasing the variance, often resulting in spuriously inflated effect sizes; (2) assuming linearity when it may be absent (e.g. middle suggestible and highly suggestible subjects may show similar brain wave patterns); and (3) rendering interpretations of group differences ambiguous (e.g. are the obtained effects due to the high group being especially suggestible, the low group being especially non-suggestible or some mixture of both possibilities?). Accordingly, the failure to include participants with medium suggestibility could create the superficial appearance of a distinctly different hypnotic state when such a state is more apparent than 'real'.

Subjects of low and high suggestibility may differ in ways that extend well beyond their responsiveness to hypnotic suggestions. Willingham and Dunn (2003) cautioned about conflating the process of interest in psychophysiological studies with some other variable. For example, if subjects with low suggestibility feel frustrated when thinking of the suggested situation, the activation (or lack of it) observed may be due to frustration. Accordingly, the alterations in consciousness that people with low suggestibility experience during hypnosis may have nothing to do with the hypnotic induction, the specific suggestion (which they might not even attempt to experience) or with suggestibility *per se*, but may instead reflect performance-based concern, negative emotions (e.g. boredom) and lack of motivation. It follows that rather than reflecting a presence of an altered state or trance in the highly suggestible participants, any differences between persons with low and high hypnotizability may be attributable to the inability of those with low suggestibility to respond to basic task demands and attendant frustration. These different cognitive and emotional correlates of hypnosis among the different sets of subjects surely have at least some corresponding neuropsychological correlates. As Meehl (1978) noted, a good deal of research in psychology suffers from an unwarranted assumption of the 'ceteris parabis' (all things being equal) clause, i.e. the assumption that one variable being manipulated by the experimenter is the only variable that is changing. This problematic assumption may apply to this body of research as well.

Horton *et al.* (2004) recently discovered differences in brain structure between participants with high and low suggestibility, as revealed by structural MRI. More specifically, highly suggestible subjects, capable of eliminating pain perception in a cold-pressor task during hypnotic analgesia, had a significantly larger rostrum (a corpus callosum area) than participants with low suggestibility. Whereas these results could be taken to imply that highly suggestible subjects have unusually effective frontal attentional systems that account for their ability to experience hypnotic analgesia, it is difficult to interpret the findings in the absence of subjects with a medium level of suggestibilty. Specifically, it may be the case that the brains of those with *low* suggestibility rather than highly suggestible people are atypical.

9.3 **Hypnosis as a state**

The attempt to demonstrate that hypnosis is an ASC or possesses unique psychophysiological correlates has motivated multiple streams of investigation. In an article in which they reanalysed their earlier study (Rainville *et al.* 1997) of pain suggestions, Rainville and his colleagues (Rainville *et al.* 1999b) focused on differences between hypnotic and non-hypnotic conditions and asked the question, 'What cortical regions are activated during the hypnotic state?' (p. 111). The authors (Rainville *et al.* 1999b) reported that hypnosis was correlated with increases in regional cerebral blood flow (rCBF) in the occipital brain areas, as well as the caudal part of the right anterior cingulate sulcus and bilaterally in the inferior frontal gyri. In their most recent report, Rainville *et al.* (2002) did not administer pain stimuli. Rather, they tested participants before and after a hypnotic relaxation induction. The findings confirmed an association between the induction and activation of the ACC, the thalamus and the brainstem. The authors suggested that their findings support a state theory characterized by a decrease in cortical arousal combined with increased attention.

In a third pain study, Faymonville *et al.* (2001) did not use suggestions to modulate either pain unpleasantness or intensity, although they measured both in response to a hot stimulus. Hypnosis not only reduced both indices of pain, but also resulted in changes in rCBF in the thalamic nuclei, anterior cingulate and insular cortices after pain stimulation.

Relatedly, Maquet *et al.* (1999) claimed that the 'hypnotic state' is related to the activation of the ACC, along with widespread activation of cortical areas involving occipital, parietal, precentral, premotor and ventrolateral prefrontal cortices. On the basis of these findings, the authors concluded that hypnosis 'is a particular cerebral waking state where the subject, seemingly somnolent, experiences a vivid, multimodal, coherent, memory-based mental imagery that invades and fills the subject's consciousness' (p. 332).

These and other studies (e.g. Crawford *et al.* 1993; Kropotov *et al.* 1997; Szechtman *et al* 1998) suggested that Gruzelier (1998) was right to single out the ACC as 'a promising candidate for involvement in hypnosis' (p. 10). Nevertheless, while undeniably interesting, the findings regarding the ACC 'do not indicate a discrete state of hypnosis' (Hasegawa and Jamieson 2000, p. 113). For instance, the ACC has been implicated in a variety of different tasks and processes (see Oschner and Gross 2004) ranging from: (1) reappraising the relationship between internal states and external events (Bush *et al.* 2000); (2) monitoring the degree of response conflict (Barch *et al.* 2001; for a review, see Botvinick *et al.* 2001); (3) overriding prepotent response tendencies (Carter *et al.* 2000); (4) lactate-induced panic (Raichle 1990); to (5) viewing a loved partner relative to friends (Baretls and Zeki 2000). Moreover, our review indicates that the overall pattern of results varies across studies, probably as a function of subtle and not so subtle differences in the suggestions given, the task demands of the situation and cognitive strategies used to modulate hypnotic experience.

For instance, in the study of Maquet *et al.* (1999), subjects were not restricted in terms of the imagery they generated from their past. Although subjects predominantly reported visual impressions, somaesthetic and olfactory perceptions were also mentioned, along with action sequences during hypnosis. Not surprisingly, hypnosis activated vast motor and sensory cortical areas. The fact that subjects in alert conditions were explicitly told they would not be hypnotized could have degraded their use of imagery or compromised its vividness, and resulted in a distinctive brain activation pattern different from hypnosis.

Danzinger *et al.* (1998) found that highly suggestible subjects use very different pain strategies to ameliorate pain associated with electrical stimuli applied to the sural nerve during hypnotically suggested analgesia. Although all of the participants reported reduced pain during hypnotic analgesia, some exhibited a strong inhibition of the nociceptive flexion reflex, whereas others showed a facilitation of the reflex, indicating 'different strategies of modulation can be operative during hypnotic analgesia' (p. 85). The findings we have reviewed do not yield a definitive or coherent picture of an unvarying hypnotic state.

As noted above, it is not clear what activation of a particular brain structure such as the ACC reveals about cognitive processes during hypnosis or a putative hypnotic state. Clearly, brain areas such as the ACC can serve multiple functions, depending on the input or overall pattern of activation (Sarter *et al.* 1996; Uttal 2001; Willingham and Dunn 2003). Moreover, many psychological processes (e.g. memory; Cabeza and Nyberg 2000) are not narrowly or clearly localized, and do not map onto a single brain structure (Cacciopo *et al.* 2003), but rather are distributed among neuronal networks (Uttal 2001).

Indeed, as Cacciopo *et al.* (2003) pointed out, localization will probably be elusive until there are coherent links between psychological–behavioural constructs and neural operations (see also Adolphs 2003). With few exceptions, the studies we have reviewed have not made predictions regarding particular patterns of activation, leaving investigators reliant on *post hoc* or vague (e.g. an 'altered state' was achieved) interpretations that are not grounded in theory. As Bentall (2000) noted, without good psychology, neuroimaging research amounts to little more than a particularly 'dazzling reincarnation of phrenology' (p. 21); see also Uttal (2001).

Barabasz's (2000) study of evoked response potentials is instructive in this regard. Barabasz assessed evoked response potentials associated with listening to 25 tone pips presented over 1 s intervals following instructions to imagine foam earplugs dampening the sound. Although individuals with low suggestibility experienced no reduction in average evoked response potentials amplitude, four of the five highly suggestible subjects showed attenuation of average evoked response potentials in hypnosis of at least 50 per cent in contrast to suggestion only. However, as Baruss (2003) observed, '... it is not exactly clear what cognitive processes are subserved by the evoked response potential changes' in Barabasz's study (p. 119). Nevertheless, Barabasz (2000) singled out the highly suggestible subject who showed no evoked response potentials changes across hypnotic and non-hypnotic conditions. He reported that in a post-hypnotic inquiry, the participant reported that when he was spanked by his father as a child he mentally travelled to 'another place' to 'turn off the pain' and that he had engaged in this coping mechanism when he received suggestions to place the earplugs in his ears. Barabasz explained these findings as a 'classical example of spontaneous hypnosis with apparent dissociation' (p. 168). Nevertheless, the assertion that a person 'slips into hypnosis' whenever there are no differences between hypnotic and non-hypnotic conditions is unfalsifiable. An alternative and, in our view, more parsimonious explanation is that imagery-based attention control strategies can be effective in hypnotic as well as non-hypnotic conditions.

9.3.1 Gruzelier's neuropsychological theory

Several welcome neuropsychological theories of hypnosis have been advanced. Gruzelier's (1996, 1998, 2000) theory posits the following sequence of neurological events associated with the enactment of cultural roles associated with the induction of hypnosis and the shifting demands of the hypnotic situation: (1) engagement of left anterior selective attention processes (e.g. fixating on the hypnotist's voice, selective attention), followed by (2) selective frontal lobe and limbic inhibition (e.g. 'letting go,' relaxation and suspension of reality testing aspect of induction) and (3) finally, posterior involvement that is greater on the right side of the brain and is associated with instructions of relaxed, passive imagery.

Wagstaff (2000) acknowledged that Gruzelier marshalled a good deal of evidence to support the inhibition of frontal lobe functioning. However, he contended that the available evidence does not sustain the hypothesis that frontal inhibition characterizes responses to a 'full and varied series of hypnotic suggestions'. For instance, a number of studies provide evidence for increased frontal lobe activity (see Crawford 1996 for hypnotic analgesia; Jasiukaitis *et al.* 1996 for hypnotic hallucinations) suggestive of increased planning among highly suggestible individuals. Wagstaff pointed out that frontal suppression and laterality shifts can also be observed in non-hypnotic circumstances, such as when people follow instructions on a computer (Morris *et al.* 1993). These concerns aside, Gruzelier has at least attempted to tie different aspects of the hypnotic proceedings to changes in brain activity, and these changes, in turn, to cultural roles and expectations.

9.3.2 Kallio and Revonsuo's hypothesis

Kallio and Revonsuo (2003) proposed an 'altered state of consciousness hypothesis' that postulates that the great majority of subjects who receive a hypnosis induction are influenced by social and cognitive variables. However, according to this view, true hypnosis is a rare phenomenon experienced only by hypnotic virtuosos (i.e. very highly suggestible subjects) who are capable of experiencing hallucinations without voluntary effort.

In one of Kallio and Revonsuo's (2003) ideal designs, neutral hypnosis is induced, with no suggestions (not even relaxation suggestions) other than the suggestion to enter the state of hypnosis. Changes in neural activity are assessed and interpreted as indications of a hypnotic trance state. However, not all changes in consciousness qualify for the term 'altered state'. According to Tart (1983, p. 19), an altered state involves 'major alterations in both the content and pattern of functioning of consciousness'. The major pattern connoted by "state" should not be trivialized by using the word "state" to refer to any change in condition' such as states like focused attention, enhanced motivation and altered expectations. If this were all that the altered state hypothesis denoted, there would be no altered state debate.

The design also fails to address the critical issue of the causal role of the trance state in producing other suggested subjective experiences. Hypnotic inductions are suggestions to experience a trance state. For that reason, they should produce altered subjective states in many people, and these altered states should possess neural substrates (Kirsch and Lynn 1995). It is not clear that the experience and neural correlates of trance would be the same for all hypnotized subjects or even all virtuosos. Having different pre-conceptions about trance might lead to different subjective states and therefore to different neural substrates. In any case, the altered state hypothesis does not concern the existence of these altered states, but rather their hypothesized causal role in producing other hypnotic phenomena.

In Kallio and Revonsuo's (2003) second ideal design, hypnotized subjects are given posthypnotic suggestions to experience hallucinations in response to a specified cue. Their prediction is that 'whenever the subject reports that they [sic] are consciously experiencing the hallucination, an increased level of activation, similar to that typically found for this type of phenomenal content, should be found in the appropriate areas' [p. 147; but see Kirsch and Lynn (1995) for a similar hypothesis from a non-state perspective]. As we have noted, studies of this general type have been conducted (e.g. Kosslyn *et al.* 2000) and are valuable. They substantiate self-reports of the subjective effect of the suggestion but, because they do not assess the causal role of trance, they do not test the altered state hypothesis.

The claim that this experimental design constitutes an ideal test of the altered state hypothesis rests on the unwarranted assumption that hallucinations are not possible without an altered background state of consciousness. Therefore, the presence of a hypnotic trance can be inferred from the verified presence of suggested hallucinations. However, the hypothesis that hallucinations and other exceptional phenomena can be elicited without a hypnotic trance state is precisely what non-state theorists propose, and self-report data are consistent with that hypothesis (Hilgard and Tart 1966; Braffman and Kirsch 1999).

Although neither 'ideal' experiment alone tests the altered state hypothesis, studies in which they are combined might well do so. One would have to induce hypnosis in exceptionally suggestible subjects, find neural changes indicating 'major alterations in both the content and pattern of functioning of consciousness' (Tart 1983, p. 19), and then find subjective and neural changes specific to both a hypnotic induction and to subsequently administered suggestions. If the altered state hypothesis is correct, these latter neural changes should not be possible without the preceding major alterations in consciousness. Note that this allows assessment of the 'slipping into hypnosis' hypothesis. Subjects who spontaneously slip into hypnosis without trance induction should show the same neural alterations as those in whom trance has been formally induced without any other suggestions being administered.

9.4 Methodological limitations

Methodological limits in the designs of much psychophysiological research preclude definitive interpretation of the findings. For example, the vast majority of brain imaging studies do not include a non-hypnotic control group given the same suggestions but with no hypnotic induction procedure. This confounds the induction of a hypothesized trance state with the suggestion for a particular change in experience.

In the rare exception in which this confound is not an issue, it is not clear that the suggested effect was experienced subjectively in the control condition. Even if the exact same suggestion were given with and without the induction of trance, a failure to find a comparable physiological change would be equivocal, especially if the experimenters had failed to induce the requisite experiential changes in the participants who had not been hypnotized. To support the hypothesis that the experiential effects of suggestion given without the induction of hypnosis are associated with brain activity that is different from that produced after a hypnotic induction, one first has to insure that the suggested experiences have been successfully induced in both conditions. Indeed, a strong version of the state hypothesis holds that there should be unique physiological changes in the hypnosis group that are not apparent in the control group, despite similar subjective experiences. Accordingly, if hypnosis and (awake) task motivation instructions evoke similar subjective experiences, yet hypnosis has distinct neurological correlates, it would constitute reasonably strong evidence for the altered state position.

Barabasz's (2000) research used a group of role-playing subjects with low suggestibility (simulators) as a control group for demand characteristics (see also Gruzelier *et al.* 1988). However, there is no way that simulators can role-play a physiological response without attempting to experience the suggestion. Indeed, simulators are exhorted to 'not go into hypnosis,' which virtually insures they will not be able to experience what is suggested, thereby guaranteeing that differences will be observed across role-playing and suggestible individuals. Also, simulators are asked to pretend to experience the response, whereas hypnotized subjects are not. The act of pretending itself must have some neural correlates.

The 'holdback effect' is a common design pitfall that can inhibit responding among non-hypnotized subjects (Zamansky *et al.* 1964). This can occur when participants are aware that their hypnotic and non-hypnotic performance is being compared, and is an issue in most of the studies reviewed in which participants are tested sequentially in waking and hypnotic conditions. Non-hypnotized individuals who know they will be hypnotized in an upcoming trial may purposefully refrain from deploying their imaginative abilities, or be less motivated to experience suggestions in non-hypnotic conditions, to demonstrate role-appropriate gains when hypnotized (see Zamansky *et al.* 1964).

To take the holdback effect into account, at least some subjects should be screened without a hypnotic induction (see Braffman and Kirsch 1999, for an example) and without any mention of hypnosis. Those scoring high in suggestibility and reporting the presence of the hypnotic phenomenon that will be assessed (e.g. the suggested hallucination) can be given the hallucination suggestion again, still without mention or induction of hypnosis, and the neurophysiological correlates of their reports can be compared with those obtained following an induction (either subsequently in the same subjects or in a separate group of subjects).

9.5 Summary and conclusions

A state theory of hypnosis posits that: (1) brain differences between hypnotized and non-hypnotized subjects will be observed in line with altered experiences and behaviours; (2) such differences are frequently observed in functional brain imaging studies; and (3) therefore, research supports a state theory of hypnosis. Yet to observe (2) and therefore conclude that prediction (1) is correct is the logician's error of affirming the consequent. Clearly, non-state theories also predict brain changes. After all, where else would such changes occur?

From a non-state perspective, if large quantitative differences on psychophysiological variables were observed across hypnotic and non-hypnotic conditions, it would beg the question of what was responsible for such differences (e.g. attitudes, expectancies, imaginative strategies). Indeed, the failure of state theorists to forward *a priori* hypotheses that link subjective experiences and behaviours specific to hypnosis with psychophysiological changes in specific areas or networks of the brain leaves many of the studies open to any number of interpretations, entirely consistent with non-state views. Among other things, to make a compelling argument for a state theory of hypnosis, it will also be necessary to outline at least preliminary criteria that cognitive neuroscience researchers could use to discriminate between state and non-state views.

These concerns aside, research in this area has succeeded in finding baseline correlates of suggestibility, effects of induction procedures and effects of other specific suggestions. Perhaps the most important finding to date is the specificity of neurological effects in response to the specific wording of suggestions. The neural concomitants of suggested analgesia, for example, seem to depend on the specific suggestion that is used

(Rainville *et al.* 1998). This finding, however, also points to one of the weaknesses of some of the research. In particular, there has been a tendency to confound induction with suggestion variables, i.e. subjects either receive or do not receive a hypnotic induction and then are given a suggestion to experience a particular effect. However, the wording of the suggestion following a hypnotic induction differs from the wording of the suggestion given without the induction. This confound renders it impossible to ascertain what is responsible for obtained differences, and this problem is compounded by the finding that neural activity may be exquisitely sensitive to suggestion wording.

Much research remains to be done. The reasons for the inconsistencies across studies are not clear, and sustained research will be needed to uncover them. In addition, the altered state hypothesis, in its traditional strong form, has not yet been tested. Although there are studies of the effects of inductions *per se* (i.e. the neurophysiology of neutral hypnosis), there is not as yet any research showing that non-mundane differences in background state of consciousness are a prerequisite to the experience of particular suggestions.

The increasing sophistication of neurophysiological methods renders altered state theories open to empirical support. It even provides a method of testing the hypothesis that some people slip into hypnosis in the absence of a hypnotic induction. If so, then the neural changes produced by inductions should also be observable without an induction and would need to be observed in responsive subjects for the altered state hypothesis to be confirmed. Until and unless it is confirmed, however, it should be considered a speculative hypothesis rather than a conventionally accepted fact.

References

Adolphs R (2003). Is the human amygdala specialized for social cognition? *Annals of the New York Academy of Sciences* **985**, 326–40.

Barabasz AF (2000). EEG markers of alert hypnosis: the induction makes a difference. *Sleep and Hypnosis*, **24**, 164–69.

Barabasz A and Lonsdale C (1983). Effects of hypnosis on P300 olfactory-evoked potential amplitudes. *Journal of Abnormal Psychology*, **92**, 520–23.

Barabasz AF, Barabasz M, Jensen SM, Calvin S, Trevison M and Wagner D (1999). Cortical event-related potentials show the structure of hypnotic suggestions is crucial. *International Journal of Clinical and Experimental Hypnosis*, **47**, 5–22.

Barber TX (1969). *Hypnosis: a scientific approach*. New York, Van Nostrand Reinhold.

Bartels A and Zeki S (2000). The neural basis of romantic love. *Neuro-Report*, **11**, 3829–34.

Baruss I (2003). *Alterations of consciousness*. Washington, DC: American Psychological Association.

Bentall RP (2000). Hypnotic and psychotic hallucinations: rich data capable of multiple interpretations. *Contemporary Hypnosis*, **17**, 21–5.

Bloom P (2004). *Advances in neuroscience relevant to the clinical practice of hypnosis: a clinician's perspective*. Keynote address to the 16th International Congress of Hypnosis and Hynotherapy. Singapore.

Botvinick M, Braver TS, Barch DM, Carter CS and Cohen JD (2001). Conflict monitoring and cognitive control. *Psychological Review*, **108**, 624–52.

Braffman W and Kirsch I (1999). Imaginative suggestibility and hypnotizability: an empirical analysis. *Journal of Personality and Social Psychology*, **77**, 578–87.

Brown RJ and Oakley DA (2004). An integrative cognitive theory of hypnosis and high hypnotizability. In: Heap M, Brown RJ, and Oakley DA. (eds), *The highly hypnotizable person*. New York: Brunner-Routledge.

Bush G, Luu P and Posner M (2000). Cognitive and emotional influences in the anterior cingulate cortex. *Trends in Cognitive Sciences*, **4**, 215–22.

Cabeza R and Nyberg L (2000). Imaging cognition II: an empirical review of 275 PET and fMRI studies. *Journal of Cognitive Neuroscience*, **12**, 1–47.

Cacioppo JT (2004). Feelings and emotions: roles for electrophysiological markers. *Biological Psychiatry*, **67**, 235–43.

Cacioppo JT, Berntson GG, Lorig TS, Norris CJ, Rickett E and Nusbaum H (2003). Just because you're imaging the brain doesn't mean you can stop using your head: a primer and set of first principles. *Journal of Personality and Social Psychology*, **85**, 650–61.

Carter CS, MacDonald AM, Botvinick M, Ross LL, Stegner VA, Noll D, *et al.* (2000). Parsing executive processes: strategic vs. evaluative funcitons of the anterior cingulate cortex. *Proceedings of the National Academy of Sciences of the USA*, **97**, 1944–48.

Christiansen C (2005). Preferences for descriptors of hypnosis: a brief communication. *International Journal of Clinical and Experimental Hypnosis*, **53**, 281–9.

Crawford HJ (1990). Cognitive and psychophysiological correlates of hypnotic responsiveness and hypnosis. In: ML Fass and D Brown, eds. *Creative mastery in hypnosis and hypnoanalysis: a festschrift for Erika Fromm*. pp. 155–168. Hillsdale, NJ, Erlbaum.

Crawford HJ (2001). Neuropsychology of hypnosis: toward an understanding of how hypnotic interventions work. In: GD Burrows, RO Stanley and PB Bloom, eds. *International handbook of clinical hypnosis*. pp. 61–84. New York, Wiley.

Crawford HJ and Gruzelier JH (1992). A midstream view of the neuropsychology of hypnosis: recent research and future directions. In: E Fromm and M Nash, eds. *Contemporary perspectives in hypnosis research*. pp. 227–66. New York, Guilford Press.

Crawford HJ, Gur RC, Skolnick B, Gur RE and Benson DM (1993). Effects of hypnosis on regional cerebral blood flow during ischemic pain with and without suggested hypnotic analgesia. *International Journal of Psychophysiology*, **15**, 181–96.

Crawford HJ, Horton JE, McClain-Furmanski D and Vandemia J (1998a). Brain dynamic shifts during the elimination of perceived pain and distress: neuroimagining studies of hypnotic analgesia. On-line Proceedings of the 5th International World Congress on Biomedical Sciences '98 at McMaster University, Canada (http://www.mcmaster.ca/inabis98/simantov/dus0133/index.html).

Crawford HJ, Knebel T and Vandemia JMC (1998b). The nature of hypnotic analgesis: neurophysiological foundation and evidence. *Contemporary Hypnosis*, **15**, 22–33.

Crawford HJ, Harrington GS, Vendemia JMC, Plantec MB, Yung S, Shamro C, *et al.* (1998c). Hypnotic analgesia (disattending pain) impacts neuronal network activation: an fMRI study of noxious somatosensory TENS stimuli, *NeuroImage*, **7**, S436.

Crawford HJ, Knebel T, Kaplan L, Vendemia J, Xie M, Jameson S, *et al.* (1998d). Hypnotic analgesia: I. Somatosensory event-related potential changes to noxious stimuli and II. Transfer learning to reduce chronic low back pain. *International Journal of Clinical and Experimental Hypnosis*, **46**, 92–132.

Crawford HJ, Horton JE, Harrington GS, Hirsch Downs T, Fox K, Daugherty S, *et al.* (2000). Attention and disattention (hypnotic analagesia) to noxious somatosensory TENS stimuli: fMRI differences in low and highly hypnotizable individuals. *NeuroImage*, **11**, S44.

Danziger N, Fournier E, Bouhassira D, Michaud D, De Broucker T, Santarcangelo E, *et al.* (1998). Different strategies of modulation can be operative during hypnotic analgesia: a neurophysiological study. *Pain*, **75**, 85–92.

De Benedittis G and Sironi VA (1988). Arousal effects of electrical deep brain stimulation in hypnosis. *International Journal of Clinical and Experimental Hypnosis*, **36**, 96–106.

De Pascalis V (1999). Psychophysiological correlates of hypnosis and hypnotic susceptibility. *International Journal of Clinical and Experimental Hypnosis*, **47**, 117–43.

De Pascalis V and Carboni G (1997). P300 event-related-potential amplitudes and evoked cardiac responses during hypnotic alteration of somatosensory perception. *International Journal of Neuroscience*, **92**, 187–208.

De Pascalis V and Palumbo G (1986). EEG alpha asymmetry: task difficulty and hypnotizability. *Perceptual and Motor Skills*, **62**, 139–50.

De Pascalis V and Perrone M (1996). EEG asymmetry and heart rate during experience of hypnotic analgesia in high and low hypnotizables. *International Journal of Psychophysiology*, **21**, 163–75.

De Pascalis V, Ray WJ, Tranquillo I and D'Amico D (1998). EEG activity and heart rate during recall of emotional events in hypnosis. Relationships with hypnotizability and suggestibility. *International Journal of Psychophysiology*, **29**, 255–75.

De Pascalis V, Magurano MR and Bellusci A (1999). Pain perception, somatosensory event-related-potentials and skin conductance responses to painful stimuli in high, mid, and low hypnotizable subjects: effects of differential pain reduction strategies. *Pain*, **96**, 393–402.

De Pascalis, V, Magurano MR, Bellusci A and Chen AC (2001). Somatosensory event-related potential and autonomic activity to varying pain reduction cognitive strategies in hypnosis. *Clinical Neurophysiology*, **112**, 1475–85.

Edmonston WE (1981). *Hypnosis and relaxation: modern verification of an old equation*. New York, Wiley.

Erickson MH (1980). Hypnosis: a general review. In: EL Rossi, ed. *The collected papers of Milton H. Erickson on hypnosis*, Vol. 3. pp. 13–20. New York, Irvington. (Original work published in 1941.)

Faymonville ME, Laureys S, Degueldre C, DelFiore G, Luxen A, Franck G, *et al.* (2000). Neural mechanisms of antinociceptive effects of hypnosis. *Anesthesiology*, **92**, 1257–67.

Graffin NF, Ray WJ and Lundy R (1995). EEG concomitants of hypnosis and hypnotic susceptibility. *Journal of Abnormal Psychology*, **104**, 123–31.

Gruzelier JH (1996). The state of hypnosis: evidence and applications. *Quarterly Journal of Medicine*, **89**, 313–17.

Gruzelier JH (1998). A working model of the neuropsychology of hypnosis: a review of the evidence. *Contemporary Hypnosis*, **15**, 3–21.

Gruzelier JH (2000). Redefining hypnosis: theory, methods, and integration. *Contemporary Hypnosis*, **17**, 51–70.

Gruzelier JH, Allison J and Conway A (2000). A psychophysiological differentiation between hypnotic behaviour and simulation. *International Journal of Psychophysiology*, **6**, 331–8.

Hasegawa H and Jamieson GA (2002). Conceptual issues in hypnosis research: explanations, definitions, and the state/non-state debate. *Contemporary Hypnosis*, **19**, 103–17.

Hilgard ER (1965). *Hypnotic susceptibility*. New York, Harcourt, Brace, and World.

Hilgard ER and Tart CT (1966). Responsiveness to suggestions following waking and imagination instructions and following induction of hypnosis. *Journal of Abnormal Psychology*, **71**, 196–208.

Hofbauer RK, Rainville P, Duncan GH and Bushnell MC (2001). Cortical representation of the sensory dimension of pain. *Journal of Neurophysiology*, **86**, 402–11.

Horton JE and Crawford HJ (2004). Neurophysiological and genetic determinants of high hypnotizability. In: M Heap, RJ Brown and DA Oakley, eds. *The highly hypnotizable person: theoretical, experimental and clinical issues*. pp. 133–51. London, Routledge.

Horton JE, Crawford HJ, Harrington G and Downs JH III (2004). Increased anterior corpus callosum size associated positively with hypnotizability and the ability to control pain. *Brain*, **127**, 1741–47.

Hyland ME (1985). Do person variables exist in different ways? *American Psychologist*, **40**, 1003–10.

Jasiukaitis P, Nouriani B and Spiegel D (1996). Left hemisphere superiority for event-related potential effects of hypnotic obstruction *Neuropsychologia*, **34**, 661–9.

Jasiukaitis P, Nouriani B, Hugdahl K and Spiegel D (1997). Relateralizing hypnosis: or, have we been barking up the wrong hemisphere? *International Journal of Clinical and Experimental Hypnosis*, **45**, 158–77.

Kalin NH, Larson CL, Shelton SE and Davidson RJ (1998). Asymmetric frontal brain activity, cortisol, and behavior associated with fearful temperament in Rhesus monkeys. *Behavioral Neuroscience*, **112**, 286–92.

Kallio S and Revonsuo A (2003). Hypnotic phenomena and altered states of consciousness: a multi-level framework of description and explanation. *Contemporary Hypnosis*, **20**, 111–64.

Kang D, Davidson RJ, Coe CL, Wheeler RE, Tomarken AJ and Ershler WB (1991). Frontal brain asymmetry and immune function. *Behavioral Neuroscience*, **105**, 860–9.

Kihlstrom JF (1985). Hypnosis. *Annual Review of Psychology*, **36**, 385–418.

Kihlstrom JF (2003). The fox, the hedgehog, and hypnosis. *International Journal of Clinical and Experimental Hypnosis*, **51**, 166–89.

Killeen PR and Nash MR (2003). The four causes of hypnosis. *International Journal of Clinical and Experimental Hypnosis*, **51**, 195–231.

Kirsch I (1991). The social learning theory of hypnosis. In: SJ Lynn and JW Rhue, eds. *Theories of hypnosis: current models and perspectives.* pp. 439–466. New York, Guilford Press.

Kirsch I and Lynn SJ (1995). The altered state of hypnosis: changes in the theoretical landscape. *American Psychologist*, **50**, 846–58.

Kirsch I and Lynn SJ (1998). Dissociation theories of hypnosis. *Psychological Bulletin*, **123**, 100–15.

Kosslyn SM (1994). Image and brain: the resolution of the imagery debate. Cambridge, MA, MIT Press.

Kosslyn SM (1999). If neuroimaging is the answer, what is the question? *Philosophical Translations of the Royal Society B: Biological Sciences*, **29**, 1283–94.

Kosslyn SM, Thompson WL, Constantine-Ferrando MF, Alpert NM and Spiegel D (2000). Hypnotic visual illusion alters color processing in the brain. *American Journal of Psychiatry*, **157**, 1279–84.

Kropotkov JD, Crawford HJ, and Polyakov YI (1997). Somatosensory event-related potential changes to painful stimuli during hypnotic analgesia: anterior cingulate cortex and anterior temporal cortex intracranial recordings. *International Journal of Psychophysiology*, **27**, 1–8.

Lynn SJ and Kirsch I (2006). *Essentials of clinical hypnosis: an evidence-based approach.* Washington, DC, American Psychological Association.

Lynn SJ and Rhue JW (1991). An integrative model of hypnosis. In: SJ Lynn and JW Rhue, eds. *Theories of hypnosis: current models and perspectives.* pp. 397–438. New York, Guilford Press.

Maquet P. Faymonville ME, Degueldre C, Delfiore G, Franck G, Luxen A, *et al.* (1999). Functional neuroanatomy of hypnotic state. *Biological Psychiatry*, **45**, 327–33.

McConkey KM (1991). The construction and resolution of experience and behavior in hypnosis. In: SJ Lynn and JW Rhue, eds. *Theories of hypnosis: current models and perspectives.* pp. 542–63. New York, Guilford Press.

Meehl PE (1978). Theoretical risks and tabular asterisks: Sir Karl, Sir Ronald, and the slow progress of soft psychology. *Journal of Consulting and Clinical Psychology*, **46**, 806–34.

Morris RG, Ahmed S, Syed GMS, and Toone BK (1993). Neural correlates of planning: frontal lobe activation during the Tower of London test. *Neuropsychologia*, **31**, 1367–1378.

Nash MR (2005). The importance of being earnest when crafting definitions: science and scientism are not the same thing. *International Journal of Clinical and Experimental Hypnosis*, **53**, 265–80.

Nitschke JB, Heller W, Etienne MA and Miller GA (2004). Prefrontal cortex activity differentiates processes affecting memory in depression. *Biological Psychology*, **67**, 125–43.

Oschner KN and Gross JJ (2004). Thinking makes it so: a social cognitive neuroscience approach to emotion regulation. In: RF. Baumeister and KD Vohs, eds. *Handbook of self-regulation: research, theory, and applications.* pp. 229–58. New York, Gulford Press.

Perlini AH and Spanos NP (1991). EEG alpha methodologies and hypnotizability: a critical review. *Psychophysiology*, **28**, 511–30.

Preacher KJ, Rucker D, MacCallum RC and Nicewander WA (2005). Use of extreme groups approach: a critical reexamination and new recommendations. *Psychological Methods*, **10**, 178–92.

Raichle ME (1990). Exploring the mind with dynamic imaging. *Seminars in Neurosciences*, **12**, 307–15.

Rainville P, Duncan GH, Price DD, Carrier B and Bushnell MC (1997). Pain affect encoded in human anterior cingulated but not somatosensory cortex. *Science*, **277**, 968–71.

Rainville P, Carrier B, Hofbauer RK, Bushnell MC and Duncan GH (1999*a*). Dissociation of sensory and affective dimensions of pain using hypnotic modulation. *Pain*, **82**, 159–71.

Rainville P, Hofbauer RK, Paus T, Duncan GH, Bushnell MC and Price DD (1999*b*). Cerebral mechanisms of hypnotic induction and suggestion. *Journal of Cognitive Neuroscience*, **11**, 110–25.

Rainville P, Bushnell CM and Duncan GH (2000). PET studies of the subjective experience of pain. In: KL Casey and CM Bushnell, eds. *Progress in pain research and mangement*, Vol. 18. pp. 123–56. Seattle, WA, IASP Press.

Rainville P, Hofbauer RK, Bushnell MC, Duncan GH and Price DD (2002). Hypnosis modulates activity in bran structures involved in the regulation of consciousness. *Journal of Cognitive Neuroscience*, **14**, 887–901.

Ray WJ (1997). EEG concomitants of hypnotic susceptibility. *International Journal of Clinical and Experimental Hypnosis*, **45**, 301–13.

Ray WJ and De Pascalis V (2003). Temporal aspects of hypnotic processes. *International Journal of Clinical and Experimental Hypnosis*, **51**, 147–65.

Ray WJ and Oathies D (2003). Brain imaging techniques. *International Journal of Clinical and Experimental Hypnosis*, **51**, 97–104.

Raz A, Kirsch I, Pollard J, and Nitkin-Kaner Y (2006). Suggestion reduces the stroop effect. *Psychological Science*, **17**, 91–95.

Raz A, Shapiro T, Fan J and Posner MI (2002). Hypnotic suggestion and the modulation of Stroop interference. *Archives of General Psychiatry*, **59**, 1155–61.

Sabourin JM, Cutcomb SD, Crawford HJ and Pribram K (1990). EEG correlates of hypnotic susceptibility and hypnotic trance: spectral analysis and coherence. *International Journal of Psychophyisiology*, **10**, 125–42.

Sarbin TR (1991). Hypnosis: a fifty-year perspective. *Contemporary Hypnosis*, **8**, 1–16.

Sarbin TR (1950). Contributions to role-taking theory: I. Hypnotic behaviour. *Psychological Review*, **57**, 225–270.

Sarter M, Berntson GG and Cacioppo JT (1996). Brain imaging and cognitive neuroscience: toward strong inference in attributing function to structure. *American Psychology*, **51**, 13–21.

Schmidt LA (1999). Frontal brain electrical activity in shyness and sociability. *Psychological Science*, **10**, 316–20.

Sheehan PW (1991). Hypnosis, context, and commitment. In: SJ Lynn and JW Rhue, eds. *Theories of hypnosis: current models and perspectives*. pp. 520–41. New York, Guilford Press.

Sheehan PW and Perry CW (1976). *Methodologies of hypnosis: a critical appraisal of contemporary paradigms of hypnosis*. Hillsdale, NJ, Lawrence Erlbaum.

Spanos NP (1986). Hypnotic behavior: a social psychological interpretation of amnesia, analgesia, and 'trance logic'. *Behavioral and Brain Sciences*, **9**, 449–467.

Spanos NP, and Barber TX (1974). Toward a convergence in hypnosis research. *American Psychologist*, **29**, 500–511.

Spiegel D (1985). The use of hypnosis in controlling cancer pain. *CA Cancer Journal for Clinicians*, **35**, 221–31.

Spiegel D (1998). Using our heads: effects of mental state and social influences on hypnosis. *Contemporary Hypnosis*, **15**, 175–77.

Spiegel D (2003). Negative and positive visual hypnotic hallucinations: attending inside and out. *International Journal of Clinical and Experimental Hypnosis*, **51**, 130–46.

Spiegel D and Barabasz A (1988). Effects of hypnotic instructions on P300 evoked potential amplitudes: research and clinical implications. *American Journal of Clinical Hypnosis*, **31**, 11–7.

Spiegel H and Spiegel D (1978). *Trance and treatment: clinical uses of hypnosis*. New York, Basic Books.

Spiegel D, Cutcomb S, Ren C and Pribram K (1985). Hypnotic hallucination alters evoked potentials. *Journal of Abnormal Psychology*, **94**, 249–55.

Spiegel D, Bierre P and Rootenberg J (1989). Hypnotic alteration of somatosensory perception. *American Journal of Psychiatry*, **146**, 749–54.

Szechtman H, Woody E, Bowers KS and Nahmias C (1998). Where the imaginal appears real. A positron emission tomography study of auditory hallucinations. *Proceedings of the National Academy of Sciences of the USA*, **95**, 1956–60.

Tart CT (1983). Altered states of consciousness. In: R Harré and R Lamb, eds. *The encyclopedic dictionary of psychology*. pp. 19–20. Cambridge, MA, MIT Press.

Tomarken AJ and Davidson RJ (1994). Frontal brain activity in repressors and nonrepressors. *Journal of Abnormal Psychology*, **103**, 339–49.

Tomarken AJ, Dichter GS, Garber J and Simien C (2004). Resting frontal brain activity: linkages to maternal depression and socioeconomic status among adolescents. *Biological Psychology*, **67**, 77–102.

Uttal WR (2001). The new phrenology: the limits of localizing cognitive processes in the brain. *Life and mind: philosophical issues in biology and psychology*. Cambridge, MA, The MIT Press.

Wagstaff GF (1991). Compliance, belief, and semantics in hypnosis: a non-state sociocognitive perspective. In: SJ Lynn and JW.Rhue, eds. *Theories of hypnosis: current models and perspectives*. pp. 362–96. New York, Guilford Press.

Wagstaff GF (1998). The semantics and physiology of hypnosis as an altered state: towards a definition of hypnosis. *Contemporary Hypnosis*, **15**, 149–65.

Wagstaff GF (2000). On the physiological redefinition of hypnosis: a reply to Gruzelier. *Contemporary Hypnosis*, **17**, 154–62.

Wik G, Fischer H, Bragée B, Finer B and Fredrikson M (1999). Functional anatomy of hypnotic analgesia: A PET study of patients with fibromyalgia. *European Journal of Pain*, **3**, 7–12.

Williams JD and Gruzelier JH (2001). Differentiation of hypnosis and relaxation by analysis of narrow band theta and alpha frequencies. *International Journal of Clinical and Experimental Hypnosis*, **49**, 185–206.

Willingham DT and Dunn EW (2003). What neuroimaging and brain localization can do and should not do for social psychology. *Journal of Personality and Social Psychology*, **85**, 662–71.

Woody EZ and McConkey KM (2003). What we don't know about the brain and hypnosis, but need to: a view from the Buckhorn Inn. *International Journal of Clinical and Experimental Hypnosis*, **51**, 309–38.

Woody EZ and Szechtman H (2000). Hypnotic hallucinations: towards a biology of epistemology. *Contemporary Hypnosis*, **17**, 4–14.

Woody EZ and Szechtman H (2003). How can brain activity and hypnosis inform each other. *International Journal of Clinical and Experimental Hypnosis*, **51**, 232–55.

Zamansky H S, Scharf B and Brightbill R (1964). The effect of expectancy for hypnosis on prehypnotic performance. *Journal of Personality*, **32**, 236–48.

Chapter 10

An empirical–phenomenological approach to quantifying consciousness and states of consciousness: with particular reference to understanding the nature of hypnosis

Ronald J Pekala and VK Kumar

Metzinger (1995) is his book, *Conscious experience*, wrote: 'Today, the problem of consciousness … marks the very limit of human striving for understanding. It appears to many to be the last great puzzle and the greatest theoretical challenge of our time' (p. 3). Research enumerated in this book suggests that consciousness can be elucidated through the scientific application of phenomenological, psychophysiological and neurobiological methodologies. In this chapter, we will delineate an approach that we have elsewhere called *psychophenomenology* (Pekala 1985a, 1991b; Pekala and Kumar 2000b); this approach combines an empirical descriptive self-report *phenomenology* with the quantitative and statistical procedures commonly employed in the *psychological* sciences to produce a reliable and valid methodology to map, quantify and statistically assess the structures (dimensions) and resulting patterns of consciousness in reference to states of consciousness such as hypnosis.

10.1 Quantifying consciousness and states of consciousness via an empirical self-report phenomenology

Nisbett and Wilson (1977) objected to the use of introspective reports as they viewed them 'not sufficient to produce generally correct or reliable reports' (p. 233), especially concerning people's attributions of their own actions, i.e. *why* people think they do what they do. However, Smith and Miller (1978), Ericsson and Simon (1980), Lieberman (1979), and Singer and Kolligian (1987) have subsequently demonstrated that 'people can generally provide reasonably valid and reliable indices of their own differential patterns of ongoing thought through relatively short questionnaires' (p. 542), i.e. the *what* of an individual's subjective experience.

Several of our studies done in the early 1980s (Pekala and Levine 1981, 1982; Pekala and Wenger 1983; Pekala *et al.* 1986) also provided evidence that subjective consciousness could be reliably and validly assessed when phenomenologically untrained individuals retrospectively reported on their subjective experiences in reference to a preceding short

(2–4 min) stimulus interval via the use of self-report questionnaires. Based on those studies, instruments were developed to measure consciousness in general: the Phenomenology of Consciousness Inventory (PCI; Pekala 1982, 1991c); and attention in particular: the Dimensions of Attention Questionnaire, DAQ (Pekala 1985b). This chapter will describe and discuss results obtained in studies using the PCI.

The 53-item PCI measures 12 major and 14 minor dimensions of subjective experience. Each item consists of two dipole items separated by a 7-point Likert scale. An example of the PCI 'altered state of awareness' item is: 'My state of awareness was not unusual or different from what it ordinarily is' versus 'I felt in an extraordinarily unusual and non-ordinary state of awareness.' The PCI is retrospectively completed in reference to a short stimulus interval. (For a more in-depth description of the approach, see Pekala 1991b; Pekala and Kumar 2000b.)

The PCI and its predecessor inventories have been found to be reliable and valid for mapping phenomenological experiences in response to such stimulus conditions as eyes open and closed, sitting quietly and hypnosis (Kumar and Pekala 1988, 1989; Pekala and Levine 1981, 1982; Pekala and Wenger 1983; Pekala et al. 2006a), progressive relaxation and deep abdominal breathing (Pekala et al. 1988/89), drumming and trance postures (Maurer et al. 1997; Woodside et al. 1997), an out of body experience (OBE) within a near death event (NDE) (Maitz and Pekala 1991) and even fire walking (Pekala and Ersek 1992/93). Over the last 20 years, we (Kumar and Pekala 1988, 1989; Kumar et al. 1996a, b, 1999; Pekala and Kumar 1984, 1986, 1987, 1989, 2000a, 2005) have used this approach to assess and quantify the subjective experience of hypnosis.

The aforementioned *psychophenomenological* approach can be contrasted with the *neurophenomenological* approach espoused by the late Francisco Varela and his colleagues. As Lutz and Thompson (2003) indicated, 'a growing number of cognitive scientists now recognize the need to make systematic use of introspective phenomenological reports in studying the brain basis of consciousness' (p. 31). In contrast to our psychophenomenological approach which uses untrained observers (college students, ordinary clients or patients), the neurophenomenological approach espoused by Varela and colleagues 'stresses the importance of gathering first-person data from phenomenologically trained subjects as a heuristic strategy for describing and quantifying the physiological processes relevant to consciousness' (2003, p. 32). The neurophenomenological approach espouses the 'importance of disciplined, phenomenological examinations of experience for cognitive science' (p. 32) and draws extensively on the approach to cognition discussed by Varela (1996, 1997). Both psychophenomenological and neurophenomenological approaches, although somewhat different, can help better understand the comprehensive nature of consciousness, especially when there is convergence of findings across differing approaches.

10.2 Mapping and quantifying states and altered states of consciousness (ASCs)

There has been a surge of interest in research on understanding the psychobiology of altered states of consciousness thanks to the recent advances in the neurosciences which have made it possible to look at the neurobiological processes associated with such states.

Vaitl *et al.* (2005) have recently summarized that research, suggesting that with 'increasing knowledge of the neural correlates of consciousness, the formerly strange and hard to explain phenomena of ASC become increasingly understandable as a natural consequence of the workings of the brain' (p. 119). Nevertheless, a neurobiological basis for altered states of consciousness can be definitively confirmed only if there is a consensually agreed upon definition for consciousness, ASCs, and related phenomena, such as hypnosis:

> If such phenomena as 'hypnosis,' 'consciousness' or 'ASC' exist at all, then for science to describe and explain them coherently, surely the relevant research community in psychology and cognitive neuroscience should aim at developing an internally coherent and widely shared theoretical vocabulary to make genuine progress in their scientific explanation.
>
> (Kallio and Revonsuo 2005, p. 51)

The original article by Kallio and Revonsuo (2003), the commentaries (Gruzelier 2005; Kihlstrom 2005; Kirsch 2005; Lynn *et al.* 2005; Naish 2005; Spiegel 2005; Wagstaff and Cole 2005; Woody and Sadler 2005) and the authors' reply (Kallio and Revonsuo 2005) suggest that 'the concept of altered state of consciousness (ASC) still lacks a commonly accepted definition and is in need of further clarification' (2005, p. 46).

We submit that the psychophenomenological methodology espoused in this chapter can help to generate consensus concerning operational definitions and phenomenological measurement of ASCs that could serve cognitive neuroscience approaches as well. We agree with Kallio and Revonsuo (2005) that an understanding of ASCs needs to be grounded in changes in the neurobiology of the brain; however, a methodology reliably and validly to quantify and statistically assess states and ASCs from a purely phenomenological perspective (Pekala 1991*b*; Pekala and Kumar 2005) should facilitate neurobiological investigations that compare and contrast states and altered states of consciousness associated with hypnosis, dreaming, meditation, etc. Additionally, advances in neurobiological approaches can help further purely phenomenological research and provide a biological basis for understanding current psychophenomenological findings.

10.3 Quantifying phenomenological intensity and pattern effects with the PCI

Tart has described a 'state of consciousness' as 'a unique configuration or system of psychological structures or subsystems, a configuration that maintains its integrity or identity as a recognizable system in spite of variations in input from the environment and in spite of various (small) changes in subsystems' (1972, p. 62). For Tart, an *altered state of consciousness* has a significantly different pattern of organization among structures or dimensions of consciousness in comparison with ordinary waking consciousness, *and* the phenomenological perception of being in a different state of awareness. Singer (in Zinberg 1977), on the other hand, suggests that intensity effects are also relevant and need to be considered in determining if an altered state of consciousness is evident.

Both intensity and pattern effects are investigated when using the PCI to quantify phenomenological experience, operationalizing both Tart's and Singer's theoretical approaches to assessing states and ASCs. A person's scores for those items making up a particular (sub)dimension of consciousness are averaged to arrive at an intensity score for each of the various (sub)dimensions of consciousness mapped by the PCI. These scores allow for intensity parameters of subjective experience to be assessed and quantified, as per the recommendation of Singer (cited in Zinberg 1977). By means of (multivariate) analyses of variance, dimension intensity scores for the dimensions of consciousness associated with differing stimulus conditions, or differing subject groups (e.g. subjects with low versus high hypnotizability) can be statistically compared.

By administering the PCI to many individuals in reference to a particular stimulus condition, a Pearson correlation coefficient matrix of the intensity scores can be computed for the various dimensions of consciousness. The intercorrelation matrix represents a quantification of the pattern of relationships among the various dimensions as per Tart's (1969, 1972, 1977) criteria for his pattern approach to defining states of consciousness (see below for Tart's definitions). The correlation matrices associated with different stimulus conditions (e.g. hypnosis versus relaxation) or differing subject groups (e.g. those with low versus high hypnotizability) can be compared and statistically evaluated via the Jennrich (1970) test (Gupta 1994; Pekala and Kumar 1985) for differences in pattern or organization among the various dimensions.

In addition, factor analysis and cluster analysis of the PCI (see below) provide strong support for the hypothesis that 'hypnotic suggestions can indeed modulate subjective experiences' using the phraseology of Rainville and Price (2003, p. 106). Consideration of the phenomenological data gathered in reference to hypnosis suggests a dynamic quality to what happens during hypnosis, a view consistent with Sheehan and McConkey (1996) that a hypnotic subject is a 'cognitively active participant in the events of a trance … who actively processes the information received in a sophisticated and skilled way, in order to arrive at a response that satisfies the demands of the hypnotic setting' (p. xii).

10.3.1 Phenomenological intensity effects associated with hypnosis and related conditions

Early studies (Pekala *et al.* 1986; Kumar and Pekala 1988, 1989) administered the PCI within the context of an eyes closed sitting quietly baseline condition and then again within the context of the HGSHS: A (Harvard Group Scale, Shor and Orne 1962) protocol, in which a sitting quietly period was embedded toward the end of the protocol. The results suggest a consistent pattern of differences in intensity ratings between the sitting quietly baseline condition and the hypnotic condition. Specifically, the hypnosis condition was associated with decreased positive affect (joy, love and sexual excitement), negative affect (anger and sadness), self-awareness, internal dialogue, rationality, volitional control and memory. Hypnosis was also associated with increased altered experiences (alterations in time sense and perception), and an increased altered state of awareness. These results are congruent with the viewpoint of hypnosis as an altered state of awareness, along with the feeling of decreased volitional control that is regarded as the hallmark of the classic suggestion effect (Brown and Fromm 1986; Bowers 1981; Kumar *et al.* 1999).

Hypnotizability is often seen as a trait and, consequently, we examined if the level of susceptibility was related to changes in subjective experiences. Considering the results reported in three studies (Pekala and Kumar 1984, 1987; Kumar *et al.* 1996), we note that many of the 26 PCI (sub)dimensions correlated significantly with the HGSHS: A scores. The dimensions (and associated subdimensions) of altered state of awareness, altered experience (altered body image, altered time sense, altered perception, altered meaning) and attention (absorption) were positively correlated with the HGSHS: A (suggesting increased intensity effects for these variables). On the other hand, the dimensions of self-awareness, volitional control, rationality and memory were negatively correlated with the HGSHS: A scores (suggesting decreased intensity effects for these variables).

Furthermore, it appears that hypnotizability interacts with stimulus condition (baseline sitting quietly versus hypnosis using the HGSHS: A) in determining subjective experiences. Specifically, hypnosis potentiated differences between stimulus conditions (sitting quietly versus HGSHS: A) for the highly susceptible subjects, relative to those with medium (to a lesser extent) and low susceptibility on altered experiences in general, altered body image, altered time sense, and altered perception, self-awareness, altered state of awareness, internal dialogue, rationality, volitional control and memory (Kumar and Pekala 1989). The afore-mentioned results provide empirical support, via replication, for 'the theorizing of Tellegen (1979) that trait and situational variables are involved in the resulting phenomenological effects associated with hypnosis' (Kumar and Pekala 1989, p. 21).

Our results are also consistent with the interesting neurophenomenological work by Rainville and Price (2003) who found that hypnosis modifies several dimensions of experience, such as 'mental ease, absorption, and the altered sense of self characterized by changes in orientation and self-agency' (p. 123); these changes were 'further associated with changes in brain activity within structures critically involved in the basic representation of the body-self and the regulation of states of consciousness' (p. 105). Specifically, they found that 'feeling of relaxation was associated with lower levels of rCBF [regional cerebral blood flow] in the mesencephalic tegmentum of the brain stem, the thalamus, and the ACC [anterior cingulated cortex] (rostral to the hypnosis-related increase in mid-ACC' (p. 118). Feelings of absorption, on the other hand, were 'associated with coordinated increases in the level of activity within the ponto-mesencephalic brain stem, thalamus and the rostral ACC' (pp. 118–119). They interpreted this contrasting pattern of findings to reflect 'either competing processes acting on the same population of neurons or, alternatively separate neurophysiological structures within the same structures acting in parallel or in interaction with those associated with relaxation' (p. 119).

Cardeña (2005) studied the phenomenology of hypnotic virtuosos using a 'neutral hypnosis' procedure wherein the only suggestion given was 'to go as deeply into hypnosis as possible' (p. 37). Using a within-subject design, he found participants to report changes on 20 out of the 26 PCI (sub)dimensions. Deep hypnosis, relative to the control condition, was associated with

> alterations in body image, time sense, perception and meaning, and the sense of being in an altered state of awareness. Affect was more intense; there was greater attentional focus, and amount as well as vividness of imagery, but there was less self-awareness, rationality, voluntary control and memory. Other variables that do not seem relevant to hypnosis per se such as 'sexual excitement' and 'arousal' showed no differences (p. 46).

Expectancy has usually been considered an important factor in hypnosis (e.g. Orne 1962; Spanos *et al.* 1989 Kirsch *et al.* 1987; Kirsch 1991; Holroyd 2003). Pekala *et al.* (1993) examined the extent to which expectancies were a factor in subjective experiences by using a hypnosis simulation condition (subjects sat quietly with their eyes closed and were asked to think what it would be like if they were experiencing hypnosis) and then completed the PCI, Form 1 'in terms of what you think you would have experienced during hypnosis' (p. 136). Subsequent to completing the PCI, Form 1, they experienced the HGSHS: A and completed the PCI, Form 2.

Pekala *et al.* (1993) reported that 'preinduction subjective expectancies' (p. 133) accounted for 11 per cent of the variance in subsequent hypnotizability; '15% of the variance (in reference to subjects' responses to the Harvard Scale) was predicted from subjects' subjective experiences during the induction' (p. 133). Expectancy interacted with hypnotizability inasmuch as the highly susceptible subjects underestimated the alterations in subjective experiences on several PCI dimensions; subjects with low susceptibility demonstrated little change from the simulation to the hypnosis condition. Pekala *et al.* concluded: 'subjective experiences during hypnosis are at least of equal importance as the preinduction subjective expectancies in predicting hypnotizability, and probably more important if the subject is highly hypnotizable' (p. 133).

10.3.2 Phenomenological pattern effects associated with hypnosis and a baseline condition

Pekala and Kumar (1986, 1989, 1991*b*, 2000*a*, 2005) have operationalized a phenomenological pattern approach to consciousness that is based upon the psychological theorizing of Tart (1977), Mandler (1985), Izard (1977) and Baars (1986, 1997). The approach is consistent at a very general level with the Parallel Distributed Processing (PDP) models of human cognition (McClelland and Rumelhart 1986; Tyron 1993) that posit parallel processing of a network of interconnected units (Matlin 1998). There is little psychological research on trying to understand hypnosis from a PDP perspective, although Dixon *et al.* (1990) used PDP theorizing to understand Stroop (1935) effects across those with low and high hypnotizability.

Intercorrelation matrices of the PCI major dimensions, computed for particular stimulus conditions, reflect the nature of association among the various subsystems of consciousness assessed for those conditions. Thus, the matrices quantify the pattern of associations among different subsystems of consciousness in reference to the stimulus condition assessed. Significant differences in the pattern of relationships in the intercorrelation matrices between the stimulus conditions can be statistically assessed via Jennrich's (1970) test (Gupta 1994; Pekala and Kumar 1985) and also diagrammed via a device called a *psygram* (Pekala 1985*a*, 1991*b*), a *graph* of the *psycho*phenomenological state. This allows for the patterns of relationships among PCI dimensions of consciousness associated with differing stimulus conditions (or subject types) to be assessed, statistically compared and even visually diagrammed.

The psygram positions the major dimensions of consciousness mapped by the PCI on the circumference of a circle and uses lines (each line represents approximately 5 per cent of the variance in common) running between subsystems to denote the percentage of variance (squared correlation coefficients or coefficients of determination) in common among two subsystems. Numbers next to the lines represent the percentages of variance (negative numbers are used to depict negative correlations). (So as not to 'clutter' the graph, only variance percentages associated with significant correlations are depicted.)

Tart described a 'state of consciousness' as 'a unique configuration or system of psychological structures or subsystems, a configuration that maintains its integrity or identity as a recognizable system in spite of variations in input from the environment and in spite of various (small) changes in subsystems' (1973, p. 62). For Tart, an 'altered state of consciousness' has a significantly different pattern of organization among structures in comparison with ordinary waking consciousness, *and* the phenomenological perception of being in an altered state of awareness, what we have earlier labelled SSAS (subjective sense of altered state, Pekala 1991b; Pekala and Kumar 2000b).

The psygram represents a 'snapshot' (across a group of individuals) of the psychophenomenological state (Pekala 1985a, 1991b; Pekala and Bieber 1989/90; Pekala and Kumar 1986, 1989, 2000a) associated with the stimulus condition assessed. By illuminating the differences in patterns of consciousness across individuals of low or high hypnotic susceptibility, researchers can use this methodology to determine *how* hypnosis may differentially affect the patterns of association (for the PCI dimensions) among those with low or high hypnotizability during hypnosis and a baseline, comparison condition.

Pekala and Kumar (1986) assessed the pattern of relationships among phenomenological subsystems of consciousness across individuals of low and high hypnotic susceptibility by means of the PCI. Participants experienced a baseline condition of eyes closed sitting quietly and then retrospectively completed the PCI in reference to that condition. They then experienced the induction procedure of the HGSHS: A (Shor and Orne 1962) and retrospectively completed the PCI in reference to the sitting quietly period embedded in that induction. These procedures were replicated in a later study (Pekala and Kumar 1989). For the purposes of analysis, data from the two studies were combined to increase the sample size. Participants were divided into four susceptibility groups based on their HGSHS: A scores: lows (scores of 0–4, $n = 111$, $M = 2.40$), low-mediums (scores of 5–6, $n = 88$, $M = 5.49$), high-mediums (scores of 7–8, $n = 99$, $M = 7.50$) and highs (scores of 9–12, $n = 106$, $M = 10.18$).

10.3.2.1 Pattern comparisons as a function of hypnotic susceptibility and between the eyes closed and hypnotic induction conditions

Correlation matrices were constructed for the four susceptibility groups using the 12 major PCI dimensions for both the eyes closed sitting quietly and the hypnotic induction conditions. The matrices were compared with Jennrich's (1970) test (Pekala and Kumar 1985). Although none of the comparisons for the eyes closed condition comparing the four susceptibility groups with each other were significant, all comparisons for the hypnotic induction condition across the four susceptibility groups were significant, except for that between highs and high-mediums.

The intercorrelation matrices of the four susceptibility groups were also compared using the Jennrich's test across the eyes-closed versus hypnosis conditions. Comparisons for lows ($\chi^2 = 150.9$, $P < 0.001$), low-mediums ($\chi^2 = 133.7$, $P < 0.001$), high-mediums ($\chi^2 = 115.7$, $P < 0.001$) and highs ($\chi^2 = 88.59$, $P < 0.05$) were all significant.

10.3.2.2 Psygram visual analysis

Psygrams were constructed using the intercorrelation matrices for the participants with low and high susceptibility for the baseline eyes closed and the hypnosis conditions. To be conservative, only those correlations significant at the 0.001 level ($r > 0.33$) were used in the psygram construction. (These psygrams were previously depicted in Pekala and Bieber 1989/90.)

Although a perusal of the psygram for those with low susceptibility during eyes closed (Fig. 10.1) and those with high susceptibility during eyes closed (Fig. 10.3) shows a higher degree of association amongst subsystems of consciousness for lows, the overall pattern of correlations was not significantly different as statistically assessed by the Jennrich (1970) test. Whereas the highly susceptibility group during eyes closed had 10 significant associations ($P < 0.001$), those with low susceptibility had 17.

For those with low susceptibilty, hypnosis appears to have potentiated the magnitude of the associations among the subsystems (compare Fig. 10.1 with Fig. 10.2). Although the number of significant associations increased from 17 to 21, the average percentage of variance in common now increased from 19 per cent (during eyes closed) to 37 per cent (during hypnosis), suggesting that hypnosis, for those with low susceptibility, was associated with the subsystems of consciousness that became more highly 'coupled' (associated) in comparison with the baseline eyes closed condition. (Jennrich's test comparing hypnosis with the baseline condition for those with low susceptibility was significant.)

A different effect occurred for highs as they move from eyes closed (Fig. 10.3) to hypnosis (see Fig. 10.4). The number of significant associations remain about the same (10 for eyes closed versus nine for hypnosis), and the average intensity of association also remained the same. However, the Jennrich test found a significant difference between correlation matrices, implying that the pattern of relationships among the subsystems of consciousness became significantly different as highs moved from eyes closed sitting quietly to hypnosis. This is illustrated by changes in the pattern of relationships shown in the psygram. Among other changes, rationality for highly susceptible individuals during the sitting quietly period was coupled with memory and an inward, attentional focus. During hypnosis, rationality became much more strongly coupled with vivid imagery, and there were no longer any significant associations with memory and attention. In addition, positive affect became much more highly coupled with vivid imagery.

Increased magnitude and frequency of associations among subsystems may make it much more difficult for lows to experience a hallucination high or to dissociate the perceptual experience of one's arm, since a change in one particular subsystem appears to lead to changes in associated subsystems. This would make it quite difficult for lows to modify the phenomenological contents of a particular subsystem of consciousness without affecting many other subsystems concurrently.

This research may shed light on a different way to operationalize dissociation (Kluft 1999), a hypothesized aspect of hypnosis. Research into the relationships between

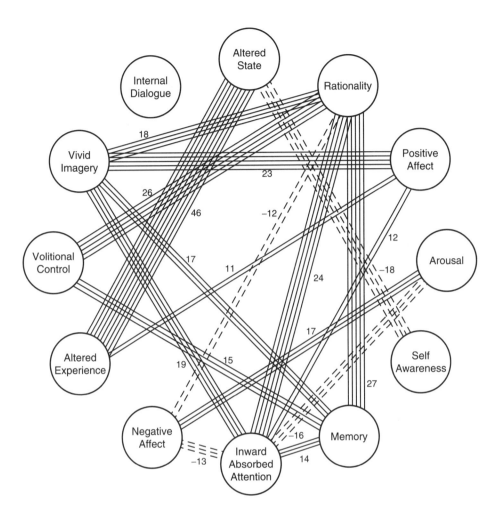

Fig. 10.1 Subjects with low susceptibility: eyes closed sitting quietly. Each line represents approximately 5 per cent of the variance in common. (All variance percentages represent correlations significant at alpha less than approximately 0.001.) n=111. [Reproduced with permission from Pekala RJ and Bieber SL (1989/90). Operationalizing pattern approaches to consciousness: an analysis of phenomenological patterns of consciousness among individuals of differing susceptibility. *Imagination, Cognition, and Personality*, 9, 308,©1989/90, Baywood Publishing Co. Inc.]

dissociation, as measured by various questionnaires such as the Dissociative Experiences Scale (DES), and hypnosis have found only weak correlations, at best (Carlson and Putnam 1992; Lynn and Rhue 1994). The above psygrams suggest a way of quantitatively operationalizing dissociation, not as a function of the dissociation of the *contents* of consciousness, as is usually assessed with such instruments as the DES (Bernstein and Putnam 1986; Carlson and Putnam 1992), but rather as a dis-association among the *processors* of consciousness for those with high, vis-à-vis, those with low susceptibility during hypnosis.

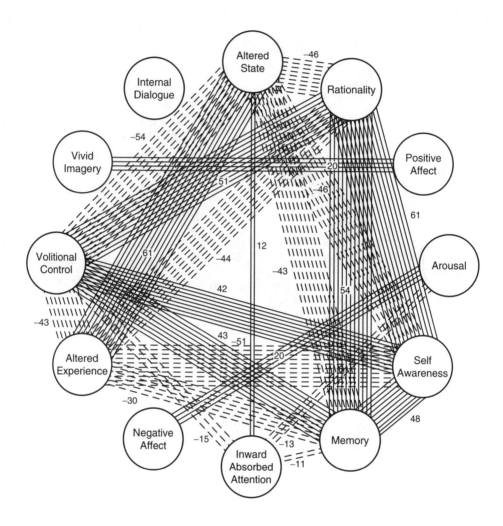

Fig. 10.2 Subjects with low susceptibility: hypnosis. Each line represents approximately 5 per cent of the variance in common. (All variance percentages represent correlations significant at alpha less than approximately 0.001.) n=111. [Reproduced with permission from Pekala RJ and Bieber SL (1989/90). Operationalizing pattern approaches to consciousness: an analysis of phenomeno-logical patterns of consciousness among individuals of differing susceptibility. *Imagination, Cognition, and Personality*, **9**, 309,©1989/90, Baywood Publishing Co. Inc.]

Egner *et al.* (2005) found that 'individual differences in hypnotic susceptibility are linked with the efficacy of the frontal attention system, and that the hypnotized condi-tion is characterized by a functional *dissociation* (our italics) of conflict monitoring and cognitive control processes' (p. 969). Egner *et al.* suggested that their findings support trait differences in hypnotic susceptibility that are a function of the disassociation of cog-nitive control systems. We believe our phenomenological pattern results engender another way to look at dissociated subsystems of consciousness.

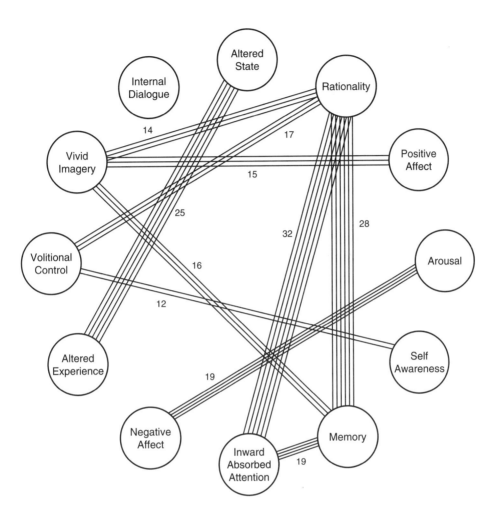

Fig. 10.3 Subjects with high susceptibility: eyes closed sitting quietly. Each line represents approximately 5 per cent of the variance in common. (All variance percentages represent correlations significant at alpha less than approximately 0.001.) n=106. [Reproduced with permission from Pekala RJ and Bieber SL (1989/90). Operationalizing pattern approaches to consciousness: an analysis of phenomenological patterns of consciousness among individuals of differing susceptibility. *Imagination, Cognition, and Personality*, **9**, 310,©1989/90, Baywood Publishing Co. Inc.]

The PDP models of cognition hypothesize that learning occurs by modification of the connections among processors of consciousness: 'Representation occurs through the pattern of connections weights across the network. Learning entails changes in these weights. New memories are written nondestructively on top of other memories up to a finite system limit, yet each memory can be fully and separately recalled' (Tyron 1993, p. 344). The psygram pattern results obtained by using the PCI across individuals with low and high

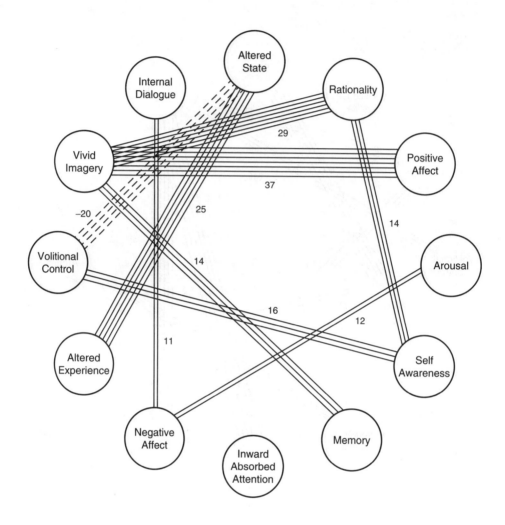

Fig. 10.4 Subjects with high susceptibility: hypnosis. Each line represents approximately 5 per cent of the variance in common. (All variance percentages represent correlations significant at alpha less than approximately 0.001.) n=106. [Reproduced with permission from Pekala RJ and Bieber SL (1989/90). Operationalizing pattern approaches to consciousness: an analysis of phenomeno-logical patterns of consciousness among individuals of differing susceptibility. *Imagination, Cognition, and Personality*, **9**, 311,©1989/90, Baywood Publishing Co. Inc.]

susceptibilities allows for such PDP models of consciousness to be phenomenologically defined and statistically assessed in reference to hypnosis. We believe the aforementioned psychophenomenological results are consistent with studies that suggest 'that hypnosis affects integrative functions of the brain and induces an alteration or even a breakdown of communication between subunits within the brain responsible for the formation of conscious experience' (Vaitl *et al.* 2005, p. 110).

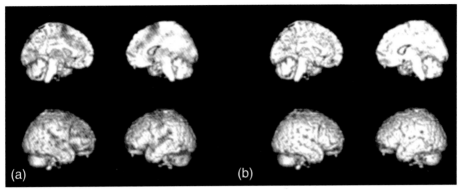

Color plate 1 Functional MRI results of an individual healthy volunteer showing dramatic differences in brain activity between normal and hypnotic states in response to intensity-matched noxious thulium-YAG laser stimuli. (A) In the normal awake state, presentation of noxious stimuli activates a large set of areas of the so-called 'pain matrix', including primary somatosensory cortex, insula, midcingulate cortex and fronto-parietal association cortices. (B) In the hypnotic state, the same stimuli only lead to activation of primary somatosensory cortex. The results are displayed at a threshold of $P < 0.001$ uncorrected. See also Figure 2.4.

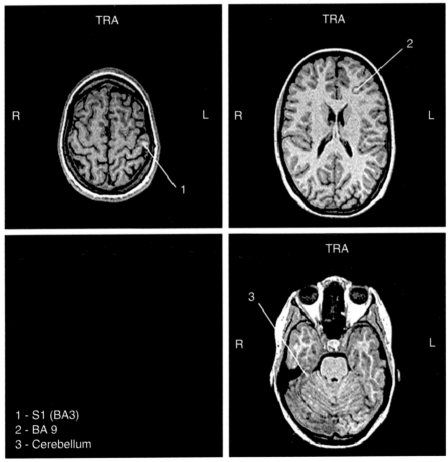

Color plate 2 Contrast of fMRI signal during painful heat between hypnotic analgesia and the control condition. Significantly higher activations were found in the prefrontal cortex (BA 9), the primary somatosensory cortex S1 and the cerebellum contralateral to the stimulation (all $P < 0.001$). See also Figure 4.3.

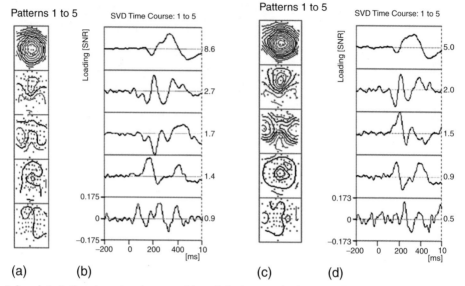

Color plate 3 Singular value decomposition of the laser-evoked potentials during suggestions of hypnotic analgesia and the control situation with the spatial patterns (a and c, respectively) and the time courses (b and d, respectively). See also Figure 4.4.

10.4 Factor analysis of the PCI dimensions in reference to hypnosis: the five factor solution and its correlations with hypnotizability and selected personality characteristics

What personality characteristics, if any, predict hypnotizability has long interested many investigators. Kumar et al. (1996) asked not only if selected personality traits are related to hypnotizability, but if the traits relate to what happens during hypnosis in terms of subjective experiences or state effects as assessed by the PCI. Four hundred and seventy-five participants completed 15 trait instruments before the administration of HGSHS: A, and the PCI was completed retrospectively in reference to a sitting quietly period embedded within the HGSHS: A.

A factor analysis of the 15 traits suggested three trait factors: absorption-permissiveness; general sensation seeking; and social desirability. A factor analysis of the 21 non-overlapping PCI (sub)dimensions generated five state effect factors: dissociated control; positive affect; negative affect; attention to internal processes; and visual imagery. The PCI factors were labelled as 'state effect' factors since the PCI intensity ratings were construed to be a product (effect) of hypnosis.

Using factor-based scores, we found that the derived trait factor, absorption-permissiveness, was not only significantly correlated with the HGSHS: A scores, but was also correlated with three of the five state effects factors: dissociative control; positive affect; and attention to internal processes. Interestingly, the HGSHS: A correlated significantly with the same three factors. Kumar et al. (1999) concluded that 'the higher the hypnotizability, the stronger the state effects of positive affect, inward absorbed attention to mental processes, and dissociated control in the sense of alterations in both trance and reality orientations as traditionally described in the literature' (p. 19). Furthermore, Kumar et al. (1996) used a hierarchical regression analysis and noted that the amount of variance accounted for by the trait factors was approximately 9 per cent; an additional 22 per cent was accounted for by state factors.

The aforementioned results with respect to the correlations between the state effects factors of dissociative control, positive affect and attention to internal processes have been replicated in a number of studies with the HGSHS: A (Angelini et al. 1999; Kumar et al. 1999; Varga et al. 2001; Manmiller et al. 2005; Robin et al. 2005), the SHSS: C (Stanford Hypnotic Susceptibility Scale: Form C; Weitzenhoffer and Hilgard 1962) (Kumar et al. 1999; Varga, et al. 2001), and with the Alman–Wexler's (1988) Indirect Hypnotic Susceptibility Scale (AWIHSS; Robin et al. 2005). The correlations were of similar magnitude and in the same direction. The correlation of the negative affect factor with hypnotizability, assessed either by the HGSHS: A, the SHSS: C or the AWIHSS, have consistently not been significant, while the correlations with respect to the visual imagery factor have been mixed.

The stability of the correlation coefficients of hypnotizability assessed via three different instruments (the HGSHS: A, the SHSS: C and the AWIHSS) with the factor-based PCI state effects scores provides strong support for the robustness of subjective experiences associated with hypnosis and for the significance of assessing phenomenological state variables for understanding the nature of hypnosis.

10.5 Operationalizing a quantitative and qualitative measure of trance depth via the PCI

10.5.1 Generating a quantitative measure of trance depth

Several years ago (Pekala and Kumar 2000*b*) we developed an empirical approach operationally to define 'trance' from both a quantitative and qualitative approach. Although there may be different types of trance, there may be at the same time some commonality across these different types of trance, analogous to Spearman's (1904, 1923) 'g' factor for general mental ability vis-à-vis different types of intelligence, a la Gardner (1983). Along a somewhat similar perspective, Woody *et al.* (2005) have hypothesized that hypnotizability involves both general and specific abilities: 'Our perspective on hypnotizability is that each distinguishable ability involves the combination of general hypnotizability with a more specific, unique component' (p. 210), such that the 'multidimensionality of hypnosis scales is not an artifact; instead multiple differentiable skills underlie hypnotic performance' (p. 209).

Using our psychophenomenological approach, we can operationally define trance as the subjective state the highly hypnotizable person reports achieving in response to a hypnotic induction. In attempting to derive a general measure of trance, we used multiple regression to predict the total HGSHS: A scores from the PCI (sub)dimensions and then used the resulting equation to compute predicted Harvard Group Scale (pHGS) scores. These pHGS scores were construed to operationalize a phenomenological measure of individual differences in *trance* or *hypnoidal* effects achieved by subjects during hypnosis. Thus, a high pHGS score reflects subjective effects typically reported by highly hypnotizable subjects.

The pHGS scores were first obtained in a study by Pekala and Kumar (1984). The multiple regression equation generated a validity coefficient of 0.62 which was cross-validated in two other studies generating validity coefficients of 0.65 (Pekala and Kumar 1987) and 0.67 (Forbes and Pekala 1993). Additionally, a validity coefficient of 0.86 (Hand *et al.* 1995) was found when correlating the actual SHSS: C (Weitzenhoffer and Hilgard 1962) scores obtained by subjects with their pHGS scores. Thus, the pHGS score was found to predict hypnotic susceptibility as measured by both the Harvard (HGSHS: A) and Stanford Scale (SHSS: C) actual scores.

In sum, the pHGS score, computed using a multiple regression equation that differentially weight particular PCI (sub)dimensions, permits an estimate of a person's 'hypnoidal state' (Pekala and Forbes 1988; Pekala and Nagler 1989) or 'depth of trance' score. Besides generating a quantitative general measure of trance depth, cluster analyses results with the PCI suggests that there are different 'types' of trance.

10.5.2 Qualitatively different 'types' of trance

In a series of studies, Pekala and colleagues (Pekala 1991*a*; Pekala *et al.* 1995; Forbes and Pekala 1996; Pekala and Forbes 1997) used K-means cluster analysis (Hartigan 1975) to determine if there might be several different 'types' or subclusters of highly hypnotizable, moderately hypnotizable, and low or non-hypnotizable subjects, based on their subjective experiences assessed by the PCI. Phenomenological experience, as assessed by the PCI, was cluster analysed using subjects as the independent variables, and the PCI major dimensions as the dependent variables.

Figure 10.5 illustrates the results of cluster analysis on the phenomenology of three groups of subjects with low susceptibility who scored 0–2 on the HGSHS: A. The group, labelled the 'classic lows', experienced the most intact self-awareness, the least drop in volitional control and the least alteration in state of awareness. They also reported very high levels of muscular tension (a high PCI 'arousal' score). The 'relaxed lows' were similar to the classic lows, except that there was not much muscular tension (low arousal). Most interesting, however, were the 'pseudolows'. Despite their low scores on the HGSHS: A, the 'pseudolows' reported moderate drops in self-awareness, rationality, volitional control and memory. They were named 'pseudolows' because even though they scored low on the HGSHS: A, they evinced phenomenological experiences consistent with that of moderately hypnotizable subjects. These results suggest that using the PCI in conjunction with the behavioural hypnotizability scales provides information as to the subtle variations in hypnotic responsiveness from a phenomenological viewpoint, which one would not otherwise get by simply using the behavioural measures.

Table 10.1 lists the nine different 'trance types' found by Pekala and Forbes (1997). From non-hypnotizable to highly hypnotizable (in terms of pHGS scores), the nine types were: classic lows, relaxed lows, nondialoguing mediums, dialoguing mediums, visualizers, rational high-mediums, dialoguing high-mediums, fantasy highs and classic highs. Here again, the classic lows had the highest level of muscle tension, and the most intact memory, rationality and self-awareness. They also had the least drop in volitional control,

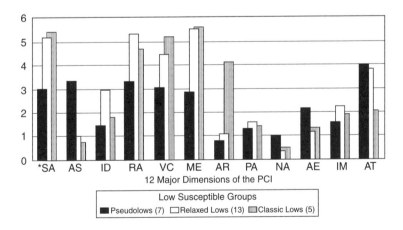

Fig. 10.5 Cluster analysis of subjects with low susceptibility. Using Ss with Harvard Scale Scores of 0–2 (unpublished data from Pekala and Forbes 1997). Intensity values (0 = none or little; 6 = much or complete). SA = self-awareness; AS = altered state; ID = internal dialogue; RA = rationality; VC = volitional control; ME = memory; AR = arousal; PA = positive affect; NA = negative affect; AE = altered experience; IM = vivid imagery; AT= inward, absorbed attention. (Originally printed in the *American Journal of Clinical Hypnosis*, Vol. 43, no. 2. Reproduced with permission of the American Society of Clinical Hypnosis.)

Table 10.1 The nine hypnotic types, average trance depth, and distinguishing characteristics

Hypnotic type	Hypnoidal state score[2]	Distinguishing characteristics of each of the nine cluster types[1] (based on intensity levels of PCI major dimensions)
Classic lows	2.88	Highest level of arousal (muscular tension); most intact memory, rationality, and self-awareness; most internal dialogue; least drop in volitional control
Relaxed lows	3.68	Similar to classic lows except have low muscle tension levels and less internal dialogue
Non-dialoguing mediums	4.87	Similar to dialoguing mediums except for lack of internal dialogue
Dialoguing mediums	5.01	Similar to non-dialoguing mediums except for more internal dialogue
Visualizers	6.06	Highest level of visual imagery; highest level of self-awareness and intact memory after classic and relaxed lows
Rational high-mediums	6.81	Similar to dialoguing high-mediums except for less internal dialogue and more rationality
Dialoguing high-mediums	6.86	Second highest level of internal dialogue after classic lows; similar to rational high-mediums except for more internal dialogue and less rationality
Fantasy highs	7.10	Second highest level of imagery after visualizers
Classic highs	7.60	Lowest level of memory, rationality, internal dialogue, imagery, and self-awareness

[1]Based on Pekala and Forbes (1997).

[2]Hypnoidal state score: average level of trance depth: scores go from approximately 1.0 (not hypnotizable) to 9.0 (highly hypnotizable).

This table was originally printed in the *American Journal of Clinical Hypnosis*, vol. 43, no. 2. Reprinted with permission of the American Society of Clinical Hypnosis.

a measure of the 'classic suggestion effect' as characterized by Bowers (1981). The classic highs, on the other hand, had the lowest level of memory, rationality, internal dialogue, imagery and self-awareness of all the groups. Especially interesting were the visualizers. They had the highest level of vivid visual imagery; and the highest level of self-awareness and intact memory after the classic and relaxed lows (the two least 'hypnotizable' groups).

10.6 The Phenomenology of Consciousness Inventory: Hypnotic Assessment Procedure: PCI-HAP

Several years ago the PCI was incorporated into a 'hypnotic assessment procedure' called the PCI-HAP (Pekala 1995a, b)[1]. The PCI-HAP consists of relaxation instructions called a 'body scan', a hypnotic induction procedure called a 'mind calm', a suggestion to have

[1] The PCI, the PCI-HAP and the EXCEL scoring protocol are available by writing to Ron Pekala, PhD, Biofeedback Clinic (116B), Coatesville VA Medical Center, Coatesville, PA 19320, USA or e-mailing him at pekalar@voicenet.com.

a vivid hypnotic dream and a few other items. Before the hypnotic induction, the client completes a pre-assessment form (recently added to the PCI-HAP) which asks if the person was hypnotized before, and to estimate their expected hypnotic depth and the expected helpfulness of hypnosis. The clinician/researcher completes a short debriefing form immediately after the hypnosis. For this debriefing, clients rate the vividness of their imagery during the hypnotic dream, and answer several other questions, including how deeply hypnotized they felt themselves to be during the hypnosis. The client then completes the PCI retrospectively in reference to the sitting quietly period embedded in the hypnosis. (An EXCEL program is used to score the PCI-HAP; it generates a 5-page printout of the results of the PCI-HAP assessment.)

10.7 Using the PCI-HAP to operationalize a recent theoretical integration of hypnosis in reference to self-reported hypnotic depth

10.7.1 Holroyd's theoretical integration

Holroyd (2003), integrating the research and theorizing on hypnosis over the last 30 years, has posited an interactive relationship between trance depth or altered state effects and suggestibility. From a synthesis of research on the neurophysiology of hypnosis (Crawford and Gruzelier 1992; Crawford 2001) and its phenomenology (Pekala and Kumar 2000*b*; Cardeña 2005), Holroyd distilled three factors to account for most of the effects we see in hypnosis: suggestibility, altered state effects and expectancy.

10.7.1.1 Suggestibility

Suggestibility is commonly defined in terms of responsiveness to suggestions given during hypnosis. (Because suggestibility means different things to different theorists, see Schumaker 1991, for a comprehensive review of these very different viewpoints.) Kirsch and Braffman (1999) distinguished two main types of suggestibility: 'if "hypnotic suggestibility" is responsiveness to suggestions given after hypnosis has been induced'; (p. 226) then 'non-hypnotic suggestibility' may be used 'to denote responsiveness to suggestions administered without the prior induction of hypnosis' (p. 226). They emphasized the role of imagination in suggestibility. They defined 'imaginative suggestions' as 'requests to experience an imaginary state of affairs as if it were real' (Kirsch and Braffman 2001, p. 59), and 'imaginative suggestibility' as the 'degree to which the person succeeds in having the suggested experiences' (p. 59), whether such experiences occur within, or outside of, hypnosis. The PCI-HAP has a hypnotic dream item which asks the client during the debriefing how vivid their imagery was during hypnosis. It is a measure of what we call imagoic suggestibility, a *subset* of Kirsch and Braffman's hypnotic imaginative suggestibility, since there may be other aspects to imaginative suggestibility besides imagery vividness.

10.7.1.2 Altered state effects

Holroyd's (2003) second factor is that of altered state effects. Holroyd, quoting Weitzenhoffer (2002), distinguished between hypnosis and hypnotism: whereas *hypnosis* 'means "altered state' and implies trance' (2003, p. 4); *hypnotism* 'means something entirely different—it means giving suggestions after you think a person is in the state of hypnosis' (p. 4). To quote Weitzenhoffer, 'I will otherwise generally reserve the term *hypnosis* for the "state" (our quotes) and the term *hypnotism*, for the production, study and use of suggestion with the state of hypnosis presumably being present, whether or not it adds anything tangible to the situation' (2002, p. 210).

Hence, hypnotism, according to Weitzenhoffer's definition, implies the giving of suggestions, via imagination, fantasy and/or other means, and the acceptance of those suggestions by individuals whether or not they are in the 'altered state' of hypnosis. Citing neurophysiological research (e.g. Crawford and Gruzelier 1992; Ray 1997; Crawford 2001), Holroyd suggested that there is a neurophysiological basis for the subjective altered state effects reported by highly hypnotizable subjects in hypnosis that parallels absorptive meditation: 'both hypnosis and concentrative meditation result in inhibitory patterns, particularly in the midline and frontal cortical areas associated with executive function and cognitive control' (p. 8). Thus, both would involve an alteration in state of consciousness associated with changes in brain wave patterns accompanying the aforementioned changes.

Holroyd suggested that both suggestibility and altered state effects associated with being hypnotized, in interaction with expectancy (Kirsch 2000), account for the phenomenon of being hypnotized: 'suggestion without an altered state is just an invitation to use imagination and fantasy. An altered state without suggestions is just trance or meditation. Not only are altered state and imagination interactive contributors, but they also interact with expectancy' (Holroyd 2003, p. 12).

All three of the processes in Holroyd's model (2003) can be operationalized using the PCI-HAP. Whereas the *pHGS score* obtained from the PCI-HAP generates a measure of altered state effects (Pekala and Kumar 2000b) via a 'hypnoidal state' score (Pekala and Nagler 1989), the *imagery vividness dream item* assessed by the PCI-HAP debriefing form taps what we call a 'imagoic suggestibility' score, an aspect of hypnotic 'imaginative suggestibility' as defined by Kirsch and Braffman (2001). Additionally, the PCI-HAP debriefing form allows participants to estimate their hypnotic depth, a self-reported Hypnotic Depth (srHD) score, by means of a single self-report item using a '1' to '10' rating scale. Finally, a pre-assessment form that was recently added to the PCI-HAP allows for hypnotic and therapeutic expectancy to be quantified.

10.7.2 Predicting self-reported hypnotic depth from the PCI-HAP

Clinicians often employ a '1' to '10' scale ('1' = 'your normal, waking state;' '10' = 'the most deeply hypnotized you can imagine') and ask their clients to estimate how deeply hypnotized they feel themselves to be at a particular moment in time. Because clinicians routinely ask their patients to estimate how deeply they felt they were hypnotized, we asked what phenomenological or behavioural processes (as assessed by the PCI-HAP) are associated with how individuals judge their depth of trance. This question was explored using correlation, 3D graphic and regression analyses (and is more fully reported in Pekala *et al.* 2006a).

10.7.2.1 Correlational and 3D graphic analyses

Participants ($n = 180$) from substance abuse treatment units, within which they were matriculated, and as part of a study on relapse prevention (reported in Pekala *et al.* 2004), completed a variety of questionnaires, including the PCI-HAP, before discharge. A correlation matrix for the following PCI-HAP-based scores was constructed: srHD (self-reported hypnotic depth), PCI pHGS (hypnoidal state), imagoic suggestibility (the imagery vividness dream item) and other PCI-HAP debriefing item scores. The imagery vividness dream item of the PCI-HAP debriefing form correlated highest with participants' srHD score ($r = 0.72$, $P < 0.001$). The second highest correlation was between the srHD score and the PCI-HAP pHGS score ($r = 0.57$, $P < 0.001$).

Figure 10.6 represents a 3D plot with imagoic suggestibility on the x-axis, the hypnoidal state on the y-axis and the srHD score on the z-axis. The figure represents a three-dimensional 'distance weighted least squares fit (of) a surface through a set of points by least squares' (Wilkinson 1988, p. 550). Visual perusal of the figure suggests that either a high hypnoidal state score or a high imagoic suggestibility score (above 7.0) was associated with a high srHD score (above 7.0) provided the other variable's score was not low (3.0 or below). To partial out the variance common to both variables, stepwise regression analyses were conducted.

10.7.2.2 Regression analyses

Regression analyses using all subjects ($n = 180$) (unpublished data from Pekala *et al.* 2006a) were completed, attempting to predict hypnotic depth from the debriefing items of the PCI-HAP and also the pHGS score. Remaining in the regression equation were the imagery vividness item (standardized regression coefficient of 0.54), the pHGS score

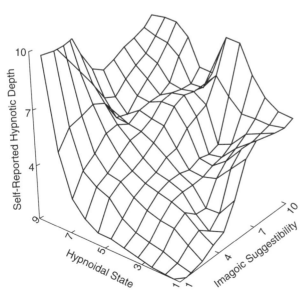

Fig. 10.6 Hypnotic depth as a function of imagoic suggestibility and hypnoidal state. [Reproduced with permission from Pekala RJ, Kumar VK, Maurer R, Elliott–Carter NC, and Moon E (2006). 'How deeply hypnotized did I get?' predicting self-reported hypnotic depth from a phenomenological assessment instrument. *International Journal of Clinical and Experimental Hypnosis*, 54, 326. ©2006, Society of Clinical and Experimental Hypnosis.]

Table 10.2 Predicting hypnotic depth using the PCI-HAP: full sample ($n = 180$)

Subscale	R	R^2	Unstandardized coefficient	Standardized coefficient	F-value	P-value
Imagery vividness dream item (imagoic suggestibility)	0.717	0.514	0.502	0.54	97.75	0.00
pHGS score (hypnoidal state)	0.770	0.594	0.586	0.34	40.12	0.00
Finger response item	0.779	0.607	0.673	0.12	5.87	0.02
Constant			−0.012			

F and P are final values for independent variables left in the regression equation.

This table is based on unpublished data taken from the study reported in Pekala *et al.* 2006a.

(regression coefficient of 0.34) and the finger-raising item (regression coefficient of 0.12), for an R of 0.78 and an R^2 of 0.61. (see Table 10.2).

Because partial regression coefficients indicate, 'with a good deal of confidence, whether specific predictors make contributions to the criterion that are unrelated to the contributions made by the other variables' (Grimm and Yarnold 1995, p. 41); the coefficients thus allow for a comparison of 'the relative contributions of each predictor to the overall effect' (p. 41). The standardized regression coefficients listed in Table 10.2 indicate that participants' imagery during the hypnotic dream vacation accounted for 54 per cent of the relative variance in srHD scores; followed by level of subjective trance as measured by the pHGS score (34 per cent of the variance); followed by the finger raising item (12 per cent) (used to determine if subjects may have fallen asleep).

These results are consistent with the theorizing and research of McConkey, Sheehan and Woody (Sheehan and McConkey 1982; Barnier and McConkey 2003; Woody and McConkey 2003) who suggest that different psychological processes are activated in the passing of differing types of hypnotic suggestions. Woody and McConkey (2003) suggest that 'different people (or the same person on different occasions) could pass an item via different underlying processes' (p. 317). A perusal of Fig. 10.6 suggests that the participant's perception of hypnotic depth does appear to be a function of both imagoic suggestibility and hypnoidal state, with higher scores in either leading to an increased hypnotic depth perception, provided the other dimension is not low.

A pre-assessment form was recently added to the PCI-HAP that allows for pre-hypnosis hypnotic expectancy ('how deeply hypnotized do you expect to be when we try to hypnotize you today?'), and pre-hypnotic therapeutic expectancy ('how helpful do you think self-hypnosis training is going to be to help you with your problems, issues, and concerns?') to be quantified.

In a pilot study currently in progress (Pekala *et al.* 2006b), a regression analysis, parallel to the regression equation mentioned above, but including the PCI-HAP pre-assessment variables, found that those variables now remaining in the regression equation included: imagoic suggestibility (with a standard regression coefficient of 0.67), hypnoidal state (with a standard regression coefficient of 0.15) and therapeutic expectancy (with a standard regression coefficient of 0.21). Although the n of this preliminary study is small ($n = 55$), pending replication, the results suggest that the participants' perception of how deeply hypnotized they felt themselves to be in was a function of imagoic suggestibility, altered state effects and therapeutic expectancy, results that provide support to the theorizing of Holroyd (2003), Weitzenhoffer (1974, 2002), Kirsch (2000) and others concerning the processes activated by 'hypnosis' and 'hypnotism.'

10.8 Potentials for combining a neurobiological approach with a multivariate psychophenomenological approach

10.8.1 Accomplishments of this multivariate psychophenomenological approach

Probably one of the most exciting potential applications of this approach to understanding hypnosis concerns its use with EEG, fMRI, positron emission tomography (PET) and related neurobiological methodologies as these methodologies become more available in hypnosis research. In the previous paragraphs, we have illustrated how we have used a 53-item self-report subjective experiences inventory to carry out the following:

1. Quantify hypnotic experience across individuals of low, medium and high susceptibility during hypnosis and baseline conditions to reveal significant phenomenological PCI intensity differences (Pekala *et al.* 1986; Kumar and Pekala 1988, 1989).

2. Diagram states of consciousness across individuals of low and high hypnotizability via psygrams (Pekala and Kumar 1986, 1989, 2000*a*; Pekala and Bieber 1989/90).

3. Account for the trait/state effects of hypnosis (Kumar *et al.* 1996, 1999) including five state effects factors that have shown consistent correlations with hypnotizability across several studies and several hypnotic assessment instruments.

4. Generate a reliable and valid measure of 'trance depth' (hypnoidal state) (Pekala and Kumar 1984, 1987, 2000*b*; Pekala *et al.* 2006).

5. Differentiate different 'types' of individuals of low to high hypnotizability via trance typology profiles (Pekala 1991*a*; Forbes and Pekala 1996; Pekala and Forbes 1997; Pekala *et al.* 1995).

6. Clinically assess hypnotic responsiveness via the PCI-HAP (Pekala 1995*a*, *b*, 2002; Pekala and Kumar 2000*b*).

7. Use the PCI-HAP to operationalize and test hypnotic theories.

10.8.2 Future directions

It seems only logical that this psychophenomenological approach should be combined with cognitive neuroscience approaches to understand more fully that puzzle we call hypnosis. PET scan research by Rainville *et al.* (2002) appears to 'support a state theory of hypnosis in which the basic changes in phenomenal experience produced by hypnotic induction reflect, at least in part, the modulation of activity within brain areas critically involved in the regulation of consciousness' (p. 887). Their research looked at two of the dimensions describing the experience of being hypnotized: mental relaxation and mental absorption. Use of the PCI to map subjective experience across its 12 major and 14 minor dimensions in a reliable and valid manner may represent a more comprehensive way to assess the phenomenological effects of hypnosis during such PET scans. Additionally, using the hypnoidal state score generated from the PCI allows for trance depth to be quantified reliably and validly so that states of consciousness associated with not only hypnosis, but other altered state induction procedures such as meditation, trance drumming, and breathing practices such as pranayama (Iyengar 1981) can be compared to determine to what extent 'hypnoidal effects' are common across these other types of altered state induction procedures.

Additionally, the aforementioned empirical phenomenological research has documented that the assessment of hypnotizability with such traditional instruments as the Harvard or the Stanford Scales fails to measure the varied and fascinating phenomenology associated with being 'hypnotized' (Pekala and Forbes 1997; Pekala and Kumar 2000b). The typology research presented above suggests that there are different types of highly hypnotizable subjects, who may achieve hypnotic effects through different mechanisms, i.e. the visualizers, possibly using very vivid imagery to pass hypnotic suggestions, and the classic highs, undergoing alterations in state of awareness or 'dissociated control' (Bowers 1992; Woody and McConkey 2003).

Kihlstrom (2003), and most recently Nash (2005) and Woody et al. (2005), argue in favour of pluralistic approaches in the understanding of hypnotic responsiveness. The provocative debates (Hammond 1998; Kihlstrom 1997; Frischholz 2000; Lynn and Sherman 2000; Kallio and Revonsuo 2003, 2005) seen in the field of hypnosis need to be balanced by equally integrated theoretical understandings that combine psychosocial, cognitive–behavioural and neurobiological explanations with reliable and valid phenomenological data. We believe psychophenomenological and neurophenomenological (Lutz and Thompson 2003) approaches to consciousness can help to quantify that elusive subjective factor in a way heretofore unavailable.

Kirsch (2004) suggested that to confirm the '"generic altered state hypothesis"—the hypothesis that there is a uniquely hypnotic state in which suggestibility is enhanced and which is the basis for some hypnotic responses' (p. 18), one needs to define what is meant by an altered state of consciousness a la Tart (1972) and provide evidence of 'physiological markers of the trance state' (p. 19). In 2003, Kallio and Revonsuo wrote that because the concepts of hypnosis and ASC 'lack a definition which can be empirically evaluated, there will be no possibility even to theorize about the possible changes in the state of consciousness associated with hypnosis' (p. 136). Two years later, in response to a series of commentaries about their provocative article, Kallio and Revonsuo (2005) remarked that 'the concept of altered state of consciousness (ASC) still lacks a commonly accepted definition and is in need of further clarification' (2005, p. 46).

We believe use of the aforementioned psychophenomenological methodology can help enrich our understanding of hypnotic responsiveness, and provide not only needed definitions, but an empirical operationalization of those definitions so that states and ASCs can be quantitatively assessed and statistically evaluated, in reference not only to hypnosis but to other putative ASCs, such as meditation, pranayama, and psychedelic, transcendental and mystical experiences (Baruš 2003).

References

Alman BM and Wexler D (1988). Alman–Wexler Indirect Hypnotic Susceptibility Scale (AWIHSS). In: GJ Pratt, DP Wood, and BM Alman, eds. *Clinical hypnosis primer. Expanded and updated.* pp. 379–88. New York, John Wiley.

Angelini FJ, Kumar VK and Chandler I (1999). The Harvard Group Scale of Hypnotic Susceptibility and related instruments; individual and group administration. *International Journal of Clinical and Experimental Hypnosis*, **47**, 236–50.

Baars BJ (1986). *The cognitive revolution in psychology.* New York, Guilford Press.

Baars BJ (1997). *In the theater of consciousness.* Oxford, Oxford University Press.

Barnier AJ and McConkey KM (2003). Hypnosis, human nature, and complexity: integrating neuro-science approaches into hypnosis research. *International Journal of Clinical and Experimental Hypnosis*, **51**, 282–308.

Baruš I. (2003) *Alterations of consciousness: an empirical analysis for social scientists.* Washington, DC, American Psychological Association.

Bernstein EM and Putnam FW (1986). Development, reliability, and validity of a dissociation scale. *Journal of Nervous and Mental Disease*, **174**, 727–35.

Bowers KS (1981). Do the Stanford scales tap the 'classic suggestion effect?' *International Journal of Clinical and Experimental Hypnosis*, **29**, 42–53.

Bowers KS (1992). Imaginative control and dissociative control in hypnotic responding. *International Journal of Clinical and Experimental Hypnosis*, **40**, 253–75.

Brown DP and Fromm E (1986). *Hypnotherapy and hypnoanalysis.* Hillsdale, NJ, Lawrence Erlbaum Associates.

Cardeña E (2005). The phenomenology of deep hypnosis: quiescent and physically active. *International Journal of Clinical and Experimental Hypnosis*, **53**, 37–59.

Carlson EB and Putnam FW (1992). *Manual for the Dissociative Experiences Scale.* Unpublished psychological manual. Beloit College, Wisconsin.

Crawford HJ (2001). Neuropsychophysiology of hypnosis: towards an understanding of how hypnotic interventions work. In: GD Burrows, RO Stanley, and PB Blood, eds. *International handbook of clinical hypnosis*, pp. 61–84. New York, Wiley.

Crawford HJ and Gruzelier JH (1992). A midstream view of the neuropsychophysiology of hypnosis: Recent research and future directions. In: E Fromm and MR Nash, eds. *Contemporary hypnosis research*, pp. 227–66. New York, Guilford Press.

Dixon M, Brunet A and Laurence J (1990). Hypnotizability and automaticity: toward a parallel distributed processing model of hypnotic responding. *Journal of Abnormal Psychology*, **99**, 336–43.

Egner T, Jamieson G and Gruzelier J (2005). Hypnosis decouples cognitive control from conflict monitoring processes of the frontal lobe. *NeuroImage*, **27**, 969–78.

Ericsson K A and Simon HA (1980). Verbal reports as data. *Psychological Review*, **87**, 215–51.

Forbes EJ and Pekala RJ (1993). Predicting hypnotic susceptibility via a phenomenological approach. *Psychological Reports*, **73**, 1251–56.

Forbes RJ and Pekala RJ (1996). Types of hypnotically (un)susceptible individuals as a function of phenomenological experience: a partial replication. *Australian Journal of Clinical and Experimental Hypnosis*, **24**, 92–109.

Frischholz EJ (2000). What is hypnosis? *American Journal of Clinical Hypnosis*, **42**, 174.

Gardner H. (1983). *Frames of mind: the theory of multiple intelligences.* New York, Basic Books.

Grimm LG and Yarnold RR (1995). *Reading and understanding multivariate statistics*. Washington, DC, American Psychological Association.

Gruzelier J (2005). Altered states of consciousness and hypnosis in the twenty-first century. *Contemporary Hypnosis*, **22**, 1–7.

Gupta SK (1994). *Jennrich's asymptotic chi square test for the equality of independent correlation matrices*. Unpublished computer program. West Chester, PA: West Chester University of Pennsylvania.

Hammond DC (1998). Guest editorial–the need for clinically relevant research. *American Journal of Clinical Hypnosis*, **41**, 2–9.

Hand J, Pekala RJ and Kumar VK (1995). Prediction of Harvard and Stanford Scale scores with a phenomenological instrument. *Australian Journal of Clinical and Experimental Hypnosis*, **23**, 124–34.

Hartigan JA (1975). *Clustering algorithms*. New York, John Wiley and Sons.

Hilgard ER (1965). *The experience of hypnosis*. New York, Harcourt Brace Jovanovich.

Holroyd J (2003). The science of meditation and the state of hypnosis. *American Journal of Clinical Hypnosis*, **46**, 109–128.

Iyengar BKS (1981). *The light on pranayama: the yogic art of breathing*. New York, Crossroad Publishing Company.

Izard CE (1977). *Human emotions*. New York, Plenum Press.

Jennrich RJ (1970). An asymptotic chi-square test for the equality of two correlation matrices. *Journal of the American Statistical Association*, **65**, 904–12.

Kallio S and Revonsuo A (2003). Hypnotic phenomena and altered states of consciousness: multilevel framework of description and explanation. *Contemporary Hypnosis*, **20**, 111–64.

Kallio S and Revonsuo A (2005). Altering the state of the altered state debate: reply to commentaries. *Contemporary Hypnosis*, **22**, 46–55.

Kihlstrom JF (1997). Convergence in understanding hypnosis? Perhaps, but not so fast. *International Journal of Clinical and Experimental Hypnosis*, **45**, 324–32.

Kihlstrom J (2003). The fox, the hedgehog, and hypnosis. *International Journal of Clinical and Experimental Hypnosis*, **51**, 166–89.

Kihlstrom JF (2005). Is hypnosis an altered state of consciousness *or what*? *Contemporary Hypnosis*, **22**, 34–8.

Kirsch I (1991). The social learning theory of hypnosis. In: SJ Lynn and JW Rhue, eds. *Theories of hypnosis: current models and perspectives*. pp. 439–465. New York, Guilford Press.

Kirsch I (2000). The response set theory of hypnosis. *American Journal of Clinical Hypnosis*, **42**, 274–92.

Kirsch I (2004). Altered states in hypnosis: the debate goes on. Abstract of the address by the winner of the distinguished scientific contributions to scientific hypnosis. *Psychological Hypnosis, Society of Psychological Hypnosis, A Bulletin of Division 30 of the American Psychological Association*, **13**, 16–9.

Kirsch I (2005). Empirical resolution of the altered state debate. *Contemporary Hypnosis*, **22**, 18–23.

Kirsch I and Braffman W (1999). Correlates of hypnotizability: the first empirical study. *Contemporary Hypnosis*, **16**, 224–30.

Kirsch I and Braffman W (2001). Imaginative suggestibility and hypnotizability. *Current Directions in Psychological Science*, **10**, 57–61.

Kirsch I, Council JR and Mobayed C (1987). Imagery and response expectancy as determinants of hypnotic behavior. *British Journal of Experimental and Clinical Hypnosis*, **4**, 25–31.

Kluft RP (1999). Current issues in dissociative identity disorder. *Journal of Practicing Psychiatry and Behavioral Health*, **5**, 3–19.

Kumar VK and Pekala RJ (1988). Hypnotizability, absorption, and individual differences in phenomenological experience. *International Journal of Clinical and Experimental Hypnosis*, **36**, 80–8.

Kumar VK and Pekala RJ (1989). Variations in phenomenological experience as a function of hypnotic susceptibility: a replication. *British Journal of Experimental and Clinical Hypnosis*, **6**, 17–22.

Kumar VK, Pekala RJ and Cummings J (1996*a*). Trait factors, state effects, and hypnotizability. *International Journal of Clinical and Experimental Hypnosis*, **44**, 232–49.

Kumar VK, Pekala RJ and Marcano G (1996*b*). Hypnotizability, dissociativity, and phenomenological experience. *Dissociation*, **9**, 143–53.

Kumar VK, Pekala RJ and McCloskey MM (1999). Phenomenological state effects during hypnosis: a cross-validation of findings. *Contemporary Hypnosis*, **16**, 9–22.

Lieberman DA (1979). Behaviorism and the mind: a (limited) call for a return to introspection. *American Psychologist*, **34**, 319–33.

Lynn SJ, Fassler O and Knox J (2005). Hypnosis and the altered state debate: sometime more or nothing more? *Contemporary Hypnosis*, **22**, 39–45.

Lynn SJ and Rhue JW, eds. (1994). *Dissociation: clinical and theoretical perspectives*. New York, Guilford Press.

Lynn SJ and Sherman SJ (2000). The clinical importance of sociocognitive models of hypnosis: response set theory and Milton Erickson's strategic interventions. *American Journal of Clinical Hypnosis*, **42**, 294–315.

Lutz A and Thompson E (2003). Neurophenomenology: integrating subjective experience and brain dynamics in the neuroscience of consciousness. *Journal of Consciousness Studies*, **10**, 31–52.

Maitz E and Pekala RJ (1991). Phenomenological quantification of an out-of-the-body experience associated with a near-death event. *OMEGA*, **22**, 199–214.

Mandler G (1985). *Consciousness: an essay in cognitive psychology*. Hillsdale, NJ, Lawrence Erlbaum.

Manmiller J, Kumar VK and Pekala RJ (2005). Hypnotizability, creative capacity, creativity styles, absorption, and phenomenological experience during hypnosis. *Creativity Research Journal*, **17**, 9–24.

Matlin MW (1998). *Cognition*, 4th edn. New York, Harcourt Brace College Publishers.

Maurer RL, Kumar VK, Woodside L and Pekala RJ (1997). Phenomenological experiences in response to monotonous drumming and hypnotizability. *American Journal of Clinical Hypnosis*, **40**, 130–45.

McClelland JL, Rumelhart DE and the PDP Research Group. (1986). *Parallel distributed processing, Vol. 2: psychological and behavioral models*. Cambridge, MA, MIT Press.

Metzinger T (1995). The problem of consciousness. In: T Metzinger, ed. *Conscious experience*. pp. 3–37. Lawrence, KS, Allen Press.

Naish P (2005). Detecting hypnotically altered states of consciousness. *Contemporary Hypnosis*, **22**, 24–30.

Nash MR (2005). The importance of being earnest when crafting definitions: science and scientism are not the same thing. *International Journal of Clinical and Experimental Hypnosis*, **53**, 265–80.

Nisbett RE and Wilson TD (1977). Telling more than we can know: verbal reports on mental processes. *Psychological Review*, **84**, 231–59.

Orne MT (1962). On the social psychology of the psychology experiment: with particular reference to demand characteristics and their implication. *American Psychologist*, **17**, 776–83.

Pekala RJ (1982). *The phenomenology of consciousness inventory*. Thorndale, PA: Psychophenomenological Concepts. (Now published by Mid-Atlantic Educational Institute. See Pekala, 1991*c*.)

Pekala RJ (1985*a*). A psychophenomenological approach to mapping and diagramming states of consciousness. *Journal of Religion and Psychical Research*, **8**, 199–214.

Pekala RJ (1985*b*). *The Dimensions of Attention Questionnaire*. West Chester, PA, Mid-Atlantic Educational Institute.

Pekala RJ (1991*a*). Hypnotic types: evidence from a cluster analysis of phenomenal experience. *Contemporary Hypnosis*, **8**, 95–104.

Pekala RJ (1991*b*) *Quantifying consciousness: an empirical approach*. New York, Plenum Press.

Pekala RJ (1991c). *The Phenomenology of Consciousness Inventory.* West Chester, PA, Mid-Atlantic Educational Institute.

Pekala RJ (1995a). A short unobtrusive hypnotic induction for assessing hypnotizability level: I. Development and research. *American Journal of Clinical Hypnosis,* **37**, 271–83.

Pekala RJ (1995b). A short unobtrusive hypnotic induction for assessing hypnotizability level: II. Clinical case reports. *American Journal of Clinical Hypnosis,* **37**, 284–93.

Pekala RJ (2002). Operationalizing 'trance': II: clinical application using a psychophenomenological approach. *American Journal of Clinical Hypnosis,* **44**, 241–55.

Pekala RJ and Bieber SL (1989/90). Operationalizing pattern approaches to consciousness: an analysis of phenomenological patterns of consciousness among individuals of differing susceptibility. *Imagination, Cognition, and Personality,* **9**, 303–20.

Pekala RJ and Ersek B (1992/93). Fire walking versus hypnosis: a preliminary study concerning consciousness, attention, and fire immunity. *Imagination, Cognition, and Personality,* **12**, 207–29.

Pekala RJ and Forbes EJ (1988). Hypnoidal effects associated with several stress management strategies. *Australian Journal of Clinical and Experimental Hypnosis,* **16**, 121–32.

Pekala RJ and Forbes EJ (1997). Types of hypnotically (un)susceptible individuals as a function of phenomenological experience: towards a typology of hypnotic types. *American Journal of Clinical Hypnosis,* **39**, 212–24.

Pekala RJ and Kumar VK (1984). Predicting hypnotic susceptibility by a self-report phenomenological state instrument. *American Journal of Clinical Hypnosis,* **27**, 114–21.

Pekala RJ and Kumar VK (1985). A short program for assessing the equality of two independent correlation matrices. *Educational and Psychological Measurement,* **45**, 175–7.

Pekala RJ and Kumar VK (1986). The differential organization of the structures of consciousness during hypnosis and a baseline condition. *Journal of Mind and Behavior,* **7**, 515–39.

Pekala RJ and Kumar VK (1987). Predicting hypnotic susceptibility via a self-report instrument: a replication. *American Journal of Clinical Hypnosis,* **30**, 57–65.

Pekala RJ and Kumar VK (1989). Patterns of consciousness during hypnosis: relevance to cognition and individual differences. *Australian Journal of Clinical and Experimental Hypnosis,* **17**, 1–20.

Pekala RJ and Kumar VK (2000a). Individual differences in patterns of hypnotic experience across low and high susceptibles. In: RG Kunzendorf and BJ Wallace, eds. *Individual differences in conscious experience.* pp. 309–323. Philadelphia, John Benjamins.

Pekala RJ and Kumar VK (2000b). Operationalizing 'trance': I: rationale and research using a psychophenomenological approach. *American Journal of Clinical Hypnosis,* **43**, 107–35.

Pekala RJ and Kumar VK (2005). States, traits, and provocative debates: the state/nonstate controversy with particular reference to operationalizing 'hypnotism'. *Psychological Hypnosis, Society of Psychological Hypnosis, A Bulletin of Division 30 of the American Psychological Association,* **14**, 13–8.

Pekala RJ and Levine RL (1981). Mapping consciousness: development of an empirical–phenomenological approach. *Imagination, Cognition, and Personality: The Scientific Study of Consciousness,* **1**, 29–47.

Pekala RJ and Levine RL (1982). Quantifying states of consciousness via an empirical–phenomenological approach. *Imagination, Cognition, and Personality: The Scientific Study of Consciousness,* **2**, 51–71.

Pekala RJ and Nagler R (1989). The assessment of hypnoidal states: rationale and clinical application. *American Journal of Clinical Hypnosis,* **31**, 231–36.

Pekala RJ and Wenger CF (1983). Retrospective phenomenological assessment: mapping consciousness in reference to specific stimulus conditions. *Journal of Mind and Behavior,* **4**, 247–74.

Pekala RJ, Steinberg J and Kumar VK (1986). Measurement of phenomenological experience: Phenomenology of Consciousness Inventory. *Perceptual and Motor Skills,* **63**, 983–9.

Pekala RJ, Forbes EJ and Contrisciani PA (1988/89). Assessing the phenomenological effects associated with several stress management strategies. *Imagination, Cognition, and Personality,* **8**, 265–81.

Pekala RJ, Kumar VK and Hand J (1993). Subjective experience, expectancy, and hypnosis: interacting effects. *Contemporary Hypnosis*, **10**, 133–43.

Pekala RJ, Kumar VK and Marcano G (1995). Hypnotic types: a partial replication concerning phenomenal experience. *Contemporary Hypnosis*, **12**, 194–200.

Pekala RJ, Maurer R, Kumar VK, Elliott NC, Masten E, Moon E and Salinger M. (2004). Self-hypnosis relapse prevention training with chronic drug/alcohol users: effects on self-esteem, affect, and relapse. *American Journal of Clinical Hypnosis*, **46**, 281–97.

Pekala RJ, Kumar VK, Maurer R, Elliott–Carter NC and Moon E (2006). 'How deeply hypnotized did I get?' predicting self-reported hypnotic depth from a phenomenological assessment instrument. *International Journal of Clinical and Experimental Hypnosis*, **54**, 316–339.

Pekala RJ, Kumar VK, Maurer R, Elliott–Carter NC, Mullen K and Moon E (2006*b*). *'How deeply hypnotized did I get?' Predicting self-reported hypnotic depth from a phenomenological assessment instrument: A possible replication.* Study in progress.

Rainville P and Price D (2003). Hypnosis phenomenology and the neurobiology of consciousness. *International Journal of Clinical and Experimental Hypnosis*, **51**, 105–29.

Rainville P, Hofbauer RK, Bushnell, MC, Duncan GH and Price DD (2002). Hypnosis modulates activity in brain structures involved in the regulation of consciousness. *Journal of Cognitive Neuroscience*, **14**, 887–901.

Ray WJ (1997). EEG concomitants of hypnotic susceptibility. *International Journal of Clinical and Experimental Hypnosis*, **45**, 301–13.

Robin BR, Kumar VK and Pekala RJ (2005). Direct and indirect scales of hypnotic susceptibility: resistance to therapy and psychometric comparability. *International Journal of Clinical and Experimental Hypnosis*, **53**, 135–47.

Schumaker JF, ed. (1991). *Human suggestibility: advances in theory, research, and application.* New York, Routledge.

Sheehan PW and McConkey KM (1982). *Hypnosis and experience. The exploration of phenomenon and process.* New York, Brunner/Mazel.

Shor RE and Orne EC (1962). *The Harvard Group Scale of Hypnotic Susceptibility.* Palo Alto, CA, Consulting Psychologists Press.

Singer JL and Kolligian J Jr (1987). Personality: developments in the study of private experience. *Annual Review of Psychology*, **38**, 533–74.

Smith E and Miller F (1978). Limits on perception of cognitive processes: a reply to Nisbett and Wilson. *Psychological Review*, **85**, 355–62.

Spearman C (1904). 'General intelligence' objectively determined and measured. *American Journal of Psychology*, **15**, 201–93.

Spearman C (1923). *The nature of 'intelligence' and the principles of cognition.* London, Macmillan.

Spanos NP, Gabora, NJ, Jarrett LE and Gwynn MI (1989). Contextual determinants of hypnotizability and of the relationships between hypnotizability scales. *Journal of Personality and Social Psychology*, **57**, 271–8.

Spiegel D (2005). Multileveling the playing field: altering our state of consciousness to understand hypnosis. *Contemporary Hypnosis*, **22**, 31–3.

Stroop JR (1935). Studies of interference in serial verbal reactions. *Journal of Experimental Psychology*, **18**, 643–62.

Tart CT (1969). *Altered states of consciousness.* New York, Wiley.

Tart CT (1972). *States of consciousness.* New York, Dutton.

Tart CT (1977). Discrete states of consciousness. In: PR Lee, RE Ornstein, D Galin, A Deikman and CT Tart, eds. *Symposium on consciousness.* pp. 89–175. New York, Penguin.

Tellegen A (1979). On measures and concepts of hypnosis. *American Journal of Clinical Hypnosis*, **21**, 219–36.

Tyron WW (1993). Neural networks: I. Theoretical unification through connectionism. *Clinical Psychology Review*, **13**, 341–52.

Vaitl D, Birbaumer N, Gruzelier J, Jamieson GA, Kotchoubey B, *et al.* (2005). Psychobiology of altered states of consciousness. *Psychological Bulletin*, **131**, 98–127.

Varela FJ (1996). Neurophenomenology: a methodological remedy to the hard problem. *Journal of Consciousness Studies*, **3**, 330–50.

Varela FJ (1997). The naturalization of phenomenology as the transcendence of nature. *Alter*, **5**, 355–81.

Varga K, Jösza E, Bányai EI, Gössi-Greuss AC and Kumar VK (2001). Phenomenological experiences associated with hypnotic susceptibility. *International Journal of Clinical and Experimental Hypnosis*, **49**, 19–29.

Wagstaff G and Cole J (2005). Levels of explanation and the concept of a hypnotic state. *Contemporary Hypnosis*, **22**, 14–7.

Weitzenhoffer AM (1974). When is an instruction an instruction? *International Journal of Clinical and Experimental Hypnosis*, **22**, 258–69.

Weitzenhoffer AM (2002). Scales, scales, and more scales. *American Journal of Clinical Hypnosis*, **44**, 209–20.

Weitzenhoffer AM and Hilgard E (1962). *Stanford Hypnotic Susceptibility Scale: form C*. Palo Alto, CA, Consulting Psychologists Press.

Wilkinson L (1988). *SYGRAPH*. Evanston, IL, SYSTAT.

Woodside N, Kumar VK and Pekala RJ (1997). Monotonous percussion drumming and trance postures: a controlled evaluation of phenomenological effects. *Anthropology of Consciousness*, **8**, 69–87.

Woody EZ and McConkey KM (2003). What we don't know about the brain and hypnosis, but need to: a view from the Buckhorn Inn. *International Journal of Clinical and Experimental Hypnosis*, **51**, 309–38.

Woody EZ and Sadler P (2005). On the virtues of virtuosos. *Contemporary Hypnosis*, **22**, 1–7.

Woody EZ, Barnier AJ and McConkey KM (2005). Multiple hypnotizabilities: differentiating the building blocks of hypnotic response. *Psychological Assessment*, **17**, 200–11.

Zinberg NE (1977). The study of consciousness states: problems and progress. In: NE Zinberg, ed. *Alternate states of consciousness*. pp. 1–36. New York, Free Press.

Chapter 11

On the contribution of neurophysiology to hypnosis research: current state and future directions

Adrian Burgess

11.1 Introduction

One of the most interesting and productive developments in hypnosis research over the last 15 years has been the growth in the number of studies that incorporate measures of neurophysiological function. Typically these studies involve samples of extreme participants with high and low susceptibility measured before and after hypnotic induction with a concurrent neurophysiological measure such as the encephalogram (EEG)[1] or functional magnetic resonance imaging (fMRI). These studies, which we might conveniently refer to as provocation tests as hypnosis is used to provoke a change in neural function, have often reported that highly susceptible participants show a change in brain physiology following hypnotic induction that is not seen before induction and is not seen in participants with low susceptibility even after induction. The inference made from these observations, either implicitly or explicitly, is that hypnotic induction effects a state change in the brains of participants who enter a hypnotized state. As such, these studies have been used as some of the most potent ammunition available in the long-standing controversy between state and non-state theorists.

   Although on the face of it, the results of provocation studies and the subsequent logic of the arguments employed in favour of the state theory of hypnosis are persuasive, they are by no means compelling. In this chapter, I will argue that the evidence currently available does not yet discriminate unambiguously between the state and non-state positions because it has not been demonstrated that the neurophysiological changes reported in these provocation studies represent a brain state that is importantly different from that seen during our normal waking lives. I go on to describe the characteristics that a change in neurophysiology would need to possess in order to compel us to accept that a change in brain state has occurred. Furthermore, I suggest that conclusive evidence on the state–non-state question is unlikely to emerge from provocation tests as they currently

---

[1] Throughout the chapter, comments about EEG can be assumed to apply also to magnetoencephalography (MEG).

exist. This is not to say that the question is irresolvable through the application of neuro-physiological measures, but I argue that if progress is to be made, then some critical changes in the way in which provocation studies have been conducted will be required. To be specific, developments from three key are of research will need to be incorporated. These are:

- Psychophysiological theories of consciousness
- The deep structure of the EEG
- The physiological origin of cortical oscillations.

11.2 Neurophysiological correlates of state changes

The results of provocation studies have shown many changes in neurophysiological meas-ures that occur in highly susceptible participants as they move from a waking to a hypno-tized state. These include alterations in background EEG such as increased theta power (Sabourin *et al.* 1990) or enhanced gamma oscillations (De Pascalis 1993), changes in functional connectivity and differences in regional brain activation (e.g. Maquet *et al.* 1999). It is not my intention to review this literature here. Rather, I intend to make a more general point about the nature of state changes and what sort of evidence would be required to compel us to accept that a state change has occurred. I shall argue that even if one accepts the results of the evidence from those provocation studies currently available, their evidence is by no means conclusive in the state versus non-state controversy.

First, it is important to clarify what is meant by a state change. Our brain moves through a continuous sequence of states in its normal waking mode; at one moment I am looking out of the window and perceiving my ginger cat in the garden, the next I remem-ber that I need to send a card for my mother's birthday, the next I am thinking about how to construct this sentence. It is a core assumption of my argument that each of these con-scious experiences, in what William James referred to as the '*stream of consciousness*', is associated with a different brain 'state' (James 1890), i.e. the physiological state of my brain is different in some important way in each of these cases. Furthermore, we can gen-eralize and hypothesize that each unique conscious state is matched by a unique neuro-physiological state and that, in principle, these neurophysiological states could be objectively measured.

This stream of consciousness that involves a continuing sequence of mental states is not, however, what is meant by 'state' in the state–non-state debate in hypnosis. If it were, then to describe hypnosis as a state change would be trivial and mean no more than saying that the hypnotic state differs from other mental states in the same way that one moment in the stream of consciousness differs from the next. Instead, the term 'state change' indicates a more profound idea which is that hypnosis involves an altered state or mode of conscious-ness. That is, there is a fundamental difference in the way the brain works during hypnosis from the way in which it operates during other states such as waking, sleeping or coma. Although all waking states are unique, and are paralleled by a unique neurophysiological state, there must be some feature of the neurophysiology that is common to all but which distinguishes them from other states such as the different stages of sleep or coma.

To avoid terminological confusion, I shall refer to these transient elements of the waking, conscious mind as 'qualic states' (from quale, or qualia) as they are characterized by a specific phenomenological experience. States that represent fundamentally different modes of operation of the brain such as the different stages of sleep, I will refer to as 'meta-states'. Our interest in this chapter is how these meta-states can be characterized and whether hypnosis should be considered to be a distinct meta-state. It is worth noting that not all meta-states consist of qualic states. Although waking, rapid eye movement (REM) sleep and hypnosis are meta-states that involve some element of conscious experience, it is by no means certain that other meta-states do. For example, is it like anything to be in deep sleep or a coma? It seems at least plausible to give the answer that it is not like anything to be in a coma.

It follows from this analysis that showing that some aspect of neurophysiology is measurably different in two conditions is not sufficient to demonstrate the existence of a meta-state. All qualic states are, at least in principle, distinguishable in terms of the concurrent physiological state of the brain, i.e. although a demonstrable difference in neurophysiology is necessary in order to prove the existence of a meta-state, it is not sufficient. What is required is the identification of a neurophysiological process that is not only always coincident with a given meta-state but is only ever coincident with that meta-state. This means that some aspect of neurophysiology must be either qualitatively different from that seen in other meta-states or operates with parameters outside the range of that seen in other meta-states.

The existence of a distinct neurophysiological marker associated with a specific state, however, is not sufficient to identify a distinct meta-state. Consider for example the observation of 'alpha blocking' first made in 1924 by Hans Berger, the discoverer of the EEG (Brazier 1961). He noticed that when his participants closed their eyes, an oscillation in the EEG around 10 Hz was visible that showed a modulating amplitude. He referred to this oscillation as the alpha rhythm and it is the dominant rhythm in the waking EEG in most adults. When his participants opened their eyes, the alpha rhythm disappeared or was 'blocked'. The classical interpretation of this is that the alpha rhythm represents the cortex's resting state and the increase in occipital alpha is due to the visual areas entering a resting state as a result of the loss of visual input that occurs when the eyes are closed. Although this interpretation has been challenged (Cooper et al. 2003), it does seem that the increase in alpha power occurs because some cortical regions are entering a different mode of function. However, from Berger's observations, it appeared that the presence of alpha spindles was uniquely associated with having ones eyes closed and could be used as an unambiguous marker of that state[2]. Does this mean that having one's eyes closed is a distinct meta-state from having them shut? Clearly not, and the reason for that is that although conscious experience with eyes open is distinct from that with eyes closed, the subjective experience is that the two conditions are, with the exception of

---

[2] This is not now believed to be the case as alpha spindles may be seen in other conditions.

visual perception, very similar. That is, the differences in conscious experience are differences between qualic states rather than between meta-states. So, in addition to a reliable neurophysiological marker of a given condition, it is also necessary to have the subjective sense that the two are experiences are of a different type, comparable with the difference between being asleep, being awake or dreaming. The problem with this criterion is that reports cannot be obtained from all meta-states. For example, to get a phenomenological account of being asleep, we need to wake the participant and get them to recall their experience and this potentially introduces distortions of recollection and other biases. Fortunately, this differential responsiveness of participants in different meta-states is in itself useful in helping us discriminate between meta-states. To sum up, in order to define a distinct meta-state it is necessary to for a state to be associated with (1) a distinct phenomenological experience or behaviour and (2) a neurophysiological correlate that is always and only present in that state.

The paradigmatic example of evidence for meta-state changes comes from the sleep–wake cycle. The obvious behavioural changes between sleeping and waking were confirmed and extended by the neurophysiological evidence obtained from concurrent EEG and electromyography (EMG) recordings together with behavioural observations. The stages of sleep can be uniquely characterized in terms of their EEG, EMG and behaviour (including subjective self-report on waking) along with other physiological changes (Niedermeyer 1999).

The first stage of sleep is characterized by theta waves, which are slower (6–8 Hz) and of greater amplitude than the alpha waves (8–13 Hz) that are dominant in the waking state. The difference in neurophysiology measured using the EEG between relaxation and stage 1 sleep is gradual and subtle, and the distinction is supplemented by changes in the subject's behaviour, although interestingly, subjects woken from stage 1 sleep will often claim not to have been asleep at all. Although intuitively we might be inclined to accept that stage 1 sleep and the waking state are distinct meta-states, there does not appear to be any clear qualitative difference in neurophysiology between the two. Instead, the difference is quantitative, as indicated by the slowing in EEG frequency which would be consistent with a continuum between waking and sleep. Perhaps we should consider stage 1 sleep to be a transitional state between waking and sleep stage 2 rather than a distinct meta-state in its own right.

The second stage of sleep involves further slowing of EEG frequency (4–7 Hz) and an increase in EEG amplitude, and is characterized by two electrophysiological phenomena that occur every minute or so, called sleep spindles and K-complexes. Sleep spindles and K-complexes uniquely identify stage 2 sleep and provide a good example of the type of neurophysiological marker that is required to demonstrate the existence of a meta-state.

Sleep stages 3 and 4 involve a further slowing of EEG frequency to delta frequencies (<3 Hz) with a concomitant increase in amplitude. Stages 3 and 4 are distinguished by the proportion of delta wave activity. Subjects awoken form these stages are hard to arouse and typically drowsy and disoriented on first waking. Although stages 3 and 4 can be distinguished from the other stages of sleep, the distinction between them is somewhat arbitrary and there seems little good reason to identify them as separate meta-states.

Rather, stages 3 and 4 might be better considered to be a single meta-state of slow wave sleep (SWS).

The final state of sleep is REM sleep named because of the eye movements that are seen during this stage. REM sleep is also characterized by a sudden and dramatic loss of muscle tone, measured using EMG. Subjects awoken from REM sleep will commonly report dreams, i.e. qualic states. Although dreams are not exclusively reported by subjects awoken from REM sleep, they are much less common during other sleep stages. Interestingly, the EEG recorded during REM is much more like that seen in the waking state. With its unique physiological profile and characteristic qualic states, REM sleep is clearly a distinct meta-state.

So, on the basis of neurophysiology and subjective report, we can identify several distinct meta-states: sleep stage 2, slow wave sleep and REM sleep. Stage 1 sleep is difficult to differentiate from deep relaxation in the waking state on either neurophysiological or phenomenological grounds, and whether it is a distinct meta-state or not is uncertain. Other meta-states occur as the result of pathological conditions such as coma and epileptic seizure, or can be drug induced such as anaesthesia. Furthermore, although we tend to think of the waking state as a distinct meta-state, there is some reason to doubt that this is in fact the case. It is a commonplace observation that monotonous and routine activities (e.g. driving a well-known route) can be completed, apparently safely and accurately, in the conscious waking state, without any subsequent recall of the actions performed while doing so. Such absent states might represent separate meta-states of consciousness, and daydreaming and meditative states might be other examples. Although good neurophysiological evidence is lacking in each case, it seems prudent to consider the possibility that the waking state may be fractionated into more than one meta-state.

Using the definition of sleep stages as a model, does hypnosis meet the criteria of being a distinct meta-state? For some individuals at least, the phenomenological experience of hypnosis is unlike any other meta-state, so hypnosis passes the subjective experience criterion. Self-report however, is prone to error, bias and outside influence, as well as deliberate distortion so, in the absence of corroborative neurophysiological evidence, such data are unpersuasive. The second criterion, that there should be a specific neurophysiological correlate of hypnosis, is more problematic, although there are many candidates. Consider, for example, the proposal that hypnosis is associated with increased levels of theta activity and assume that this finding is reliable and robust. Would an elevated level of theta be sufficient to justify defining hypnosis as a distinct meta-state? The answer is yes only if the elevation in theta is seen during the hypnotic state and only in that state. Unfortunately this is not the case, as elevations in theta occur during relaxation and stage 1 sleep but also during certain demanding cognitive processes. At best, this evidence could be considered comparable with the neurophysiological evidence suggesting a distinction between relaxation and stage 1 sleep where there is no clear boundary between the two. Certainly there is no compelling evidence for the existence of a distinct meta-state. The same argument applies to the role of the alpha rhythm and gamma oscillations in hypnosis. Although statistically significant differences in these oscillations have often been reported at the group level, in none of these cases is there evidence either of a qualitative difference between waking and hypnosis or of a quantitative difference outside of the range that might be expected during normal waking thought.

Some of the best evidence for hypnosis being a distinct meta-state comes from work showing that following hypnotic induction, highly susceptible participants show changes both in perception and in an associated neurophysiological marker. For example, painful stimuli reliably produce a somatosensory evoked potential that can be recorded at the scalp using standard EEG equipment. However, both the experience of pain and the form of the evoked response can be modified by hypnotic suggestion in susceptible individuals (Crawford et al. 1998). Similarly, hypnotic suggestion can be used to induce auditory hallucinations and an alteration in the auditory evoked response (Hogan et al. 1984). Kosslyn et al. (2000) have even shown that hypnotic suggestion can alter colour perception and simultaneously alter localized brain activity, as measured using positron emission tomography (PET). Persuasive though this evidence appears, it does not provide convincing evidence that hypnosis is a distinct meta-state. First, the neurophysiological correlates are different in each case, which means that they are neither necessary nor sufficient for the hypnosis to occur. Secondly, it is quite possible that these phenomena could also be obtained through manipulations of the normal waking state such as suggestion, focused attention or distraction. One possible response to this is that such manipulations *are* hypnosis, but if so there seems little reason to argue that hypnosis is a distinct meta-state.

It would of course be unreasonable to expect state theorists to prove that hypnotic phenomena such as induced analgesia cannot be shown in the normal waking state as this would require them to prove a negative. Rather, the solution should be to suggest a mechanism that is common to all hypnotic states and to test theory empirically. An exemplary example of this approach is provided by Egner et al. (2005). They tested Woody and Bowers' (1994) dissociated control theory (DCT) of hypnosis. This suggests that highly hypnotizable individuals are particularly adept at focusing attention at baseline, but that their attentional control is compromised following hypnosis due to a decoupling between conflict monitoring and cognitive control processes. On the basis of earlier functional imaging studies, Egner et al. (2005) attributed these functions to activity in the prefrontal cortex; specifically, they proposed that the lateral prefrontal cortex is responsible for cognitive control processes and the anterior cingulate cortex for conflict monitoring.

Egner et al. (2005) measured regional cerebral blood flow in the anterior cingulate cortex and the lateral frontal cortex during a Stroop task using event-related functional magnetic resonancce imaging (fMRI). The Stroop task is a well-known cognitive paradigm that can be used to manipulate both cognitive control and conflict monitoring. Participants of low and high hypnotic susceptibility performed the Stroop task in the waking state and after hypnotic induction. fMRI revealed that highly susceptibile participants showed a conflict-related increase in activity in the anterior cingulate cortex in the hypnosis condition compared with baseline. Furthermore, although there was evidence of control-related activation in the lateral frontal cortex, this did not differ between groups or hypnosis conditions. In a second experiment, Egner *et al.* (2005) recorded the EEG using the same participants undergoing the same experimental paradigm. They found a decrease in EEG functional connectivity in the gamma band between frontal midline and left lateral scalp sites in highly susceptible participants after hypnotic induction. The authors interpreted their results as being consistent with their hypothesis that the lateral frontal cortex controls cognitive control, the anterior cingulate cortex controls response monitoring and hypnosis induces dissociation between the two in highly susceptible individuals.

Perhaps the most impressive aspect of this study is that the authors take a psychological theory of hypnosis (i.e. that hypnotic states are a result of dissociation between two aspects of executive control) and derive testable neurophysiological predictions from it. This is particularly challenging as most psychophysiological models of hypnosis are only partially operationalized in terms of physiology. Concepts such as 'frontal inhibition' and 'neurophysiological flexibility' are more metaphor than hard physiological reality. Consequently, there remains considerable ambiguity as to how these concepts can be measured and the theories tested.

Certainly, the loss of functional connectivity between the medial and lateral prefrontal cortices, interpreted as a decoupling between conflict monitoring and cognitive control, has the potential to explain a broad range of hypnotic phenomena. Furthermore, if this loss of functional connectivity between medial and lateral prefrontal sites were found to be common to all hypnotic states, then the case in favour of hypnotic states as distinct meta-states would be compelling. However, the main difficulty in producing psychophysiological theories of this type is to match a psychological function to a neurophysiological process. Egner *et al.* (2005) make strong claims about the meaning of increased cerebral blood flow in the anterior cingulate cortex and the lateral prefrontal cortex, but the functions of these areas are by no means well understood. Similarly, with the measures of EEG coherence between central and lateral scalp sites; not only is the significance of gamma coherence unknown, but the inferred localization is at best speculative. This should not be interpreted as a counsel of despair, however, but as an acknowledgement that between psychology and neurophysiology there remains a wide explanatory gap. Studies like that by Egner *et al.* (2005) are worthwhile attempts at bridging that gap and as such are to be commended.

11.3 **Psychophysiological theories of consciousness**

If hypnosis is an altered state of consciousness that differs in some important way from the normal conscious waking state, then it follows that a fuller understanding of the nature of the hypnotic state would be facilitated by a comprehensive theory of consciousness. Over the last 15 years there has been an explosion of interest in the scientific study of consciousness and, although no consensus has emerged, certain themes such as the importance of functional connectivity and the role of cortical oscillatory activity have emerged strongly.

The starting point for most theories of consciousness is the binding problem (Treisman 1996). Put simply, the binding problem concerns the obvious dissociation between our subjective sense of a unified and coherent conscious experience and what neuroscience has led us to believe about the functional organization of the brain. In essence, the brain appears to consist of large numbers of localized specialist functional units, so, for example, our perception of the visual world is achieved by spatially separate units dealing with colour, movement, orientation, shape, and so on. Clearly, the output from these specialist modules must somehow be unified (i.e. 'bound') to give us our conscious perception of a unified and coherent visual world, but the mechanism by which this unity is achieved is not yet understood. Work by electrophysiologists making intracerebral recordings in animals suggested synchronous cortical oscillations around 40 Hz as a candidate mechanism for this binding. For example, Gray *et al.* (1989) took recordings from the visual cortex in cats from neurons that were sensitive to different objects in the visual field. When the objects moved congruently, giving the gestalt that the objects were connected, recordings at the two sites synchronously oscillated at 40 Hz. When the objects moved independently and the gestalt was lost, the 40 Hz oscillation was lost too.

On the basis of this and similar work, Crick and Koch (2003) suggested that 40 Hz oscillations were critical to the binding mechanism and consequently for consciousness itself. These ideas were supported by work by Tallon-Baudry *et al.* (1996) who showed that visual feature binding in humans measured using the scalp-recorded EEG was also associated with increases in the 40 Hz (i.e. gamma) frequency range.

If gamma oscillations are critical for normal consciousness, it is a natural step to consider how they might be different in altered states of consciousness, such as hypnosis. DePascalis (Chapter 5) provides a comprehensive review of this work and shows conclusively that gamma oscillations are altered by hypnotic induction. However, there are good reasons to doubt the critical role of gamma oscillations in consciousness. For example, gamma oscillations are seen during REM sleep and under anaesthesia, suggesting that even if they are necessary for consciousness to emerge, they are not sufficient. Certainly Crick and Koch have long since withdrawn from their advocacy of 40 Hz oscillations as a neural correlate of consciousness, and few adherents of the strong form of this theory remain.

The suggestion that cortical oscillations have a critical role in visual feature binding and consciousness, however, remains alive and well. For example, Llinas and Ribary (2001) have emphasized the role of thalamo-cortical loops for the transference of information between different cortical regions, and these thalamo-cortical loops are the physiological basis of the cortical oscillations that we record using the EEG. Transfer of information between cortical sites is controlled by two critical thalamic nuclei: the intralaminar nucleus and the reticular nucleus (Bogen 1995). Unlike the other thalamic nuclei, which have reciprocal connections with well-defined cortical areas, the intralaminar nucleus projects widely throughout the thalamus and the reticular nucleus projects diffusely across the cortex. Consequently, the intralaminar nucleus modulates communication within the thalamus and the reticular nucleus modulates communication between the thalamus and the cortex. Activity in the thalamo-cortical system is further modulated by ascending inputs from the reticular activating system (ARAS) which controls the sleep–wake cycle. It is of note that there are only three brain regions where lesions result in loss of consciousness (i.e. coma) and they are the ARAS, the reticular nucleus and the intralaminar nucleus (Bogen 1995). The interaction between the ARAS and the thalamo-cortical system is responsible for the key meta-states of waking, slow wave sleep and REM sleep; the same processes generate oscillatory activity in the brain that can be detected as the EEG. This intimate one-to-one relationship between meta-states and cerebral oscillations is one of the main reasons why so many researchers involved in studying hypnosis as an altered state of consciousness have shown such an enduring interest in EEG research.

Despite two decades of research, no EEG marker of hypnosis has yet been found. Claims have been made for the critical role of alpha, theta and gamma oscillations, but none show the specificity required to meet the criteria described above. In short, the differences in EEG power reported are neither great enough nor specific enough to qualify. This does not mean to say that an EEG marker of the hypnotic state will not be found, and there are several candidate markers that should be examined that will be discussed in the next section.

The importance of functional connectivity in the brain follows automatically from an understanding of the binding problem. If information from localized functionally specialized units is to be bound together, there must be a mechanism to achieve this connectivity and there is good evidence for the importance of long-range gamma synchrony for normal cognitive processing from scalp-recorded EEG in humans (Miltner *et al.* 1999; Rodriguez *et al.* 1999). The study described above performed by Egner *et al.* (2005) provides a good example of using gamma synchrony to test a hypothesis about functional connectivity in hypnosis, but few others have applied this approach to date. Whether the gamma oscillations are special in this respect is more doubtful, and synchrony in other frequency ranges may be no less important (von Stein and Sarnthein 2000).

Synchronous oscillations are not the only feature of the EEG that has been linked to consciousness. The spatio-temporal organization of the EEG has also been considered to play an important role in conscious processes. It is well known to researchers in the field that the EEG displays a striking spatio-temporal structure but, despite this, it remains a much under-researched area. The spatio-temporal structure can be readily observed by viewing the ongoing EEG as a series of frequency-specific power maps instead of as the usual multichannel time series. After a few minutes, it becomes apparent even to a naïve observer that similar topographical patterns repeat over and over again.

More rigorously, Lehmann in his pioneering work on the spatial organization of the EEG came up with the concept of microstates (Lehmann and Koenig 1997). These are scalp distributions of EEG power that appear and remain stable for short periods of some tens of milliseconds. Two features of these microstates are significant. First, only a relatively small set of microstates out of the very large number of possible microstates are ever seen. Secondly, they are reproducible and appear to reflect a specific functional state of the cortex. Microstates are influenced by the nature of cognitive and affective states of the cortex and are known to be abnormal in certain pathological condition such as schizophrenia.

The critical importance of the spatio-temporal organization of the EEG was also discovered in a completely different context by Walter Freeman. In a series of strikingly original studies, he investigated olfactory conditioning in rabbits (Freeman 2000). He was able to show that the pattern of amplitude-modulated EEG in the olfactory bulb of rabbits depended upon the conditioned stimulus presented, the rabbit itself and its conditioning history. That is, different aromas showed distinct patterns of EEG that were unique to each rabbit and which varied over time in ways related to the rabbit's experiences. In short, these spatio-temporal patterns showed many features of what would be expected in a neural representation of a qualic state. Perhaps the key idea here is that the neural representation was not encoded in terms of spatially localized activity but as a spatially distributed field. Freeman has gone on to develop his work to larger scales and extend it into work with humans, and currently advocates what he refers to as a field approach to understanding neo-cortical dynamics (Freeman 2005).

One recent theory, Gerald Edelman and Guilo Tononi's 'dynamic core hypothesis', provides a thought-provoking synthesis of ideas about functional connectivity and the spatio-temporal organization of information flow in the brain that makes an important contribution to the study of consciousness (Tononi and Edelman 1998; Edelman and Tononi 2000). As they point out, although functional connectivity between different brain regions is often presumed to be a necessary prerequisite for the emergence of consciousness, functional connectivity is not unique to conscious states and, consequently, functional connectivity per se cannot be a neural correlate of consciousness. One of the key aspects of our experience of consciousness is, as William James noted, that it is not a thing but a process or stream that changes from moment to moment and in which each conscious moment appears unified and coherent within itself yet is differentiated from other conscious moments (James 1890). The dynamic core hypothesis is an attempt to account for this experience of consciousness by specifying the nature of functional coordination between neural groupings that are needed for consciousness to emerge. Specifically, the dynamic core hypothesis proposes that a group of neurons can contribute to conscious experience only if it is a part of a functional cluster that achieves high levels of integration in hundreds of milliseconds and can only sustain conscious experience if this functional cluster is highly differentiated from other neurons. This combination of high integration in the context of high differentiation is called neural complexity. From the dynamic core hypothesis, conscious states can be distinguished from non-conscious ones in that consciousness is associated with high levels of neural complexity. One of the key advantages of the dynamic core hypothesis over competing models is that the concept of neural complexity is explicitly mathematically defined and can, in principle, be estimated using any measure of neural functional activation. Consequently, the hypothesis is testable.

In an unpublished study Burgess, Gruzelier and Crawford performed a provocation study with 12 participants who were highly susceptible and 11 participants who had low susceptibility, and measured EEG in the resting state using a 28-channel EEG system. It was our expectation that neural complexity would be lower in highly susceptible participants than in those with low susceptibility following hypnotic induction. There were no significant differences in neural complexity between the two groups of participants in the pre-induction baseline but, as expected, following hypnotic induction, the highly susceptible individuals showed a significantly lower level of neural complexity than those with low susceptibility in the theta frequency range. However, the highly susceptible

individuals also showed an increase in neural complexity at temporal sites for high frequencies (beta and gamma). So although the predictions of the dynamic core hypothesis
were supported in part, the pattern of change in neural complexity was more complicated
than that anticipated by the theory.

The dynamic core hypothesis has been tested in other contexts too and although there
has been some support for it (Burgess *et al.* 2003; Branston *et al.* 2005), other studies have
failed to confirm its predictions (van Putten and Stam 2001; van Cappellen van Walsum
et al. 2003). Overall, it seems that the dynamic core hypothesis in its original; format is not
correct but its emphasis on the spatio-temporal organization of patterns of functional
connectivity represents an important advance.

Although much recent interest has focused on gamma oscillations, there is no good
reason to suppose that these have a special or privileged role in hypnosis. Indeed the relationship between oscillations in different frequency ranges should also be considered.
There is good evidence, for example, from recordings in animals for a relationship
between the gamma and theta rhythms. In animals, bursts of gamma oscillations are
nested within the theta rhythm such that gamma occurs at the peaks of the theta cycle,
i.e. the theta rhythm, acts as a carrier wave for gamma oscillations. The reasons for this
are not well understood but it may be a way of improving the signal to noise ratio such
that the theta wave indicates when the information carried by the gamma oscillations
will be transmitted. Lisman (2005) claims this relationship is critical to encoding information in the cortex and is the reason why our working memory capacity is 7 ± 2 items
as seven gamma oscillations will fit into the peak of a theta wave. Whether this speculation is correct or not, there is certainly evidence of gamma/theta coordination in the
human EEG that has been associated with qualitatively distinct phenomenological states
(Burgess and Ali 2002).

To summarize, although there is no consensus as to how consciousness emerges from
activity in the central nervous system, certain features and processes are common to many
theories. These include the importance of cortical oscillations, the thalamo-cortical system, functional connectivity and the spatio-temporal structure of the EEG. For these reasons, it would seem prudent to focus on these phenomena in any attempt to determine if
and how hypnosis differs from the waking state.

11.4 The deep structure of the EEG

In this section, I shall start by examining the most commonly used techniques for the
analysis of cortical oscillations and explain why they are inadequate for the task. I shall
then go on to outline some new analytical tools that I believe have much to offer
hypnosis researchers.

Most EEG studies rely on either spectral analysis using the Fourier transform or the
method of event-related potentials (ERPs). Fourier analysis is a powerful tool for determining the power in a time series within a defined frequency range, whereas ERPs capture the
average EEG response to an event (usually, the presentation of a stimulus or a response by
the participant). ERPs in particular have been an astonishingly fruitful tool for psychologists who have found the method extremely useful for testing between competing

psychological hypotheses. In contrast, ERP analysis has proved to be an infuriating and frustrating tool for those who want to understand the physiological processes that underpin these psychological functions. In many, but by no means all cases, the functional significance of the ERP peaks and the neural sources that generate them still remain obscure.

Perhaps the primary reason for this is that ERPs confound frequency, amplitude and phase information. It is commonly believed that the ERP represents a means of extracting an evoked signal from the background 'noise', i.e. the ongoing EEG. The idea is that averaging the signal over many trials will ensure that the noise cancels out, leaving only the evoked signal. Persuasive though this idea seems, it has long been known that, in some cases at least, the ERP is not an evoked signal overlaid on the background EEG but is a phase reorganization of the background EEG (Sayers *et al.* 1974). This being the case, then measuring the peaks and troughs of the ERP is simply an indirect method of studying the frequency-dependent phase changes that are the real source of the ERP[3].

The primary problem with both these approaches, however, is that after more than 50 years of neurophysiological hypnosis research (Ravitz 1950), there is still no resolution to the state–non-state debate and it must be doubted whether these methods will ever decide the issue. I believe that the reason for this failure is that both Fourier analysis and ERPs are looking at surface features of the EEG. The EEG is generated by a highly complex neural system, and the more that we learn about it, the more it becomes clear that it there are multifarious layers of deep structure in the signal (e.g. multiple, distributed correlated sources, operating across a broad range of frequencies) that we have no access to using conventional methods of analysis. Of course, meta-states can be identified on the basis of the surface structure of the EEG (cf. the stages of sleep) but, if any such obvious marker of the hypnotic state existed, it would surely have been identified by now. Consequently, the best hope for progress lies in adopting methods of analysis that permit us to see past the surface structure of the EEG and which will allow us to probe the terra incognito of the deep structure.

11.4.1 **Source localization**

The most obvious reason to probe the deep structure of the EEG is to try to identify the anatomical locations that generate the EEG. Unfortunately, the ability to localize sources accurately using the EEG is very limited because any given distribution of EEG across the scalp could potentially have been generated by an infinite number of possible sources within in the brain (i.e. the inverse problem). Although many different methods exist that can estimate the location of sources, these are all based on simplifying assumptions of one sort or another, and it is unknown how appropriate or realistic these may be (Darvas *et al.* 2004).

---

[3] This may not be true in all cases but because of the way in which ERPs are calculated it is impossible to disentangle the contributions of evoked signals and phase reorganization.

Of course, finding that a specific brain area is selectively and specifically either active or silent during hypnosis would provide good evidence that hypnosis is a distinct meta-state, but there seems to be no more reason to hope to find a 'hypnosis centre' than there is find a 'consciousness centre'. In each case, these states probably emerge from distributed activity throughout the thalamo-cortical system, and it would seem more fruitful to examine the pattern of functional connectivity associated with the hypnotic state rather than look for specific areas of localized activity.

11.4.2 Spatio-temporal decomposition of the EEG

An alternative approach to exploring the deep structure of the EEG is to apply statistical methods, such as principal component analysis (PCA) and factor analysis (FA). These methods take a multivariate data set such as the multichannel EEG and attempt to decompose it into its fundamental elements, or factors. Although PCA and FA have a proven track record in psychometrics, when applied to ERP data, simulation studies have shown they often fail (Chapman and McCrary 1995). For this reason, PCA and FA have little to offer us in the exploration of the deep structure of the EEG.

Recently, an alternative method of exploring the deep structure of the EEG has attracted a good deal of attention: independent component analysis (ICA). ICA is a method to solve the problem of blind source separation. In the case of EEG, the scalp-recorded EEG is conceived to be the product of an unknown linear combination of statistically independent sources. Provided the number of EEG channels exceeds the number of independent sources, then ICA will separate those sources and provide a spatio-temporal decomposition of the signal. That is, ICA will reveal not only the topographical distribution of EEG that each source produces across the scalp but also its time course. ICA does not, however, solve the inverse problem, and the topographical distributions for each source should be treated with the same caution with regard to localization as any other EEG map. A good example of ICA in use is provided by Makeig et al. (2002) and more details of the method are available in Aapo et al. (2001).

There are some important limitations, however. One of these is that ICA will produce a source for each electrode or sensor entered into the analysis and, for a single case, there is no way to know which ones are important unless one has a clear a priori expectation about either the topography or time course. For group data, the problem is less severe because the critical sources can be identified because they are common to all or at least many of the individuals in the sample. The second problem is that ICA assumes the sources to be independent, which will not usually be true. However, this only becomes a problem when the level of covariance is high and persists throughout the time period examined. In fact, simulations show that ICA, unlike PCA, performs remarkably well provided the number of sources is not too high and the data are not too noisy (Lin et al. 2003; James and Hesse 2005). Overall, ICA represents a major advance in EEG analysis and provides a useful window onto the deep structure of the EEG, and as such should prove a useful tool in hypnosis research.

In many ways, partial least squares (PLS) analysis is ideally suited for the analysis of hypnosis provocation studies. PLS is a robust method for extracting spatio-temporal changes in a signal that are optimally related to the varying demands of an experimental paradigm (McIntosh *et al.* 1996; Lobaugh *et al.* 2001). Unlike ICA, it is an explicitly statistical approach designed to be used with experimental data obtained from one or more study groups. PLS produces latent variables that are associated with a specified proportion of the total covariance between a multichannel signal and an experimental design, comparable with the proportion of variance that can be attributed to the components extracted in a PCA. Like the components in ICA, each latent variable is described in terms of both the topographical distribution of EEG that it produces across the scalp and also its time course. Again, like ICA, PLS does not solve the inverse problem, and the inferences about the location of EEG sources on the basis of these topographies should be made with caution. However, the overall statistical significance of each latent variable can be determined as well as its significance at particular times and scalp locations.

One problem that may occur with PLS is that the latent variables extracted do not always match onto the experimental design in a readily interpretable way. When this occurs, it suggests that the experimental manipulation has not been successful, the effect size is too small to produce reliable neurophysiological effects or the understanding of the paradigm used is deficient. To overcome the problem of interpretability, a modified version of PLS (non-rotated PLS) has been developed in which explicit hypotheses about the relationship between the experimental design and the signal can be tested, and this should prove useful for mature research areas where explicit theoretical models are available (McIntosh and Lobaugh 2004).

In a recent simulation study, Lin *et al.* (2003) compared PCA, ICA and PLS in terms of their ability to detect the latent structure in simulated event-related fMRI data. In general, PLS performed somewhat better than either PCA or ICA, and was more robust to the effects of a low signal to noise ratio. Although these simulations were designed around event-related fMRI, they possessed the same four-dimensional structure (3D space and time) as EEG/ERP, and the results, therefore, are likely to generalize to the electrophysiology case too.

Both ICA and PLS analyses are powerful tools to help us explore the deep structure of the EEG, and both have an important role in hypnosis research. However, its explicit link with experimental design, together with its superior robustness and relative ease of use, makes PLS a particularly suitable instrument for use in EEG in provocation studies.

11.4.3 Functional connectivity

The role of cortical oscillations in functional connectivity and their relevance to consciousness should by now be clear, but the way in which functional connectivity should be measured remains uncertain. Although there are methods for measuring functional connectivity based on fMRI and PET, they provide at best a very indirect means of assessing cortical oscillatory activity and also have poor temporal resolution. The most commonly used EEG-based measure, coherence, also suffers from poor temporal resolution but does provide an effective summary of the frequency-specific phase consistency between two times series. As phase synchrony appears to be the means by which functional connectivity is achieved in the cortex, this means that coherence should be ideally suited to the task in hand. Unfortunately, there are several problems with the traditional coherence measure that limit its usefulness, including poor temporal resolution, volume conduction and linearity.

Recent developments using autoregressive models make it possible to measure coherence with much improved temporal resolution (Schack *et al.* 1999) and, even using Granger causality, to determine the direction of information flow (see Pereda *et al.* 2005 for a comprehensive review). The problem of volume conduction is more fundamental, however, and consequently more difficult to resolve. Volume conduction refers to the fact that two or more spatially separate electrode sites may appear to be functionally connected even though there is no flow of information between them. This can occur as a result of the poor spatial localization of the EEG in that both electrodes may reflect activity from a single source.

When coherence is measured between electrodes, or sensors, it is referred to as a '*sensor space*' analysis and will typically overestimate the '*true*' functional connectivity. The natural solution to this problem is to apply source localization methods to the EEG signal to identify the specific brain regions that are generating the EEG signal prior to calculating coherence, and this is referred to as a '*source space*' analysis. Unfortunately, as noted above, using source localization introduces additional simplifications and assumptions that might not always be warranted.

Another approach to minimize the effects of volume conduction involves using latent variables obtained from ICA or PLS analyses. These do not allow a true 'source space' analysis as the localization of the sources is not resolved, but it does permit the calculation of phase synchrony between latent variables which, in this context, might be thought of as 'virtual' sources. It should be remembered, however, that both PLS and ICA make assumptions about the nature of the covariance that exists between the latent variables that are extracted, and this will have implications for the type of synchrony relationships that can be observed using this approach.

Even if sources could be identified reliably, then it is by no means certain that measuring the extent of functional connectivity between them would be sufficient. The reason for this is that sources are typically identified by localizing an area of the brain where there is a change in power between two or more experimental conditions of interest, but it is quite possible for changes in functional connectivity to occur without any concurrent power changes. Indeed, coherence and most other measures of functional connectivity are independent of any changes that might have occurred in EEG power.

At present, the pros and con of '*source space*' versus '*sensor space*' analyses are finely balanced and it would seem prudent to consider both avenues of research. In some cases, there may be clear *a priori* predictions about the localization of EEG sources. For example, the study by Egner *et al.* (2005) predicted changes in coherence between the dorsolateral prefrontal cortex and the anterior cingulate following hypnotic induction. Although they reported a change in coherence between electrodes at left and midline frontal scalp sites (i.e. the sensor space), which they interpreted as being consistent with their hypothesis, their evidence would have been more compelling had they found the same change in coherence between the predicted anatomical locations instead (i.e. the source space).

In many other cases, however, aspects of the deep structure of the EEG can be examined without recourse to anatomical hypotheses, and then localization and source space analyses, with all the additional simplifications and assumptions they entail, might not be the most productive way forward. Instead, the distinction between waking and hypnosis should be sought in some difference between the two in terms of the parameters that govern the generation of the EEG in the two meta-states. For this purpose, analysis in the sensor space may be more appropriate.

The concept of phase synchronization, which coherence is well suited to assess, only makes sense in periodic, oscillatory systems. It does not, for example, address the possibility of coordination across frequencies either between signals or within the same signal such as the gamma/theta nesting noted above. Within-signal coordination across frequencies has been most actively studied in the field of anaesthesiology. Bispectral analysis is a Fourier-based method for examining the coupling between frequencies in different ranges (i.e. bicoherence) at the same electrode site (Schanze and Eckhorn 1997). Like coherence, bispectral analysis can be used to produce an index of coupling strength but, unlike coherence which measures frequency-specific coupling between recording sites, bicoherence examines the coupling between frequencies at the same recording site. It has long been known that bicoherence can be used as an index of the level of consciousness (Kearse et al. 1994), and anaesthetists wishing to ensure that their patients are adequately anaesthetized are now able to use a commercially available system in part based on this method called the Bispectral Index (BIS®). The BIS® is a patented technology produced by Aspect Medical Systems that uses an algorithm that relates the bicoherence in the EEG, the ratio of EEG power in the delta (1–4 Hz) and beta (13–30 Hz) frequency ranges and the proportion of the EEG that is isoelectric (i.e. electrical silence) (March and Muir 2005). Although extensively used by anaesthesiologists, bispectral analysis has been relatively neglected in other areas of EEG research but, because of its relevance to level of consciousness, there seems to be a natural role for this approach in hypnosis research.

More generally, signals can show dependency when they are neither oscillatory nor periodic. This raises the concept of generalized synchronicity, which is said to exist whenever the prediction of one signal is improved by knowledge of another. There are several candidate measures of generalized synchronicity, but one that is robust and has other good properties is the synchronization likelihood (SL) measure (Stam 2005). The SL, based on well-founded methods from non-linear dynamics, can be thought of as a generalization of coherence that is sensitive not only to phase synchronization but also to any form of dependency between signals. SL can also be calculated across time and sensor channels with much greater flexibility than is possible using coherence. Its only drawback in comparison with coherence is the greater computational time, but this is not prohibitive in most contexts. Its use in EEG research has now been established, and it is worth considering for use whenever a measure of functional connectivity is required. Regardless of which measure of connectivity is used, the issue of volume conduction remains and the decision to study the 'source' or the 'sensor' space will still need to be decided.

Although measures of functional connectivity are likely to prove useful, it should not be expected that hypnosis can be differentiated from the waking state either by the overall amount of synchronization or by the simple presence or absence of synchronization between specific locali\ations. Instead, the difference should be sought in some more fundamental characteristic of the pattern of connectivity in the two states. Tononi *et al*.'s (1994) concept of 'neural complexity' provides one such example, but this is problematic for a number of reasons. First, the theory from which the measure derives, the dynamic core hypothesis, has received mixed support from the handful of empirical studies that have been reported to date. Secondly, the calculation of neural complexity requires that the mutual information between every possible bipartition of the system in question is calculated. Even with relatively small set sizes, and set size here refers to the number of electrodes or sensors, the number of bipartitions rapidly escalates and the calculation becomes impractical.

An alternative approach involves studying the patterns of connectivity in EEG data in terms of graph theory measures. This is a general approach to the study of networks that has been applied in many other fields and which involves an analysis of the topological pattern of connections observed. This approach has been responsible for the discovery of 'small world' networks (Watts and Strogatz 1998) in which most elements in a system occur in clusters of intercommunicating nodes with a few sparse connections between clusters. Small world networks can be contrasted with random networks and highly structured networks. Random networks, so called because the elements in the system are connected at random, show little clustering (i.e. have a low 'cluster index') but, on average, each element can be connected with each other element through only a few intermediary steps (i.e. have a low 'characteristic path length'). Highly structured networks, in contrast, typically show a highly clustered pattern of connections (i.e. high cluster index) and much larger average distances between elements (i.e. high characteristic path length). Networks, therefore, can be characterized by these two parameters, cluster index and characteristic path length. The small world network, with its high cluster index and low characteristic path length, shows a combination of the features of random and structured networks that turns out to have a number of interesting properties.

Small world networks are commonly found in the natural world, and perhaps the most familiar example comes from human social networks. Consider your own network of friends and colleagues. Most people you know will know other people you know (i.e. social networks cluster) but a few, typically an overseas friend or colleague, may be known to you but few others in your core group. These long-distance links provide a bridge between your cluster of associates and that of your overseas friend and, in this way, it is claimed that everyone alive today can be connected to anyone else by no more than six intermediaries (i.e. six degrees of separation). Networks with these properties have the interesting property that most communication is local but communication between clusters is very efficient. Anatomical studies have shown that the neuronal structure of the brain shows 'small world' properties (Sporns *et al*. 2000) and there is some evidence that that is true in conscious states (Stam 2005). It is of note that systems with small world properties, also show high neural complexity. To date, no one has measured these 'small world' properties in other meta-states but there is good reason to expect that the pattern of connectivity will differ from that seen in the waking state, and it would seem worthwhile also to investigate these properties in hypnotic states.

Another deep structure that has recently been reported is the pattern of alternating synchronization and desynchronization that can be seen in the EEG. Far from being haphazard, it appears that there are significant temporal correlations over all time scales. Stam and De Bruin (2004) studied the time course of global synchrony measured using SL. Temporal correlations were assessed using detrended fluctuation analysis (DFA), a robust method for studying the correlation structure of a time series over a wide range of time scales. DFA gives two important measures: the characteristic time scale and the gradient. The characteristic time scale indicates whether there is any regularity in the cycle of increases and decreases seen, whereas the gradient indicates the type of temporal correlation observed. If the gradient is 0.5, then the signal is uncorrelated; if it is >0.5 the signal shows positive long-range correlations such that large amplitude fluctuations in the time scale tend to be followed by large fluctuations, and vice versa; and if it is <0.5 then the correlations are negative. Gradient values of approximately 1 are of particular interest as they are associated with 1/f noise and self-organized criticality (SOC) (Jensen 1998) which it is hypothesized indicates a near-optimal state for information processing. Stam (2005) found that in humans during rest, there was no evidence of a characteristic time scale in any of the frequency ranges studied, which means that there is no regular pattern in the increases and decreases in global synchronization that were observed. Furthermore, there was clear evidence of strong positive correlation across all time scales for all frequency ranges, which in the case of the gamma and beta ranges had a value of 1, indicating near-optimal information processing.

The importance of this is that DFA is able to reveal some of the deep structure in the temporal pattern of the global synchronization in human EEG. In the waking state, the pattern of long-range correlations and lack of a characteristic time scale are critically poised, in some frequency ranges at least, to produce highly efficient information processing. Given that other meta-states, including hypnosis, are associated with altered information processing, they should also show differences in their long-range correlations, and possibly their characteristic time scale. To date, these temporal characteristic of the EEG have only been examined in the waking state, but it would seem worthwhile to explore them in other meta-states and in hypnosis too.

11.4.4 **Non-linear dynamics**

The final approach to exploring the deep structure of the EEG that I shall mention is non-linear dynamical analysis, sometimes referred to as 'chaos theory'. A dynamic system is any system that changes over time and whose evolution can be characterized by (1) its current state and (2) the way in which it changes i.e. its dynamics. Some dynamic systems settle down to a steady state, others settle into steady periodic motion, others show quasi-periodic behaviour and others are chaotic. Chaotic systems are always non-linear and are characterized by their sensitivity to initial conditions and their apparent unpredictability. Sensitivity to initial conditions means that very small changes in the initial state of the system can rapidly have very large effects on the evolution of the system, which accounts for their unpredictability. This dependence on initial conditions is often described as the 'butterfly effect' from the idea that even a tiny cause, such as the movement of a butterfly's wing, could affect the weather across the world.

Chaos theory emerged after a long gestation in the early 1980s with the realization that apparently chaotic systems could be deterministic (although non-linear), inherently unpredictable and very simple (i.e. low dimensional). Furthermore, it was discovered that it was possible to take observations of a non-linear dynamical system and infer some of its key characteristics, i.e. for the first time, apparently chaotic processes could be studied in a way that illuminated the processes that caused them. It is beyond the scope of this chapter to cover this field in any detail, but the interested reader is referred to Stam (2005) for an excellent review of its history, application to EEG and important recent developments.

Non-linear dynamical analysis provides the tools to characterize many features of a chaotic system, but perhaps the most important are the correlation dimension, D_2, Lyapunov exponents and entropy. D_2 can be thought of as a measure of the degrees of freedom, or complexity, of the system, but it should be noted that complexity in this context is not the same as Tononi et al.'s (1994) 'neural complexity'. Whereas D_2 is a static descriptor of a system, the Lyapunov components and entropy measures describe the dynamics of the system. Lyapunov exponents (there is one for each dimension of the system) characterize the degree of divergence of the system. Positive exponents indicate that given the initial state of a system, its future states become less and less predictable over time. In contrast, negative exponents indicate that the state of a system becomes more predictable over time. All chaotic attractors have at least one positive Lyapunov exponent and all continuous systems have at least one equal to 0. The entropy of the system indicates the rate of information loss in the system over time (i.e. its overall predictability) and is obtained by summing the Lyapunov exponents.

These methods have an obvious application to the EEG as the EEG shows features that are often seen in chaotic systems; it is unpredictable and, although it never repeats exactly, it shows periodicity such that similar states recur over and over again. From the mid-1980s, non-linear analysis was applied to the EEG with enthusiasm. One of the main hopes was that it would be possible to determine whether the EEG was essentially random (i.e. stochastic) or chaotic (i.e. deterministic). At first, many claims were made to have discovered that the EEG was chaotic but, with a few exceptions, e.g. epileptic seizures (Babloyantz and Destexhe 1986) and slow wave sleep (Ferri et al. 1998), these have not stood the test of time. It soon became clear that even if the waking EEG was chaotic, it was certainly not low dimensional. This meant that the calculation of D_2 and the Lyapunov exponents required unfeasibly long noise-free EEG recordings. Furthermore, using the standard approach to calculating D_2 could give rise to spurious findings of low dimensional chaos and was not reliable for dimensions >5. The result was that the initial enthusiasm for non-linear analysis was soon doused in the cold water of experience.

The field is by no means dead, however and, due to a number of recent developments, is experiencing something of a renaissance. One of the most important advances has been the concept of generalized synchronization (see above) and the development of practical methods to measure it (e.g. the SL). Other developments have been in developing robust and more readily computable alternatives to the classical means of calculating D_2 and the Lyapunov exponents. Just as important has been the adoption of surrogate data testing. Surrogate data testing involves taking the observed time series and transforming it in such a way that it has the same linear properties as the original (i.e. power spectrum and autocorrelation) but loses its non-linear structure. If there is evidence of 'chaos', then the estimates of D_2 and the Lyapunov exponents calculated on the original data set should be significantly different from those calculated from a sample of surrogate data sets. In this way, many of the early claims of low dimensional chaos in the EEG were shown to be false.

Subsequently, the non-linear structure has been tested in different meta-states (waking, sleep, anaesthesia and coma). In the waking EEG, although there is evidence of non-linearity, the system does not appear to be low dimensional. Furthermore, in the waking EEG there is evidence for weak but significant non-linear coupling that is sensitive to the cognitive state. In sleep, there is also evidence of non-linear structure and that is strongest in stage 2 sleep (Ferri *et al.* 2002). Non-linear coupling has also been observed in sleep and increases with depth of sleep. D_2 has been shown to correlate with anaesthetic depth, and other non-linear measures have been shown to discriminate between alpha-coma and the waking state.

Overall, there is good preliminary evidence to suggest that various measurable indices of non-linear dynamical systems in the human EEG vary between meta-states. To date, however, hypnosis has not been studied in this way, at least not using up-to-date methods, so it is not known whether this approach will prove fruitful in distinguishing hypnosis from other meta-states. However, given that these non-linear indices do appear to reveal something fundamental about the deep structure of the EEG and, given the sensitivity of the EEG to different meta-states, this is surely an approach that should be applied in hypnosis research.

In this section, I have put the case for a number of analytical methods that assess some aspect of the deep structure of the EEG, which I believe have the potential to determine whether hypnosis is a distinct meta-state or not. What may surprise some readers is that most of these methods involve a mathematical abstraction derived from the system (e.g. the correlation dimension, D_2) and do not relate directly to physiology. The reason for this is that there remains a wide gap between what we can infer about the abstract characteristics of the system that produces the EEG and what we know about the way in which it is actually generated. In the next section, I suggest some ways in which that gap can be narrowed.

11.5 **The physiological origin of cortical oscillations**

Although cortical oscillations have been studied ever since they were first discovered by Richard Caton in 1875 (Brazier 1961), the relationship between the EEG and the underlying neurophysiology remains obscure. At the macro-scale, the EEG is the result of reciprocal connections between the cortex and the thalamus, and the thalamus and the ARAS. At the cellular level, it is known that the major contribution to the EEG recorded at the scalp comes from dendritic potentials of pyramidal neurons oriented perpendicular to the cortical surface. The neural networks involved have the capacity to synchronize on a massive scale, and it is estimated that 6 cm^2 of cortex is required to be synchronously active for the resulting field to be detectable at the scalp (Cooper *et al.* 1965). Oscillatory activity is the result of either the 'pacemaker' properties of some classes of cell or an emergent property of the network of intercellular connections, or most probably a combination of both.

In recent years, there has been a rapid development in our knowledge about how oscillatory activity arises both from *in vivo* animal studies and more recently from experiments on cortical or, more commonly, hippocampal slices maintained *in vitro*. From studies of this type, the nesting of theta and gamma oscillations and, more recently, the gamma–beta shift were first observed. These are potentially interesting as they represent either a characteristic state of oscillatory activity or a transition between states, and either might be useful in helping discriminate between meta-states. At present, it is too early to know whether this approach has any direct relevance to the hypnotic meta-state or not, but this area of research offers perhaps the best hope of finding a connection between the macro-scale patterns that we see in the EEG and its underlying neurophysiology.

Although developments in electrophysiology at the cellular level offer hope for the future, modelling oscillatory activity at a much larger scale may have more immediate benefits. Recently a mathematical model of the generation of the EEG has been developed at the Brain Dynamics Centre in Sydney (Robinson *et al.* 2002) that provides an elegant way of characterizing different EEG states and which, consequently, also maps meta-states. The model, which I shall refer to as the Brain Dynamic Centre Model (BDC), has been presented in a number of different forms and has developed over the years, but the account given here is from Robinson *et al.* (2002, 2005). Although the mathematical formalism of the model appears daunting and its implementation is computationally challenging, its essence is conceptually straightforward. The model sets out to show how thalamo-cortical interactions give rise to the EEG. The model consists of three core elements: the cortex, the relay nuclei of the thalamus and the reticular nucleus of the thalamus. In the model, the relay nuclei receive input from the external world, excitatory input from the cortex and inhibitory input from the reticular nucleus. Their outputs are excitatory and feed into the cortex and the reticular nucleus. The cortex receives excitatory input from the relay nuclei and feeds back both inhibitory and excitatory outputs to itself. Excitatory output from the cortex also goes to the relay nuclei and the reticular nucleus. The reticular nucleus receives excitatory input from both the cortex and the relay nuclei. Each unit is modelled as a group of neurons each of whose output is a non-linear function of its combined input. Timing is introduced into the model by incorporating rise and decay times for the summation of the input to the cell body of the neuron and by taking into account the transmission times between cortex and thalamus. In this way, the generation of the EEG can be parsimoniously characterized by only

16 parameters, including values such as the maximum neuronal firing rate, the velocity of transmission of the signals through the axons, and so on, all of which are based on physiologically realistic values.

The response of the model to an input stimulus can be easily measured and, by appropriate tuning of the model's parameters, realistic EEG for different meta-states can be readily produced. One of the most interesting findings of this model is that within the frequency range of the EEG and with realistic model parameters, the output of the model can be further simplified to a three-dimensional space where the dimensions represent cortical, corticothalamic and thalamic stability. In this 3D space, there is a stable zone where the model generates realistic EEG-like output and this is bounded by four unstable zones that lead to a degenerate output. Within this stable zone, there are areas that produce EEG matching the waking state (both eyes open and eyes closed), sleep stages 1–4, REM sleep, anaesthesia and coma. Furthermore, at least one of the unstable regions of this 3D space appears to correspond to petit-mal seizures. In short, this model provides a highly parsimonious characterization of several distinct meta-states using only three parameters: cortical, corticothalamic and thalamic stability.

Not only can this model simulate wave forms and power spectra that mimic the EEG seen in different meta-states, the model can be inverted too, i.e, it is possible to estimate the parameter values that would be needed for the model to generate any empirically recorded EEG power spectrum (Robinson *et al.* 2004). In this way, it has been possible to map EEG collected in known meta-states onto the 3D space that defines the stable zone. Consequently, any recorded EEG can, in principle, be defined in terms of three parameters that define its position in the model's parameter space and ultimately linked to the fundamental physiological processes on which the model is based. The application to hypnosis should now be obvious. If hypnosis represents a distinct meta-state, then EEGs recorded from both participants of high and low susceptibility should occupy the same region of the stable zone, i.e. the region that represents the waking state. However, following hypnotic induction, the EEG recorded from highly susceptible patients should move to a new region of the 3D parameter space and one that is not occupied by any other meta-state.

In this way, the hypothesis that hypnosis is a distinct meta-state could be empirically tested and the results might also produce some insight into how the hypnotic state differs from the waking state. The outcome of such a study, however, would critically depend upon the adequacy of the BDC model. Although the BDC model has many interesting properties and parsimoniously accounts for a wide range of EEG phenomena, it remains a highly simplified account of a very complex system and it may not characterize all features of the EEG adequately. Notwithstanding this, using the BDC or similar models in this way has the potential to provide important insights into the nature of hypnosis and is very worthy of consideration.

11.6 Summary and conclusion

In this chapter I have argued that the evidence obtained from hypnosis provocation studies that use neurophysiological measures does not conclusively resolve the state–non-state debate. If hypnosis is a distinct meta-state, then it should be associated with (1) a distinct phenomenological experience or behaviour and (2) a neurophysiological correlate that is always and only present in that state. After more than 50 years of work, these criteria have not been met and there seems little reason to hope for any imminent resolution of the question. However, progress can be made on this issue if we:

1. learn lessons from the most recent theories of consciousness many of which stress the importance of cortical oscillations, the thalamo-cortical system, functional connectivity and the spatio-temporal structure of the EEG

2. move away from conventional methods of signal analysis that measure surface features of the EEG signal and adopt instead methods that permit us to explore the deep structure instead

3. use physiologically plausible models that describe how the EEG is generated and see how their parameters change during different meta-states and the EEG.

References

Aapo H, Juha K and Erkki O (2001). *Independent component analysis*. New York, John Wiley & Sons, Inc.

Babloyantz A and Destexhe A (1986). Low-dimensional chaos in an instance of epilepsy. *Proceedings of the National Academy of Sciences of the USA*, **83**, 3513–17.

Bogen JE (1995). On the neurophysiology of consciousness: I. an overview. *Conscious Cognition*, **4**, 52–62.

Branston NM, El-Deredy W and McGlone FP (2005). Changes in neural complexity of the EEG during a visual oddball task. *Clinical Neurophysiology*, **116**, 151–9.

Brazier MAB (1961). *A history of the electrical activity of the brain; the first half-century*. New York, Macmillan.

Burgess AP and Ali L (2002). Functional connectivity of gamma EEG activity is modulated at low frequency during conscious recollection. *International Journal of Psychophysiology*, **46**, 91–100.

Burgess AP, Rehman J and Williams JD (2003). Changes in neural complexity during the perception of 3D images using random dot stereograms. *International Journal of Psychophysiology*, **48**, 35–42.

Chapman RM and McCrary JW (1995). EP component identification and measurement by principal components analysis. *Brain and Cognition*, **27**, 288–310.

Cooper NR, Croft RJ, Dominey SJ, Burgess AP and Gruzelier JH (2003). Paradox lost? Exploring the role of alpha oscillations during externally vs. internally directed attention and the implications for idling and inhibition hypotheses. *International Journal of Psychophysiology*, **47**, 65–74.

Cooper R, Winter AL, Crow HJ and Walter WG (1965). Comparison of subcortical, cortical and scalp activity using chronically indwelling electrodes in man. *Electroencephalography and Clinical Neurophysiology*, **18**, 217–28.

Crawford HJ, Knebel T, Kaplan L, Vendemia JM, Xie M, Jamison S and Pribram KH (1998). Hypnotic analgesia: 1. Somatosensory event-related potential changes to noxious stimuli and 2. Transfer learning to reduce chronic low back pain. *International Journal of Clinical and Experimental Hypnosis*, **46**, 92–132.

Crick F and Koch C (2003). A framework for consciousness. *Nature Neuroscience*, **6**, 119–26.

Darvas F, Pantazis D, Kucukaltun-Yildirim E and Leahy RM (2004). Mapping human brain function with MEG and EEG: methods and validation. *Neuroimage*, **23** Suppl 1, S289–99.

De Pascalis V (1993). EEG spectral analysis during hypnotic induction, hypnotic dream and age regression. *International Journal of Psychophysiology*, **15**, 153–66.

Edelman GM and Tononi G (2000). *Consciousness: how matter becomes imagination*. London, Allen Lane.

Egner T, Jamieson G and Gruzelier J (2005). Hypnosis decouples cognitive control from conflict monitoring processes of the frontal lobe. *Neuroimage*, **27**, 969–78.

Ferri R, Pettinato S, Alicata F, Del Gracco S, Elia M and Musumeci SA (1998). Correlation dimension of EEG slow-wave activity during sleep in children and young adults. *Electroencephalography and Clinical Neurophysiology*, **106**, 424–8.

Ferri R, Parrino L, Smerieri A, Terzano MG, Elia M, Musumeci SA, *et al.* (2002). Non-linear EEG measures during sleep: effects of the different sleep stages and cyclic alternating pattern. *International Journal of Psychophysiology*, **43**, 273–86.

Freeman WJ (2000). *Neurodynamics; an exploration of mesoscopic brain dynamics*. London, Springer-Verlag.

Freeman WJ (2005). A field-theoretic approach to understanding scale-free neocortical dynamics. *Biological Cybernetics*, **92**, 350–9.

Gray CM, Konig P, Engel AK Singer W and (1989). Oscillatory responses in cat visual cortex exhibit inter-columnar synchronization which reflects global stimulus properties. *Nature*, **338**, 334–7.

Hogan M, MacDonald J and Olness K (1984). Voluntary control of auditory evoked responses by children with and without hypnosis. *American Journal of Clinical Hypnosis*, **27**, 91–4.

James CJ and Hesse CW (2005). Independent component analysis for biomedical signals. *Physiological Measurement*, **26**, R15–39.

Jensen HJ (1998). *Self-organized criticality: emergent complex behaviour in physical and biological systems*. Cambridge, Cambridge University Press.

Kearse LA Jr, Manberg P, DeBros F, Chamoun N and Sinai V (1994). Bispectral analysis of the electroencephalogram during induction of anesthesia may predict hemodynamic responses to laryngoscopy and intubation. *Electroencephalography and Clinical Neurophysiology*, **90**, 194–200.

Kosslyn SM, Thompson WL, Costantini-Ferrando MF, Alpert NM and Spiegel D (2000). Hypnotic visual illusion alters color processing in the brain. *American Journal of Psychiatry*, **157**, 1279–84.

Lehmann D and Koenig T (1997). Spatio-temporal dynamics of alpha brain electric fields, and cognitive modes. *International Journal of Psychophysiology*, **26**, 99–112.

Lin FH, McIntosh AR, Agnew JA, Eden GF, Zeffiro TA and Belliveau JW (2003). Multivariate analysis of neuronal interactions in the generalized partial least squares framework: simulations and empirical studies. *Neuroimage*, **20**, 625–42.

Lisman J (2005). The theta/gamma discrete phase code occurring during the hippocampal phase precession may be a more general brain coding scheme. *Hippocampus*, **15**, 913–22.

Llinas R and Ribary U (2001). Consciousness and the brain. The thalamocortical dialogue in health and disease. *Annals of the New York Academy of Sciences*, **929**, 166–75.

Lobaugh NJ, West R and McIntosh AR (2001). Spatiotemporal analysis of experimental differences in event-related potential data with partial least squares. *Psychophysiology*, **38**, 517–30.

Makeig S, Westerfield M, Jung TP, Enghoff S, Townsend J, Courchesne E, *et al.* (2002). Dynamic brain sources of visual evoked responses. *Science*, **295**, 690–4.

Maquet P, Faymonville ME, Degueldre C, Delfiore G, Franck G, Luxen A, *et al.* (1999). Functional neuroanatomy of hypnotic state. *Biological Psychiatry*, **45**, 327–33.

March PA and Muir WW (2005). Bispectral analysis of the electroencephalogram: a review of its development and use in anesthesia. *Veterinary Anaesthia and Analgesia*, **32**, 241–55.

McIntosh AR, Bookstein FL, Haxby JV and Grady CL (1996). Spatial pattern analysis of functional brain images using partial least squares. *Neuroimage*, **3**, 143–57.

McIntosh AR and Lobaugh NJ (2004). Partial least squares analysis of neuroimaging data: applications and advances. *Neuroimage*, **23** Suppl 1, S250–63.

Miltner WH, Braun C, Arnold M, Witte H and Taub E (1999). Coherence of gamma-band EEG activity as a basis for associative learning. *Nature*, **397**, 434–36.

Niedermeyer E (1999). Sleep and EEG. In: E Niedermeyer and F Lopes Da Silva, eds. *Electroencephalography: basic principles, clinical applications and related fields.* Baltimore, Williams & Wilkins, pp. 174–88.

Pereda E, Quiroga RQ and Bhattacharya J (2005). Nonlinear multivariate analysis of neurophysiological signals. *Progress in Neurobiology*, **77**, 1–37.

Ravitz LJ (1950). Electrometric correlates of the hypnotic state. *Science*, **112**, 341–2.

Robinson PA, Rennie CJ and Rowe DL (2002). Dynamics of large-scale brain activity in normal arousal states and epileptic seizures. *Physical Review E*, **65**, 041924.

Robinson PA, Rennie CJ, Rowe DL and O'Connor SC (2004). Estimation of multiscale neurophysiologic parameters by electroencephalographic means. *Human Brain Mapping*, **23**, 53–72.

Robinson PA, Rennie CJ, Rowe DL, O'Connor SC and Gordon E (2005). Multiscale brain modelling. *Philosophical Transactions of the Royal Socity B: Biological Sciences*, **360**, 1043–50.

Rodriguez E, George N, Lachaux JP, Martinerie J, Renault B and Varela FJ (1999). Perception's shadow: long-distance synchronization of human brain activity. *Nature*, **397**, 430–3.

Sabourin ME, Cutcomb SD, Crawford HJ and Pribram K (1990). EEG correlates of hypnotic susceptibility and hypnotic trance: spectral analysis and coherence. *International Journal of Psychophysiology*, **10**, 125–42.

Sayers BM, Beagley HA and Henshall WR (1974). The mechansim of auditory evoked EEG responses. *Nature*, **247**, 481–3.

Schack B and Chen AC, Mescha S, Witte H (1999). Instantaneous EEG coherence analysis during the Stroop task. *Clinical Neurophysiology*, **110**, 1410–26.

Schanze T and Eckhorn R (1997). Phase correlation among rhythms present at different frequencies: spectral methods, application to microelectrode recordings from visual cortex and functional implications. *International Journal of Psychophysiology*, **26**, 171–89.

Sporns O, Tononi G and Edelman GM (2000). Theoretical neuroanatomy: relating anatomical and functional connectivity in graphs and cortical connection matrices. *Cerebral Cortex*, **10**, 127–41.

Stam CJ (2005). Nonlinear dynamical analysis of EEG and MEG: review of an emerging field. *Clinical Neurophysiology*, **116**, 2266–301.

Tallon-Baudry C, Bertrand O, Delpuech C and Pernier J (1996). Stimulus specificity of phase-locked and non-phase-locked 40 Hz visual responses in human. *Journal of Neuroscience*, **16**, 4240–9.

Tononi G and Edelman GM (1998). Consciousness and complexity. *Science*, **282**, 1846–51.

Tononi G, Sporns O and Edelman GM (1994). A measure for brain complexity: relating functional segregation and integration in the nervous system. *Proceedings of the National Academy of Sciences of the USA*, **91**, 5033–7.

Treisman A (1996). The binding problem. *Current Opinion in Neurobiology*, **6**, 171–8.

van Cappellen van Walsum AM, Pijnenburg YA, Berendse HW, van Dijk BW, Knol DL, Scheltens P, *et al.* (2003). A neural complexity measure applied to MEG data in Alzheimer's disease. *Clinical Neurophysiology*, **114**, 1034–40.

van Putten MJAM and Stam CJ (2001). Application of a neural complexity measure to multichannel EEG. *Physics Letters A*, **281**, 131–41.

von Stein A and Sarnthein J (2000). Different frequencies for different scales of cortical integration: from local gamma to long range alpha/theta synchronization. *International Journal of Psychophysiology*, **38**, 301–13.

Watts DJ and Strogatz SH (1998). Collective dynamics of 'small-world' networks. *Nature*, **393**, 440–42.

Woody E and Bowers K (1994). A frontal assault on dissociated control. In: S Lynn and J Rhue, eds. *Dissociation: clinical and theoretical perspectives.* pp. 52–79. New York, Guilford Press.

Part IV

The psychobiology of trance

Chapter 12

The experience of agency and hypnosis from an evolutionary perspective

William J Ray

Psychology is just beginning to come to grips with the manner in which evolutionary thinking can impact and shape our current conceptualizations of physiological processes. This is somewhat surprising since Darwin suggested over 150 years ago that the theoretical underpinning of psychology would come from evolutionary theory. However, the realization of this possibility has been delayed partly from an infatuation with a potentially simple scientific view that ignored internal processes and a metatheory that ignored biological foundations of human behaviour and experience. At the beginning of the twenty-first century, we are again returning to a scientific exploration of internal process including consciousness and the hypnotic experience. Such an approach draws from a variety of perspectives including cognitive and affective neuroscience, biology, human ethology and genetics, as well as psychology. The current chaptr begins to assemble the necessary perspective upon which to build a theory of internal experience which can offer insights in agency and hypnosis. Agency in this case refers to the experience that I feel myself to have controlled or willed an action. I begin with evolution itself, then consider genetic perspectives, and then possible animal models of hypnosis. At this point, I examine current perspectives of the evolution of the brain and how this may inform our understanding of the hypnotic experience. Finally, I look to human developmental processes including our historical social environment and human attachment as a potentially important mechanism. I conclude with noting the manner in which the hypnotic experience may be an advantage for humans.

12.1 Evolution

The initial perspective was historically articulated by Charles Darwin in the 1800s and emphasized variation as one of its key components. Darwin suggested that any variation, however slight, that benefits an individual in his or her interactions with the environment can predominate in future generations. The selection and preservation of such traits came to be referred to as *natural selection*. In this sense, it is the environmental conditions in which an organism lives that determines which organisms will survive and which traits will be passed on to the next generation. The classic study for Darwin was the beaks of the finches found on the Galápagos Islands (Darwin 1859; see Weiner 1994 for an overview and scientific update). Within a small geographical area, beaks of 13 different species range from long and thin to small thick hard ones. Long thin beaks would aid in obtaining seeds or other food from between rocks, as in environments such as drought in which foods were not readily available. Thicker beaks would have an advantage in environments of plenty in which nuts and other foods could develop hard shells. Overall, natural selection comprises a number of steps. First, natural selection is focused on characteristics that vary in a given species such as the physical size of the finch's beak. Secondly, natural selection focuses on those characteristics that help an organism to survive within the context of its particular environment. Thirdly, an organism that survives can mate and thus pass on these characteristics, whereas organisms that do not survive cannot. Thus, even slight changes in the environment can influence characteristics of future generations. Such changes will be passed on to future generations since those individual organisms without these characteristics will not survive and thus not reproduce.

Darwin later extended the theory of natural selection to include *sexual selection*, or the manner in which males and females chose a mate, which was described in *The descent of man* (Darwin 1874). The *Descent* was divided into three parts: the first part expanded on the theory of natural selection and more explicitly set out the case for the similarity between humans and other animals; the second and third parts of the book examined sexual selection in relation to animals (part II) and in relation to humans (part III). Darwin notes that males and females differ not only in terms of organs of sexual reproduction but also in secondary sexual characteristics such as mammary glands for the nourishment of infants in females and physical size in males. Sexual selection according to Darwin depends on the success of certain individuals over others of the same sex. In a somewhat complicated story, we now know that males compete against other males for 'attractive' females and that females compete among themselves for 'attractive' males. This may lead to structures such as the peacock's tail where females chose males with larger and more colourful tails and thus passed that characteristic on to the next generation. However, some secondary sex characteristics such as the colour of the tail of the peacock also supply additional information such as the health of the male. Thus, the female by choosing a male with a large and colourful tail is also choosing one with better health. Overall, sexual selection takes place both between and within males and females. Characteristics that make one more attractive to a mate will be passed on to future generations. Thus, if female peahens like male peacocks with larger and more colourful tails then, through mating, these characteristics will be passed on to future generations. Within the same sex, characteristics such as strength or cunning that allow one to compete and control reproduction will also have a greater chance of being passed on to future generations since those without these characteristics will have less opportunity to mate.

Although Darwin emphasized natural selection and sexual selection, he also anticipated the third major instinctual process, that of social relationships. In the twentieth century, major studies of ants, bees and other species pointed to a social instinct equally as important as survival and sexuality. In relation to humans, Darwin saw our historical arrangement of living in social groups as the basis for the evolution of cognitive development, i.e. social groups lead to both cooperation and competition. In the sense that social intelligence also contributes to survival and reproduction, then it becomes a force in the evolution of cognitive processes. Through this mechanism, the abilities of a species can be increased. With these abilities, humans also changed aspects of their environment in a variety of ways.

Bowlby (1969) reminds us that none of the environments in which we live today conform to the environment in which a variety of human systems were developed. Unlike other species, humans live in environments that are different in many respects from those that shaped our early evolutionary history. Bowlby referred to the historical environment in which humans experienced difficulties, found food, mated and raised children, formed and lived with others in social groups as the 'environment of evolutionary adaptedness.' Often referred to as the EEA, it is this *environment of evolutionary adaptedness* that we use to inform our considerations of our present-day behaviours and experiences, especially in terms of survival value. Before continuing, let us overview this environment.

The picture we have of our human ancestors begins more than 150 000 years ago in the high grasslands and wooded slopes of Eastern Africa which today would be the countries of Ethiopia, Kenya and Tanzania (Olson 2000). It is assumed that these humans looked much like we look today. Early humans lived in a group and gathered nuts, fruits and seeds. They obtained meat from hunting gazelles and rabbits as well as scavenging carcasses of animals killed by other predators. Since hunting has been estimated to be successful only 20 per cent of the time, gathering food was extremely important in supporting life. Most reconstructions of this period suggest a division of labour, with females caring for infants and gathering foods and males hunting but also involved in gathering.

Physiologically, *Homo sapiens* are characterized by a small pelvis area, a prominent chin and a forehead which rises sharply. The brain size of modern humans is somewhere around 1350 cm^3. Evidence suggests that humans began to migrate out of Africa around 90 000 years ago, initially though the Middle East. *Homo sapiens* are associated with sophisticated tool use. Beginning about 80 000 years ago, there is the appearance of bone harpoon points. By 40 000 years ago, a wide variety of materials such as flint and bone were used for tools such as needles and fishhooks. Also, clothing and art began to appear. This included objects worn as decoration on their bodies. From a psychological standpoint, symbolic behaviour is seen for the first time. A variety of art objects dating from around 30 000 years ago have been discovered. In Germany, a series of animal figurines from about 34 000 years ago were discovered. These included figures of a lion, panther, bison, horse, wren and mammoth. Carved from ivory, they were discovered in the caves of Vogelherd. In France, a series of cave paintings depicting a variety of animals dating from 32 000 years ago were discovered. The exact meaning of the cave painting of this era is unknown, although some scholars have suggested a religious significance. Based on these types of behavioural changes, it is argued that the archeological record has changed more in the last 40 000 years ago than it had in the previous million years (Klein 2000). Compared with other human species, *H. sapiens* have modified their environments in ways not seen previously and in a relatively short time. Some researchers speculate that one aspect associated with these changes some 50 000 to 40 000 years ago was changes in neural capacity that allowed for language and higher cognitive functions.

12.2 **Integration of evolution and genetics**

A step toward the modern synthesis of evolution and genetics took place in 1937 with the publication of *Genetics and the origin of species* by Theodosius Dobzhansky. Dobzhansky had been interested in studying insects in the wild since his early years as a child. After coming to America from Russia, he began studying fruit flies with Thomas Hunt Morgan at Columbia and later at the California Institute of Technology. Morgan and his group had shown spontaneous variation in genes in the laboratory fly. Dobzhansky was able to integrate this work on genetic variation with the work of those who studied species in the wild. One of his original questions had to do with the genetic variability that determines the differences in populations of a species. In studying organisms both in the laboratory and in the wild, it became clear that members of the same species can have different genetic variations. It was not the case, as some thought at the time, that each member of a species had an identical set of genes.

12.3 **Genetics**

There is a complex pathway between genes and behaviour which can be influenced by a variety of factors. To begin with, a gene is simply a part of the total length of DNA which tells the body how to manufacture particular proteins. Simplistic notions often ignore the complex turning on and off of genes in relation to internal and external environmental factors. Except for blood type, very few traits are displayed by genes without a complex input and interaction with the environment. Striking examples exist in nature such as the butterfly (*Bicyclus anyana*) which is brightly coloured if born in the rainy season, but grey if born in the dry season. The advantage of this tight coupling with the environment is that it offers a means of protection. Environmental couplings may also promote health and well-being. With some disorders, simply changing the environmental conditions in terms of the types of food a person eats can actually avoid the negative outcomes of a genetic disorder. In considering the role of genetic and environmental factors in behaviour and experience, we can recall Darwin's reminder that 'how infinitely complex and close-fitting are the mutual relations of all organic beings to each other and to their physical conditions of life.'

12.4 **Genetic influences on hypnosis**

If hypnosis is influenced by genetic processes, we would expect to find that hypnotizability would show stability across time in the same individual. This is indeed the case in that high test–re-test correlations ($r > 0.70$) have been observed for hypnotic susceptibility measured over 10, 15 and even 25 years (Piccione *et al.* 1989). Furthermore, there is a substantial correlation ($r = 0.60$) of different hypnotic susceptibility measures (Bowers 1983). Using such designs as twin studies, we should also be able compute the amount of variance in hypnotizability related to genetic factors and that related to environmental influences. Unfortunately, only a few studies have examined this question. However, the initial two showed the heritability of susceptibility to be among the highest of any psychological individual difference measure identified to date (Morgan *et al.* 1970; Morgan 1973). These results are presented in Table 12.1.

Table 12.1 Heritability of susceptibility

Study	Morgan *et al.* (1970)		Morgan (1973)	
Monozygotic twins	0.63		0.52	0.54 male; 0.49 female
Dizygotic twis	0.08 same sex	0.04 different sex	0.18 same sex	0.15 different sex
Siblings	0.22 same sex	0.01 different sex	0.25 male; 0.19 female	0.10 different sex

These data were replicated in a dissertation by Robert Rawlings at the University of New South Wales in 1977. These data from two different continents suggest that hypnotic susceptibility varies among individuals and that the similarity in identical twins reflects a strong genetic component. This is illustrated by the higher concordance between monozygotic twins who share the same genetic structure as compared with dizygotic twins who have only about 50 per cent common genetic structure. Given these results, it is also clear that environmental influences play some role. The manner in which these influences interact with each other are not well understood. Hilgard (1968), for example, suggested that there was a critical period in development which helped to set future hypnotic susceptibility limits which for him was not reversible. Overall, the available research suggests a genetic component to hypnotic susceptibility. Given a genetic component, we might expect to find similar processes or the predisposition to such processes in animals, which we discuss in the next section.

12.5 **Animal hypnosis**

Looking at the hypnotic experience from an evolutionary perspective, we can ask if similar processes are seen in non-human animals. The obvious question is what characteristics of the human hypnotic experience would one seek in animal models? In 1646, an Austrian monk published a detailed account describing how he had hypnotized a chicken by holding its head on the ground and forcing the animal to fixate on a line drawn away from its beak (Völgyesi 1966). From that time to the present, there have been a variety of stories of how alligators, rabbits, chickens and other animals could be immobilized, generally by rubbing or stroking the animal, although eye fatigue through fixation has also been used. Pavlov (1927) describes the manner in which inducing hypnosis in animals and humans utilizes similar mechanisms and its relationship to cortical inhibition. In the second half of the twentieth century, a variety of studies examined the concept of animal hypnosis (Gallup 1974), with some suggesting its value for understanding the hypnotic experience in humans (Draper and Klemm 1967). A variety of animal hypnosis studies suggest that in this condition the animals show an analgesia-like response to needle pricks and electric shock. Draper and Klemm (1967), using a conditioning procedure in rabbits, suggest that the dominant feature of animal hypnosis is a disconnection of overt motor functions without conspicuous inhibition of sensory functions.

Not unlike human hypnosis, immobilization in chickens has been characterized in three stages: (1) vocalizations and continuously open eyes; (2) suppressed vocal behaviour and eye flutters; and (3) eyes closed, occasional body twitches and lack of vocalizations (Rovec and Luciano 1973). Research has shown that once tonic immobility is induced, it remains for anywhere from 10 min in chickens to more than 8 h in lizards.

The nature of the immobilization response in animals is consistent with an action pattern described by ethologists. The survival value of the immobilization response is typically seen in the context of predator/prey responses in that predators tend to be sensitive to movement and without it they lose interest and become distracted, allowing the prey to escape. This connection is also supported by the finding that placing a stuffed hawk in the chicken's presence increased the period of tonic immobility by a factor of 5 or 6. Interestingly, human eye contact, as well as an artificial eye alone, could also prolong the immobilization response in chickens (see Gallup 1974 for a review of this literature). Overall, immobilization is both protective and related to dominance. This perspective would suggest that the hypnotic experience in humans developed from survival mechanisms which protected the organism. Whether the human hypnotic experience is related to or grew out of this evolutionarily significant event is, of course, an open question, although the development of more sophisticated neuroscience technologies is beginning to allow for the mapping of these processes in both animals and humans. With new technologies and better articulation of the evolution of brain processes, a research programme devoted to the similarities and differences in animal and human hypnosis could be achieved.

12.6 Evolution of the brain

Another perspective that can lead to evolutionary understanding of the hypnotic experience is to look at the evolution of the brain. A number of studies have examined the evolution of the brain across a variety of species (see Allman 2000 for an overview). As we look to humans, it is not only the case that our brains have become relatively larger but that this appears to be the result of our neocortex becoming larger (Striedter 2005). What is particularly interesting is that the neocortex evolved a high level of direct access to the motor neurons of the medulla and spinal cord. This allowed humans to have a high degree of dexterity in our hands as well as control the muscles of our eyes, jaws, face, tongue and vocal cords. Humans also have better control over their breathing than most other species. The obvious advantage of this arrangement is the ability it gives humans to produce vocal sounds as well as facial expressions. The enlargement of the frontal areas in humans also gave us the ability to exert voluntary control over responses, rather than just respond automatically to stimuli. Later in this chapter this will lead us to the question of what gives you a sense of willing an action or agency in the sense that the action was performed by you. To aid in the search for the underlying evolutionary mechanisms of the hypnotic experience, we can note two important and related aspects of human development. First, the complexity and plasticity of human beings are partly related to our large brains. Secondly, another important aspect is our extended juvenile period in which we are born immature and continue to develop for the next 15–25 years. We now turn to theoretical aspects of cortical development and processing that have informed evolutionary perspectives.

12.7 **Hughlings Jackson**

In the 1800s, the neurologist John Hughlings Jackson began to examine the brain from a developmental and evolutionary perspective (Jackson 1884). In the process of this research, he suggested two principles based partly on evolutionary analysis. The first principle is *hierarchical integration* through inhibitory control. By this he means that the various levels of the brain, such as the brainstem, the limbic system and the neocortex, are able to interact with each other. Further, the type of interaction from the higher levels is that of restricting or inhibiting the lower levels. Current research has supported this by showing many more inhibitory pathways going from the higher brain levels to the lower brain structures than vice versa. A simple example of this is that when a human infant is first born, she or he shows a variety of simple reflexes. One of these is the Babinski reflex. If you take your finger and run it along an infant's foot, the toes will curl up. As the infant matures, the reflex disappears. If there is cortical damage at a later point in life, then this reflex can reappear. Jackson assumed that the higher level structure which evolved later than the reflexive ones serves the purpose of inhibiting and modulating these basic reflexes. Jackson's second principle is *encephalization*. This is the principle by which special purpose control systems are taken over by a general purpose control system. For example, lateral inhibition (the tendency for activity in one area of processing to reduce activity in another area) takes place not only in the eye of birds but also in the brain of humans. Thus, over evolutionary time, human brains have developed toward a more general purpose processing system while still retaining special purpose systems.

12.8 **Paul MacLean**

Although more speculative, it may also be useful to consider the question of the evolutionary substrate of hypnotic suggestion. In many ways, this question returns us to the question of physiological mechanism, because the human brain's cognitive mechanisms are built upon circuits that cross the hierarchy of vertebrate neural architecture, including not only telencephalic (cortex, amygdala, hippocampus, neostriatum) but diencephalic (thalamus, hypothalmus) and mesencephalic (brainstem reticular system) levels. Examining fossil records along with brains of a variety of organisms has suggested that our current brain can be viewed as having the features of three basic evolutionary formations, that of reptiles, that of early mammals and that of recent mammals (MacLean 1990). MacLean's formulation, which is referred to as the triune brain, suggests that through rich interconnections our brains can process a variety of information in three somewhat independent although not autonomous manners.

The first level is that of the reptilian brain, involving the brainstem and cerebellum, that processes major life requirements such as breathing, temperature regulation and sleep–wake cycles. The second level is that of the paleomammalian which is seen to involve the limbic system and its involvement in emotional processing. MacLean points to three developments that took place evolutionarily in the transition from reptiles to mammals. These are: (1) nursing in conjunction with maternal care; (2) audio-vocal communication which maintained maternal–offspring contact; and (3) play. The third level of the triune brain is that of neomammalian and is related to the neocortex and thalamic structures. This level is generally associated with problem solving, executive control and an orientation toward the external world with an emphasis on linguistic functions. Although MacLean's anatomical framework is highly schematic, and more detailed analysis is required to understand exactly how mammalian self-regulation achieved the advances in behavioural flexibility and social coordination, his approach has been highly influential in emphasizing the integral social basis of the evolution of higher levels of psychological function. Thinking in these terms, we would conclude that processes such as a sense of control as well as conscious self-awareness and consciousness would come late in evolution.

Considering hypnosis, I propose that our ability to model or imitate others has evolutionarily preceded a fully developed sense of willed voluntary action. Current research shows that watching another person perform an action results in the firing of motor neurons similar to when performing the action for yourself (Gallese *et al.* 2004; Rizzolatti and Craighero 2004; Brass and Heyes 2005). I would further suggest that hypnosis as a process finds its evolutionary heritage in the interplay of the cortical and limbic levels. By considering the multiple levels of corticolimbic networks, we can understand the process of executive control from the perspective of not only conscious and linguistic mechanisms that are the obvious medium of hypnotic suggestion, but the pre-conscious formative processes that may be the critical mechanisms through which social influence operates.

12.9 **Hypnotic level of mechanisms**

Building on the work of Hughlings Jackson and Paul MacLean, we can ask the question as to the level of cortical processing that the hypnotic experience should be seen to manifest. To help answer an initial part of this question, in our own laboratory we asked if hypnosis could influence simple reflexive processes such as the startle response (Bjick 2001). The startle response is a predictable involuntary process involving a simple neural circuit which cannot be suppressed by voluntary inhibition. Initially studied by Landis and Hunt in 1939 as part of the overall response to surprise, it includes a bodily response including rapid eye closure to stimuli such as a loud noise. What we found was consistent with previous research which suggests that the amplitude of the startle response could be influenced by the emotional state of the person. Increased startle responses would be seen in negative emotional states and reduced ones in positive emotional states. Hypnosis itself did not influence the startle amplitude or latency of highly susceptible individuals differentially from those with low susceptibility. However, individuals with low susceptibility did subjectively experience the startle stimulus as louder, as opposed to highly susceptible individuals following a reduced hearing suggestion. What this suggests is that hypnosis does not influence basic reflexes themselves, the initial level of the MacLean tri-une brain, but does influence higher level emotional responses.

Research with the hypnotic modulation of pain also supported the conclusion that hypnosis does not influence basic reflexive processes. In this study, we used dense array (129 electrodes) electroencephalographic (EEG) activity to study the pain response in relation to hypnotic suggestion (Ray *et al.* 2002). As expected, individual of high and low hypnotic susceptibility reported differential pain experience depending on hypnotic suggestions. In terms of EEG evoked potentials, there are two evoked potential components discussed in the literature in relation to pain. The first comes early in the evoked poten-tial and relates to the sensory stimulus itself. The second comes later and relates to the emotional reaction. Both of these are experienced in the first quarter of a second and are not differentiated by individuals. What we found through factor analytic techniques was that hypnotic instructions to reduce the experience of pain did not influence the initial sensory processing in the brain. However, hypnotic suggestions greatly reduced the evoked potential component occurring at around 250 ms in highly susceptible individuals, which corresponds to the emotional experience of the person. These studies and others suggest that the level of hypnotic influence does not take place at the level of MacLean's basic reptilian brain. The best candidate appears to be the emotional level and the related limbic structures and their interaction with the higher cortical level.

12.10 Sense of agency

An important question in psychology has been what it means to perform voluntary actions (see Maasen *et al.* 2003 for an overview). This question can be divided into a number of subquestions from does one actually do anything volitionally, to what is the process that produces the experience of an action as occurring with or without our self-control. In terms of the first question, a variety of human actions, such as typing, driving or even speaking, appear to be accomplished best without awareness or conscious direc-tion. In terms of the experience of control, a variety of models have been directed at understanding this experience. This aspect has been referred to as sense of agency.

From an evolutionary perspective, we would assume that innate reflexes represent the most primitive responses. Such reflexes currently found in humans, such as moving your leg when your knee is tapped or blinking your eyes in response to a loud sound, carry with them no sense of agency. You can watch yourself make the response as if an observer of the situation, but there is no sense of agency. The next level as studied by ethologists is that of fixed action patterns such as egg rolling in geese or imprinting in ducks. Classical and operant conditioning provide the next levels. Finally, the greatest sense of agency is experienced in actions that one plans or wills, as William James would suggest. From an evolutionary perspective, moving across these successive levels involves greater plasticity and a decoupling of responses from rigid control by external stimuli. The question for the present discussion is which of these levels best represents the hypnotic experience?

Taken from this perspective, the question may be less what is taken away in the hyp-notic experience such that the person does not experience his or her own agency as what aspect of brain processing is added to give the experience of voluntary control outside the hypnotic state? An analogy to the process is the experience of pain. Electrocortical studies have shown that at least two separate components can be reflected in the evoked potential of individuals experiencing painful stimulation. The first component is related to sensory processing of the stimulus and the second to emotional processing of the stimulus. When hypnotically susceptible individuals are instructed to reduce the experience of the pain, the second evoked potential component is reduced but the first remains. Applying this type of analysis to the sense of agency, an important question for future research would be the manner in which making a movement is combined with the person's sense of making a movement in the brain. When you reach for a cup of coffee for example, you probably would describe it as a planned action on your part. However, there may be times that you reach for the coffee on your desk as you are trying to solve a mental problem without careful planning. The expectation is that the movement component in the brain would exist separately from the agency component. It is this separation of movement and the experience of agency that is commonly experienced during hypnotic experience. The experience of movement of course would be more complicated than pain since movement also has a preparatory component associated with the planning of movement.

Some researchers have suggested that the experience of goals is related to the sense of agency. That is to say, actions performed without goals may lead to the experience of lack of voluntary control. On first blush this would lead one to look to the frontal lobes of the brain and their role in executive function as one focus for the experience of agency. The prefrontal cortex is seen as the seat of preparation for action.

However, the orbitofrontal cortex with its close connections to the anterior cingulate cortex (ACC) may play an important role in the hypnotic experience. Let us briefly review these three structures, the prefrontal cortex, the orbitofrontal cortex and the ACC (see Roth 2003 for an overview in relation to movement).

The prefrontal cortex as the name implies is located at the front of the brain and is involved in the planning of actions. The dorsal part of the prefrontal cortex receives information from the parietal cortex and is assumed to be involved in locating one's body in space as well as external objects. It is also involved in the planning and preparation for movement including its temporal aspects. The lateral-ventral portion of the prefrontal cortex receives information from the temporal lobes with its access to information concerning auditory and visual perception. This area is thought to be involved in the comparison and evaluation of events as well as preparations and decisions concerning actions.

Located below the prefrontal cortex is the orbitofrontal cortex which is considered part of the limbic system and receives input from a variety of limbic structures including the hippocampus and amygdala as well as parts of the thalamus. The orbitofrontal cortex functions involve the motivational and emotional aspects of action. It appears to note if there is reward or punishment related to particular behaviours.

One structure closely connected to the orbitofrontal cortex is the ACC. The cingulate cortex was named because it forms a *cingulum* or collar around the corpus callosum and forms the dorsal part of the limbic lobe originally described by Broca. In the 1930s, Papez saw it as the area that interpreted emotional information coming from the hypothalamic region (Papez 1937). From an evolutionary developmental perspective, Papez saw the cingulate cortex as part of an ancient system. Likewise, MacLean in his concept of the tri-une brain suggested that brain development over the ages evolved in a series of three concentric structures, with the cingulate coming later than the reptilian brain and thus a part of the paleomammalian cortex (MacLean 1990). Allman *et al.* (2001) places it later in evolutionary time and suggests that the ACC may be a specialization of the neocortex rather than more primitive areas. Current research suggests that the ACC can be divided into an anterior region related to affective processing and a posterior region related to cognitive processing (see Bush *et al.* 2000 for an overview).

Overall, research has suggested that the ACC is involved in the type of executive function that allows one to drive down the street and ignore one set of signs while paying attention to another (Awh and Gehring 1999). Current research with both EEG and positron emission tomography (PET) studies suggests that within the ACC, the execution and monitoring of a response can be separated from the monitoring of the context in which the action is executed (Elliot and Dolan 1998; Luu and Tucker 2003). For example, Elliot and Dolan found that the dorsal ACC was active when subjects generated a hypothesis concerning what would be a correct response whereas the ventral ACC was active when a choice was made. Others have suggested that dorsal–ventral differences reflect cognitive versus emotional processes as well as executive versus evaluative (Bush *et al.* 2000). For example, stimulation of the central part produces intense fear or pleasure, whereas stimulation of the dorsal part produces a sense of anticipation of movement. Studying stroke patients with lesions of the anterior cingulate, Damasio and Van Hoesen (1983) described one patient who reported that her mind was empty. This patient had a remarkable recovery and knowledge of conversations which had taken place among doctors even during the early stages of her recovery. However, when asked why she did not reply, she reported that she had nothing to say and felt no will to reply to the questions. Other lesion studies have reported a similar reduction in verbal responses and spontaneous behaviour (Cohen *et al.* 1999).

The execution of voluntary action is a complex process which involves both cortical and subcortical areas in the planning and execution of motor movements. On the sub-cortical level, it is the basal ganglia that allow the action to be performed. It appears that excitatory and inhibitory network potentials representing potential motor movements are held in check through the basal ganglia. Structures in the basal ganglia use dopamine as a triggering response which initiates one of many potential motor responses. Damage to these areas, as with such pathophysiology as Parkinson's disease, results in difficulty initiating movement internally. One critical question is the manner in which the basal ganglia initiate the movement response since they lack such inputs which will convey cognitive, emotional or memory information. One possibility is the so-called limbic loop which originates in the orbitofrontal and ACC and then projects through structures of the basal ganglia and then back to the orbitofrontal and cingulate areas through the thalamus (see Roth 2003 for an overview).

In terms of hypnotic modulation of experience, the ACC is consistently shown to be an area involved. In a series of PET studies, Rainville and his colleagues have shown that neural activity in the brainstem, thalamus and ACC contribute to the experience of being hypnotized (Rainville *et al.* 1997, 1999*a*, *b*, 2002). In particular, the authors report absorption-related changes in the more rostral regions of the ACC. In an earlier hypnotic study involving painful stimuli, Rainville *et al.* (1997) found that activity in the ACC closely paralleled subjective experience, and that it reflected the emotional component (i.e. unpleasantness) but not the sensory component of the painful stimuli. The right ACC has also been implicated in the hallucination, but not the imagining of external stimuli in highly hypnotizable individuals (Szechtman *et al.* 1998).

A variety of studies have shown a connection between activity of the ACC and theta on the scalp. Also, a solid relationship between electrocortical activity, hypnosis and hypno-tizability exists in the EEG theta frequency range (see Crawford and Gruzelier 1992 for a review; see also Chapter 9 for an alternative perspective). At this point, I can suggest that EEG theta activity and the cingulate cortex are two important physiological mechanisms which are active during the hypnotic experience. The basic hypothesis to be tested in future research is that hypnosis operates by disconnecting or isolating the emotional processing of the ACC from its cognitive and motor-related processes which results in a lack of the experience of agency.

Although based on a single case study, it is tempting to speculate and note the similari-ties between a patient with a lesion in the cingulate and an individual experiencing hyp-nosis. In both cases, the individual reports a lack of desire to initiate activity although completely aware of events in the external environment. If indeed hypnosis represents a functional inhibition of normal cingulate functioning, then this would have a variety of implications. First, hypnosis would represent a simpler and more primitive cognitive/emotional/motor process than some theories have suggested. Secondly, theo-ries which place an emphasis on higher level neocortical cognitive functioning as an aspect of hypnosis would be inappropriate for understanding the basic phenomenon. Thirdly, using tools such as imaging techniques including magnetoencephalography (MEG) and EEG directed at reflecting cingulate activity or theta activity, it will now be possible to begin to address many of the questions that have plagued the field or been considered unanswerable.

12.11 Attachment and internalized self-regulation

We now turn to the development and ontogeny of the hypnotic experience. Are there developmental processes that help explain the nature of hypnosis? In terms of hypnotiz-ability, children show an increase in susceptibility until about 8–12 years of age and then begin a decline through adolescence (Morgan and Hilgard 1973). This finding is in line with Hughlings Jackson's suggestion that during cortical development in adolescence and early adulthood, inhibitory processes from higher cortical processes become expanded. Consistent with the theoretical perspective is the idea that development processes mediate the child's sensitivity to social influence and these in turn are related to hypnotic susceptibility. The complexity and plasticity of human beings are partly related to our large brains. Also important is our extended juvenile period in which we are born immature and continue to develop for the next 15–25 years. In describing development, evolutionary psychologists ask the question of what role evolved psychological mechanisms have played in adapting infants and children to their physical and social environment (see Ellis and Bjorklund 2005 for an overview). For example, human children spend a considerable amount of their available energy in play. As we consider play, we can consider both how it helps children in their current social, emotional, cognitive and physical development as well as how it prepares them for future roles in society. Thus, this perspective helps us to think about how adaptations of infants and children impact adult development. This is a complicated question since it forces us to think about the interaction between adaptations of childhood, their impact on adulthood and the manner in which these are passed to the next generation. We begin with the manner in which children at different ages relate to their environment. As we do this, we find ourselves constantly asking the question of what factors underlie these interactions. In proposing answers to this question, we find ourselves looking at the context of the situation on a variety of levels. These levels may range from the genetic one to the larger cultural one, to even the larger environmental level including weather and physical terrain. There is of course no one answer but a complex interaction of factors involving multiple layers of analysis. However, it might to useful to think of an infant as constantly giving itself experiences based on its genetic programming and environmental situation. In this spirit, evolutionary psychology has allowed us to make some predictions and test hypotheses which psychology without an evolutionary perspective did not consider.

We begin by noting that motor behaviours, in terms of either performing an action or an inability to perform, have traditionally played an important role in the hypnotic process. At an elementary level, there are neural mechanisms that plan and monitor a variety of actions. These mechanisms form the neurophysiological basis for what we experience as voluntary control over behaviour. Throughout development, the child's self-regulatory mechanisms are closely tuned to social influence. Human infants instinctually respond to parental communications. Such responses allow the infants to incorporate parental regulatory influences to supplement their immature self-regulatory capacities. The incorporation of parental control is integral to cognitive development, such that internalized parental dialogues form a foundation for self-regulation throughout life. The mind's direction of behaviour is best understood not as a pristine and powerful act of personal volition, but as an amalgam of urges and self-regulatory algorithms, and one critical algorithm for self-control is private speech. We previously approached the developmental question by proposing that hypnosis is achieved through a diversion of the normal self-regulatory algorithm of internal speech, facilitated in large part because this algorithm develops through internalization of what was initially an overt parental dialogue (see Ray and Tucker 2003).

From this perspective, we noted that human infants are neotenous. Their development is retarded, allowing an extensive period of social communication, over a decade or more, to shape their developing brains (Tucker 1993). In the first year, the normal human infant is not only highly responsive to social communication, exhibiting emotions and communications that support the attachment process, but also fails to exhibit emotions such as hostility and negativism that may disrupt the parental bond (Mahler 1968). A similar delay of hostile displays is seen in rhesus monkeys, as described by Harlow (1959) and also Suomi (2005), suggesting that the developmental progression facilitating attachment may be a generic feature of primate social development. In the second year of human development, the maturation of motor control and language acquisition are accompanied by motivational substrates, including hostility and negativism that support the child's individuation and autonomy (Mahler 1968). For both these critical developmental stages, the mechanisms of self-regulation are tightly coordinated with the mechanisms of social influence. Recent theorists have emphasized that the parent's control is important to supplement the infant's immature self-regulatory capacity (Rothbart and Posner 1985). Because self- and social regulation inevitably diverge as causal influences on behaviour, the coordination of dependence and independence is a key theme not only for early development, but also for psychological organization throughout the life span.

In considering how hypnotic suggestion could become effective in controlling an individual's experience and behaviour, it may be important to consider early psychological orientations, both those that facilitate the incorporation of social influences within self-regulatory systems, and those that reject social influences in order to establish autonomy. Effective hypnosis would seem to require a strong dominance of the incorporation orientation over the rejection orientation. Whether this could inform research in individual differences in hypnotic susceptibility would be an interesting question.

Although the early, pre-verbal motivational and cognitive orientation must be a critical substrate for experience in a social context, the child's capacity for verbal representation of thought soon becomes an essential medium not only for social influence, but also for internal control of behaviour. Developmental theorists have emphasized the self-regulatory functions of the child's own speech, which is often used overtly to organize behavioural plans in young children, and then becomes internalized as a private guide for actions (Vygotsky 1934).

Although the explicit verbal form of private speech may be important as an organization and memory device in the child's behaviour planning, there also may be more abstract social representational functions provided by private speech, in which the child guides his or her actions by representing the viewpoint of the parent or other significant figure as an observer of the behaviour. Freud's (1940) formulation of the superego emphasized the importance of incorporated parental viewpoints and directives as elements of the self. Later, object relations theorists came to understand that the early social relation patterns, while they may result in parental introjects, are also fundamental to the development of the ego itself (e.g. Horney 1945; Mahler 1968). Recent research on language acquisition (Baldwin 1993) has converged with these traditional formulations in an interesting way. The young child learns the meaning of words in large part through careful attention to the perspective and intention of the parent. Although classical approaches to language have long emphasized the need to represent the speaker's intention in interpreting the utterance, it has only been recently that we have recognized that forming a mental representation of the parent's intention is an elementary process that is formative in the development of verbal thought as early as the second year of life. Research on representation of others' mental states has also emphasized the importance of the cognitive representation of social perspective and the intention of others for the development of the self. The normal volitional control of behaviour emerges out of these elementary structures of self in social context. Although the complexities of social cognition remain poorly understood, we can expect that hypnotic control must be understood in relation to the social influences that engage, at a primitive level, the mental representations that motivate, direct and monitor behavioural actions.

12.12 **Evolutionary advantage of hypnosis**

I now approach the question of what is the function and survival value of being able to enter into the hypnotic experience, i.e. we ask the question of whether there is any survival value to those individuals who are able to enter a hypnotic experience as compared with those who are not. We first must consider the possibility that there is no value to the hypnotic experience and that it remains as an epiphenomenon that may have served a purpose in the past but does not any longer. For example, human infants at birth will close their fingers and toes around an object such as a rope tightly enough to allow them to hold their own weight. Clearly this is not a task that human infants are required to do in their environment. However, given that one of the best stimuli for eliciting the response is a clump of hair, it may be that the response is related to the non-human primate infant grasping his mother as she moves through the trees, which does have great survival value. Thus, what has functional significant for non-human primates may have little for human infants. However, the grasping reflex still exists in humans.

The alternative to considering hypnosis as a vestigial response is to examine areas in which there is functional value. If we examine the data in terms of the current functional value of hypnosis, we are drawn to such areas as pain management through hypnosis (Holroyd 1996), modulation of the immune system through hypnosis (Kiecolt-Glaser *et al.* 2001), and its ability to enhance treatment effectiveness (Kirsch *et al.* 1995). A variety of studies including a special issue of the *International Journal of Clinical and Experimental Hypnosis* (April 2000) have reviewed these areas and shown that hypnotic procedures enhance cognitive behavioural treatments for a variety of problems. Given that one meta-analysis (Kirsch *et al.* 1995) suggested that there existed few procedural differences between the hypnotic and non-hypnotic treatments, one might conclude that the positive benefits of hypnotic procedures lie with the individual and his or her susceptibility to hypnotic procedures. Whether this susceptibility level can in turn result in a greater level of adaptability or ability to produce offspring as would be suggested by evolutionary fitness is an open question. However, the fact that hypnotizability is associated with an ability to reduce the experience of pain, modulate the immune system and achieve greater benefits of psychosocial therapies is of course of great functional significance. On a larger scale, this would suggest that the hypnotic experience plays an important role in the process of internal self-regulation involving the ACC and theta activity as described previously. Other chapters in this book lay out in more detail the manner in which these ideas may be related to absorption as well as internal self-regulation (see Chapters 8, 13 and 14).

12.13 **Summary and conclusion**

There have been few articulations of how the hypnotic experience reflects evolutionary pressures based on the adaptive history of human beings. In the present chapter, I have begun to bring together a variety of perspectives that would inform such theoretical speculation. The initial question of is there evidence for a genetic involvement in the hypnotic experience was answered in the affirmative. The next unanswered question in the genetic relationship to hypnosis is which genes turn on and off during the experience and the environmental conditions that bring forth these processes. Utilizing the historical speculation of Hughlings Jackson and Paul MacLean, the chapter further suggested that the hypnotic experience is not a process found at the earliest evolutionary structures but rather one involved in the interface between the limbic and neocortical systems. Specifically, the anatomical structure of the ACC with its close connections to the neocortex appears to play an important role. ACC activity appears to be reflected in EEG theta activity which has a strong association with hypnosis. One important hypothesis to be tested is that hypnosis operates by disconnecting or isolating the emotional processing of the ACC from its cognitive and motor-related processes which results in a lack of the experience of agency. In terms of our evolutionary history, it is further suggested that hypnosis may be related to the developmental concept of attachment and other human social processes which may have helped to promote cohesion in the community. In terms of current adaptive features, hypnotizability is associated with an ability to reduce the experience of pain, to modulate the immune system and to achieve greater benefits of psychosocial therapies. This would suggest that the hypnotic experience has its roots in processes which initially evolved to protect the organism in a variety of both internal and external situations.

References

Allman JM (2000). *Evolving brains*. New York, Scientific American Library.

Allman JM, Hakeem A, Erwin JM, Nimchinsky E and Hof P (2001). The anterior cingulate cortex: the evolution of an interface between emotion and cognition. *Annals of the New York Academy of Sciences*, **935**, 107–17.

Awh E and Gehring W (1999). The anterior cingulate cortex lends a hand in response selection. *Nature Neuroscience*, **2**, 853–54.

Baldwin DA (1993). Infants' ability to consult the speaker for clues to word reference. *Journal of Child Language*, **20**, 395–418.

Bjick E (2001). *Physiological reactivity, startle, and suggestion: an investigation into the mechanism of hypnotic alteration of experience*. Penn State University Dissertation.

Bowers K (1976). *Hypnosis for the seriously curious*. Pacific Grove, CA, Brooks Cole.

Bowers K (1983). *Hypnosis for the seriously curious, 2nd ed*. New York: Norton.

Bowlby J (1969). Attachment and loss: Vol. 1. Attachment. London, Hogarth.

Brass M and Heyes C (2005). Imitation: is cognitive neuroscience solving the correspondence problem? *Trends in Cognitive Sciences*, **9**, 489–95.

Bush G, Luu P and Posner M (2000). Cognitive and emotional influences in the anterior cingulate cortex. *Trends in Cognitive Sciences*, **4**, 215–22.

Cohen R, Kaplan R, Zuffante P, Moser D, Jenkins M, Salloway S, *et al* (1999). Alteration of intention and self-initiated action associated with bilateral anterior cingulotomy. *Journal of Neuropsychiatry and Clinical Neuroscience*, **11**, 444–53

Crawford H and Gruzelier J (1992). A midstream view of the neuropsychophysiology of hypnosis: Recent research and future direction. In: E Fromm and M Nash eds, *Contemporary hypnosis research*. New York, Guilford Press, pp. 227–266.

Damasio A and Van Hoesen G (1983). Emotional disturbances associated with focal lesions of the limbic frontal lobe. In: K Heilman and P Sata, eds. *Neuropsychology of human emotion*. pp. 85–110. New York, Guilford.

Darwin C (1859). *On the origin of species by means of natural selection*. London, J Murray.

Darwin C (1874). *The descent of man and selection in relation to sex*. Chicago, Rand McNally.

Draper D and Klemm W (1967). Behavioral responses associated with animal hypnosis. *The Psychological Record*, **17**, 13–21.

Elliott R and Dolan R (1998). Activation of different anterior cingulate foci in association with hypothesis testing and response selection. *NeuroImage*, **8**, 17–29.

Ellis B and Bjorklund D, eds. (2005). *Origins of the social mind: evolutionary psychology and child development*. New York, The Guilford Press.

Freud S (1940). *An outline of psychoanalysis*. Wiltshire: Redwood Press Ltd.

Gallup G (1974). Animal hypnosis: factual status of a fictional concept. *Psychological Bulletin*, **81**, 836–53.

Gallese V, Keysers C and Rizzolatti G (2004). A unifying view of the basis of social cognition. *Trends in Cognitive Sciences*, **8**, 396–403.

Harlow H (1959). Love in infant monkeys. *Scientific American*, **200**, 68–74.

Hilgard E (1968). *The experience of hypnosis*. New York, Harcourt Brace Jovanovich.

Holroyd J (1996). Hypnosis treatment of clinical pain: understanding why hypnosis is useful. *International Journal of Clinical and Experimental Hypnosis*, **44**, 33–51.

Horney K (1945). *Our inner conflicts*. New York, WW Norton.

Jackson JH (1884). Evolution and dissolution of the nervous system (the Croonian Lectures). *British Medicial Journal*, **1**, 591–754.

Kiecolt-Glaser J, Maruch P, Atkinson C and Glaser R (2001). Hypnosis as a modulator of cellular immune dysregulation during acute stress. *Journal of Consulting and Clinical Psychology*, **69**, 674–82.

Kirsch I, Montgomery G and Sapirstein G (1995). Hypnosis as an adjunct to cognitive–behavioral psychotherapy: a meta-analysis. *Journal of Consulting and Clinical Psychology*, **63**, 214–20.

Klein R (2000). Archeology and the evolution of human behavior. *Evolutionary Anthropology*, **9**, 17–36.

Landis C and Hunt W (1939). *The startle pattern*. New York, Farrar and Rinehard.

Luu P and Tucker D (2003). Self-regulation and the executive functions: electrophysiological clues. In: A Zani and AM Preverbio, eds. *The cognitive electrophysiology of mind and brain*, pp. 199–223. San Diego, Academic Press.

Maasen S, Prinz W and Roth G (2003). *Voluntary action: brains, minds, and sociality*. Oxford, Oxford University Press.

MacLean P (1990). *The triune brain in evolution*. New York, Plenum.

Mahler MS (1968). *On human symbiosis and the vicissitudes of individuation*. New York, International University Press.

Morgan A (1973). The heritability of hypnotic susceptibility in twins. *Journal of Abnormal Psychology*, **82**, 55–61.

Morgan A and Hilgard E (1973). Age differences in susceptibility to hypnosis. *International Journal of Clinical and Experimental Hypnosis*, **21**, 78–85.

Morgan A, Hilgard E and Davert E (1970). The heritability of hypnotic susceptibility of twins: a preliminary report. *Behavioral Genetics*, **1**, 213–24.

Olson S (2000). *Mapping human history*. Boston, Houghton Mifflin.

Papez J (1937). A proposed mechanism of emotion. *Archives of neurology and pathology*, **38**, 725–743.

Pavlov (1927; 1960) *Conditioned reflexes: an investigation of the physiological activity of the cerebral cortex* (GV Anrep, Transl.). New York, Dover.

Piccione C, Hilgard E and Zimbardo P (1989). On the degree of stability of measured hypnotizability over a 25-year period. *Journal of Personality and Social Psychology*, **56**, 289–95.

Rawlings R (1977). *The genetics of hypnotisability*. Dissertation, University of New South Wales.

Rainville P, Duncan GH, Price DD, Carrier B and Bushnell MC (1997). Pain affect encoded in human anterior cingulate but not somatosensory cortex. *Science*, **277**, 968–71.

Rainville P, Carrier B, Hofbauer RK, Bushnell MC and Duncan GH (1999a). Dissociation of sensory and affective dimensions of pain using hypnotic modulation. *Pain*, **82**, 159–71.

Rainville P, Hofbauer RK, Paus T, Duncan GH, Bushnell MC and Price DD (1999b). Cerebral mechanisms of hypnotic induction and suggestion. *Journal of Cognitive Neuroscience*, **11**, 110–25.

Rainville P, Hafbauer R, Bushnell M, Duncan G and Price D (2002). Hypnosis modulates activity in brain structures involved in the regulation of consciousness. *Journal of Cognitive Neuroscience*, **14**, 887–901.

Ray WJ and Tucker D (2003). Evolutionary approaches to understanding the hypnotic experience. *International Journal of Clinical and Experimental Hypnosis*, **51**, 256–81.

Ray WJ, Keil A, Mikuteit A, Bongartz W and Elbert T (2002). High resolution EEG indicators of pain responses in relation to hypnotic susceptibility and suggestion. *Biological Psychology*, **60**, 17–36.

Rizzolatti G and Craighero L (2004). The mirror-neuron system. *Annual Review of Neuroscience*, **27**, 169–92.

Roth G (2003). The interaction of cortex and basal ganglia in the controls of voluntary actions. In: S Maasen, W Prinz and G Roth, eds. *Voluntary action*. pp. 115–132. Oxford, Oxford University Press.

Rothbart MK and Posner MI (1985). Temperament and the development of self-regulation. In: LC Hartlage and CF Telzrow, eds. *The neuropsychology of individual differences: a developmental perspective*. pp. 93–123. New York, Plenum Press.

Rovec C and Luciano D (1973). Rearing influences on tonic immobility in three day old chicks (*Gallus gallus*). *Journal of Comparative and Physiological Psychology*, **83**, 351–54.

Striedter G (2005). *Principles of brain evolution*. Sunderland, MA, Sinauer Associates.

Suomi S (2005). Mother–infant attachment, peer relationships, and the development of social networks in rhesus monkeys. *Human Development*, **48**, 67–79.

Szechtman H, Woody E, Bowers K, and Nahmias C (1998). Where the imaginal appears real: A positron emission tomography study of auditory hallucinations. *Proceedings of the National Academy of Sciences of the USA*, **95**, 1956–60.

Tucker DM (1993). Emotional experience and the problem of vertical integration. *Neuropsychology*, **7**, 500–9.

Völgyesi F (1966). *Hypnosis of man and animals*. Baltimore, MD, Williams and Wilkins.

Vygotsky L (1934, reprinted 1962). *Thought and language*. Cambridge, MA, MIT Press.

Weiner J (1994). *The beak of the finch*. New York, Alfred A Knopf.

Chapter 13

To see feelingly: emotion, motivation and hypnosis

Erik Woody and Henry Szechtman

King Lear (to Gloucester, who has become blind): 'Yet you see how this world works'.
Gloucester: 'I see it feelingly'.

(Shakespeare's *King Lear*, Act IV, scene vi)

13.1 Behaviour and experience in hypnosis

In the late 1950s and early 1960s, Weitzenhoffer and Hilgard laid the foundation for modern hypnosis research by devising standardized hypnosis scales. They modified the earlier hypnosis scale of Friedlander and Sarbin (1938) by adding additional comparatively easy test suggestions, particularly direct motor suggestions, resulting in two alternate forms, the Stanford Hypnotic Susceptibility Scales, Forms A and B (SHSS: A and SHSS: B; Weitzenhoffer and Hilgard 1959). They then devised another hypnosis scale with a better representation of relatively difficult suggestions, such as hallucinations and age regression, resulting in the Stanford Hypnotic Susceptibility Scale, Form C (SHSS: C; Weitzenhoffer and Hilgard 1962). The SHSS: C is now widely regarded as the gold standard of hypnosis research (Woody and Barnier 1996).

Later developments in hypnosis scales have closely followed this pioneering work. For example, the world's most widely used hypnosis scale is the Harvard Group Scale of Hypnotic Susceptibility, Form A (HGSHS: A; Shor and Orne 1962), which is simply a group adaptation format of the SHSS: A. Similarly, the Waterloo–Stanford Group Scale of Hypnotic Susceptibility, Form C (WSGC; Bowers 1993, 1998) reproduces the psychometric properties of the SHSS: C in a group format.

To a considerable extent, these hypnosis scales provide a working operational definition of what a hypnotic response is. Thus, it is very interesting that the Stanford scales and their kin measure hypnotic response purely in terms of the observable motor behaviours that may be elicited by the test suggestions. The hypnotist records these responses in individually administered scales such as the SHSS: C, and the participants themselves record them, taking the point of view of an objective observer, in group scales such as the HGSHS: A. For each response, there is a dichotomous scoring criterion. To illustrate, for the arm immobilization suggestion, the response is scored as a pass if the hand and arm did not lift by at least 1 inch, and as a fail if they lifted by 1 inch or more. The underlying assumption is clearly that overt behavioural responses, in and of themselves, provide a valid index of true hypnotic response (Weitzenhoffer 1997).

However, it is important not to confuse what is readily measured with what is truly essential. All these overt motor responses can be faked or simulated by people who are not actually responding to hypnosis at all. Fortunately, there is evidence that hypnotic subjects are generally not faking their responses (Kinnunen *et al.* 1994). Nonetheless, the possibility of faking or simulating indicates that behavioural response alone cannot adequately define the essence of a truly hypnotic response. Instead, the crucial effect of hypnosis is not on observable behaviour *per se*, but on subjective experience. Orne (1972) remarked that the 'hallmark of the hypnotic phenomena … is the nature and quality of the concomitant subjective events' (p. 421).

The most widely recognized attempt to characterize the essential subjective experience in hypnosis is Weitzenhoffer's (1980) notion of the 'classic suggestion effect'. He argued that a true hypnotic response necessarily involves an alteration in the sense of agency, in which one's own will or volition is not experienced as the origin of the response. What the hypnotist suggests seems to happen of itself, extra-volitionally. For example, if the hypnotist suggests that the subject's arm is rigid, the truly hypnotic response is the experience that one's arm has become rigid on its own. In contrast, the experience that one is purposely holding one's arm stiff would not be a true hypnotic response, even though it could be associated with the same objective behaviour. Thus, true hypnotic responses have an essential quality of involuntariness or non-volition.

Although this characterization fits motor suggestions quite well, it applies less well to some hypnotic phenomena, such as hallucinations. For phenomena such as hallucinations, the crucial subjective experience is the conviction of the reality of the suggested state of affairs. Tellegen (1978/1979) argued that regardless of how vividly a perception is imagined, it does not meet the minimal definition of a hypnotic response unless it is experienced as real: 'it is the *act* of positing something imagined as real that characterizes a response as hypnotic rather than the *content* of the imagined event' (p. 220). Similarly, Kallio and Revonsuo (2003) maintained that a true hypnotic response is not 'to imagine some alternative state of affairs', but instead 'to believe that such a state of affairs is really the case' (p. 129).

In summary, although hypnotic suggestions can produce measurable changes in overt behaviour, these overt behaviours alone do not define the essence of hypnosis. Instead, certain subjective experiences are the crux of hypnosis. These experiences involve changes in the sense of volition and the sense of reality.

13.2 **Feelings of knowing**

A number of theorists have pointed out that the senses of volition and of reality are feelings, i.e. they are irreducibly emotive in nature, rather than rationally inferential.

For example, the philosopher Proust (2003) characterized the sense of volition as follows:

> The impression of being or not being the agent in one's actions is not *inferred* from what one believes and desires. It is a genuine, direct feeling, experienced dynamically in the changing world, a feeling functionally independent of the specific content of the corresponding intention (p. 317).

Likewise, William James (1890, p. 283) characterized the sense of reality as emotive rather than rational: 'In its inner nature, belief or the sense of reality, is a sort of feeling more allied to the emotions than anything else'. In a similar vein, he noted the following:

> The recesses of feeling … are the only places where we catch real fact in the making, and directly perceive how events happen, and how work is actually done. Compared with this world of living individualized feelings, the world of generalized objects which the intellect contemplates is without solidity or life.
>
> (James 1902/1977, p. 770)

In discussing the relevance of such felt experiences to hypnotic phenomena, Woody and Szechtman (2000*a*, *b*) dubbed them 'feelings of knowing'. In the cognitive literature, the term 'feeling of knowing' has most often been employed to refer to intuitions about one's memory: namely, the feeling that one knows some information even though at the moment one cannot bring it to mind (e.g. Nelson *et al.* 1984). This basic distinction between the subjective conviction of knowing and one's objectively verifiable knowledge can be usefully extended to other spheres of mental activity, including perception and action (Whittlesea 2002).

Although feelings of knowing can appear to be merely epiphenomenal, they actually have extremely potent effects on behaviour (Woody and Szechtman 2002). For example, Jaspers (1913/1963) pointed out that the emotive component of knowing has a somewhat concealed, yet crucial role in mental life, which becomes more frankly evident in certain kinds of psychopathology:

> Conceptual reality carries conviction only if a kind of presence is experienced. … Our attention gets drawn to it because it can be disturbed pathologically and so we appreciate that it exists (pp. 93–94).

Imagine being faced by very clear external information, yet unable to produce a conviction of knowing. What would this be like? Rapoport (1989*a*, *b*) proposed that this is, in fact, the predicament faced by suffers of obsessive–compulsive disorder (OCD). She characterized OCD patients as follows:

> The doorknob must be turned again and again; the light switched on and off, on and off. These acts bring immediate information, yet it doesn't get through. They can't say, 'Yes, I have checked this out and now I know …'.
>
> (Rapoport 1989*b*, p. 238)

That is, the perceptions of OCD patients are objectively sound, but do not generate the normally accompanying conviction. The failure to generate this sense of conviction outweighs evidence before the senses that most people would find obvious and compelling. In addition, it leads to repetition of the relevant thoughts and actions, which yield conviction only weakly and slowly. Accordingly, Rapoport suggested that OCD patients may have a deficit in a feeling-based ability to know which we all normally take for granted.

Building on the ideas of Rapoport (1989a, b) and Reed (1985), we have recently hypothesized that the symptoms of OCD have what might be called an 'epistemic' basis, involving a disturbance in subjective convictions about reality (Szechtman and Woody 2004; Woody and Szechtman 2005). For OCD sufferers, knowing objectively does not translate into believing subjectively. For example, even though the compulsive hand washer sees hands that look objectively clean, he or she cannot readily generate the subjective conviction that they are truly clean, and so continues to wash.

Other psychopathological conditions, such as delusional misidentification syndromes (Ellis et al. 1994; Halligan and Marshall 1996), also illustrate the powerful role that feelings of knowing have on behaviour. The most fully studied of such syndromes is Capgras delusion, in which the patient believes that a close relative has been replaced by an identical-looking imposter. Such patients recognize that the objective characteristics of the relative are correct, such as the face, tone of voice, and so forth; however, they fail to experience the emotional 'glow' that they would normally feel in the presence of the person (Ellis and Young 1990; Ramachandran and Blakeslee 1998). The lack of this covert, felt response outweighs all the more objective evidence, leading to the delusional belief that the person in front of them cannot possibly be the real person. Hence, in Capgras delusion, as in OCD, the lack of feelings of knowing leads to far-reaching effects on perception and behaviour.

There is a wide spectrum of delusional misidentification problems, and it has been proposed that they lie along a continuum of disturbances of feelings of knowing (Sno 1994). At the opposite end from Capgras delusion, in which such feelings are lacking, are conditions such as chronic déjà vu, in which people have a surfeit of feelings of knowing, leading to the continuing delusion that events that are actually new have all happened before (Moulin et al. 2005). An example is a man who, travelling in Europe for the first time, complained that he had already been everywhere before (Kirkey 2006).

In summary, the foregoing psychopathological conditions demonstrate the considerable potency of feelings of knowing. At least some kinds of compulsions and delusions appear to stem from disturbances in patients' felt experiences. In addition, these felt experiences are so primary that they overturn strong objective evidence, which such patients may continue to process normally and accurately.

13.3 Hypnosis and feelings of knowing

In highly hypnotizable individuals, hypnotic suggestions produce changes in behaviour that resemble the forgoing psychopathological conditions. Indeed, Kihlstrom (2006) characterized hypnosis as involving two essential qualities: 'involuntariness bordering on compulsion' and 'conviction bordering on delusion'. Accordingly, we hypothesized that because hypnosis alters feelings of knowing, such as the sense of volition and the sense of reality, these feelings may be the mechanism by which hypnotic suggestions produce classic hypnotic responses (Woody and Szechtman 2000a, b).

What initially led us to this hypothesis was consideration of the results of our positron emission tomography (PET) study of hypnotic auditory hallucinations

(Szechtman *et al.* 1998). We designed this study to locate the brain regions involved in discriminating whether an auditory event comes from the external world or not. We found that, while hallucinating, highly hypnotizable participants showed elevated regional cerebral blood flow (rCBF) in the right, rostral anterior cingulate (Brodmann area 32). Compared with baseline, adjusted blood flow in this region during hallucination was as elevated as it was during hearing, whereas there was no elevation during imagining. In addition, during hallucination, rCBF in this region correlated very strongly with participants' subjective ratings of externality ($r = 0.95$) and clarity ($r = 0.85$). Finally, participants pre-screened as incapable of hypnotic hallucinations, when run under the same conditions, showed no significant activation in this region. Thus, the right anterior cingulate appeared to be critically implicated in the perception that an auditory event originated in external reality.

The further question, then, was what activation of this particular brain region might indicate about the underlying nature of hypnotic hallucinations. The anterior cingulate, as part of the limbic system, is strongly involved in emotional experience and regulation, especially the determination of the motivational significance of stimuli (Devinsky *et al.* 1995; Damasio 1997). This role suggested to us that the conviction of the reality of a suggested state of affairs may require a crucial affect, or feeling of knowing. By creating such a feeling, i.e. a felt conviction that something is out there in external reality, a hypnotic suggestion would provide the core around which the subject could construct a percept based on expectations, prior knowledge, and the like. Thus, hypnosis, via feelings of knowing, would produce a dissociation between perceptual experience and reality (Woody and Szechtman 2000a).

Recall our previous characterization of the OCD patient: despite sensory evidence most people would find self-evident—such as washing one's hands or checking a locked door—the OCD patient remains subjectively unconvinced because he or she cannot generate the feeling of knowing. Although a dissociation between subjective conviction and external reality characterizes both the OCD patient and the hypnotic hallucinator, the circumstances of the two individuals are, in an important sense, opposites. For the OCD patient, the external stimulus is present, yet the feeling of knowing is absent; for the hallucinator, the external stimulus is absent, yet the feeling of knowing is present. The effect of hypnotic suggestions in highly hypnotizable participants can be likened to other conditions that may produce a surfeit of the feeling of knowing, such as the subjectively insight-enhancing effects of marijuana (Tart 1970; Woody and Szechtman 2000a, 2002).

Further, we argued that, just as positive hallucinations may stem from a heightened feeling of knowing, negative hallucinations could likewise be explained by a weakened feeling of knowing (Woody and Szechtman 2000a). To illustrate, Spanos *et al.* (1989) suggested to highly hypnotizable participants that they would see only a blank sheet of paper, but then showed them a clear, large numeral eight. The participants who reported seeing nothing were later pressed by a second experimenter, whereupon almost all could guess the number correctly. Spanos (1991) interpreted this result as showing that when hypnotic participants claim they see nothing, they are merely complying with the hypnotist and exaggerating dishonestly. However, this interpretation is inconsistent with other

evidence showing that hypnotic subjects report truthfully about their subjective experiences (Kinnunen *et al.* 1994). We proposed an alternative explanation in terms of the
hypnotic weakening of the feeling of knowing: 'These subjects behaved in accordance
with not knowing what they knew; that is, they didn't *feel* as if they knew' (Woody and
Szechtman 2000*a*, p. 11). Accordingly, we posited that hypnosis may 'provide particular
access to the experiential or emotional (rather than rational) underpinnings of mental
processes' (p. 11; see also Brown and Oakley 1997).

In a similar vein, Kihlstrom (1994) attempted to specify which aspects of behaviour are
influenced by hypnosis and which are not. He argued that hypnosis affects 'explicit'
forms of memory, perception and action, while preserving their 'implicit' forms.
For example, explicit memory refers to the conscious, intentionally directed recall of
events, whereas implicit memory refers to other behavioural changes stemming from
previous events, such as priming effects, which are independent of conscious recall.
Hypnotic suggestions for amnesia tend to disrupt explicit memory, while preserving
implicit memory (Kihlstrom and Hoyt 1990). Similarly, explicit perception refers to the
conscious perception of stimuli, whereas implicit perception refers to effects of exposure
to stimuli, such as priming effects, that do not depend on conscious detection (Kihlstrom
et al. 1992). Hypnotic suggestions tend to affect explicit perception while sparing implicit
perception. For example, in hypnotically suggested blindness, subjects avoid walking into
obstructions, such as a table, that they cannot consciously see. Likewise, hypnotic suggestions for motor behaviours exert their effects on explicit forms of action, which are
consciously directed and volitional, rather than implicit forms, which are stimulus driven
and relatively automatic.

It is important to be clear about where feelings of knowing fit into this explicit versus
implicit distinction. Work by Ellis and Lewis (2001) on face recognition indicates that
feelings of knowing are an essential component of the explicit forms of behaviour, not
their implicit forms. Explicit perception, in Kihlstrom's (1994) sense, appears to consist
of two parallel streams of processing, an overt–cognitive route and a covert–affective
route, which are subsequently integrated. In addition, evidence shows that the
covert–affective component (i.e. the feeling of knowing) is independent of implicit
perceptual phenomena such as priming effects. Thus, this work suggests that explicit
perception, as discussed by Kihlstrom, can be fractionated into an overt, cognitive
component and a covert, affective component; in addition, the covert, affective
component (feeling of knowing) appears to be distinct from implicit perception.

In summary, our core hypothesis is that hypnotic suggestions exert their effects by
altering the covert, affective components of behaviour, which we broadly label as 'feelings
of knowing'. The next step is to address how a suitable neural model could be derived
from this hypothesis.

13.4 Approach to deriving a neural model of hypnosis

Like neural models of behaviour in general, so too models of hypnosis must be consti-
tuted from known functional neuroanatomical systems—after all, hypnotic phenomena

must be mediated by the same brain that mediates all of behaviour. This neuroscience logic forces two immediate issues that must be addressed as a prerequisite for model construction. The first issue relates to our hypothesis that hypnosis works indirectly by altering the 'feeling of knowing' associated with perception or performance of motor acts rather than by a direct influence on mechanisms of perception, reasoning or motor performance. The necessary question that such a foundational hypothesis raises is this: what are the naturally occurring conditions where feeling states dominate over information provided by other sensory inputs or sources of information? In other words, is the normal brain so constructed that under particular circumstances the output of the system mediating feelings has precedence in guiding behaviour over outputs from other sensory and motor systems, even when those other sources of information contradict the feeling information? A positive answer to this question leads immediately to the second issue, namely what is it about hypnosis that brings about those particular circumstances where behaviour is guided by feelings? Answers to these questions are considered below and form the conceptual basis of the proposed neural model of hypnotic phenomena as resulting from alterations in the feeling of knowing.

13.5 **When feelings are enough**

An evolutionary perspective on brain and behaviour highlights the hierarchical nature of nervous system organization, with different neural systems specialized for distinct modes of processing and responding to changes in the external environmental and internal milieu. Although there are various proposals regarding the actual details of this organization, all share the notion of a gradient in the complexity of neural systems and their function. At one end of the gradient are neural circuits that mediate reflex actions, which are relatively rapid and inborn responses to particular types of stimuli. Such circuits are generally genetically determined (i.e. the organism is born with the circuit pre-wired to detect particular stimuli and produce a stereotyped response); have simple wiring composed of relatively few connections (synapses); and are under immediate control of the appropriate environmental stimuli. At the other extreme are circuits that mediate processes such as language, evaluation of alternatives, decision making, planning, reasoning, abstract thoughts, and the like. Such circuits require extensive learning and practice for optimum performance; have complicated neural wiring specialized to integrate and perform complex calculations on diverse inputs; and even though very open to modulation by learning and experience they are not subject to immediate control by environmental stimuli as they lack pre-set connections with sensory and motor systems. Between the two extremes lie circuits of varying complexity having various combinations of dependence on genetics and the environment for their establishment, various amounts of selectivity for the type of stimuli they process and diversity of motor outputs they generate, and variously subject to control by immediate changes in the environment or internal milieu. Circuits of feelings fall within this intermediate layer of nervous system organization as they integrate interoceptive and exteroceptive inputs and control internal bodily processes that are the substrates of feelings; these circuits mediate various survival-related motivations and a range of affective responses to a multitude of external and internal events (Panksepp 1998).

Comparative neuroanatomy and evolutionary theory suggest that the various circuits have a rough anatomical localization according to the degree of complexity and function. Circuits mediating most complex functions are localized predominantly in the neocortex. The neocortex forms the outermost part of the forebrain and constitutes the bulk of it; the forebrain as a whole underwent the greatest expansion along an evolutionary scale and compromises nearly 85 per cent of the human central nervous system by volume as compared with about 45 per cent in the rat (Swanson 1995). At the other end, circuits mediating simple reflexes, chains of reflexes, as well as complex automatisms and species-typical motor acts, are confined predominantly to an area that forms the central core of the central nervous system and includes the spinal cord and the medulla, parts of the midbrain, diencephalon and basal ganglia (Ploog 2003). Circuits mediating motivated behaviours and emotions are located in the middle layer, comprising the limbic system (MacLean 1952). These rough localizations and functional divisions are embodied in the concept of the triune brain elaborated by MacLean (Lambert 2003; Ploog 2003).

While under normal circumstances all parts of the nervous system work in concert, the activity of one or the other system may occasionally predominate. For instance, in particular conditions such as sudden perturbation of postural stability, reflex systems will engage first and provide rapid corrective actions. Because perturbations of equilibrium may signal external threats to the organism, a suitable motivational system may be engaged next, thereby heightening perceptual mechanisms for danger cues and facilitating activation of appropriate species-typical motor behaviours. Neocortical systems would come into play last—these systems would be engaged for a comprehensive appraisal of the situation in light of past experiences and if needed to elaborate a plan of action that extends beyond the immediate situation (Shuren and Grafman 2002).

The activity of the limbic and neocortical systems is normally mutually interactive; however, there may be conditions under which the balance between the two systems is shifted toward one or the other. Conditions of high motivational significance tend to shift the balance toward the limbic system at the expense of neocortical processes. From an evolutionary perspective, the limbic system contains systems that are hard wired and specially tuned to the processing of survival-related events so that processing is fast and requires fewer resources, although at the cost of reduced flexibility. In addition, strong motivational states are associated with changes in neurotransmitters and hormones that reduce the contribution of the prefrontal cortex in processing information (Arnsten 1998; Seamans and Yang 2004; Arnsten and Li 2005; Robbins 2005; Floresco and Magyar 2006). In such states, behaviour is principally guided by the immediate situation and evoked feelings, at the expense of higher level goals and flexible use of prior knowledge.

13.6 **The emotive nature of hypnosis**

Our contention is that the hypnotic circumstance engages a particular motivational system of great importance. This is the system that manages the dominance hierarchy that characterizes organized mammalian societies (Wilson 1975). As Wilson (1999) has pointed out,

> Countless studies of animal species ... have shown that membership in dominance order pays off in survival ... not just for the dominant individuals, but for the subordinates as well. ... It would be surprising to find out that modern humans had managed to erase the old mammalian means of distributing power. All the evidence suggests that they have not. True to their primate heritage, people are easily seduced by confident, charismatic leaders (pp. 283–284).

From this vantage point, the position of the hypnotic subject is essentially that of a subordinate in a social hierarchy, with the hypnotist assuming the role of the dominant individual. The crucial motivationally driven processes elicited by this subordinate position include suppression of one's own will in favour of the will of the dominant individual.

Jaynes (1976) characterized hypnosis in this way. First, he observed the close link between hearing and obedience: 'To hear is actually a kind of obedience. Indeed, both words come from the same root and therefore were probably the same word originally' (p. 97). Next, he noted that a key aspect of a hypnotic induction is a narrowing of consciousness in which the hypnotist confines the subject's attention to only the hypnotist's voice and thereby suppresses internal narrating that denotes the sense of self. Finally, he referred to the 'archaic authorization' (p. 393) that the hypnotist offers the subject, in which the hypnotist assumes the position of a powerful authority figure. Indeed, Nash and Spinler (1989) verified that many hypnotic subjects experience the hypnotist as a larger-than-life figure, an experience Shor (1962) labelled 'archaic involvement'.

In a review of research on consciousness, Banks and Farber (2002) criticized current theories of hypnosis for not addressing the mechanism by which the hypnotist acquires control over hypnotically susceptible individuals. Their proposal for this mechanism is highly congruent with the point of view advanced here:

> We suggest that the mechanism may lie in a receptivity to control by others that is part of our nature as social animals. By this account hypnotic techniques are shortcuts to manipulating—for a brief time but with great force—the social levers and strings that are engaged by leaders, demagogues, peers, and groups in many situations (p. 16).

In summary, we hypothesize that the hypnotic circumstance engages a system for responding in a subordinate role to a dominant other. Under this motivational system, which originated to coordinate a group under a dominant leader, the words of the hypnotist elicit immediate feelings that direct perception and behaviour. In addition, the activation of this limbic-based system tends to suppresses prefrontal contributions to information processing, such that the individual fails to question the state of affairs suggested by the hypnotist's words. The lack of normal critical perspective about the suggestions of the hypnotist and their implications was labelled 'trance logic' by Orne (1959).

It is important to note that the social processes to which we are referring are fundamentally different from both compliance and rational persuasion. In compliance, individuals knowingly set aside their own views and wishes in temporary submission to those of another person because of that person's power or control over important outcomes. In rational persuasion, individuals are won over to the views and wishes of another person on the basis of some cognitive recognition of the merits of those views. In contrast, we posit that the motivational system engaged by hypnosis has the relatively automatic effect of entraining group members' perceptions and actions to the views and wishes of a leader. In this way, the group can function as if it has a single, unified level of executive control. From an evolutionary point of view, the capacity for such entrainment had considerable survival value (Wilson 1975).

13.7 **Model of hypnosis and the neurology of interoception**

Our conception of hypnosis as mediated causally by alteration in feelings as opposed to some higher order processes, such as, for instance, attention (Raz 2005), readily suggests a rudimentary schema of the neuroanatomical territories involved and their functional relation as depicted in Fig. 13.1. In a nutshell, the neuroanatomical embodiment of our conceptual model corresponds to the major jobs performed by the neocortex and the limbic system (critical analysis and affective processing, respectively) and stresses that by some means the limbic mode of information processing becomes dominant in higly hypnotizable subjects but not in those with a low susceptilility to hypnosis. In usual everyday circumstances, sensory input, including spoken words, is processed in parallel and interactively by neocortical and subcortical systems; nevertheless, neocortical processing dominates over lower subcortical inputs as evidenced, for example, by reduced limbic activity in conditions of high cognitive demand (Pochon *et al.* 2002). According to our model, this is the situation that tends to characterize subjects with a low susceptibility to hypnosis (see upper panel of Fig. 13.1): the neocortical route predominates, ensuring critical scrutiny of the hypnotist words, a scrutiny that extends to behavioural checking and hence failing the suggestion.

In contrast, in highly hypnotizable subjects, the limbic route is dominant because for those subjects the hypnotic situation activates a motivational or highly charged affective state (see lower panel of Fig. 13.1). With the limbic system thus primed, feeling states become altered to agree with the intent of the hypnotist's suggestions. Because the effect of motivational/emotional activity is to reduce prefrontal cortex processing (Arnsten 1998; Seamans and Yang 2004; Arnsten and Li 2005; Robbins 2005; Floresco and Magyar 2006), critical analysis is minimized. Consequently, behaviour becomes controlled by feelings with no active challenge afforded by neocortical processing.

We suggest that the motivational/affective state primed in the highly hypnotizable subject is one related to maintenance of social hierarchy and in particular to the appraisal and maintenance of subordinate status in a dominant/subordinate relationship. A number of studies have documented the involvement of the limbic system in the maintenance and establishment of social hierarchy in animals (Ferris 1992; Korzan *et al.* 2000; Hardy *et al.* 2002; Summers *et al.* 2003). Although we do not know the factors that account for the high but not the low hypnotizable subjects responding to the hypnotic situation in terms of a dominant/subordinate relation, the model implies that their respective hypnotic susceptibilities might be reversed by a manipulation that reverses the appraisal of their social status in the hypnotic situation.

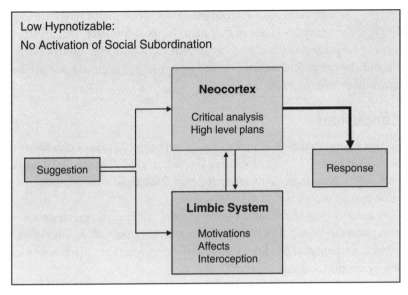

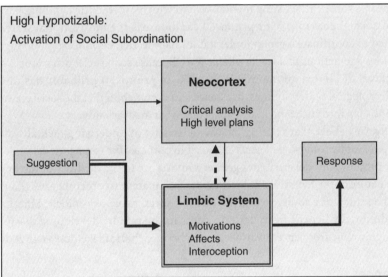

Fig. 13.1 Model of response to hypnotic suggestions for individuals with low hypnotizability (upper panel) and high hypnotizability (lower panel).

Although our neuroanatomical model of hypnosis is at present very global in specifying its components, it should be amendable to refinement along the lines elaborated in other contexts by others (Craig 2003; Price 2005). A most fruitful approach will no doubt involve the network of autonomic afferent inputs to higher regions of the brain (including the limbic system) conveying information about the physiological condition of the body—the sense of interoception (Craig 2003). As Craig (2003, p. 3) noted, 'Re-representation of interoceptive … activity in the right anterior insula is associated with subjective feelings … [providing] … the subjective image of the "material me'". It is likely that auditory input in the form of language and possibly other sounds has a powerful influence over insula function, and the congruent feelings evoked by hypnotic suggestion are produced by affecting neural processing in the insula.

13.8 Conclusions

In developing a comprehensive neural model of hypnosis, there are other issues of relevance, which we have discussed elsewhere (Woody and McConkey 2003; Woody and Szechtman 2003). Nonetheless, the foregoing initial sketch of a model advances several themes that may be generative.

First, we believe that the emotive components in hypnosis merit greater study. Hypnosis appears to manipulate covert affects, which we termed 'feelings of knowing'. Various psychopathological conditions show that changes in these affects have the capacity to alter perception and behaviour profoundly.

Secondly, we believe that it is promising to conceptualize hypnosis as a circumstance that captures some pre-existing mental system which evolved for handling particular types of social behaviour. Our proposed candidate is the motivational system that originated to coordinate a group under a dominant leader, entraining group members' perceptions and actions to a leader's behaviour. Because such social behaviour is vital to the survival of almost all mammals that live in groups, it probably has universal neurophysiological underpinnings. In essence, our argument is that the social conventions of hypnosis tap into such a mental system somewhat inadvertently.

Thirdly, we believe that relating the characteristics of underlying mental systems to core hypnotic phenomena will generate novel hypotheses for testing models. For example, our proposed model attributes greater importance to the qualities of the hypnotist and the nature of the hypnotist–subject interaction than most other theories of hypnosis do. In the future, our ability to link hypnosis to social neurophysiological mechanisms will undoubtedly benefit from developments in the rapidly developing discipline of social cognitive neuroscience (Ochsner and Lieberman 2001; Blakemore et al. 2004).

References

Arnsten AF (1998). The biology of being frazzled. *Science*, **280**, 1711–2.

Arnsten AF and Li BM (2005). Neurobiology of executive functions: catecholamine influences on prefrontal cortical functions. *Biological Psychiatry*, **57**, 1377–84.

Banks WP and Farber I (2002). Consciousness. In: A Healey and R Proctor, eds. *Handbook of psychology, vol. 4: experimental psychology*. pp. 3–31. Hoboken, NJ, Wiley.

Blakemore SJ, Winston J and Frith U (2004). Social cognitive neuroscience: where are we heading? *Trends in Cognitive Sciences*, **8**, 191–238.

Bowers KS (1993). The Waterloo–Stanford Group C (WSGC) scale of hypnotic susceptibility: normative and comparative data. *International Journal of Clinical and Experimental Hypnosis*, **41**, 35–46.

Bowers KS (1998). Waterloo–Stanford Group Scale of Hypnotic Susceptibility, Form C: manual and response booklet. *International Journal of Clinical and Experimental Hypnosis*, **46**, 250–68.

Brown RJ and Oakley DA (1997). Hypnosis and cognitive-experiential self-theory: a new conceptualization for hypnosis? *Contemporary Hypnosis*, **14**, 94–9.

Craig AD (2003). Interoception: the sense of the physiological condition of the body. *Current Opinion in Neurobiology*, **13**, 500–5.

Damasio AR (1997). Towards a neuropathology of emotion and mood. *Nature*, **386**, 769–70.

Devinsky O, Morrell MJ and Vogt BA (1995). Contributions of anterior cingulate cortex to behaviour. *Brain*, **118**, 279–306.

Ellis HD and Lewis MB (2001). Capgras delusion: a window on face recognition. *Trends in Cognitive Sciences*, **5**, 149–56.

Ellis HD and Young AW (1990). Accounting for delusional misidentifications. *British Journal of Psychiatry*, **157**, 239–48.

Ellis HD, Luauté, JP and Retterstol N (1994). Delusional misidentification syndromes. *Psychopathology*, **27**, 117–20.

Ferris C (1992). Role of vasopressin in aggressive and dominant/subordinate behaviors. *Annals of the New York Academy of Sciences*, **652**, 212–26.

Floresco SB and Magyar O (2006). Mesocortical dopamine modulation of executive functions: beyond working memory. *Psychopharmacology*, **188**, 567–585, DOI: 10.1007/s00213–006–0404–5

Friedlander JW and Sarbin TR (1938). The depth of hypnosis. *Journal of Abnormal and Social Psychology*, **33**, 453–75.

Halligan PW and Marshall JC, eds. (1996). *Method in madness: case studies in cognitive neuropsychiatry.* East Sussex, UK, Psychology Press.

Hardy MP, Sottas CM, Ge R, McKittrick CR, Tamashiro KL, McKewen BS, *et al.* (2002). Trends of reproductive hormones in male rats during psychosocial stress: role of glucocorticoid metabolism in behavioral dominance. *Biology of Reproduction*, **67**, 1750–5.

James W (1890). *The principles of psychology.* New York, Holt.

James W (1902/1977). *The varieties of religious experience.* Reprinted in JJ McDermott, ed. *The writings of William James: a comprehensive edition.* Chicago, University of Chicago Press.

Jaspers K (1913/1963). *General psychopathology.* Translated by J Henig and MW Hamilton. Chicago, University of Chicago Press.

Jaynes J (1976). *The origin of consciousness in the breakdown of the bicameral mind.* Boston, Houghton Mifflin.

Kallio S and Revonsuo A (2003). Hypnotic phenomena and altered states of consciousness: a multilevel framework of description and explanation. *Contemporary Hypnosis*, **20**, 111–64.

Kihlstrom JF (1994). One hundred years of hysteria. In: SJ Lynn and JW Rhue, eds. *Dissociation: clinical and theoretical perspectives.* pp. 365–94. New York, Guilford Press.

Kihlstrom JF (in press). Consciousness in hypnosis. In: PD Zelazo M Moscovitch and E Thompson, eds. *Cambridge handbook of consciousness.* New York, Cambridge University Press.

Kihlstrom JF and Hoyt IP (1990). Repression, dissociation, and hypnosis. In: JL Singer, ed. *Repression and dissociation: implications for personality theory, psychopathology, and health.* pp. 181–208. Chicago, University of Chicago Press.

Kihlstrom JF, Barnhardt TM and Tataryn DJ (1992). Implicit perception. In: RF Bornstein and TS Pittman, eds. *Perception without awareness.* pp. 17–54. New York, Guilford Press.

Kinnunen T, Zamansky HS and Block ML (1994). Is the hypnotized subject lying? *Journal of Abnormal Psychology*, **103**, 184–91.

Kirkey S (2006). When déjà vu is more than just an odd feeling. *Ottawa Citizen*, February 13.

Korzan WJ, Summers TR and Summers CH (2000). Monoaminergic activities of limbic regions are elevated during aggression: influence of sympathetic social signaling. *Brain Research*, **870**, 170–8.

Lambert KG (2003). The life and career of Paul MacLean: a journey toward neurobiological and social harmony. *Physiology and Behavior*, **79**, 343–9.

MacLean PD (1952). Some psychiatric implications of physiological studies on frontotemporal portion of limbic system (visceral brain). *Electroencephalography and Clinical Neurophysiology Supplement,* **4**, 407–18.

Moulin CJA, Conway MA, Thompson RG, James N, Jones RW (2005). Disordered memory awareness: recollective confabulation in two cases of persistent *déjà vecu*. *Neuropsychologia*, **43**, 1362–1378.

Nash MR and Spinler D (1989). Hypnosis and transference: a measure of archaic involvement. *International Journal of Clinical and Experimental Hypnosis*, **37**, 129–44.

Nelson TO, Gerler D and Narens L (1984). Accuracy of feeling-of-knowing judgments for predicting perceptual identification and relearning. *Journal of Experimental Psychology: General*, **113**, 282–300.

Ochsner KN and Lieberman MD (2001). The emergence of social cognitive neuroscience. *American Psychologist*, **56**, 717–34.

Orne MT (1959). The nature of hypnosis: artifact and essence. *Journal of Abnormal and Social Psychology*, **58**, 277–99.

Orne MT (1972). On the simulating subject as a quasi-control group in hypnosis research: what, why, and how. In: E Fromm and RE Shor, eds. *Hypnosis: research developments and perspectives*, pp. 519–65. Chicago. Aldine-Atherton.

Panksepp J (1998). *Affective neuroscience: the foundations of human and animal emotions.* New York, Oxford University Press.

Ploog DW (2003). The place of the Triune Brain in psychiatry. *Physiology and Behavior*, **79**, 487–93.

Pochon JB, Levy R, Fossati P, Lehericy S, Polin JB, Pillon B, *et al.* (2002). The neural system that bridges reward and cognition in humans: an fMRI study. *Proceedings of the National Academy of Sciences of the USA*, **99**, 5669–74.

Price JL (2005). Free will versus survival: brain systems that underlie intrinsic constraints on behavior. *Journal of Comparative Neurology*, **493**, 132–9.

Proust J (2003). Perceiving intentions. In: J Roessler and N Eilan, eds. *Agency and self-awareness: issues in philosophy and psychology.* pp. 296–320. Oxford, Oxford University Press.

Ramachandran VS and Blakeslee S (1998). *Phantoms in the brain: probing the mysteries of the human mind.* New York, William Morrow.

Rapoport JL (1989*a*). The biology of obsessions and compulsions. *Scientific American*, **260**, 82–89.

Rapoport JL (1989*b*) *The boy who couldn't stop washing: the experience and treatment of obsessive–compulsive disorder.* New York, Dutton.

Raz A (2005). Attention and hypnosis: neural substrates and genetic associations of two converging processes. *International Journal of Clinical and Experimental Hypnosis*, **53**, 237–58.

Reed GF (1985). *Obsessional experience and compulsive behaviour: a cognitive-structural approach.* Orlando, FL, Academic Press.

Robbins TW (2005). Chemistry of the mind: neurochemical modulation of prefrontal cortical function. *Journal of Comparative Neurology*, **493**, 140–6.

Seamans JK and Yang CR (2004). The principal features and mechanisms of dopamine modulation in the prefrontal cortex. *Progress in Neurobiology*, **74**, 1–58.

Shor RE (1962). Three dimensions of hypnotic depth. *International Journal of Clinical and Experimental Hypnosis*, **10**, 23–38.

Shor RE and Orne EC (1962). *Harvard Group Scale of Hypnotic Susceptibility, Form A.* Palo Alto, CA, Consulting Psychologists Press.

Shuren JE and Grafman J (2002). The neurology of reasoning. *Archives of Neurology*, **59**, 916–9.

Sno HN (1994). A continuum of misidentification symptoms. *Psychopathology*, **27**, 144–7.

Spanos NP (1991). A sociocognitive approach to hypnosis. In: SJ Lynn and JW Rhue, eds. *Theories of hypnosis: current models and perspectives.* pp. 324–61. New York, Guilford Press.

Spanos NP, Flynn DM and Gabora NJ (1989). Suggested negative visual hallucinations in hypnotic subjects: when no means yes. *British Journal of Experimental and Clinical Hypnosis*, **6**, 63–7.

Summers CH, Summers TR, Moore MC, Korzan WJ, Woodley SK, Ronan PJ, *et al.* (2003). Temporal patterns of limbic monoamine and plasma corticosterone response during social stress. *Neuroscience*, **116**, 553–63.

Swanson LW (1995). Mapping the human brain: past, present, and future. *Trends in Neurosciences*, **18**, 471–4.

Szechtman H and Woody E (2004). Obsessive–compulsive disorder as a disturbance of security motivation. *Psychological Review*, **111**, 111–27.

Szechtman H, Woody E, Bowers KS and Nahmias C (1998). Where the imaginal appears real: a positron emission tomography study of auditory hallucinations. *Proceedings of the National Academy of Sciences of the USA*, **95**, 1956–60.

Tart CT (1970). Marijuana intoxication: common experiences. *Nature*, **226**, 701–4.

Tellegen A (1978/1979). On measures and conceptions of hypnosis. *American Journal of Clinical Hypnosis*, **21**, 219–37.

Weitzenhoffer AM (1980). Hypnotic susceptibility revisited. *American Journal of Clinical Hypnosis*, **22**, 130–46.

Weitzenhoffer AM (1997). Hypnotic susceptibility: a personal and historical note regarding the development and naming of the Stanford scales. *International Journal of Clinical and Experimental Hypnosis*, **45**, 126–43.

Weitzenhoffer AM and Hilgard ER (1959). *Stanford Hypnotic Susceptibility Scale, Forms A and B*. Palo Alto, CA, Consulting Psychologists Press.

Weitzenhoffer AM and Hilgard ER (1962). *Stanford Hypnotic Susceptibility Scale, Form C*. Palo Alto, CA, Consulting Psychologists Press.

Whittlesea BW (2002). False memory and the discrepancy-attribution hypothesis: the prototype–familiarity illusion. *Journal of Experimental Psychology: General*, **131**, 96–115.

Wilson EO (1975). *Sociobiology: the new synthesis*. Cambridge, MA, Harvard University Press.

Wilson EO (1999). *Consilience: the unity of knowledge*. New York, Vintage Books.

Woody EZ and Barnier AJ (in press). Hypnosis scales for the 21st century: what do we need and how should we use them? In: MR Nash and AJ Barnier, eds. *The Oxford handbook of hypnosis*. Oxford, Oxford University Press.

Woody EZ and McConkey KM (2003). What we don't know about the brain and hypnosis, but need to: a view from the Buckhorn Inn. *International Journal of Clinical and Experimental Hypnosis*, **51**, 309–38.

Woody E and Szechtman H (2000*a*). Hypnotic hallucinations: toward a biology of epistemology. *Contemporary Hypnosis*, **17**, 4–14.

Woody E and Szechtman H (2000*b*). Hypnotic hallucinations and yedasentience. *Contemporary Hypnosis*, **17**, 26–31.

Woody E and Szechtman H (2002). The sensation of making sense: motivational properties of the 'fringe.' *PSYCHE*, **8**(20). Available at <http://psyche.cs.monash.edu.au/v8/psyche-8-20-woody.html>

Woody E and Szechtman H (2003). How can brain activity and hypnosis inform each other? *International Journal of Clinical and Experimental Hypnosis*, **51**, 232–55.

Woody E and Szechtman H (2005). Motivation, time course, and heterogeneity in obsessive–compulsive disorder: response to Taylor, McKay, & Abramowitz (2005). *Psychological Review*, **112**, 658–61.

Chapter 14

States of absorption: in search of neurobiological foundations

Ulrich Ott

14.1 Tellegen's Absorption Scale and related inventories

For many people, states of absorption are part of everyday live. When watching television or reading a book, they become so engrossed in the presented story that they completely forget their surroundings. The same can happen spontaneously, in the absence of external stimulation, such as when daydreaming or when remembering past events.

14.1.1 Absorption scale

In 1974 Tellegen and Atkinson presented the *Tellegen Absorption Scale* (TAS) to assess interindividual differences in the tendency to experience states of absorption. They described absorption as 'a disposition for having episodes of "total" attention that fully engage one's representational (i.e., perceptual, enactive, imaginative, and ideational) resources' and explained that absorbed attending was believed to 'result in a heightened sense of reality of the attentional object, imperviousness to distracting events, and an altered sense of reality in general, including an empathically altered sense of self' (p. 268).

The TAS consists of 34 items that are answered using a true/false response format. An English version utilizing a 5-point Likert scaled response format with improved psychometric properties is also available (Jamieson 2005). To illustrate the range of phenomena covered by the scale, the six factors revealed in an analysis by Tellegen (1992) based on a data set of $n = 2000$ are described below with example items in parentheses:

1. *Responsiveness to engaging stimuli*. Intensive and emotional response to the beauty of nature and art. ('I can be deeply moved by a sunset'.)

2. *Synaesthesia*. Cross-modal associations. ('Some music reminds me of pictures or changing colour patterns'.)

3. *Enhanced cognition*. Extra-sensory perception and imaginational thinking. ('I can often somehow sense the presence of another person before I can actually see or hear her/him'. 'My thoughts often don't occur as words but as visual images'.)

4. *Oblivious/dissociative involvement*. States of absorption during daydreaming, watching a film or listening to music. ('While watching a film, a TV show, or a play, I may become so involved that I may forget about myself and my surroundings and experience the film as if it were real and as if I were taking part in it'.)

5. *Vivid reminiscence.* Past events are remembered vividly. ('I can sometimes recollect certain past experiences in my life with such clarity and vividness that it is like living them again or almost so'.)

6. *Enhanced awareness.* Mystical peak experiences. ('Sometimes I feel as if my mind could envelop the whole world'.)

However, the high correlations found between the factors (oblique rotation) speak for a general absorption dimension and discourage the use of subscales (Tellegen 1992).

A review by Roche and McConkey (1990) revealed that the absorption trait—measured by the total score on all TAS items—is related to several other psychological constructs, namely synaesthesia, daydreaming, imagery ability, imaginative involvement, fantasy proneness, openness to experience and hypnotic susceptibility.

Tellegen and Atkinson (1974) originally reported a significant correlation between TAS scores and hypnotic susceptibility. However, research by Kirsch and Council (1992) suggested that the true correlation dropped to about $r = 0.1$ when context effects were controlled for. Yet, the concept of a personality trait that predicts hypnotic responding has been attractive for many researchers in the field of hypnosis, and the TAS is probably the scale most frequently applied to this end.

14.1.2 **Self-transcendence scale**

As will be shown in subsequent sections, only a few of the studies that utilized the TAS were concerned with the biological foundations of personality. The very opposite is true for research using Cloninger's *Temperament and Character Inventory* (TCI; Cloninger *et al.* 1994). Together with its predecessor, the *Tridimensional Personality Questionnaire* (TPQ), it is the most frequently applied psychometric instrument in molecular genetic studies of personality (see Munafo *et al.* 2003; Reif and Lesch 2003). This predominance is due to the fact that Cloningers's psychobiological model connects the three temperament dimensions assessed with the TPQ and the TCI ('novelty seeking', 'harm avoidance' and 'reward dependence') with different neurotransmitter systems (Cloninger *et al.* 1993). The TCI contains 'persistence' as a fourth temperament dimension as well as three character dimensions of 'self-directedness', 'cooperativeness' and 'self-transcendence'.

Self-transcendence (TCI-ST) consists of the three following bipolar subscales (Cloninger *et al.* 1994; example items in parentheses):

1. *Creative self-forgetfulness vs. self-consciousness* (ST1). Experiences of absorption. ('Often I become so involved in what I am doing that I forget where I am for a while'.)

2. *Transpersonal identification versus personal identification* (ST2). Experiences of mystical union. ('I often feel a strong sense of unity with all the things around me'.)

3. *Spiritual acceptance versus rational materialism* (ST3). Paranormal experiences; belief in spiritual forces and miracles. ('I seem to have a "sixth sense" that sometimes allows me to know what is going to happen'. 'Sometimes I have felt my life was being directed by a spiritual force greater than any human being'.)

It is obvious that these subscales of TCI-ST overlap considerably with the factors of the TAS presented above. First, the self-forgetfulness (ST1) items are quite similar to those that constitute the TAS factor 'oblivious/dissociative involvement', stressing the intensive focusing of attention, deep involvement, and disorientation in place and time. States of mystical union, represented by transpersonal identification (ST2), are also mentioned in several items of the sixth TAS factor. According to Tellegen and Atkinson (1974), they are characteristic for absorption states because 'objects of absorbed attention acquire an importance and intimacy that are normally reserved for the self and may, therefore, acquire a temporary self-like quality. These object identifications have mystical overtones. And, indeed, one would expect high-absorption persons to have an affinity for mystical experience …' (p. 275). Finally, extra-sensory perceptions are part of the third subscale of TCI-ST and also of the third TAS factor.

Recently, Laidlaw *et al.* (2005) reported a correlation of $r = 0.64$ ($P < 0.001$; $n = 80$) between the two scales. In two of our own screening studies, the German version of the TAS (Ritz and Dahme, 1995) using a 5-point scale ranging from 'does not apply' to 'does fully apply' was administered together with a questionnaire which contained 33 TCI-ST items in German form (Cloninger *et al.* 1999). The correlation of $r = 0.66$ ($P < 0.001$; $n = 195$), found between the two scales, confirms the impression that many facets of absorption and self-transcendence are quite similar. Therefore, in the following section, findings on TCI-ST are also considered to be relevant for absorption.

14.1.3 Transliminality scale

Finally, the construct of 'transliminality' is worth mentioning because it is also highly correlated with absorption (Thalbourne *et al.* 1997). Five items of the *Transliminality Scale* (TS) were actually taken from the TAS, which had the highest loading of the nine scales included in the factor analytic procedure used to build this scale (Thalbourne 1998). Other relevant domains spanned by the TS are mystical experience, paranormal belief and experience, and magical thinking. Recently, a revised version of the TS with improved psychometric properties has been presented (Lange *et al.* 2000) and hypotheses regarding neurobiological correlates have been formulated (Thalbourne *et al.* 2001, 2003).

14.2 The disposition to become absorbed: genetic influences

Studies of heritability and molecular genetics have provided evidence in support of the notion that individual differences in absorption can be linked to genetic differences at birth. These studies suggest that a large proportion of the variance in this trait cannot be explained by environmental influence, but is rather due to biological differences.

14.2.1 Studies on heritability

Finkel and McGue (1997) investigated the heredity of the traits included in Tellegen's *Multidimensional Personality Questionnaire* (MPQ) based on the data of $n = 4300$ twins and relatives drawn from the Minnesota Twin-Family Registry. For the scale 'absorption', they found a broad-sense heritability (additive genetic variance and dominance variance) of 0.26 for males and 0.44 for females. This sex difference in heritability reached significance. In the review and meta-analysis by Bouchard (2003), no other study on the heredity of the absorption trait assessed with MPQ or TAS was mentioned. However, absorption and self-transcendence were grouped together, in line with the broader 'openness' factor of the 'Big Five' (Costa and McCrae 1992).

For self-transcendence, several studies on heredity are available. Kirk *et al.* (1999) used a subset of 15 items of the TCI-ST scale as a measure of spirituality in a sample of $n = 2733$ older Australian twins and their relatives. The genetic factor for self-transcendence was estimated as 0.37 for males and 0.41 for females. Ando *et al.* (2002) analysed the TCI data of 296 young Japanese twin pairs (between 14 and 28 years old; 381 females, 211 males). They found self-transcendence to be the only character dimension that consti-tuted a genetic factor, with an estimated heredity of 0.39. Further evidence for the relative genetic independence of TCI-ST was provided by the twin study of Gillespie *et al.* (2003), who administered the abbreviated TCI with 15 self-transcendence items to a sample of 2517 older Australians. Against expectations, the TCI-ST showed the highest genetic effect of all seven dimensions, with an estimated heredity of 0.44, as well as proving to be the character dimension with the lowest percentage of genetic variance explained by tem-perament (only 10 per cent compared with 26 and 37 per cent for self-directedness and cooperativeness, respectively).

Taken together, the reported findings of the heritability of absorption and self-transcendence of about 40 per cent point to a biological foundation for the disposition to enter states of absorption.

14.2.2 Molecular genetic association studies

Association studies can help to identify specific genes that contribute to the absorption disposition. Typically, this approach is focused on genetic polymorphisms known to influence certain neurotransmitter systems. By comparing subjects with different geno-types, the impact on the trait under study can be estimated. However, significant results require large samples because the effects rarely exceed 10 per cent of explained variance.

To date, the TAS has been used in two association studies. In a sample of $n = 109$ subjects, Lichtenberg *et al.* (2000) found no association between absorption and the catechol-O-methyltransferase (COMT) polymorphism, which influences dopamine metabolism. The COMT genotype also showed no main effect in the study by Ott *et al.* (2005). However, based on the data of $n = 336$ subjects, a main effect of the T102C polymorphism and an interaction between COMT and T102C was revealed. Subjects with the T/T genotype, implying a stronger binding capacity of the 5-HT$_{2a}$ receptors, had significantly higher TAS scores than those with the T/C or C/C genotypes of the T102C polymorphism. This increase was higher in subjects with the VAL/VAL genotype of the COMT polymorphism, which is related to higher catabolic enzyme activity and faster inactivation of dopamine. Since the 5-HT$_{2a}$ receptors are known to be the target site of hallucinogens such as LSD, the authors suggest that similar mechanisms may be involved in naturally occurring and drug-induced hallucinations and mystical states (see also Goodman 2002).

Molecular genetics studies using the TCI (e.g. Comings *et al.* 2000*a*, *b*; Kusumi *et al.* 2002; Golimbet *et al.* 2004; Ham *et al.* 2004) suffer from small sample sizes and have shown conflicting results that do not permit firm conclusions to be drawn. Methodological refinements and promising candidate genes are discussed in the concluding section.

14.3 Physiological markers of high absorption

Recent findings suggest that absorption is related to a range of psychophysiological markers and may play an important role in the psychobiology of self-regulation as well as selective cortical inhibition and activation.

14.3.1 Differences in autonomic sensitivity

Zachariae *et al.* (2000) investigated the influence of hypnotic susceptibility and absorption on physiological responses to relaxation and to an acute stressor (electro-shock). Only absorption scores were able significantly to predict changes in heart rate variability (HRV) during the two experimental conditions. During induced stress, HRV in the low and in the high frequency displayed a greater increase in subjects with higher absorption scores. In another study by the same research group (Ehrnrooth *et al.* 2002), arithmetic tasks and mild electric shocks were used to induce stress. High absorption subjects exhibited significantly higher cortisol levels after the stressor than low absorption subjects, supporting the finding that high absorption is associated with greater autonomic stress reactivity.

Further evidence for a connection between the absorption trait and cardiovascular responsiveness was provided by two studies that used rhythmic tilting to manipulate HRV (Ott *et al.* 2002; Vaitl and Ott 2005). In the first study, in half of the $n = 56$ subjects, different tilting protocols could be successfully used either to amplify or to dampen respiratory sinus arrhythmia (RSA). A *post hoc* analysis revealed that responders had significantly higher TAS scores. This finding was replicated and extended in the second study, which included continuous blood pressure measurements. Again, the absorption trait was found to be significantly correlated with cardiovascular parameters related to baroreflex sensitivity (BRS). In another study by our group (Hempel and Ott 2006), no correlation of TAS scores with BRS was present in a sample of $n = 31$ students before they participated in a 10-week yoga training. Yet, after the training, the correlation reached significance ($r = 0.50$, $P = 0.003$) due to stronger increases in BRS in subjects with higher absorption scores.

In summary, the reviewed findings suggest an association between high absorption and cardiovascular responsiveness to stress, baroreflex stimulation and yoga training.

14.3.2 Selective cortical inhibition and activation

Soon after the introduction of the absorption trait, Davidson *et al.* (1976 *b*) published an electroencepholagraphic (EEG) study, which compared 10 high- and 10 low-scoring subjects on the TAS. Subjects were asked to either attend to a flashing light or to a tapping sensation on the forearm. When asked to count the flashes and taps to increase task demand, the cortical activation patterns in these two conditions differed between the groups. The group scoring high on the TAS displayed stronger inhibition in the occipital region when attending to the taps. According to the authors, this mode-specific patterning of cortical activation is indicative of a more flexible attentional style in persons with a high absorption capacity.

An EEG study by De Pascalis *et al.* (1989) points in the same direction. In this case, subjects were asked vividly to imagine emotional experiences with positive or negative valence. The 40 Hz EEG activity over the right and the left hemisphere was used as an indicator for cortical activation. Only subjects with high absorption scores showed an emotion-specific lateralization, with more 40 Hz EEG activity over the right hemisphere when imagining negative experiences. This finding points to a stronger activation of the right hemisphere which has been linked to the processing of negative emotions (Davidson 1995).

14.4 States of absorption during hypnosis and meditation: new theories and findings

In contrast to the absorption trait, which can be measured and operationally defined by the administration of the absorption scale (Tellegen and Atkinson 1974), standards for the definition and assessment of *states* of absorption have not been established thus far. The theoretical approaches of altered states of consciousness as well as the empirical studies reviewed below emphasize the aspects of focused attention, relinquished self-control and reduced meta-cognitions. However, focused attention or oblivious involvement is only one facet of the absorption trait, which also involves perceptual, cognitive and affective changes in consciousness. This limitation has to be kept in mind, if the degree of absorption is assessed by a single rating scale only (e.g. Rainville *et al.* 2002). Future research could profit from instruments that allow a more comprehensive assessment of subjective experiences such as the Phenomenology of Consciousness Inventory (PCI; see Pekala and Kumar, Chapter 10).

14.4.1 Altered states of consciousness

The definition of absorption by Tellegen and Atkinson (1974) cited in the first section includes alterations in the experience of reality and self. Fundamental changes of this type are a hallmark of altered states of consciousness (ASCs). Recently, several reviews have addressed potential brain mechanisms involved in a variety of ASCs (Vollenweider and Geyer 2001; Dietrich 2003; Vaitl *et al.* 2005).

The general hypothesis of Dietrich (2003) claims that changes in the functioning of the prefrontal cortex (PFC) are critically involved in all kinds of ASC. While he stresses the role of hypofrontality, i.e. reduced PFC activation, he also considers exceptions where increased activity could be observed in certain areas of the PFC. Namely, sustained attention during concentrative meditation should be accompanied by an activation of the attentional network of the PFC while other frontal functions could be selectively disengaged, resulting in 'a sense of timelessness, denial of self, little if any self-reflection and analysis, little emotional content, little abstract thinking, no planning, and a sensation of unity' (p. 243).

According to Dietrich, the hypnotic state is characterized by a similar pattern, with focused attention and PFC activation on the one hand and inhibition of dorsolateral PFC on the other hand, affecting cognitive functions 'such as willed action, initiative, critical self-reflection, memory accessibility, cognitive flexibility, and independent thinking and logic' (p. 245).

This inhibition of monitoring and control functions of the PFC fits well with Tellegen's (1981) description of an 'experiential set' said to be characteristic for persons scoring high on the absorption scale. The experiential set is defined as an effortless, non-striving, and non-volitional attentional style opposed to the 'instrumental set' which is characterized by reality-orientated, effortful and goal-directed striving.

Critical, self-reflective cognitive facilities are typically reduced during states of absorption in hallucinating subjects, too. Vollenweider and Geyer (2001) point out the parallels between hallucinogen-induced and acute psychotic states, which are both associated with a pattern of hyperfrontality. Within their model of ASC, the distortion of thalamic filtering leads to sensory overload and symptoms such as ego dissolution and de-realization. Based on the analysis of target sites of hallucinogens and antipsychotic drugs, they conclude that several interacting neurotransmitter systems are involved including the serotonergic ($5\text{-}HT_{2a}$) and dopaminergic system, which are also associated with the absorption trait (see Section 2.2).

Thus, changes in PFC and thalamic functioning are considered to be crucial elements of drug-induced and self-induced ASCs. States of absorption induced by psychological procedures such as hypnosis and meditation have already been investigated in several imaging studies. In the two following sections, the discovered patterns of brain activation are reviewed.

14.4.2 Hypnosis

The idea that highly hypnotizable subjects are characterized in particular by an efficient executive control system was propagated early on by Crawford (1994), who stressed the importance of the ability to focus attention as well as to ignore irrelevant stimuli. The sole imaging study to differentiate between states of relaxation and absorption during hypnosis was done by Rainville et al. (2002). In this positron emission tomography (PET) study, subjects were asked to rate their level of relaxation and absorption during four PET scans before and after hypnotic induction. Increased absorption-related activity was found in the anterior cingulate cortex, the thalamus and the upper pons, providing 'very strong evidence that mental absorption is an experiential correlate of the activation of the brain's "executive attentional network" and suggests that this system plays a critical role in the production of hypnotic states' (p. 897).

The anterior cingulate cortex (ACC) is an important structure in the attentional network for executive control described by Posner (Raz and Shapiro 2002). Differences in ACC activation between subjects with low and high susceptibility have also been found in a functional magnetic resonance imaging (fMRI) study by Egner et al. (2005). Performing a Stroop task, highly susceptible subjects displayed significantly greater conflict-related ACC activation under hypnosis than those with low susceptibility.

This was taken as an indicator for decreased attentional efficiency but could also be interpreted as a compensatory mechanism since task demands required the highly susceptible subjects to engage cognitive control functions typically suspended during hypnosis (see description of Dietrich in the preceding section) and thus impeding hypnotic trance. Interestingly, EEG gamma band coherence between left lateral and medial frontal cortex was reduced in highly susceptible subjects under hypnosis. This finding of a decreased functional coupling shows that hypnosis specifically affects the coordination of cognitive control processes in the PFC as predicted by the dissociated control theory of Woody and Bowers (Jamieson and Sheehan 2004).

14.4.3 Meditation

The first study to demonstrate a connection between meditation and the absorption trait was conducted by Davidson et al. (1976a). The TAS was administered to three groups of subjects with different meditation experience, and higher absorption scores were found in the long-term practitioners. However, this cross-sectional study leaves the question open as to whether the absorption capacity was actually enhanced by the meditation training or if those with a low absorption trait simply dropped out early on in the training.

The first fMRI study on meditation was conducted by Lazar et al. (2000). Five practitioners of mantra-meditation were studied during meditation and a control condition (generation of a list of animals). During meditation, significant signal increases were found in 'neural structures involved in attention (frontal and parietal cortex) and arousal/autonomic control (pregenual anterior cingulate, amygdala, midbrain and hypothalamus)' (p. 2).

Further imaging studies have been conducted since and their results have been summarized in two recent review articles (Newberg and Iversen 2003; Cahn and Polich 2006). Although the great variety of meditation techniques is mirrored in heterogeneous results, some overlap regarding activated brain areas could be delineated. The changes during meditation described by Newberg and Iversen (2003) include an activation of the prefrontal and cingulated cortex associated with volitional aspects of meditation, especially the will to focus attention. Other changes include a thalamic activation, reduced activity in the posterior superior parietal lobule (associated with the representation of the own body in three-dimensional space) and activations in structures regulating emotions and the autonomic nervous system. Newberg and Iversen (2003) presented a model with neural structures and neurotransmitters involved in meditative states. In commenting on this model, Grant and Rainville (2005) argued that hypnosis could be conceived as a kind of guided meditation due to the large degree of correspondence of subjective experiences and physiological changes.

According to Cahn and Polich (2006), the ACC and dorsolateral PFC are the key structures for understanding the generation and neurophysiology of meditative states. Attention-demanding tasks such as meditation and hypnosis would be associated with frontal midline theta EEG activity and increased blood flow in the ACC. The authors state that the increased activity in the ACC found in the majority of non-guided meditation studies could be seen as 'a marker of the increased attentional focus in meditative states'.

14.5 **Future perspectives**

Systematic, theory-guided research on the physiological correlates of absorption states is scarce, despite their omnipresence in everyday life, hypnosis and meditation. Basic research on attention has largely neglected receptive modes of sustained focused attention but rather concentrated on constructs such as vigilance and selective or divided attention studied within the confines of stimulus–response paradigms. Natural states of absorption occurring during reading or imagining require carefully designed settings that allow subjects to forget their surroundings and to reduce meta-cognitions about participating in an experiment. In addition, the level of absorption is difficult to determine, since complete involvement and lack of self-awareness are incompatible with concurrent reports of the actual state. The same holds true for states of absorption induced by a hypnotic induction procedure or a meditation technique. For fMRI studies, the situation is aggravated by the annoying scanner noise and the motionless supine position required.

14.5.1 **Disposition-focused approach**

In view of these constraints, it is necessary that research into states of absorption requires careful selection of subjects, i.e. those who are able to become absorbed even in environments that are not optimal. In order to identify specific correlates of absorption, groups with different absorption capacities could then be compared or control conditions could be devised that include comparable stimulation but prevent absorption. Afterwards, as a manipulation check, the depth of absorption has to be assessed with instruments such as the PCI (Pekala 1991), that provides a hypnoidal score which can be used to estimate trance depth.

For a first screening of subjects, the absorption scale could be employed. However, little is known about the predictive power of the TAS for the absorption realized in different conducive conditions or induction procedures. In view of the rather low correlation with hypnotic susceptibility, it seems wise to use as a second criterion for the selection of subjects a behavioural test which is similar to the procedure used later to induce a state of absorption.

Besides experimental studies of absorption states in extreme groups, correlation studies can be helpful to identify correlates of the absorption trait. Tellegen himself did not develop hypotheses about neuronal correlates of absorption (personal communication, 22 May 2002). The findings reviewed above provide some evidence that this disposition has neurobiological correlates ranging from genetic factors and neurotransmitters to differences in cardiovascular regulation and the efficient task-related allocation of attentional resources. However, the empirical basis is still thin, and most findings urgently need replication. For instance, the early EEG study of Davidson *et al.* (1976*b*) described above could easily be replicated and extended by applying modern imaging techniques that allow a full investigation of the attention networks involved in the cortical inhibition of the unattended modality.

Future molecular association studies should also include polymorphisms related to the 5-HT_{1a} receptor that appears to be associated with self-transcendence (Borg *et al.* 2003; Lorenzi *et al.* 2005). Finally, the combination of genotyping and fMRI studies

(Fossella *et al.* 2002) seems to hold promise in elucidating the role of attention networks in absorption. Differences in the serotonergic system, especially the 5-HT$_{2a}$ receptor, could also be responsible for the observed differences in cardiovascular regulation which is strongly modulated by this receptor subtype (Raul 2003).

14.5.2 Training-focused approach

The study of the *plasticity* of the absorption capacity represents an interesting second empirical approach. Concentrative, object-based meditation techniques can be conceptualized as mental training to cultivate the faculty of absorption (Ott 2003). In order to avoid the ambiguity of cross-sectional, correlation studies (see Davidson *et al.* 1976*a*), long-term studies should be undertaken in order to examine the extent to which meditation practice enhances the ability to enter states of absorption, spontaneously as well as voluntarily.

In combining repeated physiological measurements, administration of questionnaires and tests probing the efficiency of attentional control, the relationships between brain activity, subjective experience and performance could be determined. At the University of California, Davis, a corresponding research project on the effects of an intensive meditation retreat lasting for 1 year is in the advanced planning stage (Center for Mind and Brain n.d.). fMRI could be used to study the brain structures engaged during focusing on the meditation object and how activation patterns change in the course of skill development. Morphometric analyses of anatomical high-resolution MRI volumes could also help to identify structural changes caused by the intensive training (Draganski *et al.* 2004).

14.5.3 Self-regulation approach

Finally, recent methodological progress in EEG and especially fMRI technology has rendered a third approach possible. Nowadays, presumed indicators of focused attention, such as frontal midline theta EEG activity or haemodynamic activation of the ACC, can be directly fed back to subjects. For EEG biofeedback, the time delay is less than a second; for real-time fMRI, only a few seconds are required for measurement, computation and display of a feedback signal (Weiskopf *et al.* 2003).

Research by Qualls and Sheehan (1981) suggests that for participants already high in absorption, biofeedback can interfere with their degree of relaxation. Thus, caution is needed in order to tailor the attentional demands of the biofeedback task and the feedback signal to the non-striving, receptive characteristics of the intended absorption state.

It has already been demonstrated that training with different EEG biofeedback training protocols is able to influence cognitive functions (Vernon *et al.* 2003). A systematic comparison of subjective alterations that accompany successful sessions with distinct biofeedback protocols could help to identify frequency bands and locations associated with absorption states. The high-frequency gamma EEG band should also be taken into account since it has been related to intensive concentration during meditation (Sheer 1984) and seems to be enhanced in subjects with long-standing meditation practice (Lutz *et al.* 2004). The identification of feedback protocols effective in supporting subjects in developing their absorption capacity could also be of clinical use, e.g. in the treatment of patients suffering from attention deficit disorder who are unable to ignore distracting stimuli.

In summary, the findings reviewed above give an incomplete picture, like the scattered pieces of a jigsaw-puzzle. At the same time, they provide clear evidence that absorption has specific neurobiological foundations. The empirical approaches outlined here will continue to build upon our knowledge of the neurochemistry and the brain dynamics underlying both the trait and the state of absorption, and so perhaps further our ability to utilize the brain's capacity for extended self-regulation.

References

Ando J, Ono Y, Yoshimura K, Onoda N, Shinohara M, Kanba S, *et al.* (2002). The genetic structure of Cloninger's seven-factor model of temperament and character in a Japanese sample. *Journal of Personality*, **70**, 583–609.

Borg J, Andre B, Soderstrom H and Farde L (2003). The serotonin system and spiritual experiences. *American Journal of Psychiatry*, **160**, 1965–9.

Bouchard TJ and McGue M (2003). Genetic and environmental influences on human psychological differences. *Journal of Neurobiology*, **54**, 4–45.

Cahn BR and Polich J (2006). Meditation states and traits: EEG, ERP, and neuroimaging studies. *Psychological Bulletin*, **132**, 180–211.

Center for Mind and Brain (n.d.). University of California, Davis. *The Shamatha Project*. Retrieved 31 August 2005 from http://mindbrain.ucdavis.edu/content/ShamathaInfo

Cloninger CR, Svrakic DM and Przybeck TR (1993). A psychobiological model of temperament and character. *Archives of General Psychiatry*, **50**, 975–89.

Cloninger CR, Przybeck TR, Svrakic DM and Wetzel RD (1994). *The Temperament and Character Inventory: a guide to its development and use.* St Louis, Washington University Center for Psychobiology of Personality.

Cloninger CR, Przybeck TR, Svrakic DM and Wetzel RD (1999). *Das Temperament und Charakter-Inventar (TCI): Ein Leitfaden über seine Entwicklung und Anwendung.* [The Temperament and Character Inventory: a guide to its development and use] Translated and revised by J Richter, M Eisemann, G Richter and CR Cloninger. Frankfurt am Main, Swets Test Services.

Comings DE, Gade-Andavolu R, Gonzalez N, Wu S, Muhleman D. Blake H, *et al.* (2000a). A multivariate analysis of 59 candidate genes in personality traits: the temperament and character inventory. *Clinical Genetics*, **58**, 375–85.

Comings DE, Gonzales N, Saucier G, Johnson JP and MacMurray JP (2000b). The DRD4 gene and the spiritual transcendence scale of the character temperament index. *Psychiatric Genetics*, **10**, 185–9.

Costa PT and McCrae RR (1992). *Revised NEO Personality Inventory (NEO-PI-R) and NEO Five-Factor Inventory (NEO-FFI) professional manual.* Odessa, FL, Psychological Assessment Resources, Inc.

Crawford HJ (1994). Brain dynamics and hypnosis—attentional and disattentional processes. *International Journal of Clinical and Experimental Hypnosis*, **42**, 204–32.

Davidson RJ (1995). Cerebral asymmetry, emotion, and affective style. In: RJ Davidson and K Hugdahl, eds. *Brain asymmetry.* pp. 361–87. Cambridge, MA, MIT Press.

Davidson RJ, Goleman D and Schwartz GE (1976a). Attentional and affective concomitants of meditation: a cross-sectional study. *Journal of Abnormal Psychology*, **85**, 235–8.

Davidson RJ, Schwartz GE and Rothman LP (1976b). Attentional style and the self-regulation of mode-specific attention: an electroencephalographic study. *Journal of Abnormal Psychology*, **85**, 611–21.

De Pascalis V, Marucci FS and Penna PM (1989). 40-Hz EEG asymmetry during recall of emotional events in waking and hypnosis: differences between low and high hypnotisables. *International Journal of Psychophysiology*, **7**, 85–96.

A (2003). Functional neuroanatomy of altered states of consciousness: the transient ɔfrontality hypothesis. *Consciousness and Cognition*, **12**, 231–56.

ski B, Gaser C, Busch V, Schuierer G, Bogdahn U and May A (2004). Changes in grey matter induced by training. *Nature*, **427**, 311–2.

Egner T, Jamieson G and Gruzelier J (2005). Hypnosis decouples cognitive control from conflict monitoring processes of the frontal lobe. *Neuroimage*, **27**, 969–78.

Ehrnrooth E, Zachariae R, Svendsen G, Jørgensen MM, Yishay M, Sørensen BS, *et al.* (2002). Increased thymidylate synthase mRNA concentration in blood leukocytes following an experimental stressor. *Psychotherapy and Psychosomatics*, **71**, 97–103.

Finkel D and McGue M (1997). Sex differences and nonadditivity in heritability of the Multidimensional Personality Questionnaire Scales. *Journal of Personality and Social Psychology*, **72**, 929–38.

Fossella J, Sommer T, Fan J, Wu Y, Swanson JM, Pfaff DW, *et al.* (2002). Assessing the molecular genetics of attention networks. *BMC Neuroscience* **3**, 14.

Gillespie NA, Cloninger CR, Heath AC and Martin NG (2003). The genetic and environmental relationship between Cloninger's dimensions of temperament and character. *Personality and Individual Differences*, **35**, 1931–46.

Golimbet VE, Alfimova MV and Mityushina NG (2004). Polymorphism of the serotonin 2A receptor gene (5HTR2A) and personality traits. *Molecular Biology*, **38**, 337–44.

Goodman N (2002). The serotonergic system and mysticism: could LSD and the nondrug-induced mystical experience share common neural mechanisms? *Journal of Psychoactive Drugs*, **34**, 263–72.

Grant JA and Rainville P (2005). Hypnosis and meditation: similar experiential changes and shared brain mechanisms. *Medical Hypotheses*, **65**, 625–6.

Ham B-J, Kim Y-H, Choi M-J, Cha J-H, Choi Y-K and Lee M-S (2004). Serotonergic genes and personality traits in the Korean population. *Neuroscience Letters*, **354**, 2–5.

Hempel H and Ott U (2006). Effects of Hatha-yoga: autonomic balance, absorption, and health. Unpublished manuscript.

Jamieson GA (2005). The modified Tellegen Absorption Scale: a clearer window on the structure and meaning of absorption. *Australian Journal of Clinical and Experimental Hypnosis*, **33**, 119–39.

Jamieson GA and Sheehan PW (2004). An empirical test of Woody and Bower's dissociated control theory of hypnosis. *International Journal of Clinical and Experimental Hypnosis*, **52**, 232–49.

Kirk KM, Eaves LJ and Martin NG (1999). Self-transcendence as a measure of spirituality in a sample of older Australian twins. *Twin Research*, **2**, 81–7.

Kirsch I and Council JR (1992). Situational and personality correlates of hypnotic responsiveness. In: F Fromm and EN Nash, eds. *Contemporary hypnosis research*. pp. 267–91. New York, Guilford Press.

Kusumi I, Suzuki K, Sasaki Y, Kameda K, Sasaki T and Koyama T (2002). Serotonin 5-HT$_{2A}$ receptor gene polymorphism, 5-HT$_{2A}$ receptor function and personality traits in healthy subjects: a negative study. *Journal of Affective Disorders*, **68**, 235–41.

Laidlaw TM, Dwivedi P, Naito A and Gruzelier JH (2005). Low self-directedness (TCI), mood, schizotypy and hypnotic susceptibility. *Personality and Individual Differences*, **39**, 469–80.

Lange R, Thalbourne MA, Houran J and Storm L (2000). The Revised Transliminality Scale: reliability and validity data from a Rasch top-down purification procedure. *Consciousness and Cognition*, **9**, 591–617.

Lazar SW, Bush G, Gollub RL, Fricchione GL, Khalsa G and Benson H (2000). Functional brain mapping of the relaxation response and meditation. *NeuroReport*, **11**, 1581–5.

Lichtenberg P, Bachner-Melman R, Gritsenko I and Ebstein RP (2000). Exploratory association study between catechol-O-methyltransferase (COMT) high/low enzyme activity polymorphism and hypnotizability. *American Journal of Medical Genetics (Neuropsychiatric Genetics)*, **96**, 771–4.

Lorenzi C, Serretti A, Mandelli L, Tubazio V, Ploia C and Smeraldi E (2005). 5-HT1A polymorphism and self-transcendence in mood disorders. *American Journal of Medical Genetics (Neuropsychiatric Genetics)*, **137**, 33–5.

Lutz A, Greischar LL, Rawlings NB, Ricard M and Davidson RJ (2004). Long-term meditators self-induce high-amplitude gamma synchrony during mental practice. *Proceedings of the National Academy of Sciences of the USA*, **101**, 16369–73.

Munafo MR, Clark TG, Moore LR, Payne E, Walton R and Flint J (2003). Genetic polymorphisms and personality in healthy adults: a systematic review and meta-analysis. *Molecular Psychiatry*, **8**, 471–84.

Newberg AB and Iversen J (2003). The neural basis of the complex mental task of meditation: neurotransmitter and neurochemical considerations. *Medical Hypotheses*, **61**, 282–91.

Ott U (2003). The role of absorption for the study of yoga. *Journal for Meditation and Meditation Research*, **3**, 21–6.

Ott U, Sammer G and Vaitl D (2002). Baroreflex responsiveness correlates with the trait of absorption. *International Journal of Psychophysiology*, **45**, 16–7.

Ott U, Reuter M, Hennig J and Vaitl D (2005). Evidence for a common biological basis of the Absorption trait, hallucinogen effects and positive symptoms: epistasis between 5-HT2a and COMT polymorphisms. *American Journal of Medical Genetics (Neuropsychiatric Genetics)*, **137**, 29–32.

Pekala RJ (1991). *Quantifying consciousness: an empirical approach*. New York, Plenum Press.

Qualls PJ and Sheehan PW (1981). Role of the feedback signal in electromyograph biofeedback: the relevance of attention. *Journal of Experimental Psychology: General*, **110**, 204–16.

Rainville P, Hofbauer RK, Bushnell MC, Duncan GH and Price DD (2002). Hypnosis modulates activity in brain structures involved in the regulation of consciousness. *Journal of Cognitive Neuroscience*, **14**, 887–901.

Raul L (2003). Serotonin$_2$ receptors in the nucleus tractus solitarius: characterization and role in the baroreceptor reflex arc. *Cellular and Molecular Neurobiology*, **23**, 709–26.

Raz A and Shapiro T (2002). Hypnosis and neuroscience: a cross talk between clinical and cognitive research. *Archives of General Psychiatry*, **59**, 85–90.

Reif A and Lesch K-P (2003). Toward a molecular architecture of personality. *Behavioral Brain Research*, **139**, 1–20.

Ritz T and Dahme B (1995). Die Absorption-Skala: Konzeptuelle Aspekte, psychometrische Kennwerte und Dimensionalität einer deutschsprachigen Adaptation [The Absorption Scale: Conceptual aspects, psychometric properties, and dimensionality of a German adaptation]. *Diagnostica*, **41**, 53–61.

Roche SM and McConkey KM (1990). Absorption: nature, assessment, and correlates. *Journal of Personality and Social Psychology*, **59**, 91–101.

Sheer DE (1984). Focused arousal, 40-Hz EEG, and dysfunction. In: T Elbert, B Rockstroh, W Lutzenberger and N Birbaumer, eds. *Self-regulation of the brain and behavior*. pp. 64–84. Berlin, Springer.

Tellegen A (1981). Practicing the two disciplines for relaxation and enlightenment: comment on 'Role of the feedback signal in electromyograph biofeedback: the relevance of attention' by Qualls and Sheehan. *Journal of Experimental Psychology: General*, **110**, 217–26.

Tellegen A (1992). *Note on the structure and meaning of the MPQ absorption scale*. Unpublished manuscript, University of Minnesota, Minneapolis.

Tellegen A and Atkinson G (1974). Openness to absorbing and self-altering experiences ('absorption'), a trait related to hypnotic susceptibility. *Journal of Abnormal Psychology*, **83**, 268–77.

Thalbourne MA (1998). Transliminality: further correlates and a short measure. *Journal of the American Society for Psychical Research*, **92**, 402–19.

Thalbourne MA, Bartemucci L, Delin PS, Fox B and Nofi O (1997). Transliminality: its nature and correlates. *Journal of the American Society for Psychical Research*, **91**, 305–31.

Thalbourne MA, Crawley SE and Houran J (2003). Temporal lobe lability in the highly transliminal mind. *Personality and Individual Differences*, **35**, 1965–74.

Thalbourne MA, Houran J, Alias AG and Brugger P (2001). Transliminality, brain function, and synesthesia. *The Journal of Nervous and Mental Disease*, **189**, 190–2.

Vaitl D and Ott U (2005). Altered states of consciousness induced by psychophysiological techniques. *Mind and Matter*, **3**, 9–30.

Vaitl D, Birbaumer N, Gruzelier J, Jamieson GA, Kotchoubev B, Kubler A, *et al.* (2005). Psychobiology of altered states of consciousness. *Psychological Bulletin*, **131**, 98–127.

Vernon D, Egner T, Cooper N, Compton T, Neilands C, Sheri A, *et al.* (2003). The effect of training distinct neurofeedback protocols on aspects of cognitive performance. *International Journal of Psychophysiology*, **47**, 75–85.

Vollenweider FX and Geyer MA (2001). A systems model of altered consciousness: integrating natural and drug-induced psychosis. *Brain Research Bulletin*, **56**, 495–507.

Weiskopf N, Veit R, Erb M, Mathiak K, Grodd W, Goebel R, *et al.* (2003). Physiological self-regulation of regional brain activity using real-time functional magnetic resonance imaging (fMRI): methodology and exemplary data. *NeuroImage*, **19**, 577–86.

Zachariae R, Jorgensen MM, Bjerring P and Svendsen G (2000). Autonomic and psychological responses to an acute psychological stressor and relaxation: the influence of hypnotizability and absorption. *International Journal of Clinical and Experimental Hypnosis*, **48**, 388–403.

Chapter 15

Time distortion, and the nature of hypnosis and consciousness

Peter LN Naish

15.1 Behaviour and experience

Of all the phenomena and claims that have been linked to hypnosis, such as pain control, memory modification or even enhancement of the immune system (Gruzelier *et al.* 2002*a*), it may seem strange to focus upon something as obscure as its effect on timing. In fact, among the alleged effects of hypnosis, time distortion seems to have a rather special characteristic, making it valuable when trying to understand the nature of hypnosis itself. Before I explain that characteristic, and describe the associated research, I will begin by showing why research on the other phenomena (while valuable for other reasons) may not be best placed to explain the nature of hypnosis.

It has seemed to me for a long time that a good case could be made for saying that researchers should concentrate upon the *perceptual*, rather than *behavioural* aspects of hypnosis (Naish 1986, 2005*a*). Thus, although the behaviour of hypnotized people may sometimes appear strange (a characteristic encouraged by stage hypnotists), it can be re-interpreted as reasonable, when it is seen to be the result of strange experiences. For example, a person may speak to an empty chair, but that is not unreasonable if they see a friend sitting in it. Clearly, the phenomenon to investigate then becomes the false perception, not the speaking.

Kalio and Revonsuo (2003) also concluded that perceptual phenomena were likely to be the most profitable area to address, when trying to elucidate the nature of hypnosis. They reached this conclusion by taking a 'levels of explanation' approach, showing that, in principle, anything from the underpinning neural mechanisms to the facilitating social context might be investigated. However, they concluded that the broad phenomena of hypnosis would be best accounted for if the underlying perceptions were explained. This paper was important, not just because it selected subjective experience as the correct level to address, but also because it demonstrated the need to explain from the 'level below'. That is, hypnotic behaviour should be explained in terms of the underlying perceptions, and not the overarching social mediators. It is recognized that there are strong social influences in hypnotic responding, but so there are in many other situations: to focus upon these influences is unlikely to reveal anything very informative about the hypnotic process. Later in this chapter it will be seen that it is also profitable to dig a little deeper, to explain the perceptions by looking for their possible neural correlates.

The preceding analysis contrasts rather starkly with the actual stance of many researchers over the latter part of the twentieth century. Many (e.g. Barber 1969; Wagstaff 1981; Spanos 1986) produced accounts of hypnosis from a perspective that came to be known as 'socio-cognitive'. A principal element of this approach has been the demonstration that, when put in a situation labelled 'hypnotic', people produce exactly the behaviour that they were led to believe *was* hypnotic. Thus, there appears to be nothing in hypnotic behaviour that is intrinsic to the process of being hypnotized; rather, people shape their actions to meet whatever the hypnotist implies is expected of hypnotized people. I have argued (Naish 2005b) that there is little to be gained in pursuing further experiments to demonstrate this, since it is now clear beyond reasonable doubt that people who are susceptible to hypnosis will perform in very much the way they believe appropriate to the hypnotic role. This should come as no surprise because, in the absence of suggestion or implication, participants have no guidance as to how to behave. They simply remain rather passive until a suggestion has been received; then they can set about producing the appropriate phenomena. Those may be observable behaviours but, far more interestingly, they are likely to include unusual experiences.

15.2 Searching for a genuine experience

The problem with researching a participant's experiences is a difficulty well known to psychology: the data are subjective, hence hard to verify. In the past, some researchers (e.g. Wagstaff 1981) have even considered it plausible that the subjective accounts were simply fabrications, generated to comply with the obvious expectations of the hypnotist. Many would dispute the likelihood of that, especially those in clinical practice, perhaps having witnessed a subjective change that was unlikely to be fabricated, such as the alleviation of previously intractable pain. Nevertheless, it is an explanation that must be addressed if the topic is to be treated with scientific rigour. At first sight, the obvious solution is to find an objective correlate of the experience, such as talking to an empty chair. The problem with this is that, not only are we all capable of talking to empty chairs, but we are also capable of acting out *all* the feats traditionally associated with being hypnotized.

It was Orne (1979) who first demonstrated that people told to act as if hypnotized could do so, without any training as to what that behaviour should entail: they simply followed the hypnotist's suggestions. Indeed, they did this so well that an expert was unable to distinguish between the actors and those who were genuinely hypnotized. Naturally, this has led researchers to question exactly what is meant by 'genuine', for those who are supposedly hypnotized. The finding that non-hypnotized people can act the part so convincingly has resulted in the use of a 'simulator group' in many hypnosis studies. Since they receive no training in their role, the simulators' success or otherwise serves as an indicator of what cues the hypnotized participants may be assumed to have gleaned from the situation. Not surprisingly, in the light of the earlier comments on suggestion, it turns out that the hypnotized and simulating groups glean very much the same, and hence behave similarly. At the very least, these observations reinforce the assertion that, if we are to learn anything about the true nature of what it is to be hypnotized (as opposed to acting hypnotized), then it is the experience and not the behaviour that must be investigated.

Recently, a new set of tools has become available, capable of lending a degree of objectivity to private experience: the techniques of neuroimaging. Methods such as positron emission tomography (PET) and functional magnetic resonance imaging (fMRI) reveal which areas of the brain are particularly active during specific mental tasks, including the act of perceiving. If an appropriate region is active, both when the participant perceives a real event and also when he or she *claims* to be having the experience in hypnosis, then this is good evidence that the claim is genuine. This approach has been used for a wide range of experiences, such as pain control (Crawford *et al.* 1998), paralysis (Halligan *et al.* 2000), visual hallucination (Kosslyn *et al.* 2000) and auditory hallucination (Szechtman *et al.* 1998). In every case, although the research was not necessarily conducted with that purpose, the neural activity could reasonably be described as supporting the reality of the claimed experience.

Although the brain imaging findings broadly support the position that people really do have the experiences they claim, further interpretation is not entirely straightforward. For example, Kosslyn *et al.* (2000) obtained hard-to-explain hemispheric effects. They used PET scanning, while their participants viewed either coloured patterns or grey-scale equivalents of the patterns. In some conditions, they were asked to see the grey pattern as if it were coloured; this request was made either during or outside hypnosis. As a result of the request, the pattern of brain activity when observing the grey actually resembled the activity when looking at the coloured display. This effect was obtained in the right hemisphere, whether or not hypnosis was used; it appeared to result from any attempt to imagine colour. On the other hand, in the left hemisphere, the colour response to a grey stimulus occurred only during hypnosis. Two questions are prompted. First, if activity during hypnosis is not fully like 'the real thing', has the scanning told us very much? Secondly, if the pattern during hypnosis has a good deal in common with the pattern during imagination, is hypnosis anything more than imagining (and hence perhaps not worthy of further study)?

I will leave those questions hanging, and raise another which is perhaps more problematic. The presence of similar brain activity, during both real perception and hypnotic hallucination, may be useful in convincing sceptics that hypnotic experiences are 'real', but what does it tell us about the nature of the underlying processes? As I will argue later, some brain mapping results do help with generating theories of hypnosis, but simply demonstrating the kind of equivalence reported by Kosslyn *et al.* (2000) does little to further theoretical issues. We are no nearer to discovering *how* people generate activity associated with perception, in the absence of a driving stimulus. In the framework of Kallio and Revonsuo (2003), perhaps neural activity is too low a level in which to seek explanation; we need for the present to return to the perceptual.

15.3 **Perception without suggestion**

It has already been explained that traditional hypnotic experiences and their consequent behaviour are liable faithfully to follow suggestion. This is unsatisfactory as an avenue of research, since simulators can produce exactly the same behaviour, and it seems to tell us more about the ability to recognize what is expected, than about the mechanisms of hypnosis. What is required is a perceptual change that is *intrinsic* to hypnosis, and occurs in the absence of any suggestion that might indicate it was expected. There is a candidate.

I claimed earlier that a hypnotized person does very little, unless given a suggestion. However, there does seem to be one change in the underlying experience, which becomes apparent when the participant is questioned later. It has been recognized for a long time (Bowers 1979; Bowers and Brenneman 1979) that if a person is asked at the end of a session of hypnosis how long it seemed to last, then the answer is almost always a considerable underestimate. No suggestion is required to achieve this effect; it appears to be spontaneous and almost universal. Clearly, a perception has been changed, and it would appear to be the result of the hypnosis, without any overt suggestion. Could there be anything in a typical hypnotic induction procedure that might be interpreted as signalling that the duration should seem short? That can be tested by using simulators, instructed to behave exactly as they imagine hypnotized people would. Mozenter and Kurtz (1992) did just that, and found that simulators failed to produce the marked truncation of the time judgement.

Time estimation thus appears to be a rare, perhaps unique, window upon the perceptions of a hypnotized person. The time distortion occurs spontaneously, apparently as a result of being hypnotized, so if the distortion mechanisms could be understood, this might also lead to a greater understanding of the mechanisms of hypnosis (Naish 2001, 2003).

15.4 Is hypnosis the cause of time distortion?

Having claimed that faulty time judgements are a window upon the mechanisms of hypnosis, it may seem strange to ask whether hypnosis causes the errors. However, for a long time it has been far from clear exactly how, or indeed if, the two were really linked. The problem begins with the absence of a correlation. People vary in the extent to which they underestimate the duration of hypnosis, and of course they also vary in hypnotic susceptibility. If the timing effect is associated with hypnosis, then it is reasonable to suppose that it will be exhibited more strongly by those who are more responsive, in other words that there will be a correlation with hypnotic susceptibility. Surprisingly, neither the original Bowers and Brenneman (1979) study, nor many subsequently (see St Jean *et al.* 1994, for a review) have found such a relationship. This is extremely puzzling. It is far from clear how an effect so strongly associated with hypnosis can fail to be influenced by responsiveness to hypnosis.

Possible explanations can, in broad terms, seek a reason for the lack of correlation in the hypnosis domain or the time domain. Thus, an extreme explanation related to hypnosis would be that susceptibility scales do not measure anything related to the 'true' responsiveness to hypnosis. In effect, one would be claiming that time distortion is a better measure of susceptibility than the standard scales: a difficult position to defend. A less extreme version of this account would suggest that, whereas traditional scales incorporate a range of dimensions, perhaps the timing effects are linked to only one. If this were true, a subject might score highly on the other dimensions, and hence gain an overall high susceptibility score, but crucially be deficient in the measure that correlates with time distortion.

A similar pair of explanations can be constructed from the timing perspective. The extreme version is that the effect is linked to something that often accompanies hypnosis, but has nothing to do with hypnosis itself. Certainly, two decades ago this would have been a reasonable position to adopt, and St Jean (1988) pointed out, 'It has not been established that underestimation is due to the employment of hypnotic procedures' (p. 83). Nevertheless, a less extreme explanation can preserve the hypnosis–timing link. It is that the timing effect is partly brought about by hypnosis, but is also influenced by other factors. These would increase the variance in the timing data and reduce the correlation with susceptibility.

Studies of hypnotic time distortion, many of them conducted by St Jean and his colleagues, can be characterized as searching in the two domains outlined above. Some research has attempted to find the elements of hypnosis that might influence time perception; other studies have taken known influences upon time judgement, and looked for them in hypnosis. As will be explained, the investigations did not meet with any great success.

15.5 Do amnesia and absorption distract from timing?

Following hypnosis, subjects may be amnesic for some of the events that took place, or for the suggestions that were given during hypnosis (especially if these included suggestions for amnesia). It has been proposed (Ornstein 1969) that one of the factors that influences our judgement of how long a period lasted is the number of activities that took place within it. Someone who, through amnesia, could remember only a few activities might conclude that the period had been rather brief. However, St Jean et al. (1982) failed to find any correlation between the extent of hypnotic amnesia and the degree of time distortion. Amnesia appears not to be the element of hypnosis that accounts for the effect.

Absorption is seen as another element of hypnotic responding; it can be measured, and is known to correlate with hypnotic susceptibility (Tellegen and Atkinson 1974). Since susceptibility itself has seldom been shown to correlate with time judgements, it might have been expected that time judgements would also fail to correlate with absorption. Nevertheless, it is tempting to propose that becoming thoroughly absorbed in the experiences of hypnosis might be a distraction from detecting the passage of time. St Jean and MacLeod (1983) tested this proposal, by reading subjects absorbing stories, following which the subjects judged the story's duration. The procedure was carried out both within and outside hypnosis. Substantial underestimation was found only when two conditions applied: (1) the subjects were highly susceptible; and (2) they were hypnotized. In other words, this study showed hypnosis producing its traditional timing effect, but in particular with those who scored high on susceptibility. The effect was not found if the material listened to was not involving, suggesting that the absorption component of hypnosis was indeed the dimension associated with the timing effects.

This study looked as if it had finally proved the link with susceptibility, but St Jean soon rejected the absorption account (St Jean and Robertson 1986). It was shown in this latter study that the attentional demands of the task, rather than the involving nature of the story, determined the degree of time underestimation. The effect of having to pay close attention to a task has been well known for some time. Thus, outside the hypnosis context, it has been shown that high attentional demand leads to time underestimation (e.g. Brown and Boltz 2002). It is assumed that attention is a finite resource, and that an increase in mental workload, such as occurs when a task is difficult, makes more demands upon the resource, so leaving less available to monitor the passage of time (e.g. Zakay 1989). This observation is pertinent to two of the possibilities for non-correlation raised earlier. First, it suggests a plausible non-hypnotic influence upon time judgements, which might dilute any hypnotic effects. Secondly, mental workload may actually be a varying element of hypnosis itself, and thus be the component that gives rise to the timing effects. This will now be considered.

15.6 **Hypnosis and mental workload**

St Jean *et al.* (1994) reasoned similarly to the above, and set about demonstrating the effects of workload upon time estimation in hypnosis. In the first of two experiments, hypnotized subjects took part in one of two conditions; both included listening to a story, and at the end they were asked to estimate how long the story had lasted. Listening was all that was required in the low workload condition, but the high workload group had simultaneously to solve word puzzles and count the number of occurrences of a particular name in the story. The two groups were themselves divided, to contain equal numbers of low and high susceptibility subjects (commonly referred to as 'lows' and 'highs').

St Jean *et al.* found that time estimates were shortened for both workload groups. People in the low workload condition averaged 63 per cent of the true time, but the high workload subjects reduced their estimates to 43 per cent of the actual duration of the story. Interestingly, the results hint at an apparently non-significant interaction (the statistics are not quoted). Whereas there was no difference between the estimates of hypnotic 'highs' and 'lows' in the low workload condition, under high workload the 'highs' and 'lows' gave estimates of 38 and 48 per cent (of true time), respectively. This suggests that 'highs' might be more vulnerable to the time-shortening effect, when subjected to higher workload. A similar effect appeared to be present in the earlier, rejected experiment (St Jean and MacLeod 1983), where time distortion seemed to be restricted to the 'highs'. Although the results are thus far non-significant, they begin to suggest that 'highs' and 'lows' might differ in the way hypnosis affects their time judgement, a theme which will be revisited later.

The basic finding of St Jean *et al.* (1994) of an effect of workload upon time judgement is not of great interest, since it merely confirms an effect known outside hypnosis. There was no particular reason to suppose that hypnosis would modify the effect. However, St Jean *et al.* went on to a second experiment, comparing the magnitudes of the misjudgement obtained in and out of hypnosis. Unfortunately, in this experiment, there seems not to have been a separation into 'highs' and 'lows', so the effects are averaged across subjects with a range of susceptibilities. Moreover, it is reported that the tasks had been modified somewhat, so it is not possible to make meaningful comparisons with the first experiment. The results obtained were hard to explain.

Under low workload, the time estimates were 92 per cent outside hypnosis and 80 per cent in hypnosis. Thus, hypnosis appeared to be having the usual effect of reducing the perceived duration. However, under high workload, the situation was different: 'waking', 45 per cent and 'hypnosis' 64 per cent of true duration, i.e. in hypnosis the time distortion was actually *less* pronounced. This puzzling interaction just missed statistical significance ($P = 0.08$), and the only significant main effect was of workload, i.e. increased workload caused a time period to seem shorter, but whether or not a subject was hypnotized made no difference. Since it is effectively a universal finding that hypnosis *does* make a difference to time estimation, we must conclude that some very unusual factors were influencing these results.

A partial explanation might be that the high workload condition was so demanding that subjects were unable to maintain a significant degree of hypnosis, and consequently produced less time distortion. However, the subjects in the corresponding non-hypnosis condition (who clearly were not maintaining *any* degree of hypnosis) actually experienced *greater* time distortion. This was a 'between-subjects' study, with only 15, non-selected participants per group, so perhaps the best explanation for this strange reversal is that it was brought about by inadequate randomization of subjects. That, however, was not the conclusion reached by St Jean *et al.*

St Jean's group concluded that the time reduction customarily associated with hypnosis was indeed due to the demands (i.e. workload) of being hypnotized. This was encapsulated in what they called their 'Busy Beaver' hypothesis:

> The processing resources of the hypnotic subject are so fully occupied by the demands of the hypnotic task that the residual capacity available for the processing of time-related [...] cues is minimal. [Hypnotic time underestimation] may simply be a by-product of the attentional demands of the hypnotic task (p. 568).

This position does not seem to be justified by the data. Their first experiment showed that, although the hypnotized 'beaver' may well be busy, there was still capacity to take on another task, and thus increase the time distortion. The second experiment was even more problematic for the busy beaver hypothesis. If hypnosis is demanding, then adding it to a task that is already causing time distortion should lead to even greater timing effects. The experiment showed that there was no such increase (if anything a *decrease*), so the hypothesis is completely unsupported. We must look elsewhere for more plausible explanations of hypnotic time distortion.

15.7 **Hypnosis and the internal clock**

Researchers in the field of time perception assume that the impact of increasing workload comes about through the reduction in resources available to count some kind of 'clock tick' (e.g. Brown and Boltz 2002). This would result in a proportion of 'ticks' being missed, so the accumulated score at the end of a timed period would be less than normal. That in turn would lead to the perception that less time had passed. Although the timing effects associated with manipulations of workload and attention are indeed plausibly related to the number of timing units counted or missed, there is another possible candidate for bringing about changes: the tick rate itself. If this were to change speed, then the number of ticks counted in a given period would also change, giving rise to changed estimates of duration. Whether the effects of increased workload (outside hypnosis) should be conceptualized as a distraction from counting, or a slowing of the clock to 'fit everything in', is an issue not relevant to this chapter; we will be concerned only with the possibility that hypnosis might slow the clock.

How plausible is it that there actually is a 'clock' to slow? While its exact nature remains unclear, many experiments have suggested that we do have a form of internal oscillator. Treisman and colleagues (e.g. Treisman et al. 1990, 1992) have proposed that it is neurologically based. We were even able to suggest the rate at which it appeared to tick: approximately 12 Hz (Treisman et al. 1994). The estimate was made by attempting to 'pull' the frequency of the putative internal oscillator, by means of external rhythmic stimuli of various frequencies. The degree and direction of shift were deduced from alterations in time judgements, and the results were used to compute the underlying master frequency. The rate can be shifted in ways other than by using external driving frequencies: Fox et al. (1967) showed that a patient with a fever behaved as if her internal clock was ticking more quickly, presumably because the neural circuitry functioned more rapidly at elevated temperatures. There is thus good evidence for a clock, and there are certainly some circumstances in which its rate can change.

What would be the observed effects, if hypnosis caused an inner clock to run more slowly? With fewer ticks being counted per unit of real time, the overall number accumulated over a session of hypnosis would be relatively small, leading the subject to conclude that a shorter length of time had passed. That of course is the usual observation. A further prediction can be made. If it is true that the clock ticks slowly, a subject waiting for a period of time to pass will wait too long. Suppose, for example, that they try to wait 2 min, before carrying out some action. From previous experience they will have in mind what 2 min feels like, presumably based upon some conscious representation of the tick-accumulation value for this duration. If the clock begins to tick more slowly than usual, then inevitably the person has to wait longer for the appropriate tick value to accumulate. I tested the 'waiting 2 min' idea (Naish 2001), asking hypnotized subjects to interrupt me when they believed 2 min to have passed. They did indeed 'overshoot', producing an average duration 21 per cent longer than a true 2 min. I also asked the traditional question about the length of the session; the mean judgement was 64 per cent of the actual time. This study used an opportunity sample of subjects, and no attempt was made to divide them into low and high susceptibility groups.

The two kinds of timing test, 'interrupt me in 2 min' and 'judge the duration of the session', can be described as prospective and retrospective. The usual test in hypnosis, asking how long it lasted, seeks a retrospective estimate. Requesting the subject to keep track of time, for a specified interval, is a prospective task. Outside the hypnosis field, it is well known that prospective estimates are generally longer (and as a result usually more accurate) than retrospective estimates (e.g. Zakay 1989), and the observation is commented upon by St Jean *et al.* (1994). These authors claimed that the principal difference between the two tasks was that the retrospective measure was unexpected by the subject, hence leading to a reduced level of attention to the timing task. Prospective timing, by definition, requires that the subject knows what is required, and presumably deploys the necessary resources to carry out the task. Consequently, retrospective timing will have missed ticks, whereas prospective timing is likely to catch more of them.

The possibility that the prospective effect that I found was due merely to foreknowledge and a shift of attention needs to be addressed. An effective way of looking at the impact of hypnosis itself (and incidentally removing other individual differences) is to compare the timing estimates made in hypnosis with those made outside hypnosis, when carrying out similar tasks. Importantly, an individual's hypnosis results should be expressed as a fraction of their 'waking' results. In this way, any general tendency for an individual to over- or underestimate time intervals is eliminated from the result; only the impact of hypnosis upon the timing is recorded. In my experiment, I had taken similar prospective and retrospective measures outside hypnosis, so it was possible to recalculate the data in this way.

When comparing subjects' ability to interrupt me in what they felt was 2 min, both during and before hypnosis, it was found that the time they waited within hypnosis was 60 per cent *longer* than the time delay during 'waking'. Corresponding calculations of the retrospective effect showed that the estimate in hypnosis was 32 per cent *shorter* than the estimate made out of hypnosis. It was clear that hypnosis was having an impact upon both measures of time estimation, and the directions of the changes were consistent with the slow clock hypothesis. Nevertheless, although the hypnosis–waking comparison reveals some kind of effect of hypnosis, it does not entirely rule out the possibility that the effect was, at least in part, something to do with a prepared–unprepared difference between prospective and retrospective tests. The next experiments were attempts to eliminate this possibility.

15.8 Hypnosis and brief interval assessment

The time estimates investigated in hypnosis have tended to be for periods in the range of several minutes, whereas most experiments reported in the time perception literature consider intervals of a few seconds or less (Fortin and Couture 2002). There would be merit in using brief periods in hypnosis. The first advantage would be that, with the tests appropriately administered, there could be no claim that the subject had not expected the task, and in consequence had paid insufficient attention to it. Another advantage of testing over a brief time interval is that this would eliminate some of the variability introduced by other tasks taking place during the hypnosis. St Jean *et al.* (1994, Experiment I) showed that higher workload tasks within hypnosis produced greater time distortion. Most retrospective estimates published have been for periods during which subjects were involved in a variety of activities, such as undertaking susceptibility tests. These periods of unknown and varying workload may have contributed to the variability in the magnitude of the effects reported. In a brief time estimation study it is not possible for subjects to be engaged in any other activity.

The tasks I used (Naish 2001) were button pressing and tone duration judgements. For the prospective task, subjects were required to depress a push-button for an estimated 5 s. In the retrospective task, they listened to computer-generated 'beeps', of durations ranging from 2 to 8 s (mean 5 s), and had to judge how long each beep had lasted. Clearly, subjects were warned that they were required to make these judgements, so this form of retrospective estimate was in no sense unexpected. It should be noted that, if the internal clock were running slowly, then the prospective task would result in the button being depressed for too long, while the retrospective task would have beeps judged as being of shorter duration than they would be at a normal clock speed. I found that the button pressing was indeed 17 per cent longer in hypnosis, while the beeps were judged to be 19 per cent shorter in hypnosis (both being compared with the corresponding 'waking' estimates).

The four sets of results I have described show that, whether making a prospective or retrospective judgement, and whether it is for a long or short interval, the resultant timing shifts are consistent with the proposal that hypnosis causes the inner clock to tick more slowly. The short interval results are unlikely to be attributable to the subject in some sense 'attending away from', or forgetting the task; all appeared to be as focused upon what was required of them as they seemed to be when performing the task outside hypnosis. It is possible that, as St Jean et al. (1994) suggested, the hypnosis acted as an additional task and that, as in many other timing studies, this produced the familiar 'workload' effect. However, while this might be plausible in some phases of hypnosis, when for example a subject could be engaged in trying to enact the suggested experiences (Spanos 1986, 1991), it seems less likely when no experience is being demanded. These subjects were already hypnotized (without pre-judging what that term might mean), and were merely being asked to focus upon simple timing tasks. The resulting effects seem more reasonably attributable to the slowing of an internal clock than to an increase in workload. If this conclusion is reasonable, it invites the question: why does hypnosis slow the clock? An answer may have something to say about the nature of hypnosis itself.

15.9 **Consciousness and its modification**

If hypnosis has an impact upon subjects' experience of time, then in some sense it could be said to be modifying their consciousness. In fact, hypnosis has been referred to as 'an altered state of consciousness', although the appropriateness of this description has been a matter for debate (see Kalio and Revonsuo 2003, for an analysis of this controversy; also Hasegawa and Jamieson 2002). Whatever the rights and wrongs of that particular debate, it is pertinent to consider the nature of consciousness, not least because some accounts of the phenomenon appear to offer explanations for timing misjudgements. Moreover, the accounts of consciousness I shall address have been developed around the notion of changed experiences, although not in the context of hypnosis; they are concerned with illness-related hallucinations.

A significant model of consciousness was outlined by Gray (1995). It was significant, not just because it was an attempt to link the phenomenon to specific neural circuitry, but also, and importantly for the theme of this chapter, it incorporated a timing element. Gray's starting point can be reached from an evolutionary perspective; as animals developed behaviours to interact with their environments, so they would also need to develop monitoring systems, to ensure that a behaviour was progressing as required and that it continued to be appropriate for the environmental demands. Part of the monitoring would necessitate access to long-term memories, to provide predictive 'templates', against which to compare the developing outcome of an action. Any mismatch detected by the monitoring system would be required to trigger corrective actions. In more advanced animals, the mismatch could be described as capturing attention and, at least in humans, attention can be equated with consciousness (Naish 2005c).

The behavioural and the monitoring components of Gray's model comprise interlocked neural circuits within the brain. The motor and data gathering element, he proposed, included the basal ganglia, thalamic nuclei and ascending dopaminergic pathways. The predictive loop he claimed to be based on the septo-hippocampal system, taking in regions of the prefrontal cortex, including the cingulate. These two systems, Gray suggested, operate together to carry out a test-and-predict cycle. The dopaminergic components are concerned with gathering data on the current state, while the monitoring system uses information such as goals, and memories of previous experiences, to predict what should be registered in the next cycle of data gathering. As explained, mismatches detected between data and prediction are presumed to capture attention and become part of consciousness.

More recent studies have confirmed the role of the frontal cortex (including the cingulate region) in its supervisory/regulatory role. Thus, Ridderinkhof *et al.* (2004) concluded, from a review of the literature, that the posterior medial frontal cortex acted in a monitoring role, in association with the lateral prefrontal cortex, the latter having a controlling function. Botvinick *et al.* (2004) reviewed the large literature showing that activity in the anterior cingulate cortex (ACC) is associated with the recognition of conflicts during information processing. (Egner and Raz, Chapter 3, address this aspect from a slightly different perspective.) Botvinick *et al.* (2004) suggested that conflict-related activity may be a reflection of a larger role for the region: that of monitoring and evaluating actions. Luu and Pederson (2004) have taken this proposal further, concluding that the ACC plays a key role when actions need either to be corrected, or modified to suit changing demands. Additionally, they believe that the region is implicated in monitoring for departures from the expected, and also in evaluating the affective consequences of detected mismatches.

It was suggested above that mismatches may determine which elements enter consciousness. While these determinants are clearly important to the theory, so too are the factors controlling what fails to reach consciousness. Duncan (2001) has demonstrated the 'uncommitted' quality of neurons in the prefrontal cortex. Unlike most neurons, whose activity appears to be associated with specific stimuli, the prefrontal area seems to be reconfigurable, to suit the requirements of the task in hand. It would seem that the region acts as the 'working memory', holding current action plans and predictions. The work of Fletcher *et al.* (1999) suggests that these predictive activities of the prefrontal cortex serve to inhibit activation in the monitoring regions of the superior temporal cortex. Inhibition appears to prevent correctly predicted material from entering consciousness, but crucially (for the account that will be developed) the extent of inhibition seems to be modulated by the ACC region.

In a complex neural system there is the inevitable possibility of faults occurring, and in this system faults might be expected to influence the content of consciousness. Indeed, much of Gray's work was concerned with the neurological basis of the symptoms of schizophrenia, including the problems of attention and the generation of hallucinations. He proposed that, in schizophrenia, there is a problem with the system that compares the observed with the predicted, resulting in much of the normally predictable data being treated as unpredicted. Even the patient's own 'inner voice', Gray suggested, could be treated as unexpected, and hence attributed to an external agent. This, of course, accounts for the classic symptom of auditory hallucination. The suggestion that normal events are experienced as unpredicted has gained support from subsequent studies. Thus Fletcher *et al.* (1999) showed, with PET scanning, that the normal cingulate modulation (described above) was deficient in schizophrenia patients, so leaving the temporal regions more than normally active. Using fMRI, Lawrie *et al.* (2002) showed that, compared with controls, patients with schizophrenia exhibited a lower correlation between the activities of the prefrontal cortex and temporal cortex. Moreover, those who suffered most from auditory hallucinations displayed the weakest correlations. These studies highlight the role of prefrontal/temporal circuits in monitoring sensory experiences. Prefrontal/parietal circuits may serve a similar role for proprioceptive activity; thus, Frith *et al.* (2000) suggest that breakdown in control of the parietal from the frontal cortex accounts for the schizophrenic illusion of one's behaviour being externally controlled.

Before this account of non-hypnotic consciousness is taken further, it is worth noting that there are parallels between the hallucinations of schizophrenia, and those that can occur in hypnosis. Szechtman *et al.* (1998) went so far as to use hypnotically induced auditory hallucinations as an analogue for the schizophrenic form. Similarly, Blakemore *et al.* (2003) hypnotized subjects, and gave the familiar suggestion for movements that would 'happen by themselves' (such as arm levitation). PET scans showed that when the hypnotized participants experienced movements as being outside their control there was simultaneously a higher level of activity in the parietal cortex. This, of course, is exactly analogous to the findings of Frith *et al.* (2000) in schizophrenia patients. Hypnotic susceptibility and schizotypy are positively correlated (Jamieson and Gruzelier 2001; Gruzelier *et al.* 2004); Gruzelier (2003) proposes that schizophrenia and hypnosis have common neurophysiological features.

Since Gray's proposed circuitry includes significant dopaminergic pathways, it is not surprising to find that it can also account for some of the phenomena of Parkinson's disease (PD), a condition resulting from dopamine deficiency. Here again, there is a link with consciousness, since patients can suffer from visual and auditory hallucinations; Fénelon *et al.* (2000) report that hallucinations in PD patients are far more common than has hitherto been supposed. The well-known 'freezing' behaviour of PD sufferers appears to be a problem in trying to allow well-rehearsed motor 'programmes' (such as climbing stairs) to run without conscious monitoring. If the patient brings the activity into consciousness, by clearly imagining the intended goal, the actions can sometimes be recommenced. It will be proposed that imagination is an important element of consciousness, as will now be briefly explained. The topic will be revisited later.

Gray himself admitted that his model did not fully explain how the phenomenon of consciousness emerges from the circuits he describes, and subsequent studies have done little to elucidate the issue. From a logical perspective, consciousness seems not to be necessary to the processes of behaving and monitoring: machines can do that. Nevertheless, we can all attest to a sense of 'awareness of being aware'. A possible evolutionary driver for the sense of consciousness was the valuable skill of imagining, of being able to plan, and ask 'what if?' questions. This ability appears to use many of the same neural structures as would be active if external stimuli were really present, although during imagining the neural activity is self-generated. The process is very much like using a computer 'off-line', as is sometimes done with the computers used to control complex systems. By disconnecting the computer's sensors, and feeding it with dummy data, it can be used in training, or to test emergency scenarios. Just as it is important that operators know the procedure is an exercise, so it is important that humans have the ability to recognize that imagination is not real. Whitty and Lewin (1957) showed that the region of brain apparently responsible for making the distinction is in the ACC. Patients with damage to this area experienced great difficulty in differentiating between events that had actually occurred, and those that they had only imagined. Hypnosis, of course, enables some people to have very realistic (imagined) experiences, and it carries with it the danger of creating false memories (e.g. Home Office Circular 1988). In view of this, it is particularly interesting to note that all hypnosis brain-scanning studies appear to show unusual activity in the ACC, irrespective of what other regions are active. This region, it will be recalled, was a component in Gray's proposed circuitry, and it has a central role in many of the accounts of consciousness and hallucination cited earlier.

15.10 **Consciousness and the clock**

For a prediction system to generate representations of an expected state, at just the moment when the sensory-motor systems are acquiring data about the actual state, requires precise temporal intermeshing. This kind of synchronization is achieved in a computer by means of a 'clock', an oscillator that ensures all the processes remain in step. Gray proposed that it was the septo-hippocampal system that maintained synchrony in the system that gives rise to consciousness, suggesting that its 'tick rate' was about 10 Hz. This frequency is remarkably close to the 12 Hz clock identified by Treisman *et al.* (1994); there is additional evidence to suggest that they may be driven by one and the same system.

If it is the case that the tick rate of the inner clock is determined by the rate of the test-and-predict loop proposed by Gray, then it is reasonable to suppose that a breakdown in the integrity of the loop might disrupt the timing. This effect is indeed observed, in the two classes of patient considered above. Thus, Elvevåg *et al.* (2004) tested schizophrenic patients on a series of tasks, including time estimation, and concluded that schizophrenia is associated with a selective impairment in temporal processing ability. Similarly, Harrington *et al.* (1998) showed that PD patients too have impaired time perception abilities.

Drawing these evidential strands together, it seems possible that the time distortions of hypnosis could also reflect some form of disruption to the smooth running of the 'consciousness cycle'. If this were the case, then hypnosis could legitimately be called an altered state of consciousness, and an examination of the temporal effects may reveal how that consciousness is altered. It has already been pointed out that hypnosis appears to impact the cingulate region, a central element of the putative timing structure; how this might occur will now be considered.

15.11 **Self-generated consciousness and the clock**

As explained, the ACC appears to be involved in reality checking (Whitty and Lewin 1957); it is a common description of hypnosis that it involves the abandonment of reality checking (e.g. Naish 1986). This implies that the 'predict' part of the test-and-predict cycle runs without meshing with the corresponding 'test' subcomponent. In effect, this is another way of describing what happens when we engage in imagination, the difference with the latter being that we do not attempt the testing process, because we are aware that our experience is not being driven by external stimuli. Those susceptible to hypnosis also appear not to test, but additionally, seem not to be *aware* that they are avoiding the process. If the ACC has a central role in determining what is experienced as real [a role supported by Szechtman *et al*'s (1998) study of auditory hallucinations], then in hypnosis it seems to be indicating 'real', when in fact the system is in 'self-generate' mode. There are circumstances in which the results of this self-deception can surprise the hypnotized person, in much the same way as schizophrenic patients can be surprised by the 'sound' of their own inner voice. Thus, the failure properly to monitor the motor programmes that cause an arm to lift, following arm levitation suggestions, leads a hypnotized participant to believe that the arm has levitated 'all by itself'. The Blakemore *et al.* (2003) PET study, concerning the sense of non-volition, has already been described. Haggard *et al.* (2004) reported a related study in which hypnotized subjects were asked to indicate the moment in time (not a duration) when they moved a finger. When the movement was perceived as non-voluntary (i.e. like arm levitation), the indication that movement had occurred was made later than when the movement was made consciously. In fact the 'non-voluntary' timing was very similar to that obtained when the movement was experimenter initiated, i.e. truly involuntary. This finding supports the claim that, in hypnosis, the link between monitoring and self-generated behaviour can be in some way modified.

Clearly, hypnotized participants maintain a considerable link with reality; for one thing, without it they would be unable to follow the hypnotist's suggestions. Moreover, to be aware of the results of a suggestion, such as for arm levitation, while failing to monitor their own enactment of the suggestion, implies that successful hypnosis requires a complex blend of attending and detaching. If this is an accurate account of hypnosis, then it is not surprising that relatively few have the skill to reach the level of hypnotic 'highs'.

If it is true that the abandonment of the reality testing cycle disrupts the clock and causes time distortion, then presumably those subjects who are better able to generate their own 'reality', while keeping the 'real thing' out of consciousness, will exhibit more distortion. However, as just pointed out, hypnosis requires some level of reality monitoring to be maintained; exactly how much may depend upon the particular circumstances. It is possible that even hypnotic 'highs' may not always need to engage in a great deal of reality generating, and consequently the extent of the resultant time distortion may be less than the 'high' status would lead one to expect. This is another possible explanation for the weak timing–susceptibility correlations that have been reported. Nevertheless, when required to generate a 'world of their own', those participants who are most successful should, if this account is correct, produce the largest timing effects.

I carried out an experiment (Naish 2003) that tested that prediction. Subjects were given the traditional task of imagining a beach scene, with the additional element that they were waiting on the beach for a friend, who was due in precisely 5 min. They were given stopwatches, which they were told to press at the moment they judged the friend to be due. While waiting for that moment, it was suggested that they should do whatever they liked on their beach; subsequently some reported sunbathing, others paddling, and so on. The resulting times ranged from close to 2 min, to over 7 min.

After the participants had completed the timing task, they were asked to make two self-ratings, both on 7-point scales. The first was of the vividness and reality of the scene they had been trying to visualize, and the second asked for the extent to which the real world intruded (awareness of outside sounds, etc.). The intrusion score was subtracted from the vividness rating, to yield a measure of 'detachment'. Thus, a subject who rated the vividness as high and the intrusion as low would score high on detachment. This measure was taken to reflect the extent to which a subject was able to engage in generating a personal reality, while ceasing to monitor the real thing.

There was a highly significant correlation between the detachment scores and the time estimates ($r = 0.75$, $P < 0.001$). In terms of the clock, it was, as predicted, running more slowly for those who were able to detach more successfully. Neither of the individual 7-point instruments correlated with time judgements as strongly as the combined detachment measure; the implications are discussed below.

15.12 How does detachment slow the clock?

Thus far, the proposition has been that failure to engage in reality testing disrupts the cycle that supports the clock function. However, this proposal does not, as it stands, predict a *slowing* of the clock; it could just as well run fast. It is possible that the system 'free-wheels' slowly when the test and predict elements become disengaged. (The body's circadian rhythm shows this slowing effect, producing a period of greater than 24 h, in the absence of sunlight to lock it to the day/night frequency.) As an alternative to the free-wheeling explanation, the partial engagement of the timing components (as explained above, to support a measure of contact with reality) may result in the detection of only some of the 'ticks'. This second explanation is not dissimilar from the traditional account of high workload taking attention away from a 'tick counter', except that hypnosis is not being described as a high workload situation.

If the 'missing ticks' account were correct, it might be expected that the subjects in my detachment study who reported the least awareness of outside reality would also be cutting themselves off most successfully from the source of the ticks. However, the correlation between intrusion and timing scores was relatively low ($r = -0.62$, $P < 0.001$). Missing ticks may not be the reason for the clock seeming to run more slowly. To develop an alternative account, a situation far removed from hypnosis will first be considered.

The experience of events unfolding as if in slow motion may offer a clue concerning the processes in hypnosis. People frequently report that at times of heightened arousal, such as in an accident situation, all the action appears to be slowed down. This may be the result of a speeding of the test-and-predict cycle (and with it the clock). To be certain of capturing timely data, the cycle might run more quickly, resulting in each captured scene differing only slightly from its predecessor. The person experiencing this phenomenon would be familiar with the usual extent of alteration between data captures, so encountering a smaller change would lead to the perception that an on-coming car, say, was approaching unusually slowly.

The opposite situation may occur in hypnosis. If the content of consciousness is in large part self-generated, then there is little need to initiate another data capture cycle: the content would be much the same as for the current situation. As a result, the cycle rate would be reduced, and the ticks would be more widely spaced. This explanation might lead one to expect that people better able to generate a vivid inner experience would be the ones to suffer a greater time distortion effect. However, in the detachment study, this correlation was the lowest of all ($r = 0.57$, $P < 0.005$). Perhaps the ability to generate a vivid and convincing experience need not necessarily demand that a slower test-and-predict cycle be maintained.

Clearly, there is as yet no complete explanation for the impact of hypnosis upon the inner clock. Nevertheless, some facts seem to emerge:

- Disruption to the circuits associated with monitoring and prediction results in poor time estimation.
- The ACC is a part of the timing-sensitive circuitry.
- The ACC is involved in determining the content of consciousness, and whether that content feels 'expected' or 'surprising', i.e. in reality checking.
- People who are able to abandon reality checking produce timing errors.
- Neuroimaging shows that hypnosis impacts the ACC.

To summarize, there is good reason to believe that the neural circuits associated with generating conscious experience are also involved in making time judgements. When there are faults in the system, as in schizophrenia or PD, they change both the nature of consciousness and the ability to make accurate time judgements. Hypnosis behaves like a temporary and controllable 'fault in the system'. Consequently, hypnosis modifies the conscious experience, and also changes the clock rate.

15.13 Is there a correlation between clock rate and susceptibility?

Throughout this chapter several possible reasons have been offered for the weakness, or indeed absence of the expected tick rate–susceptibility correlation. Nevertheless, the developing account has shown that there is good reason to propose strong links between hypnosis, modifications to conscious experience and the clock. These links seem inescapably to imply that people better able to achieve the effects of hypnosis would normally experience more time distortion. Why has this effect been so hard to demonstrate?

It has been pointed out that the hypnotic component of any temporal distortions is more apparent if the timing data collected in hypnosis are compared with the same subject's data gathered during waking. In addition, if modest numbers of subjects are to be used, it is more likely that differences would be found between 'highs' and 'lows', rather than seeking a correlation using subjects with a range of susceptibilities. I have been able to take this approach, in a small, as yet unpublished study, which formed part of a larger series of trials, being conducted by colleagues John Gruzelier and Tobias Egner (then both at Imperial College, London). They were engaged in research using 'highs' and 'lows', and it included periods of making EEG recordings, while the participants were in hypnosis. I was able to make use of both the recording phase, and also the preceding period, during which participants were having the scalp electrodes attached (and were not hypnotized).

At the conclusions of both the electrode-fitting stage and the period of EEG testing (when they were hypnotized), participants were asked how long they believed that phase to have lasted. Additionally, during each phase they were required to carry out the beep estimation and 5 s button press tests described earlier. With respect to the overall period judgement, the 'highs' and 'lows' did not differ significantly outside hypnosis: as a percentage of actual time, they estimated the electrode fitting to have taken 86 per cent ('highs') and 80 per cent ('lows'). Thus, both groups underestimated the time somewhat. However, in hypnosis, the 'highs' decreased their estimation much further, reducing it to 65 per cent of the true value. This change, which was in the traditional direction, was significant ($P < 0.05$). In contrast, the 'lows' *increased* their assessment to 92 per cent of the actual time: another significant shift ($P < 0.05$). The group ('high'/'low') × condition (waking/hypnosis) interaction was also significant ($P < 0.01$).

When estimating beep duration, the 'highs' reduced their judgement by 12 per cent in hypnosis. In this test, although the 'lows' also reduced their estimates, it was by less than 2 per cent. This interaction was again significant ($P < 0.05$). Consistent with the slow-running clock hypothesis, during hypnosis the 'highs' increased the duration of their button pressing by 6 per cent. The 'lows', in contrast, actually reduced their button pressing time by 4 per cent, producing yet another significant interaction ($P < 0.05$).

It can be seen that by every measure there was a 'high'–'low' difference, with those scoring high on susceptibility producing the typical 'slow clock' effects, while the low scorers tended to produce little, or even a reverse effect. There seems to be no doubt that, at least with this method of testing, susceptibility modulates the hypnotic time distortion effect.

It will be recalled that in the St Jean and MacLeod (1983) study, the effects also appeared to be restricted to the highly hypnotizable. It is possible that, rather than exhibiting the quantitative differences of a behavioural continuum, the temporal effects of hypnosis in 'highs' and 'lows' are qualitatively different.

15.14 The neural correlates of hypnotic susceptibility

The timing effects evident in my own studies, and apparent in some of those reported by St Jean and his colleagues, suggest that hypnotic 'highs' and 'lows' respond differently. By definition, they report different experiences when tested on susceptibility measures, but they also show either marked time distortion ('highs'), or negligible and possibly reversed timing effects ('lows'). It has been argued in this chapter that changed experiences are brought about by changes in the frontal cortex, particularly in the anterior cingulate. This is the region presumed to be involved in directing attention to the unexpected, which as we have seen is a function that breaks down in schizophrenia (Lawrie *et al.* 2002). This attention-directing role, and its modulation by hypnosis, seems to have been demonstrated by Gruzelier *et al.* (2002*b*).

Gruzelier *et al.* (2002*b*) used EEG recording techniques, which lack the discriminatory power to identify the precise location of an electrical response. Thus, it was not possible with their methodology to localize activity specifically to the cingulate, but it was possible to identify responses as being located more generally in the frontal cortex. The researchers looked for differences in evoked responses to predictable and unexpected events. The events used were tone bursts, most being of low pitch, but with a small proportion having higher pitch, and hence, in a sense, being surprising. Typically, events give rise to a negative-going electrical response in the frontal region, at about 100 ms after the event took place; the signal is labelled N100. Approximately 200 ms later (300 ms after the event), a positive transient is detected, termed the P300 wave. The N100 wave has been identified as a marker of attention-directing activity. The P300 is particularly associated with surprise, and has high amplitude when a signal is unexpected.

Gruzelier *et al.* tested 'low' and 'high' hypnotizable subjects, both in and out of hypnosis. In both groups, the N100 response to *expected* tones was not greatly influenced by hypnosis; there was a tendency for it to reduce slightly. However, when the signal was one of the rare, higher pitched tones, the two groups behaved very differently. The 'highs', who produced large amplitude N100 responses to rare signals outside hypnosis, reduced the amplitude down to 'expected' values when hypnotized. In contrast, the 'lows' produced even higher amplitude waves when hypnotized.

These effects could be interpreted as showing that the 'highs', when hypnotized, detached from a complete monitoring of outside stimuli. The stimuli were detected, but no special 'attend' signals were initiated. The 'lows' appear to have done the reverse, and became, if anything, even more alert to unexpected stimuli. The P300 responses bear out this interpretation. For the 'highs' in hypnosis, the P300 amplitude fell to almost zero, implying that no 'surprise' was registered. Contrastingly, the 'lows' maintained a significant level of P300.

15.15 A final look at the clock

The findings of Gruzelier *et al.* (2002*b*) reinforce the suggestion that 'lows' do not simply do less of whatever it takes to be hypnotized; they actually do something different. How moderately susceptible subjects fit into this range of behaviour will be a matter for future research, but it seems clear that the complexity of these responses will have been a major factor in making it difficult to detect timing–susceptibility correlations.

The N100/P300 results are concerned with attention, and raise again the question of whether hypnotic time distortion has more to do with tick missing than clock slowing. If hypnosis reduces the level of attention, it perhaps reduces the attention to the ticks. However, the evoked responses demonstrate a changed response to the unexpected. Presumably, 'ticks', whatever their precise nature, are not unexpected: they are ever-present. Moreover, when subjects are asked to engage in timing tasks such as button pressing, or judging a tone duration, they must inevitably be attending to the activity. These sorts of task, and also the results of Gruzelier *et al.* (2002) show 'lows' to be behaving differently: time distortion going 'the wrong way', and attention increasing. Unless it is assumed that 'lows' are chronic 'tick missers', it is difficult to see how hypnosis could make them miss fewer ticks. It seems altogether more plausible to suppose that hypnosis tends to speed their clock rates. Taking this together with the N100 attentional changes, the situation for hypnotized 'lows' can be likened to that proposed for people in an accident situation, where it was also suggested that the clock may run faster.

A speculative summary of the above is that 'highs' and 'lows' respond to hypnosis differently. 'Highs' cease to monitor for the unexpected; instead they generate their own experiences, and consequently do not need to maintain a high tick rate in the consciousness cycle. In contrast, 'lows' actively *seek* hypnotic experiences as if they are to be expected from outside. Their response is to raise the general level of attention, so as not to miss whatever effects hypnosis might bring, and thus they maintain a higher rate in the consciousness cycle. Sadly for the 'lows', this is not the right way to ensure a hypnotic experience.

15.16 Conclusions

Time distortion is a hallmark of hypnosis. The direction of the distortion is such as would be produced by a slow-running internal clock, and its magnitude correlates with hypnotic susceptibility. However, the correlation is often blurred by many other possible influences, and it seems possible that people low on susceptibility may actually produce reverse timing effects.

Time distortion effects are also observed in other consciousness-modifying conditions, such as schizophrenia. These parallels, taken together with the rather similar experiences of hallucinations and loss of volition, lead to the conclusion that similar neural circuits are involved. In fact brain imaging studies may be interpreted as showing that identical circuits are involved, although hypnosis and other time-modifying conditions may affect different components within the circuits.

The circuits associated with changing perceptions of time are also implicated in the generation of other changes to perception; they are part of the system apparently responsible for determining the content of consciousness.

When hypnosis changes a perception, it does so, it is concluded, by changing the behaviour of the system that gives rise to consciousness. Hypnosis may thus be seen not only as a cause of temporal changes, but also as an altered state of consciousness.

This kind of account, that hypnosis is both a cause and a condition, might be accused of circularity. In defence of this position, I would argue that the nature of consciousness and the content of consciousness must inevitably be driven by circular processes. This will be the case whether or not the generation of consciousness has hypnosis as one of its contributing elements.

References

Barber TX (1969). *Hypnosis: a scientific approach*. New York, Van Nostrand Reinhold.

Blakemore S-J, Oakley DA and Frith CD (2003). Delusions of alien control in the normal brain. *Neuropsychologia*, **41**, 1058–67.

Botvinick MM, Cohen JD, and Carter CS (2004). Conflict monitoring and anterior cingulate cortex: an update. *Trends in Cognitive Science*, **8**, 539–46.

Bowers KS. (1979). Time distortion and hypnotic ability: underestimating the duration of hypnosis. *Journal of Abnormal Psychology*, **88**, 435–39.

Bowers KS and Brenneman HA (1979). Hypnosis and the perception of time. *International Journal of Clinical and Experimental Hypnosis*, **27**, 29–41.

Brown SW and Boltz MG (2002). Attentional processes in time perception: effects of mental workload and event structure. *Journal of Experimental Psychology: Human Perception and Performance*, **28**, 600–15.

Crawford HJ, Horton JE, Hirsch TB, Harrington GS, Plantec MB, Vendemia JMC, *et al* (1998). Attention and disattention (hypnotic analgesia). to painful somatosensory TENS stimuli differentially affects brain dynamics: a functional magnetic resonance imaging study. *International Journal of Psychophysiology*, **30**, 77.

Duncan J (2001). An adaptive coding model of neural function in prefrontal cortex. *Nature Reviews Neuroscience*, **2**, 820–29.

Elvevåg B, Brown GDA, McCormack T, Vousden JI and Goldberg TE (2004). Identification of tone duration, line length, and letter position: an experimental approach to timing and working memory deficits in schizophrenia. *Journal of Abnormal Psychology*, **113**, 509–21.

Fénelon G, Mahieux F, Huon R and Ziégler M (2000). Hallucinations in Parkinson's disease. *Brain*, **123**, 733–45.

Fletcher P, McKenna PJ, Friston KJ, Frith CD and Dolan RJ (1999). Abnormal cingulate modulation of fronto-temporal connectivity in schizophrenia. *NeuroImage*, **9**, 337–42.

Fortin C and Couture E (2002). Short-term memory and time estimation: beyond the 2-second 'critical' value. *Canadian Journal of Experimental Psychology*, **56**, 120–27.

Fox RH, Bradbury PA, Hampton IFG and Legg CF (1967). Time judgment and body temperature. *Journal of Experimental Psychology*, **75**, 88–96.

Frith CD, Blakemore S-J and Wolpert DM (2000). Explaining the symptoms of schizophrenia: abnormalities in the awareness of action. *Brain Research Reviews*, **31**, 357–63.

Gray JA (1995). The contents of consciousness—a neuropsychological conjecture. *Behavioural and Brain Sciences*, **18**, 659–76.

Gruzelier JH (2003). Theory, methods and new directions in the psychophysiology of the schizophrenic process and schitzotypy. *International Journal of Psychophysiology*, **48**, 221–45.

Gruzelier J, Champion A, Fox P, Rollin M, McCormack S, Catalan P, *et al.* (2002*a*). Individual differences in personality, immunology and mood in patients undergoing self-hypnosis training for the successful treatment of a chronic viral illness, HSV-2. *Contemporary Hypnosis*, **19**, 149–66.

Gruzelier J, Gray M and Horn P (2002*b*). The involvement of frontally modulated attention in hypnosis and hypnotic susceptibility: cortical evoked potential evidence. *Contemporary Hypnosis*, **19**, 179–89.

Gruzelier JH, De Pascalis V, Jamieson G, Laidlaw T, Naito A, Bennett B, *et al.* (2004). Relations between hypnotizability and psychopathology revisited. *Contemporary Hypnosis*, **21**, 169–76.

Haggard P, Cartledge P, Dafydd, M and Oakley DA (2004). Anomalous control: when 'free-will' is not conscious. *Consciousness and Cognition*, **13**, 646–54.

Halligan PW, Athwal BS, Oakley DA and Frackowiak RSJ (2000). Imaging hypnotic paralysis: implications for conversion hysteria. *Lancet*, **355**, 986–87.

Harrington DL, Haaland KY and Hermanowicz N (1998). Temporal processing in the basal ganglia. *Neuropsychology*, **12**, 3–12.

Hasegawa H and Jamieson GA (2002). Conceptual issues in hypnosis research: explanations, definitions and the state/non-state debate. *Contemporary Hypnosis*, **19**, 103–17.

Home Office Circular 66 (1988). *The use of hypnosis by the police in the investigation of crime.* Queen Anne's Gate, London.

Jamieson G and Gruzelier JH (2001). Hypnotic susceptibility is positively related to a subset of schizotypy items. *Contemporary Hypnosis*, **18**, 32–7.

Kallio S and Revonsuo A (2003). Hypnotic phenomena and altered states of consciousness: a multilevel framework of description and explanation. *Contemporary Hypnosis*, **20**, 111–64.

Kosslyn SM, Thompson WL, Costantini-Ferrando MF, Alpert NM and Spiegel D (2000). Hypnotic visual illusion alters color processing in the brain. *American Journal of Psychiatry*, **157**, 1279–284.

Lawrie SM, Buechel C, Whalley HC, Frith CD, Friston KJ and Johnstone EC (2002). Reduced frontotemporal functional connectivity in schizophrenia associated with auditory hallucinations. *Biological Psychiatry*, **51**, 1008–11.

Luu P and Pederson SM (2004). The anterior cingulate cortex: regulating actions in context. In: MI Posner, ed. *Cognitive neuroscience of attention.* pp. 232–242. New York, Guilford Press.

Mozenter RH, Kurtz RM. (1992). Prospective time estimation and hypnotizability in a simulator design. *International Journal of Clinical and Experimental Hypnosis*, **40**, 169–79.

Naish PLN (1986). Hypnosis and signal detection: an information processing account. In: PLN Naish, ed. *What is hypnosis? Current theories and research.* pp. 121–44. Milton Keynes, UK, Open University Press.

Naish PLN (2001). Hypnotic time perception: busy beaver or tardy timekeeper? *Contemporary Hypnosis*, **18**, 87–99.

Naish PLN (2003). The production of hypnotic time-distortion: determining the necessary conditions. *Contemporary Hypnosis*, **20**, 3–15.

Naish PLN (2005*a*). Detecting hypnotically altered states of consciousness. *Contemporary Hypnosis*, **22**, 24–30.

Naish PLN (2005*b*). On the inevitability of finding hypnosis–simulator equivalence. *Contemporary Hypnosis*, **22**, 154–57.

Naish PLN (2005*c*). Attention. In: N Braisby and A Gellatly, eds. *Cognitive psychology.* pp. 37–70. Oxford, Oxford University Press.

Orne MT (1979). On the simulating subject as a quasi-control group in hypnosis research: what, why and how. In: E Fromm and RE Shor, eds. *Hypnosis: developments in research and new perspectives*, pp. 399–443. New York, Aldine.

Ornstein RF (1969). *On the experience of time*. Harmondsworth, UK, Penguin Books.

Ridderinkhof KR, Ullsperger M, Crone EA and Nieuwenhuis S (2004). The role of the medial frontal cortex in cognitive control. *Science*, **306**, 443–47.

St Jean R (1988). Hypnotic underestimation of time: fact or artifact. *British Journal of Experimental and Clinical Hypnosis*, **5**, 83–5.

St Jean R and MacLeod C (1983). Hypnosis, absorption and time perception. *Journal of Abnormal Psychology*, **92**, 81–6.

St Jean R and Robertson L (1986). Attentional versus absorptive processing in hypnotic time estimation. *Journal of Abnormal Psychology*, **95**, 40–2.

St Jean R, MacLeod C, Coe WC and Howard M (1982). Amnesia and hypnotic time estimation. *International Journal of Clinical and Experimental Hypnosis*, **30**, 127–37.

St Jean R, McInnis K, Campbell-Mayne L and Swainson P (1994). Hypnotic underestimation of time: the Busy Beaver hypothesis. *Journal of Abnormal Psychology*, **103**, 565–69.

Spanos NP (1986). Hypnosis and the modification of hypnotic susceptibility: a social psychological perspective. In: PLN Naish, ed. *What is hypnosis? Current theories and research.* pp. 85–120. Milton Keynes, UK, Open University Press.

Spanos NP (1991). A sosciocognitive approach to hypnosis. In: SJ Lynn and JW Rhue, eds. *Theories of hypnosis: current models and perspectives.* pp. 324–361. New York, Guilford Press.

Szechtman H, Woody E, Bowers KS and Nahmias C (1998). Where the imaginal appears real: a positron emission tomography study of auditory hallucinations. *Proceedings of the National Academy of Sciences of the USA*, **95**, 1956–60.

Tellegen A and Atkinson G (1974). Openness to absorbing and self-altering experiences ('absorption'), a trait related to hypnotic susceptibility. *Journal of Abnormal Psychology*, **83**, 268–77.

Treisman M, Faulkener A, Naish PLN and Brognan D (1990). The internal clock: evidence for a temporal oscillator underlying time perception with some estimates of its characteristic frequency. *Perception*, **19**, 705–43.

Treisman M, Faulkner A and Naish PLN (1992). On the relation between time perception and the timing of motor action: evidence for a temporal oscillator controlling the timing of movement. *Quarterly Journal of Experimental Psychology (A)*, **45**, 235–63.

Treisman M, Cook N, Naish PLN and MacCrone JK (1994). The internal clock—electroencephalo-graphic evidence for oscillatory processes underlying time perception. *Quarterly Journal of Experimental Psychology (A)*, **47**, 241–89.

Wagstaff GF (1981). *Hypnosis, compliance and belief*. Brighton, UK, Harvester.

Whitty CWM and Lewin W (1957). Vivid day-dreaming: an unusual form of confusion following anterior cingulectomy. *Brain*, **80**, 72–6.

Zakay D (1989). An integrated model of time estimation. In: I Levin and D Zakav, eds. *Time and human cognition: a life-span perspective*, pp. 365–397. Amsterdam, North Holland Press.

Chapter 16

Executive control without conscious awareness: the cold control theory of hypnosis

Zoltán Dienes and Josef Perner

16.1 Introduction

Control and awareness seem intimately related (e.g. Norman and Shallice 1986; Jacoby 1991). Of course, some forms of control occur quite unconsciously (plausibly, for example, the detailed configuring of motor movements; Milner and Goodale 1995). However, there are some forms of control, such as planning or overcoming strong response tendencies (the 'executive tasks' of Norman and Shallice) that are so commonly associated with conscious awareness that it would seem bizarre if they occurred without it. In fact, unconscious executive control is not possible in the theories of Norman and Shallice and Jacoby. In this chapter, we argue for the theoretical possibility of unconscious executive control, based on the higher order thought (HOT) theory of Rosenthal (1986, 2002, 2005), and then argue that hypnosis provides an example of executive control without conscious awareness (cf. Hilgard 1977; Spanos 1986; Oakley 1999).

A fundamental explanatory problem in hypnosis is how activities that are normally performed voluntarily out of the hypnotic setting can be performed with the experience of involuntariness after hypnotic suggestion (see Lynn and Rhue 1991; Fromm and Nash, 1992 for reviews). Of course, hypnotic phenomena present the researcher with many interesting problems to be explored, but a central if not defining issue is the experience of involuntariness, singled out as the 'classical suggestion effect' by Weizenhoffer (1974). It is this experience of involuntariness under hypnotic suggestion which makes the experience of carrying out otherwise mundane actions, such as slowly raising one's arm, holding one's arm out straight and rigidly, acting like a child, and so on, hypnotic rather than mundane. Other counterintuitive hypnotic phenomena, such as alterations in perception (positive and negative hallucinations), may also be examples of this process of creating the experience of involuntariness (cf. Bentall 1990; Frith 1992). Hypnotic behaviour involves planning, and yet can be performed without conscious awareness of the contents of the plans, and without conscious awareness of intentions to perform the behaviours (Hilgard 1977; Sheehan and McConkey 1982; Spanos 1986; Oakley 1999).

In this chapter, we first review different types of control, and then we consider the distinction between control and awareness of control in the light of Rosenthal's (2002)

HOT theory. The framework we develop provides a number of ways of accounting for hypnotic phenomena, in particular the experience of involuntariness.

16.2 Two types of control

Hilgard (1977) suggested a model of cognitive control in which action schemata (which he called cognitive control structures) compete amongst themselves such that the strongest at any given moment comes to control behaviour. An executive ego can override the strongest so that some other control structure actually controls behaviour. Hilgard presented this model as part of his neo-dissociation theory of hypnosis. Later, Norman and Shallice (1986) provided a very similar and influential theory of cognitive control, motivated independently and without reference to hypnosis. They suggested that action schemata compete to control behaviour. The schema with the most activation is the one that wins. The level of activation of a schema is determined by the match of the schema's trigger conditions with the conditions that actually obtain, and by the lateral excitation and inhibition between schemata (mutually incompatible schemata inhibit each other; cooperating schemata excite each other). This process by which a schema comes to be sufficiently active that it is the one that controls behaviour is called contention scheduling. In addition, there is a supervisory attentional system (SAS) that can send additional excitation or inhibition to a chosen schema, biasing its chances of winning. The SAS is attention demanding and is involved in conscious control, according to Norman and Shallice. The SAS achieves its function by forming intentions: a particular type of imperative representation with the function of bringing about its content.

Norman and Shallice (1986) suggested particular executive function tasks that the SAS was needed for, for example learning new actions or overcoming a strong pre-existing response. If contention scheduling were just left to itself, we would be entirely creatures of habit. If we always drive a certain route from home to work, that route is likely to be taken every time if contention scheduling were the only control process at work. However, sometimes we can decide to do something new; for example, to make a detour at the traffic lights by turning left rather than right in order to buy milk at the supermarket. This new action requires the SAS. Typically the new action would only be accomplished if we were consciously aware of wanting to do it at the appropriate juncture. Hence, Norman and Shallice regarded the SAS as being intimately related to conscious awareness of what one is doing. Jack and Shallice (2001) indicated that they regarded that relationship, between intentional action (SAS) and conscious awareness, as a contingent one that has to be demonstrated (unlike Jacoby 1991, who takes intentional control to be constitutive of conscious awareness). We will argue that the contingent relationship can systematically break down.

16.3 Conscious awareness

We now explore the relationship between control and conscious awareness by use of Rosenthal's (1986, 2002) HOT theory. Rosenthal provided an account of when a mental state is conscious, e.g. when is seeing a case of conscious seeing and when is it unconscious?

Blindsight patients can indicate highly accurately whether an object is moving up or down, even while they claim to have no visual experience whatsoever (Weiskrantz 1986, 1997). Their accurate responses indicate they do see that, for example, an object is moving up. However, their verbal reports indicate that they do not consciously see that an object is moving up. The data indicate that we need a distinction between seeing and consciously seeing, or more generally between being simply *conscious* or *aware of something* and being *consciously aware of something* (Carruthers 2000).

A mental state (e.g. of seeing) makes us conscious of some state of affairs, in the minimal sense of 'conscious of' that applies to the seeing that occurs in a blindsight patient's blind field. What the blindsight patient fails to have is awareness of being in the mental state of seeing that state of affairs. Indeed, Rosenthal argues that a mental state, like seeing, is a conscious mental state only when we are conscious of being in that mental state. Consistently, it sounds bizarre to say the blindsight patients could consciously see but were not conscious of seeing. When we are conscious of seeing, we consciously see.

In Rosenthal's account, we are conscious of mental states by having thoughts about those states. A thought about being in a mental state is a second-order thought (SOT), because it is a mental state about a mental state. For example, the first-order state could be seeing that 'the object in front of me is black'. By virtue of this first-order state, we are conscious of the object in front of me being black. By virtue of the SOT that 'I see that the object in front of me is black', we are conscious of the first-order state of seeing. The seeing is then a conscious mental state, we consciously see that the object in front is black. In summary, according to HOT theory, a mental state is a conscious mental state when the person has a HOT to the effect that they are in that mental state (for elaboration, see Rosenthal 2002; for review, criticism and discussion of higher order theories of consciousness, see chapters in Gennaro 2004).

A SOT (e.g. 'I see that the cat is black') constitutes awareness of the first-order thought ('the cat is black') resulting in the first-order thought being a conscious thought. The SOT itself is not a conscious thought until one becomes conscious of it—by a third-order thought (TOT; 'I am aware that I am seeing that the cat is black'). It is by virtue of the TOT that one is consciously aware or introspectively aware that it is *me* who is *seeing*. TOTs rather than SOTs constitute introspection because being consciously aware of the world is not introspection; introspection is being consciously aware of one's mental states.

We will make use of the distinction between SOTs and TOTs later when discussing hypnosis. Consider the intention to 'lift the left arm!' This is not a conscious intention unless there is the SOT that 'I am intending to lift my left arm'. Due to this SOT, one is conscious of the intention, but not consciously aware of having the intention. To be consciously aware (or introspectively aware) of intending, there needs to be a TOT that 'I am aware that I am intending to lift my left arm'.

HOT theory in principle allows intentions (including those used in executive control) without HOTs of intending. The theory allows unconscious intentions; thus, on the theory, unconscious intentions should sometimes happen. This prediction is counterintuitive and directly contradicts the theories of Norman and Shallice (1986) and Jacoby (1991).

If executive functioning were always performed consciously, HOT theory would prima facie be in trouble. By the same token, the counterintuitive finding of unconscious performance of executive tasks would corroborate HOT theory. We call executive control without a HOT (without conscious intentions) 'cold control'.

The every day use of the term 'intention' does not clearly distinguish the first-order imperative representation that controls the action schema ('Do A!', 'If C do A!') from the HOTs about that representation (e.g. 'I am intending to do A', 'I am intending to do A if C'). For clarity, we use the term 'intending' (or 'intention') to refer to the first-order imperative representation (just as 'seeing' refers to the first-order visual representation and not to the HOT that one is seeing). Thus, intending is genuinely causal. The SOT about intending has the function of tracking this causal process. The SOT, as a representation, can misrepresent, and hence occasionally gets things wrong (cf. Wegner, 2002)[1], and this allows an explanation of hypnotic phenomena: the cold control theory of hypnosis, or executive control without accurate HOTs.

16.4 **Cold control: executive control without a HOT**

16.4.1 **The theory**

The cold control theory of hypnosis states that a successful response to hypnotic suggestions can be achieved by forming an intention (imperative representation in the SAS) to perform the action or cognitive activity required, without forming the HOTs about intending that action that would normally accompany the reflective performance of the action. The first part of the theory claims that hypnosis typically involves the SAS (i.e. executive control). We first consider the evidence for this, and then consider the consequence of not forming suitable HOTs about intending. Claims amounting to cold control theory have been made before (e.g. Spanos, 1986; Kihlstrom, 1992). In this sense, cold control theory is not novel; however, we pursue the claim in a single-minded way (Spanos and Kihlstrom also made other claims we do not make) and drawing on HOT theory (Rosenthal 2002) to look at data in a new way (making claims that Spanos and Kihlstrom did not make). The relationship of cold control theory to previous theories is considered below.

Hypnotic suggestions can involve the subject engaging in executive function tasks. For example, a standard suggestion used in stage hypnosis, and that can be reproduced in the laboratory (Evans 1980), is the suggestion to forget, for example, the number '4'. The subject will count, e.g. '1, 2, 3, 5, 6' fingers on a hand. This must involve executive control (overcoming a strong pre-existing habit), but the person denies awareness of why they count unusual numbers of fingers on their hands. [According to the logic of Jacoby (1991), the ability of the subject to exclude '4' from its habitual production implies conscious awareness of 4; this is just what the subjects themselves deny having.]

---

[1] However, that does not mean that conscious will is an illusion (contrast Wegner, 2002). Most of the time the HOTs accurately track and make us aware of the underlying causal intentions (executive control) and/or the consistency of actions made by contention scheduling (interacting with the environment) with executive control (compare Wegner and Wheatley, 1999).

Sackheim *et al.* (1979) found that with strong motivation instructions for blindness, a highly hypnotizable subject performed significantly *below* chance in reporting the emotion shown in photographed faces. Bertrand and Spanos (1985) gave subjects a list of three words in three different categories, and highly hypnotizable subjects ('highs'), when suggested, could selectively forget one word from each category. Subjects recalled on a category-by-category basis, and must have inhibited the to-be-forgotten word when recalling each category. Spanos *et al.* (1982) found that under suggestion to forget certain words in any type of task given to them, 'highs' produced those words at a *below* baseline level in a word association test. This requires executive control, because the existing associations that would be produced by contention scheduling must be suppressed. Strikingly, Raz *et al.* (2002) found that 'highs' could eliminate or dramatically reduce the Stroop effect when given the suggestion that they could not read the words. Remarkably, the habit of reading was apparently suppressed. Challenge suggestions also require executive control. In a challenge suggestion, the subject is asked to try to perform some action, such as bending the arm, while being told the arm is rigid and unbendable. People often respond to this suggestion by trying to contract both triceps and biceps simultaneously (Comey and Kirsch 1999). However, contention scheduling ensures the smooth performance of actions by inhibiting contradictory actions, and so does not lead to a muscular stalemate.

In general, virtually any arbitrary behaviour can be hypnotically suggested despite the fact that such behaviour might be novel to the person, at least novel in context, and many hypnotic suggestions require the person to ignore some salient aspect of the situation (e.g. analgesia or amnesia suggestions). At least many hypnotic responses are under executive control.

A curious relationship between HOTs of intending and task performance in some situations may be illustrated by Wegner's (1994) task of asking people to not think of white bears for a specified time. People find this extraordinarily difficult. In this task, an intention is formed by the SAS 'Do not produce representations of white bears'[2]. This representation can be used to guide the lower system, and also monitor its success. However, if a SOT is automatically formed 'I am intending not to produce representations of white bears', the HOT about intending makes the content of the intention, which includes the concept white bear, the content of a conscious mental state. That is, if engaging in the task to not think of white bears itself leads to a HOT of intending, that makes one consciously think of the concept of white bears[3].

---

[2] Alternatively, the intention could be phrased: 'do not think of white bears!' Although this intention is a mental state about a mental state (an intention about thinking), it is not the right sort of HOT to produce awareness of being in a mental state (it does not assert that one is in a certain mental state). Thus, in the following, we will still refer to this intention as a first-order state.

[3] Wegner (1994) postulates a monitoring process that constantly looks for mental contents indicative of failure of control, and it is the action of the monitor that leads to the dramatic failures of thought suppression. We are not arguing against this account, just pointing out that successfully not consciously thinking of the concept of white bears entails not having any HOTs about the intention to not think of white bears.

Highly hypnotizable subjects may be especially good at avoiding accurate HOTs about intending. Bowers and Woody (1996; also King and Council 1998) found that after hypnosis, 'highs' could *not* think of their favourite car for 2 min more effectively than 'lows'[4]. Prima facie, the 'highs' could engage in executive control without corresponding HOTs. Consistently, the fact that 'highs' can pass the forget-4 task implies that 'highs' need not become consciously aware of the labels for concepts that figure in their intentions, i.e. their intentions can indeed remain unconscious.

It can be difficult to dissociate HOTs from certain first-order states. Consider HOTs of perception. It is very difficult now to form the HOT that 'I am seeing a pink elephant' when in fact you are not (not to be confused with forming the HOT that 'I am imagining seeing a pink elephant'). Conversely, try performing the 'I am not seeing a white bear' task while looking at a white bear for 2 min. The link between intention and HOTs about intending may be weaker than the link between perception and HOTs about perceiving, allowing HOTs of intending to be more loosely triggered by relevant actions (Wegner and Wheatley 1999; Wegner 2002). The SAS can delegate control to contention scheduling, so it is not always easy to check whether an action was intentional by checking the SAS's description of the act. The specific action selected by contention scheduling will be but one way of implementing the SAS's more general intention in relation to the environmental flux of stimulation, e.g. switching gears in traffic. In any case, for simplicity we will presume that all that is required in hypnotic response is dissociating HOTs about intending from actual intentions.

16.4.2 How can HOTs about intending be prevented?

According to HOT theory, HOTs are just thoughts and so their occurrence will be sensitive to the same influences as other thoughts, i.e. consistent with socio-cognitive approaches to hypnosis (e.g. Spanos 1986, 1991), formation of a HOT about intentions might be prevented by activation of beliefs and expectations inconsistent with it.

Kirsch and Lynn (1999) have especially emphasized the importance of expectation in hypnotic responding. However, there is a powerful argument against hypnotic responsiveness being directly caused by expectations. Kallio and Revonsuo (2003) point out that in everyday life we can fully expect to, for example, see our keys where we left them on the table, but in clear viewing conditions this does not cause us to see our keys on the table if they are not there. Alternatively, consider expecting not to see something. With hypnotic suggestion, 'highs' can fail to see, for example, words (e.g. Bryant and McConkey 1989). Wagstaff *et al.* (2002) found that when non-hypnotized subjects were 100% confident they would not see something on a sheet of paper (all the previous pieces of paper had been blank), they all did still see the '8' that was on it. Surely evolution has led us to see or not see what the data rather than our expectations indicate, when the data are

---

[4] The difference between 'highs' and 'lows' occurred only after hypnotic induction. However, Woody *et al.* (1992) point out that in general 'highs' can respond in the same way with or without hypnotic induction so long as they notice the contextual appropriateness to do so.

clear. In everyday life, expecting to see our keys does not in itself make us see them when they are not there.

Cold control theory offers a solution to the problem of why we can have illusions in a hypnotic context but not normally in non-hypnotic contexts, with good viewing conditions. Expectations need only affect the formation or otherwise of HOTs of intending. In order to hallucinate keys, we would need to intend to imagine keys being there. Expectation can lead us to not have HOTs about intending the imagery but, in order to hallucinate hypnotically, the intention to imagine has to be there for some reason, i.e. that it fits in with other intentions, plans and strategies. Cold control theory does not need to postulate that expectations affect first-order perceptual or other first-order states in clear viewing conditions; expectations need only affect HOTs about intending. Thus, hallucinations and the other phenomena of hypnosis will only occur when they are strategically appropriate (White 1941; Barber 1969; Sarbin and Coe 1972; Spanos 1986), because relevant intentions will only be formed when strategically and contextually appropriate. In the absence of intentions to visualize, seeing can be strongly guided by the actual state of affairs in clear viewing conditions.

While expectations seem the most natural candidate for preventing the formation of HOTs about intending, they may not be the only effective means for preventing formation of HOTs about intending. Cold control theory would allow for any other mechanism by which HOTs are avoided, or even a special state in which HOTs can be readily avoided [we are not personally partial to a state explanation of hypnosis; see Kirsch and Lynn (1995) for the arguments against state theory; Kallio and Revonsuo (2003) for arguments sympathetic with state theory].

We will now consider whether cold control theory sheds any light on differences in difficulty in different hypnotic suggestions and also any light on individual differences in hypnotizability.

16.4.3 Why are some hypnotic suggestions easier than others?

Hypnotic suggestions can be roughly divided into simple motor suggestions ('Your arm is becoming so heavy it is falling'), challenge suggestions ('Try to bend your arm' in a rigid arm suggestion) and cognitive suggestions (amnesia, hallucination, the 'forget 4' suggestion, etc.). In general, more people can reliably pass motor suggestions (about 80 per cent of people for, for example, hand lowering and hands moving apart) than challenge suggestions, and more people pass challenge suggestions than cognitive suggestions (from 50 to 10 per cent of people, depending on the suggestion) (e.g. Hilgard, 1965; Perry *et al.* 1992; Kallio and Ihamuotila 1999). Cold control theory provides two ways of accounting for different degrees of item difficulty: first, different orders of HOTs to be avoided; and secondly, different degrees of effort involved in implementing first-order intentions. We consider each in turn.

16.4.3.1 The order of the thought: SOTs versus TOTs

Rosenthal (2005) suggested that most of the time when we have HOTs we simply have SOTS. Only occasionally, when we introspect, do we have TOTs. Given that TOTs are less automatically created than SOTs, it is plausible to assume that accurate TOTS (that: 'I am aware I am intending to do X') would be easier to prevent than SOTs (that: 'I am intending to do X'). Given this plausible assumption, the individuals most skilled at preventing accurate HOTs, i.e. highly hypnotizable subjects, would be able to avoid both accurate TOTs and SOTs about intending. Less skilled individuals ('mediums' and 'lows') may only be able to avoid accurate TOTs about intending (and only form inaccurate TOTs but not inaccurate SOTs).

Assume that 'lows' can only prevent accurate TOTs of intending but not SOTs. For instance, the SOT that 'I am intending to not say four' is still there, making them consciously think of the content of the relevant intention ('do not say four'), hence making them have a conscious thought about 'four'. Even if they then had an inaccurate TOT ('I think I am not intending to not say four'), they may not be introspectively aware of intending to not say four, but they would still be thinking of four in a conscious mental state. So they could not do the 'forget 4' task. However, 'lows' could do other tasks such as arm heaviness. They would have an unavoidable SOT (with the content 'I am intending to lower my arm'), making them consciously think of lowering their arms, but, by virtue of preventing accurate TOTs ('I am aware I am intending to lower my arm'), they would not be introspectively aware of *intending* the arm to fall, so the action would appear involuntary.

If highly hypnotizable subjects can even avoid accurate SOTs of intending, then they can do the 'forget 4' task, because the SOT about intention can be avoided. Further, when performing motor suggestions, they can avoid SOTs about the motor suggestion and not be consciously thinking about the action in any way. Zamansky and Clark (1986) asked subjects with high and low hypnotizability to engage in imagery inconsistent with the hypnotic suggestions given (e.g. for a rigid arm suggestion, to imagine bending the arm). 'Highs' were just as responsive to suggestions (e.g. that the arm is unbendable) when engaged in imagery inconsistent with the suggestion as when having consistent imagery. In contrast, the performance of 'lows' was severely degraded by contradictory imagery, strongly supporting the notion that 'highs' but not 'lows' can avoid SOTs of intention. In order to implement the required executive control, 'lows' need to be consciously thinking about the action to be performed. 'Highs' do not need to be consciously thinking of the action to be performed. Similarly, Hargadon et al. (1995) found that 'highs' were just as responsive to an analgesia suggestion when involved in counter-pain imagery as in an image-less condition where imagery and even suggestion-related thoughts were proscribed. 'Highs' do not need accurate SOTs to respond effectively to suggestions. These results directly falsify theories of hypnosis that postulate that hypnotic response is based simply on absorption in response-consistent thoughts and imagery (Arnold 1946; Barber et al. 1974; Baars 1988, 1997), but corroborate cold control theory. Cold control theory also predicts that 'highs' should be able to produce analgesia just as effectively in or out of the hypnotic context (in both contexts, the same pain control strategies can be used, the only difference being that in the hypnotic context the pain reduction would feel more like a 'happening' than a 'doing'); this prediction is indeed supported (see Milling et al. 2002, 2005 for recent data and review).

The ability to avoid accurate SOTs would facilitate the performance of any hypnotic task that needs to be performed with intentions whose contents remain unconscious. Consider, for example, the task used by Spanos *et al.* (1982) in which subjects were to forget the use of a specific set of words in any context. One way to perform this task is to form an intention, the content of which involves reference to the specific words that are to be forgotten. However, the content would have to remain unconscious or else the words would be part of a conscious mental state and hence not forgotten. It is not obvious how else the task could be performed. It is an executive task so an intention must be formed; yet the intention should remain unconscious. Thus, similar cognitive tasks that involve not being consciously aware of some specific stimulus should be especially difficult, and more difficult than, for example, motor tasks where there is not a problem in being consciously aware of any concepts or stimuli in order to respond successfully.

16.4.3.2 First-order effort

The second way cold control theory can account for different degrees of difficulty for following hypnotic suggestions consists of the amount of effort required to implement first-order intentions.

Positive hallucination can be one of the more difficult hypnotic suggestions, depending on what needs to be hallucinated. According to Hilgard (1965), about 50 per cent of people pass the taste hallucination (experiencing a sweet or sour taste in the mouth) and about 50 per cent pass the mosquito hallucination (hearing or feeling a mosquito), but only about 10 per cent of people hallucinate a voice. How can cold control theory account for hallucinations and their degrees of difficulty? Positive hallucinations could be produced by the executive-controlled production of relevant imagery; the lack of accurate HOTs about intending the imagery might lead the person to experience the image as a perception because the image is not experienced as intended (cf. Bentall 1990; Frith 1992). However, why is this difficult?

First, to experience the image as a perception requires not only the avoidance of a TOT about intending but also the creation of an inaccurate HOT representing oneself as *perceiving* (rather than imagining) the target of the image (it is the triggering of this HOT that corresponds to experiencing the hallucination as 'real'). Such a HOT of perception may be facilitated by preventing any HOTs of imagining from occurring. Thus, hallucinations may involve preventing accurate SOTs and not just TOTs of intending.

A second (compatible) explanation is that there exist individual differences in ability to prevent accurate HOTs of intention depending on the amount of cognitive effort required in executing the first-order intention. Performing a simple motor action may be less cognitively demanding than forming an image. Thus, it may be more difficult to suppress HOTs about forming images than performing motor actions. Images of tastes and simple noises (such as the sound of a mosquito) might be easier to form than images of voices. Similarly, ignoring intensely painful stimuli, or not perceiving a stimulus that has been primed by instructions (as in a negative hallucination), may be especially demanding. These are all proposals that are open to be being tested. Lifting an arm is harder than letting it drop; consistently, arm lowering is more easily experienced as involuntary than arm raising (Kirsch and Lynn 1995, in their sample found a response rate of 51 per cent for hand lowering compared with 23 per cent for hand raising).

The greater skills of 'highs' in avoiding accurate HOTs may allow them to avoid HOTs even when large amounts of cognitive effort are required in implementing the first-order intention. This could be tested by acquiring effort ratings, or measuring interference of each task with, say, random number generation, for different types of tasks outside of the hypnotic setting and determining the correlation with assessed effort and difficulty of the corresponding hypnotic suggestion.

The idea that more difficult tasks make it harder to suppress HOTs of intention can also explain why challenge suggestions are more difficult than simple motor suggestions. A simple motor suggestion that one's arm is so light it is rising requires the effort needed to lift one's arm. However, the challenge to lift one's arm—while being told the arm is so heavy that it cannot be lifted—in principle involves both an attempt to lift the arm and an attempt to stop the lifting from happening. For some people, this will involve some considerable muscular effort using antagonistic muscles to prevent the lift (Comey and Kirsch 1999) and cognitive effort in intending to try to lift the arm while remembering to make it heavy. The greater effort involved in successful responding to the challenge suggestion rather than the simple motor suggestion may be one reason why it is harder to suppress HOTs of intending with challenge rather than simple motor suggestions. We will consider another way of successfully responding to challenge suggestions later, one that involves no muscular effort at all.

In summary, cold control theory enables us to get a handle on the order of difficulty of different hypnotic suggestions in a principled way. Suggestions that require avoiding accurate SOTs of intending will be more difficult than suggestions that require only the avoidance of accurate TOTs of intending; and the more effort involved in performing the task, the harder it may be to avoid accurate HOTs, so the more difficult the task will be as a hypnotic suggestion.

We cannot claim to have explained the rank order of difficulty of all hypnotic responses (e.g. why do only about a fifth of people pass post-hypnotic suggestion compared with a third of people passing amnesia suggestions?), but cold control theory does provide a means for thinking about why some suggestions are harder than others within the context of a single theory, a single mechanism for producing hypnotic responses.

16.4.4 Difference between subjects with high and low hypnotizability on non-hypnotic tasks

Cold control theory can generate predictions about how 'highs' and 'lows' may differ in various tasks outside the hypnotic context. The fundamental skill postulated by cold control theory is unlinking HOTs about intending from intentions. So the ability to produce actions in any context that feel like they happen by themselves should be the main correlate of susceptibility. Indeed, the best correlate of hypnotizability is suggestibility without a hypnotic induction; the correlation goes from about 0.65 (Hilgard and Tart 1966) to 0.85 (Barber and Glass 1962).

Hypnotizability should also correlate with other sorts of tasks. Being good at executive control is a likely correlate of hypnotizability, because if one is good at executive control without HOTs, then plausibly (but not inevitably) one is simply good at executive control. Correlates for hypnotizability are notoriously difficult to find. Any non-hypnotic measures that do correlate with hypnotizability do so only moderately, if not sporadically. Nonetheless, despite the chequered pattern, findings can be usefully summarized in a broad-brush way in terms of executive function ability (Crawford *et al.* 1993). For example, maintaining attention is an example of an executive function task, because it involves successfully overcoming distraction. One of the most frequently replicated correlates of hypnotizability (with $r \sim 0.30$) is self-reported absorption in imaginative activities (e.g. Van Nuys 1973; Hilgard 1974; Tellegen and Atkinson 1974; Karlin 1979; Wilson and Barber 1981; Roche and McConkey 1990; Lyons and Crawford 1997; Barnier and McConkey 1999; contrast Jamieson and Sheehan 2002). Note that the relationship between executive control and hypnotizability is not strong (and is even less when context is controlled; Kirsch and Council 1992). Any theory that actually required 'highs' to be strong on executive control would have difficulty explaining the weak relationships found. 'Highs' are not 'highs' *because* they can, for example, concentrate well. Cold control theory does not need to make such assumptions: 'highs' are 'highs' because they can avoid HOTs of intending when actually intending, and this does not demand being especially good at executive control. Being good at executive control is just a likely correlate of hypnotizability, because one can allow oneself to prevent relevant HOTs if one is good at executive control without HOTs.

16.4.5 Motivation for further research

Cold control theory opens new alleys to explore. For example, we have already noted the need to measure difficulty with independent ratings or secondary tasks when considering the order of difficulty of different hypnotic suggestions. Cold control theory predicts that if the performance of the executive system is compromised, hypnotic response is likely to be affected as well (see Kirsch *et al.* 1999). For example, repetitive transcranial magnetic stimulation (rTMS) applied to the frontal areas should lower hypnotic response particularly to suggestions demanding special executive control, such as selective amnesias. In contrast, the dissociated control theory of Woody and Bowers (1994) predicts an increase in hypnotizability with a disruption of frontal lobe activity. Similarly, cold control theory, unlike dissociated control theory, predicts that frontal lobe patients should have low hypnotizability scores. The commitment to HOTs also motivates research contrasting cold control with 'empty heat', which is discussed below.

16.4.6 Summary

Cold control theory postulates that hypnotic responding is based on executive control without HOTs about intending. It thus explains why many hypnotic responses can be executive tasks. It also gives us a handle on the order of difficulty of hypnotic suggestions (e.g. whether the suggestion requires SOT or just TOT avoidance), on individual differences in hypnotizability (e.g. the weak relationship between executive ability and hypnotizability), and on why expectations seem to have much larger effects in a hypnotic rather than a non-hypnotic context. It also allows subjects different routes to achieving a given hypnotic response.

16.5 **Other accounts suggested by HOT theory**

Cold control theory postulates that hypnotic experiences of lack of voluntariness arise due to the unusual separation of intendings from the usually accompanying HOTs about intendings. However, HOT theory itself can produce two other explanations of hypnosis. First, HOT theory proposes a distinction between HOTs and first-order states, and the converse of first-order states without HOTs (cold control theory) is HOTs without first-order states (*empty heat theory*). Secondly, in HOT theory, mental states seem to belong to a person because the HOT represents that person—the 'I'—as being in the state. However, if somehow there could be multiple selves, one of those 'I's may not be aware of the experiences of the other Is (Kihlstrom 1997): the *multiple-selves theory of hypnosis*.

16.5.1 **Empty heat: HOTs without first-order states**

According to Rosenthal (2000), one can have a SOT that one is in a certain first-order state, without actually being in that state. Mistaken HOTs could produce many of the experiences brought about by hypnotic suggestion, in particular hallucinations, by representing one as being in a state one is not actually in.

If hypnotic suggestions operate directly on HOTs, then hypnotic hallucinations would not involve actual first-order perceptual states. So hypnotic hallucinations would not, for example, facilitate implicit perceptual tasks, or involve the use of visual pathways in the brain, or at least they would involve only areas concerned with HOTs about perception.

On the other hand, if, as cold control theory postulates, hypnotic hallucinations operate via preventing HOTs about intentions to imagine, hypnotic hallucinations would activate brain pathways involved in perception to the extent that those pathways are used by the imagination. Kosslyn and Thompson (2003) provided a meta-analysis of positron emission tomography (PET), functional magnetic resonance imaging (fMRI) and single photon emission computed tomography (SPECT) studies of visual imagery, showing that imagery can activate early visual cortex, as early as V1 or V2. Conversely, Rees *et al.* (2002) argued that visual awareness depends on prefrontal and parietal cortex rather than just specifically visual cortical areas, and Rees (2001) also speculates that conscious awareness depends on dorsal frontoparietal cortex. If we accept both these claims, finding a context in which hypnotic hallucinations causes activity in primary visual cortex would support cold control theory but falsify empty heat theory in that context. This is the sort of logic we now pursue in one example.

Kosslyn *et al.* (2000) asked highly hypnotizable subjects either to see a colour pattern in colour, or to see a grey-scale pattern in colour. PET scanning indicated that the left and right fusiform areas were active in 'highs' either seeing genuine colour or hallucinating colour, but not when veridically seeing grey-scale. To be consistent with empty heat theory, the fusiform area would need to be responsible for the formation of HOTs of seeing. However, Dehaene *et al.* (2001) found that both conscious and unconscious (masked) words produced activity in the fusiform area, so activity in this area is not sufficient for HOTs of perception. Similarly, Driver *et al.* (2001) reported activation in the fusiform area for extinguished (i.e. not consciously seen) visual stimuli, i.e. empty heat theory is falsified as an account of the colour hallucinations reported in Kosslyn *et al.*

On the other hand, for cold control theory to account for the results, imagination would need to be sufficient to induce activity in the fusiform areas. Indeed, when subjects were instructed without hypnosis to 'remember and visualize' the colour pattern, the same degree of activation of the right fusiform region was found as when subjects were hallucinating. However, the 'remember and visualize' instructions led to less activation in the left fusiform region than when hallucinating, challenging cold control theory. In interpreting the latter result, however, one should bear in mind Kosslyn *et al.*'s concern that the subjects did not 'drift into hypnosis' and hallucinate in the 'remember and visualize' condition. The wording was chosen to 'lead the subjects to attend to the visible stimulus and alter it rather than to substitute a complete hallucination', i.e. the demand characteristics entailed forming a less convincing image in the 'remember and visualize' condition rather than the hallucinate condition. It is thus not surprising that this was reflected in less relevant activity in the fusiform area for the 'remember and visualize' condition than the hallucination condition. Cold control theory predicts that if subjects capable of producing activation in the left fusiform gyrus when hypnotically hallucinating colour are tested out of hypnosis, activation will be produced in the left fusiform gyrus when subjects are asked intentionally to produce the same vivid experience as when hallucinating—but these results are not yet in.

Future research might identify separate populations of cold control and empty heat hallucinators. Brain imaging may find some people who reliably show no activation in V1–V5 while hallucinating and some people who reliably do. Cold control and empty heat would be then both supported as individual strategies in responding to hallucination suggestions.

Empty heat theory could in principle apply to challenge suggestions, such as being asked to try to bend one's arm, while being told one's arm is as rigid as an iron bar. In this case, to pass the suggestion, the subject must fail to move. On cold control theory, the subject might intend to 'go through the motions of trying to move but do not move', while being unaware of intending this. Empty heat theory offers an alternative strategy. The subject does not intend to move at all, but forms the 'empty' (with no actual first-order intention) SOT that 'I am intending to move' and/or the TOT that 'I am aware I am intending to move'. However, without the intention to move, the subject will not move (even while the subject believes that he or she is trying), so the suggestion is passed. With the cold control strategy, muscular effort is exerted in both trying to move and resisting that attempt. With the empty heat strategy, no muscular effort would be exerted at all. Comey and Kirsch (1999) found that about 70 per cent of people passing a challenge suggestion reported that they did try to respond to the challenge.

16.5.2 **Multiple selves**

Kihlstrom (1997) suggested that hypnotic subjects could create an additional 'hypnotic I' which is the cause of hypnotic responding. Because the hypnotic I's intentions (causes of hypnotic responding) are not linked to the normal I, the person does not experience himself as intending to make the actions occur. This theory corresponds to Hilgard's (1977) neo-dissociation theory in that Hilgard postulated that in hypnosis the executive ego was split in two so that there are two conscious streams, one controlling the hypnotic responses and the other unaware of this control.

Rosenthal (2003) elaborates how apparently separate selves could arise in terms of HOT theory. We will not pursue the idea further, however, because this approach predicts a hidden observer, and the notion of a hidden observer has generated much controversy (see, for example, Kirsch and Lynn 1998, for an overview, and comments by Kihlstrom 1998, and Woody and Sadler 1998). For example, hidden observer responses can in principle arise by attending to the pain or away from the pain depending on the demands of the situation (Spanos 1986), and this is consistent with cold control theory. While it may be open how best to interpret the processes producing hidden observer responses, one fact about hidden observer responses is uncontroversial: people often pass all sorts of hypnotic suggestions without demonstrating a hidden observer on request. While the level of hidden observer responding can vary dramatically according to the overt demands for it and the type of suggestion (see Kirsch and Lynn 1998, for a review), in many studies about 50 per cent of 'highs' show hidden observer responding. That would be roughly 5 per cent of the population, whereas a majority of people are responsive to at least some hypnotic suggestions. Bowers (1992) and Kirsch and Lynn argue that one cannot use phenomena so rare as hypnotic amnesia or the hidden observer to support the notion of multiple selves (separated by amnesic barriers) as an explanation of hypnotic responding in general. We conclude that multiple selves is at least a rare route to hypnotic response compared with cold control.

16.6 Comparison with other theories

Cold control theory's emphasis on executive function brings it in line with the two most prominent theories of hypnosis in the 1970s and 1980s, namely Hilgard's neo-dissociation theory and the socio-cognitive approach, the latter argued for vigorously by Spanos, amongst others. The 1990s saw theories emerge in which hypnotic responding involved contention scheduling rather than executive control (e.g. Woody and Bowers 1996; Brown and Oakley 2004). We briefly compare cold control with these different theories.

16.6.1 Dissociation theory

In Hilgard's neo-dissociation theory (1977, 1986, 1992), the 'executive ego' (SAS) was postulated as being the cause of any hypnotic response, consistent with cold control theory. The potential incompatibility between the theories is whether there is some part of the person that is aware of the first-order states the hypnotized person denies having. According to cold control theory, when a highly hypnotizable person produces, for example, hypnotic analgesia, there simply are no HOTs about the pain (nor HOTs about intending to engage in cognitive strategies to relieve the pain). According to Hilgard, the monitoring and executive functions of the executive ego (SAS) are split into two. 'The two parts differ only in that they are separated by an amnesic barrier' (Hilgard 1986, p. 234).

This might imply that the two parts are quite capable of their own HOTs, and this makes Hilgard's theory a multiple selves theory (Kihlstrom 1997), different from cold control. However, Hilgard (1986) also said that there are 'two experiences going on simultaneously; of one the subject is aware, of the other he is unaware' (p. 236). The streams are also referred to as subconscious versus conscious. There are two interpretations of these phrasings. In one, the stream about which one lacks awareness, the subconscious stream, is a stream of first-order states for which there are no accurate HOTs. This is the 'no HOTs' interpretation. In the other interpretation, the lack of awareness refers only to the lack of awareness of the stream by one of the selves; it is the hypnotized self that is unaware, though another self is aware of the first-order contents.

The 'no HOTs' interpretation makes neo-dissociation theory compatible with cold control. Many suggestions could be carried out by forming intentions, but failing to be aware of those intentions, i.e. by cold control (Kihlstrom 1992). Dissociative responses could also come about in negative hallucinations by having only first-order states of perceiving in the absence of accurate HOTs of perception, a perceptual analogue of cold control (i.e. cold perception). Kihlstrom (1998) prima facie accepted the 'no HOTs' interpretation of neo-dissociation theory in reviewing implicit–explicit distinctions generally (e.g. in blindsight) as supporting evidence for Hilgard's theory. Blindsight consists of first-order visual states without HOTs of seeing; there is no evidence that blindsight involves multiple selves (Kirsch and Lynn 1998).

The prime evidence for neo-dissociation theory is the hidden observer, and the hidden observer can express HOTs. This strongly implies that Hilgard did not intend the 'no-HOTs' interpretation of his theory. Cold control theory and neo-dissociation theory are then clearly different theories. However, they have in common the postulate that hypnotic responding involves executive functions.

Woody and Bowers (1994) provided another take on dissociation theory. They described hypnosis as a weakening of frontal lobe function so that contention scheduling could control behaviour (hence the feeling of involuntariness). In dissociation terms, the dissociative split did not render the supervisory attention system in two (as in Hilgard's theory, or a version of it), it split one or more action schemata from the supervisory attentional system, so that the schemata could become directly triggered by hypnotic suggestion. Thus, they call their theory the dissociated control theory. However, uniquely associating actions experienced as involuntary with contention scheduling creates a problem. Hypnotic responding cannot be based simply upon contention scheduling, because hypnotic responses can involve performing executive function tasks, as reviewed above. Our primary criticism of dissociated control theory, and its primary difference from cold control theory, is that the theory fails to get to grips with the highly strategic and, when necessary, executive nature of hypnotic responding. In cold control theory, like dissociated control theory, control is split off from consciousness, but the supervisory attentional system is still involved.

Bowers and Woody (1996) used Wegner's white bear task to provide support for their theory. They argued that the absence of the ironic conscious awareness of bears (or cars, in their study) indicated that the highly hypnotizable subjects simply did not have the intention to not think about bears. However, as indicated above, the success of 'highs' on the white bear task does not necessitate the conclusion that the task is performed non-intentionally (it could be performed intentionally and with avoiding relevant HOTs).

A further difference between cold control and dissociated control theories is that dissociated control theory is committed to a special state of hypnosis, specifically a state in which frontal lobe function is weakened. However, consistent with the idea that 'highs' in hypnosis actually have good executive abilities which can be used when expectations allow, when 'highs' were given hypnotic suggestions to eliminate the Stroop effect altogether, remarkably they could do this (Raz *et al.* 2002).

16.6.2 Socio-cognitive approach

The other great strand of theorizing about hypnosis has been broadly called the social psychological (e.g. Sarbin and Coe 1972; Spanos 1986) or socio-cognitive (Spanos 1991; Kirsch and Lynn 1997) perspective. These approaches view hypnotic behaviour as fundamentally similar to other more mundane forms of social behaviour, behaviour to be explained by personal (rather than subpersonal) states such as expectations, beliefs, purposes and attributions. The body of empirical work showing that hypnotic responses are indeed contextually appropriate, flexible, planned and goal directed (e.g. Spanos 1986) inspired a central notion in cold control theory, namely that executive functions are involved (consistent also with Hilgard's neo-dissociation theory). Cold control can also be simply described at the personal level, i.e. as the use of intentions without awareness of having those intentions, a description entirely consistent with the social psychological approach (and also, on a certain reading, with neo-dissociation theory). Where cold control theory goes beyond social psychological approaches is in a specific commitment to HOT theory (Rosenthal 1986); and social psychological approaches go beyond cold control theory in having a specific commitment to there being no special state of hypnosis. The social psychological approach is also consistent with empty heat theory, but cold control is the opposite of empty heat. We have seen above how a commitment to HOT theory leads to predictions concerning, for example, the order of difficulty of hypnotic suggestions, and also to considering brain imaging to distinguish cold control and empty heat theories. Different approaches—such as the social psychological and cold control—need not be incompatible to inspire different research questions, different types of answers and different agendas.

16.6.3 Neurophysiological accounts

Crawford and Gruzelier (1992) and Guzelier (1998) proposed a neurophysiological account of hypnosis. They postulate that 'highs' have better executive skills than 'lows' (e.g. Crawford *et al.* 1993) and hence can deploy their attention in different ways. Gruzelier (1998) and Gruzelier and Warren (1993) argue that the better ability of 'highs' to focus attention allows them during an induction to exhaust their frontal abilities, and hence end up frontally impaired in a hypnotic state. In contrast, Crawford *et al.* (1998) see hypnotic responding to, for example, pain as dependent on the effective functioning of the supervisory attentional system in 'highs'. Crawford's idea is, of course, consistent with cold control theory, but, as noted above, cold control theory does not rely on any superior ability of 'highs' over 'lows' in frontal tasks, and the evidence for hypnotizability differences in frontal task performance indicates an effect probably too weak actually to form the basis of the capacity for hypnotic responding.

16.7 **Evolutionary context**

Why does hypnotic behaviour exist? At first blush, hypnotic experience and behaviour are an unlikely product of natural selection. Surely natural selection favours accurate perception without hallucinations, and awareness of one's own control over one's actions (or at least not a systematic misrepresentation of the intentional causes of actions)? One possibility is that hypnosis was not specifically selected for at all. For whatever reason HOTs evolved, only a certain amount of accuracy was required of them, and the residual amount of slack between intentions and HOTs about intending—the slack that allows hypnotic experience—was simply tolerated by selective processes. However, another answer is suggested by the observation that hypnotic-like experiences are extremely common cross-culturally and seem to serve definite functions (Lewis 1973, 2003). We take the intentional control of cognition and behaviour without awareness of intention as the essential nature of hypnotic experiences. These types of experiences occur largely associated with religious rituals and in the form of spirit possession (Lewis 2003). Presumably, for our ancestors tens of thousands of years ago, hypnotic experiences also occurred in divine and spiritual contexts. If our distant human ancestors performed actions, or saw images, etc. that it seemed to them they did not produce, the obvious conclusion might have been that a spirit or divine force caused them.

One speculative function of such possession experiences is to support religious beliefs. If there were selective pressure on people to have religious beliefs, as some have argued (e.g. Alper 1996), then the experience of being taken over by a spiritual force would help strengthen spiritual beliefs (Oesterreich 1930), and hence could be selected for as well. Cold control would be the perfect way of achieving this end. The strategic nature of cold control allows the experience to correspond to whatever is required by the religious beliefs held, and to make sure the experiences occur in appropriate contexts. The lack of accurate HOTs provides the necessary self-deception (so that the cognition or behaviour can be attributed to divine intervention). The claim that hypnotic-like possession experiences can bolster religious beliefs is supported by large number of possession instances in religions struggling to obtain power; once religion has power, there is less need for such experiences to give authority to the religion, and indeed the experiences occur less often (Lewis 2003).

Lewis (1971, 2003) reviews the various sociological functions of possession experiences. For example, a possessed person can perform behaviours for which they are not held responsible. A socially marginalized person (such as in many cultures, a woman in a struggling marriage) can demand (with the voice of a mighty spirit) from the husband the gifts necessary for the spirit to be exorcized. In general, a person who speaks with the voice of a spirit acquires the authority of the spirit. If this performance is convincing to others, then the person (male or female) can climb the social ladder to achieve a status they could never have been accorded otherwise, including becoming the most senior political figure. Lewis (2003) documents just how culturally and globally widespread this phenomenon is. Again cold control provides the perfect mechanism. The behaviour and experience can be planned so as to be as contextually appropriate as possible, depending on the assumptions of the particular culture. The self-deception afforded by inaccurate HOTs enables the performance to be convincing to oneself, which in turn makes it more convincing to others.

In this respect, hypnosis is just one particular cultural expression of a more general phenomenon, and many of the particular characteristics of hypnotic behaviours are historical accidents frozen in time. The association of hypnosis with sleep (long discredited in the academic world), or the notion that the hypnotized person is passive, apparently lobotomized as it were, are simply particular cultural beliefs.

16.8 Concluding note

While we call cold control theory a 'theory', in truth we regard it more as a means of theoretically orienting in the right direction rather than as a final explanation of hypnosis. However, we hope our arguments convince psychologists, philosophers and cognitive scientists generally that hypnosis offers a rich domain for testing ideas of consciousness and control.

References

Alper M (1996). *The 'God' part of the brain: a scientific interpretation of human spirituality and God.* New York, Rogue Press.

Arnold MB (1946). On the mechanism of suggestion and hypnosis. *Journal of Abnormal and Social Psychology*, **41**, 107–28.

Baars B (1988). *A cognitive theory of consciousness*. Cambridge, Cambridge University Press

Baars B (1997). *In the theatre of consciousness*. Oxford, Oxford University Press.

Barber TX (1969). *Hypnosis: a scientific approach*. New York, Van Nostrand.

Barber TX and Glass LB (1962). Significant factors in hypnotic behaviour. *Journal of Abnormal and Social Psychology*, **64**, 222–8.

Barber TX, Spanos NP and Chaves JF (1974). *Hypnosis, imagination, and human potentialities.* New York, Pergamon.

Barnier A and McConkey KM (1999). Absorption, hypnotisability, and context: nonhypnotic contexts are not all the same. *Contemporary Hypnosis*, **16**, 1–8.

Bentall RP (1990). The illusion of reality: a review and integration of psychological research on hallucinations. *Psychological Bulletin*, **107**, 82–95.

Bertrand LD and Spanos NP (1985). The organization of recall during hypnotic suggestions for complete and selective amnesia. *Imagination, Cognition, and Personality*, **4**, 249–61.

Bowers KS (1992). Imagination and dissociation in hypnotic responding. *International Journal of Clinical and Experimental Hypnosis*, **40**, 253–75.

Bowers KS and Woody EZ (1996). Hypnotic amnesia and the paradox of intentional forgetting. *Journal of Abnormal Psychology*, **105**, 381–90.

Brown RJ and Oakley DA (2004). An integrative cognitive theory of hypnosis and high hypnotizability. In: M Heap, RJ Brown and DA Oakley (eds), *The highly hypnotizable person*, pp. 152–186. Routledge.

Bryant RA and McConkey KM (1989). Hypnotic blindness, awareness, and attribution. *Journal of Abnormal Psychology*, **98**, 443–7.

Carruthers P (2000). *Phenomenal consciousness naturally*. Cambridge, Cambridge University Press.

Comey G and Kirsch I (1999). Intentional and spontaneous imagery in hypnosis: the phenomenology of hypnotic responding. *International Journal of Clinical and Experimental Hypnosis*, **47**, 65–85.

Crawford HJ and Gruzelier JH (1992). A midstream view of the neuropsychophysiology of hypnosis: recent research and future directions. In: E Fromm and MR Nash, eds. *Contemporary hypnosis research*. pp. 227–66. New York, Guilford Press.

Crawford HJ, Brown AM and Moon CE (1993). Sustained attentional and disattentional abilities: difference between low and highly hypnotisable persons. *Journal of Abnormal Psychology*, **102**, 534–43.

Crawford HJ, Knebel T and Vendemia JMC (1998). The nature of hypnotic analgesia: neurophysiological foundation and evidence. *Contemporary Hypnosis*, **15**, 24–35.

Dehaene S, Naccache L, Cohen L, Bihan DL, Mangin JF, Poline JB, *et al.* (2001). Cerebral mechanisms of word masking and unconscious repetition priming. *Nature Neuroscience*, **4**, 752–58.

Driver J, Vuilleumier, P Eimer, M and Rees G (2001). Functional magnetic resonance imaging and evoked potential correlates of conscious and unconscious vision in parietal extinction patients. *NeuroImage*, **14**, S68–75.

Evans FJ (1980). Posthypnotic amnesia. In: GD Burrows and L Dennerstein, eds. *Handbook of hypnosis and psychosomatic medicine*. pp. 85–103. Amsterdam, Elsevier/North-Holland.

Frith CD (1992). *The cognitive neuropsychology of schizophrenia*. Hove, UK, Psychology Press.

Fromm E and Nash MR, eds (1992). *Contemporary hypnosis research*. New York, Guilford Press.

Gennaro RW, ed. (2004) *Higher-order theories of consciousness*. Amsterdam, John Benjamins Publishers.

Gruzelier J (1998). A working model of the neurophysiology of hypnosis: a review of evidence. *Contemporary Hypnosis*, **15**, 3–21.

Gruzelier J and Warren K. (1993). Neuropsychological evidence of reductions on left frontal tests with hypnosis. *Psychological Medicine, **23**, 93–101.

Hargadon R., Bowers KS and Woody EZ (1995). Does counterpain imagery mediate hypnotic analgesia? *Journal of Abnormal Psychology*, **104**, 508–16.

Hilgard ER (1965). *Hypnotic susceptibility*. New York, Harcourt, Brace, and World.

Hilgard ER (1977). *Divided consciousness: multiple controls in human thought and action*. New York, Wiley-Interscience.

Hilgard ER (1986). *Divided consciousness: multiple controls in human thought and action*, 2nd edn. New York, Wiley-Interscience.

Hilgard ER (1992). Dissociation and theories of hypnosis. In: E Fromm and MR Nash, eds. *Contemporary hypnosis research*. pp. 69–101. New York, Guilford Press.

Hilgard ER and Tart CT (1966). Responsiveness to suggestions following waking and imagination suggestions and following induction of hypnosis. *Journal of Abnormal Psychology*, **71**, 196–208.

Hilgard JR (1974). Imaginative involvement: some characteristics of the highly hypnotizable and the nonhypnotisable. *International Journal of Clinical and Experimental Hypnosis*, **22**, 138–56.

Jack AI and Shallice T (2001) Introspective physicalism as an approach to the science of consciousness. *Cognition*, **79**, 161–96.

Jacoby LL (1991). A process dissociation framework: separating automatic from intentional uses of memory. *Journal of Memory and Language*, **30**, 513–41.

Jamieson GA and Sheehan PW (2002). A critical evaluation of the relationship between sustained attentional abilities and hypnotic susceptibility. *Contemporary Hypnosis*, **119**, 62–74.

Kalio S and Ihamoutila M (1999). The Finnish norms for the Harvard Group Scale of Hypnotic Susceptibility form A. *International Journal of Clinical and Experimental Hypnosis*, **47**, 227–35.

Kallio S and Revonsuo A. (2003). Hypnotic phenomena and altered states of consciousness: a multilevel framework of description and explanation. *Contemporary Hypnosis*, **20**, 111–64.

Karlin RA (1979). Hypnotisability and attention. *Journal of Abnormal Psychology*, **88**, 92–95.

Kihlstrom JF (1992). Hypnosis: a sesquicentennial essay. *International Journal of Clinical and Experimental Hypnosis*, **50**, 301–14.

Kihlstrom JF (1997). Consciousness and me-ness. In: J Cohen and J Schooler, eds. *Scientific approaches to consciousness*. pp. 451–68. Mahwah, NJ, Lawrence Erlbaum Associates, Inc.

Kihlstrom JF (1998). Dissociations and dissociation theory in hypnosis: comment on Kirsch and Lynn (1998). *Psychological Bulletin*, **123**, 186–91.

King BJ and Council JR (1998). Intentionality during hypnosis: an ironic process analysis. *International Journal of Clinical and Experimental Hypnosis*, **46**, 295–313.

Kirsch I and Council JR (1992). Situational and personality correlates of hypnotic responsiveness. In: E Fromm and MR Nash, eds. *Contemporary hypnosis research*. pp. 267–91. New York, Guilford Press.

Kirsch I and Lynn SJ (1995). The altered state of hypnosis: changes in the theoretical landscape. *American Psychologist*, **50**, 846–58.

Kirsch I and Lynn SJ (1997). Hypnotic involuntariness and the automaticity of everyday life. *American Journal of Clinical Hypnosis*, **40**, 329–48.

Kirsch I and Lynn SJ (1998). Dissociation theories of hypnosis. *Psychological Bulletin*, **123**, 100–15.

Kirsch I and Lynn SJ (1999). Automaticity in clinical psychology. *American Psychologist*, **54**, 504–15.

Kirsch I, Burgess CA and Braffman W (1999). Attentional resources in hypnotic responding. *International Journal of Clinical and Experimental Hypnosis*, **47**, 175–91.

Kosslyn SM and Thompson WL (2003). When is early visual cortex activated during visual mental imagery? *Psychological Bulletin*, **129**, 723–46.

Kosslyn SM and Thompson WL, Constantini-Ferrando MF, Alpert NM and Spiegel D (2000). Hypnotic visual illusion alters colour processing in the brain. *American Journal of Psychiatry*, **157**, 1279–84.

Lewis IM (1971). *Ecstatic religion: a study of shamanism and spirit possession*. London, Routledge.

Lewis IM (2003). *Ecstatic religion: a study of shamanism and spirit possession*, 3rd edn. London, Routledge.

Lynn SJ and Rhue JW, eds (1991). *Theories of hypnosis: current models and perspectives*. New York, Guilford Press.

Lyons LC and Crawford HJ (1997). Sustained attentional and disattentional abilities and arousability: factor analysis and relationship to hypnotic susceptibility. *Personality and Individual Differences*, **26**, 1071–84.

Milling LS, Kirsch I, Meunier SA and Levine MR (2002). Hypnotic analgesia and stress innoculation training: individual and combined effects in analog treatment of experimental pain. *Cognitive Therapy and Research*, **26**, 355–71.

Milling LS, Kirsch I, Allen GJ and Reutenauer EL (2005). The effects of hypnotic and nonhypnotic imaginative suggestion on pain. *Annals of Behavioural Medicine*, **29**, 116–27.

Milner AD and Goodale MA (1995) *The visual brain in action*. Oxford, Oxford University Press.

Norman D and Shallice T (1986). Attention to action: willed and automatic control of behavior. In: Davidson R, Schwartz G and Shapiro D, eds. *Consciousness and self regulation: advances in research and theory*, Vol. 4. pp. 1–18. New York, Plenum.

Oakley DA (1999). Hypnosis and consciousness: a structural model. *Contemporary Hypnosis*, **16**, 215–23.

Oesterreich TK (1930). *Possession, demoniacal and other, among primitive races, in antiquity, the Middle Ages, and modern times*. Routledge and Keegan Paul Ltd. London.

Perry C, Nadon R and Button J (1992). The measurement of hypnotic ability. In: E Fromm and MR Nash, eds. *Contemporary hypnosis research*. pp. 459–90. New York, Guilford Press.

Raz A, Shapiro T, Fan J and Posner MI (2002) Hypnotic suggestion and the modulation of Stroop interference. *Archives of General Psychiatry*, **59**, 1155–61.

Rees G (2001). Seeing is not perceiving. *Nature Neuroscience*, **4**, 678–80.

Rees G, Kreiman G and Koch, C. (2002). Neural correlates of consciousness in humans. *Nature Reviews Neuroscience*, **3**, 261–70.

Roche SM and McKonkey KM (1990). Absorption: nature, assessment, and correlates. *Journal of Personality and Social Psychology*, **59**, 91–101.

Rosenthal DM (1986). Two concepts of consciousness. *Philosophical Studies*, **49**, 329–59.

Rosenthal DM (2000). Consciousness, content, and metacognitive judgments. *Consciousness and Cognition*, **9**, 203–14.

Rosenthal DM (2002). Consciousness and higher-order thought. In: *Macmillan encyclopedia of cognitive science*. pp. 717–26. Basingstoke, UK, Macmillan Publishers Ltd.

Rosenthal DM (2003). Unity of consciousness and the self. *Proceedings of the Aristotelian Society*, **103**, 325–52.

Rosenthal DM (2005). *Consciousness and mind*. Oxford, Clarendon Press.

Sackheim HA, Nordlie JW and Gur RC (1979). A model of hysterical and hypnotic blindness: cognition, motivation, and awareness. *Journal of Abnormal Psychology*, **88**, 474–89.

Sarbin TR and Coe WC (1972). *Hypnosis: a social psychological analysis of influence communication*. New York, Holt Rinehart and Winston.

Sheehan PW and McConkey KM (1982). *Hypnosis and experience: the exploration of phenomena and process*. Hillsdale, NJ, Erlbaum.

Spanos N (1986). Hypnotic behaviour: a social–psychological interpretation of amnesia, analgesia, and 'trance logic.' *Behavioural and Brain Sciences*, **9**, 449–502.

Spanos NP (1991). A sociocognitive approach to hypnosis. In: SJ Lynn and JW Rhue, eds. *Theories of hypnosis: current models and perspectives*, pp. 324–61. New York, Guilford Press.

Spanos NP, Radtke HL and Dubreuil DL (1982). Episodic and semantic memory in post-hypnotic amnesia: a re-evaluation. *Journal of Personality and Social psychology*, **43**, 565–73.

Tellegen A and Atkinson G (1974). Openness to absorbing and self-altering experiences ('absorption'), a trait related to hypnotic susceptibility. *Journal of Abnormal Psychology*, **83**, 268–77.

van Nuys D (1973). Meditation, attention, and hypnotic susceptibility: a correlational study. *International Journal of Clinical and Experimental Hypnosis*, **21**, 59–69.

Wagstaff GF, Toner S and Cole J (2002). Is response expectancy sufficient to account for hypnotic negative hallucinations? *Contemporary Hypnosis*, **19**, 133–58.

Wegner DM (1994). Ironic processes of mental control. *Psychological Review*, **101**, 34–52.

Wegner DM (2002). *The illusion of conscious will*. Cambridge, MA, MIT Press.

Wegner DM and Wheatley TP (1999). Apparent mental causation: sources of the experience of will. *American Psychologist*, **54**, 480–92.

Weizenhoffer AM (1974). When is an 'instruction' an 'instruction'? *International Journal of Clinical and Experimental Hypnosis*, **22**, 258–69.

Weiskrantz L (1986). *Blindsight: a case study and implications*. Oxford, Oxford University Press.

Weiskrantz L (1997) *Consciousness lost and found*. Oxford, Oxford University Press.

White RW (1941). A preface to a theory of hypnotism. *Journal of Abnormal and Social Psychology*, **36**, 477–505.

Wilson SC and Barber TX (1981). Vivid fantasy and hallucinatory abilities in the life histories of excellent hypnotic subjects ('somnambules'): preliminary report with female subjects. In: E Klinger, ed. *Imagery: Vol 2. Concepts, results, and applications*. pp. 133–52. New York, Plenum Press.

Woody E and Bowers KS (1994). A frontal assault on dissociated control. In: SJ Lynn and JW Rhue, eds. *Dissociation: clinical and theoretical perspectives*. pp. 52–79. New York, Guilford Publications.

Woody E and Sadler P (1998). On re-integrating dissociated theories: comment on Kirsch and Lynn (1998). *Psychological Bulletin*, **123**, 192–7.

Woody EZ, Bowers K and Oakman JM (1992). A conceptual analysis of hypnotic responsiveness: experience, individual differences, and context. In: E. Fromm and M.R. Nash (eds), *Contemporary hypnosis research*, pp 3–33. The Guilford Press.

Zamansky HS and Clark LE (1986). Cognitive competition and hypnotic behaviour: whither absorption? *International Journal of Clinical and Experimental Hypnosis*, **34**, 205–14.

Index

Note: page numbers in italic indicate diagrams and tables.